SCHOOL AND THE END OF INTELLIGENCE

The Erosion of Civilized Society

PRAISE
FOR SCHOOL AND THE END OF INTELLIGENCE

The power of this new book lies in its ambition, its scope, its un-expected connections, and its clarity. The beauty of this book is found in its alternating current of fury and compassion, realism and hope, humour and common sense. It is an exceptional ride.

Durrie, now 92 and standing on a long career as educator in both public and private systems, begins with a searing critique of what has gone wrong, and why and how, in conventional teacher-directed education. His examples are often appalling.

He continues with an assessment of the price our culture has paid in its mediocrity, in collapse of the arts, and in corrosion of liberal values and authentic democracy. In every debate, he centres children and their innate curiosity, capacity, and eloquence.

He buttresses all of this with a long central essay that deals, pri-marily in the English-speaking world, with a history of the many reformers who sought to build an architecture of public education. These are often sad but redeeming tales, amply sourced and cited in 676 (!) footnotes. He concludes with a three-part look at futures.

Durrie paints on a vast canvas. He has the gift of uncovering <u>for-gotten links, and turning dots into through-lines. He does all</u> of this in a conversational tone chosen to make every reader feel wel-come, and to leave inspired. Highly recommended.

--Dr Charles Barber (MA, DMA Stanford) Author of 'Correspond-ing With Carlos: A Biography of Carlos Kleiber' (Rowman and Littlefield)

For 60 years, ever since Neill's Summerhill, Tom Durrie kept thinking about the horrible state of education and its departure from Neill's philosophy. Tom's book is a product of those many years of accumulated wisdom and knowledge. He brings Neill's reasoning to a new level by confronting it with all aspects of modern life. This is a fascinating read even for those well-versed in the legacy of great authors in the field of educational freedom. The book is jam-packed with curious tidbits from all imaginable sources to boost core theses of the author. In his exposure of human ignorance, the author's caustic language is likely to make you laugh more than once.

--Piotr Wozniak, PhD, SuperMemo Research, Poland

In this book Tom Durrie gives us the results of his more than 50 years of research and thinking about how the world might look if we put children at the centre of their own learning. During the past few decades a few changes have occurred within the formal schooling system. For example, the strap is gone and other forms of assault on children in classrooms have mostly disappeared in Canada. Some parents with the means have created a home schooling culture that is less formal. But that is not what Tom is focused on here. Two sentences gave me the essence of this rich and detailed book: "Children are endlessly curious, they are learning machines. Until the routines of school intervene". But don't take Tom's word for it, he also calls in Albert Einstein who said, "I have no special talents. I am only passionately curious." What would education be like if it was focused on passionate curiosity?

--Lynn Curtis, retired Community Social Worker, Province of B.C.

Interested in homeschooling your children? Looking for reasons why? Read this book. Filled with facts and astute humorous observations, this book exposes the many ironic results of school, i.e. the reduced literacy rates in the past 100 years. Anyone interested in education and how to support children to thrive will benefit from the author's many years of experience working with children both in and outside of the educational system and his many years of observing how humans learn.

--Marty Layne, homeschool mom of four, author of Learning At Home: A Mother's Guide To Homeschooling, Newly Revised Edition

ABOUT THE AUTHOR

Tom Durrie (b. 1931) is a school critic, a nonagenarian giant, and a poster boy for longevity and vitality of a happy brain. His biography is rich beyond description, and reflects Durrie's infinite passion for life. His CV would suffice to fill in a few lifetimes, and is the best testimony that a rich and productive life is a self-sustaining process.
  --Piotr Wozniak, PhD, SuperMemo Research, Poland

Tom Durrie has degrees in music history, opera, and psychology. After spending ten years as a teacher, in the 1960s, he developed a fixation on school and what's wrong with it. Aside from that, a long life has led him down many paths. Besides teaching, he has been a vocal coach and accompanist, piano technician, actor and director, arts administrator, psychotherapist, university lecturer, caterer, handyman, community activist and organizer, father of three grown children and grandfather of six. He now lives in the small community of Boston Bar, in British Columbia, where he gives piano lessons and is active in community affairs.

If you want to read more. Here's my blog and website.

"Some thoughts from an aging radical on society, politics, art, opera, literature, and then some."

https://tdurrie.wordpress.com/

PREFACE

Maybe I shouldn't admit this, but I rarely read prefaces. They seem more like those *Terms of Agreement* that we never read but still click OK. Nevertheless, I do have a few words to say here.

As I mention somewhere in the book, I started this project at least thirty-five years ago, with the title *Ten Arguments for the Elimination of School*. If you've ever read Jerry Mander's *Four Arguments for the Elimination of Television*, you'll know where I got the idea. After having written half of the ten arguments, I got involved in other projects, and put this one aside, though maintaining the feeling that I really should write a book slamming school once and for all. The closest I came to it was when, in 2001, I wrote a master's thesis titled *Making Schools That Are Good for Kids*. This was for Prescott College, in Arizona, where I was obtaining an MA in Counselling Psychology. My thesis didn't have much to do with counselling, at least not directly, but it was accepted anyway. By the way, Prescott College is a fine example of how student-directed education can work. I won't go into that here, but it would be well worth your time to look into. By the way, I still think that my 2001 thesis is pretty good. If you're interested, let me know, I'll send it to you.

Then came the pandemic. Stuck at home for who knows how long, I felt the urge to get on with the anti-school book. When I started writing, I had little idea of where I was going. I just began poking around at various ideas about school and education. That's why you might find that much of this book seems like putting forward statistics and histories that don't add up to a persuasive case. At least, I have to admit that it looks that way to me. I hope I'm wrong and that readers will draw their own conclusions, maybe even finding something of interest.

If you get the impression that I can find no redeeming value in public school as it exists, you're on the right track. I know that everything I write about school in the book is negative. Rightly so, because the more I learned and thought about school, the more I concluded that the system not only does not do what it says it does but also that it is extremely damaging to learning, curiosity, and a sense of participation in a democratic society.

I'm sure this book will make some people very angry. They probably believe that if we don't regulate and control young people anarchy and chaos will result. My experience teaches me that exactly the opposite is true. We need to deinstitutionalize and become more primitive. Given the freedom to conduct their own lives in association with intelligent and responsible adults, children and youth will co-operate with and learn from each other and from those grownups with whom they associate. Simple enough, remove the frustration, anger, and rebellion, and the natural intelligence and curiosity of children will emerge.

More easily said than done? As I've said, this book is not about "School is bad and here's how to fix it." School cannot be "fixed." I'll bet that if all elementary and high schools were closed tomorrow, nothing horrible would happen. Everything would perk along the way it does now during holiday breaks and summer vacations. This does imply a society that welcomes the participation of young people in its work and in its culture. This also implies that there will be adults around who will spend time with kids. I have touched on the idea of something like neighbourhood one-room schools (Let's call them something else.) as centres of socialization and learning. I hope you find in this book that I believe that learning takes place spontaneously and effortlessly all the time. I urge you to read Frank Smith's excellent book that I refer to so frequently.

I could go on and on here, but why not just go ahead, click OK, and read the book. Or, if you're like me, you'll be reading it already, having skipped this Preface entirely.

SCHOOL AND THE END OF INTELLIGENCE

The Erosion of Civilized Society

Tom Durrie

The author has made every effort to ensure the accuracy of the information within this book was correct at time of publication. The author does not assume and hereby disclaims any liability to any party for any loss, damage, or disruption caused errors or omissions, whether such errors or omissions result from accident, negligence, or any other cause.

ISBN   978-1-7389351-0-9

FREE SCHOOL PRESS
PO Box 299
Boston Bar, BC
Canada
V0K 1C0

For my son Miles
1957-2021

TABLE OF CONTENTS

Introduction
Something About Me   3

PART ONE

What School Has Done For Us
Let's See   11
Reading   12
"Words Words Words"   12
Writing   13
Emotional Health   14
Bullying   15
And Then There's Cyberbullying   16
Dropout Teachers and Students   16
Suicide   18
Loss of Creativity   19
Higher Learning?   20
In Case You Missed Anything   20
So What's Going On Around Here?   21

PART TWO

The Erosion of Civilized Society
Bowling Alone   27
Supermarkets and Big Boxes   29
Self-Checkout   33
Popular Music   34
Yay Team! The World of Sports   36
Fast Food   38
Fill 'er Up   40
ATMs   41
The Decline of Print   42
Are You Paying Attention?   46
TED   48

Once Upon a Time 50

And So— 52

The Readymade Teenage Market 53

PART THREE

The World of Fun and Games

A. Shoot To Kill

This Changes Everything 59

And On The Other Hand 65

Reality is Broken 68

What You See Is What You Get 70

B. Learning As Fun or The Erosion of Childhood

Edutainment for Preschoolers and Babies 70

The Mozart Effect 77

Why All This Stuff? 79

Bringing Up Baby 81

Television for Children 83

Learning As Fun 90

The Oregon Trail 92

Now Let's Get Serious 94

And Now, The Gamified Classroom 97

There Will Be No Escape 99

Now Wait a Minute 102

So What? 107

C. Social Media

Even Better Than TV or Games 108

Facebook and Friends 108

All About Instagram 110

Are We Having Fun Yet? 113

Sextortion 117

A Peer-Oriented Culture 120

PART FOUR

How Did We End Up With School?—And Why

A. How and Why It All Started

The Fredericks   127

Now What Do We Do?   135

B. Visitors from North America

Horace Mann and Egerton Ryerson   139

Calvin Ellis Stowe   142

On Second Thought   144

C. Locke and Friends: The Philosophy of Education

John Locke   147

Locke on Education   149

The Pervasive Influence of Locke   159

Jean-Jacques Rousseau   160

Johann Heinrich Pestalozzi   171

John Dewey   188

Lev Vygotsky   193

A. S. Neill   200

The Lord of the Flies   206

A Question of Freedom   208

Protecting Children—Sort Of   212

D. The Denial of Freedom

Control and Educate   213

What's the Point of It All?   216

The Curriculum as Recipe   217

E. And Then What Happened?

The School Before School   221

Divide and Conquer   224

The Efficiency Revolution   226

The Latest Wrinkle: Taylorism   228

Scientific Management in Action   229

Scientific Management Goes to School   231

B. F. Skinner Is Alive and Well   235

PART FIVE

The Next Big Thing

STEM Invades the U.S.A. 245
Which Child Gets Left Behind? 253
Testing for Profit 254
Standardized Teaching and Standardized Learning 256
STEMing the Tide in Canada 265
Standardized Testing in Canada 268
Another Kind of Test 270

PART SIX

The School and Its Agenda

Is School Necessary? 277
School as Corporation 281
Promises, Promises 283
Teachers: Good, Bad, and Indifferent 386
The Training of Teachers 292
Paradigms of the Classroom 295
What Teacher Wants, Teacher Gets 298
Neoliberal Economics in the Classroom 299
The Disappearance of the Liberal Arts 303
Grades, Marks, Rewards, and Punishments 307
Reports and Report Cards 313
A More Subtle Punishment 323
Getting the Kids to Read? 327
The First and the Last Day of School 329

PART SEVEN

In Conclusion

What Is Education? 339
Why I Believe in Freedom 343
Kids These Days—And Beyond 346
The Beginning of Intelligence 349

Epilogue

Epilogue 359

Appendix

From 1966   365

What's this?   375

Acknowledgements

378

Bibliography

Bibliography of Books Cited and Referenced   379

Notes

386

Introduction

Something About Me

How did I ever get involved in school and education? Well, outside of my own twelve years in schools and uncounted years in universities, it started in 1955. At the time, I was a graduate student in Music History at the University of Southern California in Los Angeles. I had some sort of scholarship or teaching assistantship that helped, and my wife Gretel worked as a receptionist in a doctor's office. In March of the second semester, we discovered that our first child was on the way. That meant that Gretel would quit working and that I would have to support the family. At the time, there was a shortage of school teachers and jobs were readily available. So the easiest way seemed to be for me to become a school teacher, and I would write my master's thesis in my spare time.

After one summer course in "How To Teach," I landed a job in a rural school in Santa Paula, California, a small orchard and farming community near Oxnard. I was assigned grades seven and eight mathematics and art. This was quite nonsensical because I knew nothing about how art was supposed to be taught in elementary school. The math was OK because I was able to keep a step or two ahead of the kids when it came to factoring fractions and deriving square root. The real challenge was maintaining some kind of control over these teenage kids, most of whom were from migrant farm-worker families. That made them a wonderfully varied and rambunctious bunch, and I could have gotten along with any one or two of them, but a classroom full was a different matter. Struggle I did. It was stressful and no fun at all. The school was run by a rarely-seen back-country-bureaucrat-type principal and a lunk-headed vice-principal who coached sports and provided discipline. There are stories I could tell about that year, but I won't take your time. Amazingly enough, it all turned out pretty well and I was invited to return the next year. But I had other plans.

I dreamed of a more up-to-date kind of school and of younger—and more tractable—kids, so I applied to an in-town school that ran from kindergarten to grade five. The lower grades were all taught by women, and the two grade five classes were reserved for male teachers. Seemed like a great improvement. I was hired and given a class of delightful ten-year-old boys and girls. This was a time of Deweyism, and this school was right in the running. It was a lovely modern school building, run by Principal Dorothy Pinkerton. (I suppressed my fantasy of her connection to Benjamin Franklin Pinkerton of *Madama Butterfly* fame. If only her name had been Kate! As I discovered later, an association with Pinkerton's Detective Agency would have been more likely.) Oh well, everyone got along well, I liked the other teachers mostly, and the kids were great. During the two years I was there, I did all kinds of neat things in music and just about everything else. I was able to bootleg opera, music, and art into my classes. There was even one bunch of kids that, without being asked, acted out *Madama Butterfly* after I had told them the story and played some of the music. That wasn't all though. I remember how much they loved the Bacchanale from *Samson and Delilah* and the art reproductions I would hang in the classroom. I read to them every day after lunch for at least a half hour, sometimes more: *Wind in the Willows, The Yearling, The Bastable Children, Doctor Dolittle, The Jungle Book*, and many more. It was a great time.

Why did I leave such a pleasant situation? First of all, you'll notice that there has been no mention of the thesis. It was obvious right from the start that this was not going to happen. I was now stuck with being a teacher. However, that did not stop me from being an activist, and toward the end of year two, I was in trouble. It was because I was outspoken about the proposed introduction of a merit-rating system. All the teachers were against it, but they were too timid or scared to say anything. Not me. There was a teachers' meeting at which I gave a speech condemning the administration and merit rating in general. It turned out that the superintendent and Ms. Pinkerton the principal were listening to the meeting on the school intercom. A few days later I was called into the office where the superintendent awaited. He pronounced various warnings and told me that I would be "watched." Furious, I went home and told Gretel that we were moving to Canada.

I haven't mentioned it yet, but we had been talking about moving to Canada for a couple of years. There was some foolhardy youthful notion of buying land and taking up subsistence farming. That was about as realistic as writing a master's thesis in my spare time. And, to our great joy, our daughter Emily was born in January of that second year of teaching grade five.

So, move to Canada we did. That was a move I have never regretted in the sixty-some years that I have lived in this wonderful country. During the first summer, in Vancouver, British Columbia, I took some education courses at the University of British Columbia (UBC) in order to qualify for a teaching certificate, and I was soon to join the staff of a junior secondary school (grades eight, nine, and ten). I taught music and English literature. The school was known as a rough one in a rough neighbourhood full of delinquent kids. I managed OK, but I should tell you—and this is a confession—that I strapped several kids that year. Yes, it was a rough school and, in 1960, corporal punishment of that sort was common. Looking back on it, I can't believe that I could have been so heartless and brutal. What was I then? Twenty-nine or thirty. I hope I've learned something in the last sixty years.

The fantasy of subsistence farming hadn't died yet, so I signed on to teach in a two-room school in a small village in central British Columbia. I taught the upper grades. The farming idea began to fade (*Deo gratias!*) and, after two years, we moved on to another school in another town. Well, actually a city, and a nice one. There it was that I taught grade seven and the special class that I shall write about later.

Practically from the start, I was questioning what school was actually for. What the hell was going on there? It was obvious that in spite of all the rigmarole, lessons, discipline, and textbooks, the kids weren't learning much. Most of the energy seemed to be directed at keeping the kids under control and harassing them about paying attention and doing their homework. To me, it did not seem very beneficial or educational. I knew that I was not going to last in this profession. A life-changing revelation came with A. S. Neill's *Summerhill*, published in 1960. Reading that book confirmed my underlying, though as yet unrealized, thoughts about learning and children.

During my last year in the school system, I had written an article or two about my experience with the special class. That attracted the attention of some progressive people in Vancouver who had set up an independent school, known as The New School, for their kids. They, too, had read *Summerhill* (more about that later) and wanted what they thought of as freedom in their school. I was hired as Director, Headmaster, Principal, whatever you want to call it. With me came my brand of almost unbridled liberty for the kids. They were free to do whatever they wanted, and they did. It was wild! You can read about the "breakaway" period later.

About half of the parents at the school were appalled at what they saw their kids doing. What? Playing all day, wrecking things, running about, teasing each other—how were they ever going to learn anything? Nevertheless, I stood by my principles of freedom. The other half of the parents thought it was all just fine. They saw their kids having a whale of a time and talking about it all with intelligence and interest. Those were the parents that supported me in the founding of another school, a free school, soundly based on Summerhill.

That chaotic year ended with the creation of the Saturna Island Free School, located on a beautiful acreage with a beach and a heritage house on the southernmost of the Gulf Islands. We had chickens, rabbits, and horses. I think there were five of us who formed the staff of the school, and our first enrollment consisted of about thirty kids aged six to seventeen. There was a hay barn, an orchard, and in the spring, fields of daffodils. It was an idyllic setting and an overall happy one for all involved. Naturally, it wasn't all a picnic. There were endless meetings and discussions, finances were problematic to say the least, and who was supposed to do what was top on every agenda.

The glory of the Saturna Island Free School was short-lived: three years as I recall. There are many reasons why it ended, one of the main ones being that enrollment dropped because the public schools had co-opted some of our ideas, setting up so-called alternative programs and schools. Ha! Those were a far cry from the real thing, but they satisfied the parents who might have considered a free school. By the way, there were at least five free schools in B.C. at that time, all aiming at the Summerhill ideal. Those were great days—the late 1960s— and change was in the air. What ever happened to the idealistic, dope-smoking, politically active, and radical-thinking kids of those days?

Was the free school a success? For me, and I think most everyone else, the answer is yes. Obviously, the Saturna Island Free School had its shortcomings. None of us really knew what we were doing. Nevertheless, it was a great experience for all involved. I still firmly believe that children deserve to be free of directive constraints. The best possible learning experience is freedom.

So what happened to the kids that went there? As at Summerhill, kids of all ages mixed together and mostly got along; there was no bullying, and play and talk of all kinds were prevalent. A couple of things I remember especially: one group got together and wrote a school newspaper. It was well-written and illustrated, very funny and irreverent. Listening to music was a common practice, and there were one or two who would listen to the Saturday opera broadcast with me. There was one little boy who found the big first-edition book of *Paradise Lost* in the school library. He called it "the God book" because he loved the beautiful and dramatic Doré illustrations. He would listen attentively, at least for a little while, when any of the verses were read to him. Several of the kids looked after the rabbits and chickens, but there was never any compulsion or direction that they do so. The older girls loved the horses and were meticulous in their care of them. Above all, it was a place of freedom, enthusiasm, and laughter.

What happened to our "graduates"? I know of but a few: One boy wrote a book about a jazz musician, another boy became a journalist, editor, and writer, a girl became an opera singer, a boy embarked on an adventurous life and wrote a book about it, another boy became a business consultant, and a girl became a department of highways manager. I don't know what happened to the others.

If you're interested in reading more, there are two excellent papers by PhD candidate Harley Rothstein. The first one, his master's thesis, is about the New School. The second, his PhD

Tom Durrie

dissertation is a detailed study of free schools, including the Saturna Island Free School. Both are very interesting, well researched
and well-written. Highly recommended.

Harley Rothstein, *The New School, 1962-1977*, January 1992[1]

Harley Rothstein, *Alternative schools in British Columbia,
1960-1975*, 1999[2]

PART ONE

What School Has Done For Us

Let's See

For over one hundred and seventy years, children have been compelled by law to attend school in the United States and Canada. Why?

In eighteenth-century Prussia, compulsory school attendance was instigated to bring uppity peasants under control and to provide a source of obedient young men for the military. In nineteenth-century North America, the growth of cities with their factories and offices created a need for well-trained and compliant workers. The efficiency movements of the twentieth century reemphasized the need for punctuality and discipline in the workplace, somewhat softened by the influence of John Dewey, until the ominous beeping of Sputnik in 1957 got everyone worrying. Then it was *We'd better toughen up and produce more scientists.*

School serves as a conduit of unexamined societal values, solidifying those values in the minds of the young, and, since the 1970s, the pervasive influence of neoliberal[3] thought has emphasized competition and the production of wealth. While school is proclaimed as a means of nurturing the intellectual and cultural growth of children, aiming toward citizens who are socially and politically aware and able to contribute to a society that is inclusive and just, it has instead become a job preparation factory now taken over by competition for grades and high stakes testing, with many dropping off the lower levels into unemployment and poverty. The effects seeping into society are undermining human contact and communication. Instead of intelligent social and political discourse, school is unwittingly promoting ignorance and mistrust.

When Horace Mann retired from the Massachusetts State Board of Education, in 1849, after twelve years of actively promoting the establishment of public schools and compulsory attendance, he reflected on what he saw as the salutary effects of school on the young:

> When I made my first circuit over the State, I saw hundreds and thousands of little boys and girls

11

wending their unconscious way to the school-room, or sitting upon its seats, or sporting around its door, as happy in the first-born joys of life, and in their ignorance of coming events, as are the birds of spring. But now, they are fledged; they are poised, and, with outstretched wings, are ready for a flight into this uncertain world.[4]

That was in the 1840s. Let's see what's being learned in the schools of the 2020s. Are "the birds of spring" prepared for "this uncertain world?"

Reading

There is every reason to believe that literacy has been on a steady decline ever since the introduction of compulsory school attendance in the 1840s. Approximately thirty-two million adults in the United States can't read, according to the U.S. Department of Education and the National Institute of Literacy.[5] Also noted is a steady decline in literacy from 1992 to 2003. The Organization for Economic Cooperation and Development found that 50 per cent of U.S. adults can't read a book written at an eighth-grade level.[6]

Forty-eight per cent of adult Canadians have literacy skills that fall below high school equivalency and affect their ability to function at work and in their personal lives. Seventeen per cent function at the lowest level, where individuals may, for example, be unable to read the dosage instructions on a medicine bottle.[7]

"Words Words Words"

If I mention that this is a line from *Hamlet*, most people won't know what I'm talking about or, perhaps worse, wouldn't care. The point is that reading involves words, and the more you read the more words you will know. So, if most people either can't or won't read, what happens to their vocabulary? Expression will be limited to slogans, clichés, and a handful of over-used adjectives. (Isn't that *awesome* or *incredible*?)

According to a study by Jean Twenge of San Diego State University, vocabulary, or the number of words a person knows, has steadily declined in spite of an increase in the number of people attending higher education. In fact, there is little difference between college graduates and high school dropouts. Another website reports the decline in teenagers' verbal skills: "Vocabulary of average U.S. fourteen-year-old in 1950: 25,000 words; Average vocabulary in 1999: 10,000 words." [8] As a reason for this, other studies seem to agree that fewer young people these days are reading books, magazines, or newspapers.[9] Jean Twenge concludes her report saying, "The average college graduate now has considerably lower verbal ability than the average college graduate of forty years ago." [10]

Writing

According to Maggie Gilmour in *Maclean's*, "The class of 2011 is opinionated and expressive but they can't structure an essay, don't know how to write an introduction, write paragraphs that are two pages long, and have murderously bad grammar." In the same article, Paul Budra, associate dean and English professor at Simon Fraser University, is quoted as saying: "The grammar sucks and the writing is awful. . . . High school teachers are failing students.'"[11]

A report from the *Higher Education Quality Council of Ontario—October 2013* tells us that "while Canada has one of the most highly educated populations in the world, 42 per cent of the adult population still lacks the literacy skills required to thrive in the global economy." And "As early as 1998, Thomas J. Collins, an administrator and English professor with twenty years of experience at Western University, notes that incoming university students at his institution lack basic reading and writing skills to such an extent that he 'cannot assume even a moderate degree of litera-cy from those who elect to study first-year English'"[12]

Emotional Health

Julia Martin Burch, PhD, of the Harvard Medical School wrote, "Heading back to school sparks an upswing in anxiety for many children. The average child's school day is packed with po-tential stressors."[13]

The American Psychological Association found that teens are more stressed than adults. "Teens report that their stress level during the school year far exceeds what they believe to be healthy. . . . Many teens also report feeling overwhelmed (31 per cent) and depressed or sad (30 per cent) as a result of stress."[14]

Boston College psychology professor, Peter Gray, looked more closely at these data and found that children's mental health is directly related to school attendance. "The available evidence suggests quite strongly that school is bad for children's mental health. Of course, it's bad for their physical health, too; nature did not design children to be cooped up all day at a micromanaged, sedentary job."[15]

Indications are that attention deficit hyperactivity disorder (ADHD) is on the rise among school children. Over a twenty-year period, the estimated prevalence of diagnosed ADHD in U.S. chil-dren and adolescents increased from 6.1 per cent in 1997-1998 to 10.2 per cent in 2015-2016.[16] As of 2019, of the 11 per cent of American children, ages 4-17, diagnosed with ADHD, nearly 70 per cent were taking various prescription drugs,[17] a blessing to big pharma if there ever was one. Profits were amounting to thirteen billion dollars in 2019,[18] and there is little doubt that the figure has continued to rise, especially considering the advantages to teachers in having a classroom full of tractable, medicated, and spaced-out kids.

In her novel *Paradise*, the American writer Toni Morrison describes high school in these words:

> She was back in that place where final wars are waged, the organized trenches of high school. . . Where smugness reigns, judgments instant, dismissals permanent. And the adults haven't a clue. Only prison could be as blatant and as frightening, for beneath its rules and rituals scratched a life of growing violence. Those who came from peaceful well-regulated homes were overtaken by a cruelty that visited them as soon as they entered the gates, Cruelty decked out in juvenile glee.[19]

Does this sound like an institution of higher learning?

Bullying

According to the American Psychological Association, 40 to 80 per cent of school-age children experience bullying at some point during their school careers.[20]

While dedicated to improving matters, The Stop Bullying Now Foundation (based in Florida) admits, "The overall outlook of the long-term effects of bullying upon society is grim."[21] In fact, according to their statistics:

- Sixty per cent of middle school students say that they have been bullied.
- One hundred sixty thousand students stay home from school every day due to bullying. (NEA)
- Thirty per cent of students who reported they had been bullied said they had at times brought weapons to school.
- Twenty per cent of all children say they have been bullied.
- Twenty per cent of high school students say they have seriously considered suicide within the last twelve months, and
- **The average child has watched 8,000 televised murders and 100,000 acts of violence before finishing elementary school.** (emphasis added)

Let's not forget that the biggest bullies in school are the teachers. No matter what clever tactics of "classroom management" might be employed, the message is Do what you're told— or else!

And Then There's Cyberbullying

Cyberbullying, or cyberharassment, involves the posting of denigrating or insulting comments about an individual or group of individuals on social media. The well-publicized case of Amanda Todd, which I will address below, is a sad but far from unusual example.

- Overall, 36.5 per cent of people feel they have been cyberbullied in their lifetimes, 17.4 per cent have reported it has happened at some point in the last thirty days, and 60 per cent of teenagers have experienced some sort of cyberbullying.[22]
- All indications are that cyberbullying is on the increase, suggesting we are heading in the wrong direction when it comes to stopping bullying of all kinds.[23]
- So all of the pink-shirt days and playground buddies programs are not only ineffective but may intensify bullying.[24]

School seems to have a knack for producing an effect opposite the intended one.

Dropout Teachers and Students

Every year, over 1.2 million students drop out of high school in the United States alone. That's a student every twenty-six seconds—or seven thousand a day. About 25 per cent of high school freshmen fail to graduate from high school on time.[25]

According to *Learning Liftoff*, students list many reasons for dropping out of high school. More than 27 per cent say that they leave school because they are failing too many classes. Nearly 26 per cent report boredom as a contributing cause.[26]

Writing in *GenFKD*, homeschooling mother Caitlin Curley suggests: "Standardized testing may be the primary culprit behind the declining public high school graduation rates since No Child Left Behind expanded their use in 2002. The development has led many researchers to conclude that the tests serve to push children out of school rather than keep them in it."[27]

From *The Guardian*: "Almost a quarter of the teachers who have qualified since 2011 have already left the profession, according to official figures that have prompted further concerns about the pressures on the profession. Of those who qualified in 2011 alone, 31 per cent had quit within five years of becoming teachers, the figures show." [28]

In the 2022-23 academic year, the Economic Research Institute reports that the average B.C. teacher's salary is $68,499. The salary of a teacher in elementary school ranges from $48,703 to $82,815. [29] Considering that the school year runs around ten months of the year, with considerable time off for holidays, spring break, and professional days, that doesn't look so bad. Nevertheless, fewer people are opting to enter the teaching profession. Clint Johnston, president of the British Columbia Teachers' Federation, was quoted as saying, "The teacher shortage in B.C. has been growing for quite some time and we are not producing enough teachers in the province for ourselves."[30] In addition to a shortage of new teachers, low salaries and poor working conditions are often cited as reasons why teachers drop out.

The problem is also endemic in U.S. schools. The chief academic officer of *SchoolMint, Inc.* wrote:

> A major challenge in schools today is for all children to receive a quality education from "highly-qualified" teachers. However, over the past decade, education researchers and district leaders have increasingly called attention to the growing problem of a teacher shortage in the nation's K–12 schools as massive numbers of teachers are leaving the classroom in pursuit of other opportunities or eschewing the field altogether.[31]

In the *Canadian Journal of Educational Administration and Policy*, "Much attention is given to the development of novice teachers According to a study. However, many beginning teachers, despite their initial enthusiasm, abandon the profession, depressed and discouraged, with the most talented beginning teachers among those most apt to leave." [32] Note *most talented.* Why is that?

I probably don't need to answer that question, but I can't help pointing out that the anti-intellectual, test-obsessed, and discipline-oriented atmosphere of school is sure to stultify and drive out any person of more than mediocre intelligence.

Suicide

The suicide rates for adolescent boys and girls have been steadily rising since 2007, according to a report from the *U.S. Centers for Disease Control and Prevention.* The suicide rate for girls ages fifteen to nineteen doubled from 2007 to 2015, when it reached its highest point in forty years, according to the CDC. The suicide rate for boys ages fifteen to nineteen increased by 30 per cent over the same time period. The suicide rate for teen boys increased from twelve suicides per 100,000 individuals in 1975 to eighteen suicides per 100,000 in 1990, when it reached a high point. The numbers declined from 1990 to 2007 and then climbed again by 2015.[33] "The rate of death by suicide in people from 10-24 years old increased 57.4 per cent over the ten-year period from 2007 to 2018, according to new data released by the CDC," said *Insider*, September, 2020.[34]

According to Stephen Singer in *The HuffPost*, "For the first time, suicide surpassed car crashes as a leading cause of death for middle school children. In 2014, the last year for which data was available, 425 middle schoolers nationwide took their own lives. To be fair, researchers, educators, and psychologists say several factors are responsible for the spike; however, pressure from standardized testing is high on the list."[35]

A study on hospitalization by Vanderbilt University found that children's hospitals saw higher rates of suicidal patients during the fall and the spring, but not during the summer. "There is a seasonality to suicide," said Dr. Gregory Plemmons, the lead author on the study. "If you look at adult data, most adults tend to commit suicide in summer and the spring, we noticed that our biggest time (for children) was in the fall."[36] And fall means back to school.

Loss of Creativity

Line Dalile, a 14-year-old student and writer in the *Huff-Post*—

> Remember being a kid and wanting to play around? No one told you how to use your imagination or taught you how to be creative. You played with LEGOS. You pretended you were an astronaut and imagined traveling in space. Being naturally creative, you asked questions like "Why is the grass green?" and "Are we alone?" — questions no wise man could answer.
> Then came school, a child's worst nightmare. You learned to live in a rotten environment. You were bullied, made fun of, and you had this teacher that told you to stop dreaming and live in reality. So what did you learn at school? You learned to stop questioning the world, to go with the flow, and that there's only one right answer to each question.
> The "whys" you have always wanted to ask are never on the test, and they are omitted from the curriculum.
> So what did you learn at school? You learned to stop questioning. To stop wondering, to stop thinking, to stop being curious.[37]

In the most watched TED Talk of all time, educationalist Sir Ken Robinson FRSA[38] claims that "schools kill creativity," arguing that "we don't grow into creativity, we grow out of it. Or rather we get educated out of it." Yet to Robinson, "creativity is as important as literacy and we should afford it the same status."[39]

Higher Learning?

In *The Unschooled Mind,*[40] a book by Howard Gardner, several studies cited show "that even students who have been well trained and who exhibit all the overt signs of success—faithful attendance at good schools, high grades and high test scores, accolades from their teachers—typically do not display an adequate understanding of the materials and concepts with which they have been working." For example, 70 per cent of students in physics, mechanics in particular, could give only the most naïve explanation of a simple coin toss question, a naïve explanation similar to students who had studied no physics whatsoever. "Indeed, in dozens of studies of this sort, young adults trained in science continue to exhibit the very same misconceptions and misunderstandings that one encounters in primary school children."[41] And, as for students of literature: "Those who have studied the intricacies of modern poetry, learning to esteem T. S. Eliot and Ezra Pound, show little capacity to distinguish masterworks from amateurish drivel, once the identity of the author has been hidden from view."[42]

In Case You Missed Anything

1. Nearly 50 per cent of Americans and Canadians are functionally illiterate.
2. Vocabulary across all levels of education and society is decreasing.
3. High school graduates are woefully deficient in writing skills.
4. School is bad for children's mental and physical health.
5. Up to 80 per cent of school age children have been bullied at school.

6. Large numbers of young people drop out of school because of a sense of failure. Thirty per cent of beginning teachers drop out of the profession within five years.

7. More teenagers die by suicide than in car crashes. Pressure from standardized testing is blamed.

8. "Then came school, a child's worst nightmare." We are "educated" out of creativity.

9. University students show little understanding of the subjects they have studied.

These results present a rather dismal view of a society that accepts compulsory schooling as a necessary part of childhood and what is called "education." If school is actually a complete failure at doing what it says it does, why do we keep spending vast sums of money on it and insisting that every child be subjected to its influences? These are the questions I shall address in the rest of this book.

So What's Going On Around Here?

If school fails at doing what it says it's doing, what does it succeed at? What is really going on around here? This is the question I asked myself during the ten years I spent teaching in public elementary schools in the United States and Canada. I came to the unavoidable conclusion that school is there to kill curiosity and promote ignorance.[43] Why and how this happens can be revealed by a study of the history of universal and compulsory public school as well as a consideration of the theories and practices of education and childhood. It's worth remembering (and I'll come to this again later) that John Stuart Mill wrote, in *On Liberty* (1849) that the state should insist, and even legislate, that all children be educated, but that the state should not be providing or controlling that education. He thought that would be giving governments far too much control of people's thoughts and ideas. I ask this question: To whose advantage is it to maintain a complacent, unquestioning, and even non-voting populace?

Most school curricula proclaim that the purpose of putting children through this process is to end up with a populace of intelligent, well-informed, articulate, and thoughtful people. The following stories of the erosion of civilized society will illustrate that the one hundred or more years of "education" have had quite the opposite effect. This is because, as I said earlier, school serves as a conduit of the unexamined values of society, without providing a critical examination of trends in popular thought, entertainment, or social discourse. I also maintain that school plays a major role in guiding those social values.

For a striking example, let's turn back the clock some two hundred years. In 1884, Horace Mann, the idealist who brought compulsory public schooling to North America, addressed the Massachusetts State Board of Education with these words:

> I suppose it to be the universal sentiment of all those who mingle any ingredient of benevolence with their notions on Political Economy, that vast and overshadowing private fortunes are among the greatest dangers to which the happiness of the people in a republic can be subjected. Such fortunes would create a feudalism of a new kind, but one more oppressive and unrelenting than that of the Middle Ages. The feudal lords in England, and on the continent, never held their retainers in a more abject condition of servitude, than the great majority of foreign manufactures and capitalists hold their operatives and laborers at the present day. The means employed are different, but the similarity in results is striking. What force did then, money does now.[44]

Remember that he said this nearly one hundred fifty years ago. At the present time, wealth inequality has increased to such a point that a visitor to any city in the United States or Canada would be confronted with sites of homeless encampments, people living on the streets, and line-ups at food banks, while a visit to the "better" parts of town will reveal gated communities, elaborate mansions, and other displays of wealth. Horace Mann would have to accept that his idealistic vision of schooling had gone completely awry.

How is it that we can be faced with impending disaster from climate change? It has now become so obvious that no sensible person can deny that it's happening, and yet a passive and complacent public sits in front of their televisions or computers while governments fume, fuss, and do nothing. I'm saying that school is responsible for this passivity because it teaches, for twelve years, that as an individual you have no say about what the institution decides is best for you. It's better to shut up, do what you're told, and escape into entertainment or drugs that will distract you from what's happening as the world over which you have no power crumbles all around.

PART TWO

The Erosion of Civilized Society

Bowling Alone

In 1995, *The Journal of Democracy* published an article by Robert Putnam with the intriguing title "Bowling Alone."[45] Putnam, a professor of Public Policy at Harvard University, made the point that *social capital* in the United States was losing ground because of declining individual involvement in organizations like the PTA (Parent Teachers Association), political groups, labour unions, and, yes, bowling leagues. The article was followed, in 2000, by a book[46] in which Putnam enlarges on and documents, in exhaustive detail, the propositions he made in 1995.

The term *social capital* seems to have been first mentioned by Lyda J. Hanifan,[47] a state supervisor of rural schools in West Virginia, in a 1916 article describing how people could be brought together by a variety of social and community activities centered on rural schools. Here, he defines the notion of social capital:

> In the use of the phrase social capital I make no reference to the usual acceptation of the term capital, except in a figurative sense. I do not refer to real estate, or to personal property or to cold cash, but rather to . . . good-will, fellowship, mutual sympathy, and social intercourse among a group of individuals and families . . . **The individual is helpless socially, if left entirely to himself.**[48] (emphasis added)

Simple enough. When people get together they tend to talk about issues that are of concern to them; they tend to share personal and family stories; they talk about the weather, about food prices, about "kids these days," the condition of roads and highways, stray dogs, and what they might do to change or influence matters. In doing this they are expressing themselves in words and recognizing the existence and equality of other members of their community.

It is often argued that "communities" are now flourishing on social media and the Internet, and that these provide the sense of fellowship that used to be found in the associations whose demise is lamented by Putnam in his article and book. However, Facebook "friends," video game opponents, Twitter feeds, Instagram networks, Linkedin profiles, and a plethora of social media do not supply face-to-face communication and expanded social networking; they tend to focus on single issues or the exchange of trivial bits of information. (Of course, they also provide a vast and arable acreage for misinformation and targeted advertising.) While we sit at our computers or stare at our smartphones we imagine that we are part of some kind of community and that all kinds of people want to "friend" us. Nevertheless, we are still bowling alone.

This is a far cry from what Hanifan describes as growing out of social events like potlucks, PTA meetings, concerts, lectures, the school Christmas concert, and the Ratepayers' association—coffee and doughnuts will be served. Hanifan writes about the need for "accumulation of community social capital."

> Such accumulation may be effected by means of public entertainments, "sociables," picnics and a variety of other community gatherings. When the people of a given community have become acquainted with one another and have formed a habit of coming together upon occasions for entertainment, social intercourse and personal enjoyment.[49]

Such gatherings can also involve a public speaker addressing issues of concern. In the early twentieth-century communities described by Hanifan, people felt empowered in improving matters like school attendance, local history, economics of agriculture, patriotism, public libraries, and adult literacy.[50] In other words, social capital was invested in a range of benefits to members of the community.

On the subject of literacy, or at least as an indication of what people read, Robert Putnam, writing in the year 2000, discusses the demise of newspaper readership: "In 1948, daily newspaper circulation . . . was 1.3 papers per household. That is, half a century ago the *average* American family read *more* than one newspaper a day. Fifty years later . . . newspaper readership had fallen by 57 per cent."[51] Subsequent to the publication of *Bowling Alone*, between 2000 and 2014, the number of newspaper publishers in the U.S. declined from nearly 6,200 to around 4,500. Looking at weekly circulation, the decline is even more dramatic: From 1994 to 2018, print circulation fell from nearly 60,000 to 35,000. The second figure includes digital subscriptions.[52]

Even more alarming, though perhaps not surprising, is the inverse relation between newspaper readership and education. According to Putnam's sources, in 1948 the median American adult had nine years of formal schooling and, by 1998, that figure had risen to thirteen years. Yet, at the same time, readership had declined dramatically, "despite the fact that newspaper reading is highly correlated to education." And, newspaper readers are less likely to bowl alone. "Compared to demographically identical non-readers, regular newspaper readers belong to more organizations, participate more actively in clubs and civic associations, attend local meetings more frequently, volunteer and work on community projects more often, and even visit with friends more frequently, and trust their neighbors more."[53] Could it be that more school means less education?

Supermarkets and Big Boxes

"Good morning, Mrs. Jones, good to see you here today. How's Johnny doing now that he's started school and did Judy get over that cold she had? By the way, we have some very nice fresh beans, just in from farmer Brown, and Joe tells me that the spring lamb is especially good this year." So begins a visit to the grocer circa 1920. After a few moments of friendly conversation, Mrs. Jones would read off her list of desired purchases, and the grocer would assemble and package everything for her. She may well look at the fresh green beans and decide to buy some. "I'll cook those for dinner tonight, so may I have just the right amount?"

Since the grocer was familiar with her family and their eating habits, he would measure out the appropriate amount, place the beans in a paper bag, weigh them, and ring up the correct price. If she decided to buy some of the lamb, that, too, would be cut to order in chops, roast, or whatever Mrs. Jones wanted. Since most grocery items that now come prepackaged were in bulk at the store, the grocer and his helpers would be kept busy serving customers, measuring and packaging the amounts requested, all the while engaged in friendly conversation. Mrs. Jones could have her purchases delivered to her house if she wished. While at the store, Mrs. Jones may have taken the opportunity to chat with her neighbours and other shoppers, turning the event into a social occasion. Within the next few decades this was all to change.

As early as 1915, as the efficiency movement gathered momentum, the notion of one large market containing a wide assortment of products was promoted in a short-lived project by Vincent Astor in New York. The idea was to reduce prices to the consumer by stocking large quantities of goods that could be purchased at lower bulk prices. However, "he failed to consider the whims of human nature."[54] That is, people were not yet willing to travel to a central location when they could still shop at their local grocery store.

That was also about to change--

Another harbinger of the future was Clarence Saunders, who introduced self-service into his Piggly Wiggly store in Memphis, Tennessee in 1916. Innovations included entryway turn-stiles, individually price-marked items, checkout stands, and the soon-to-come shopping cart. Saunders obviously knew he was on to something, acquiring patents for his ideas and offering franchises to other entrepreneurs. (Incidentally, he never revealed the origin of the curious name of his stores.) Offshoots of self-service were the need for name brands and advertising, the significance of the shopping cart (size matters), and customers who are compliant, impressionable, uncritical, and obedient.

With quantities of goods displayed on open shelves, customers were likely to choose a recognizable brand label, one that would be advertised in newspapers, magazines, and on the radio. Recommendations from the grocer were not possible because self-service meant that there would be no one there to offer advice. And those green beans that Mrs. Jones bought were now prepackaged and may have been shipped in from distant farms. She no longer could buy the exact amount she wanted.

As Mrs. Jones entered this store, she would have taken a shopping cart, another highly effective marketing tool. The original shopping cart was a simple trolley designed to carry a regular-sized shopping basket of the kind that housewives would have carried when they went shopping. Compare that image to the giant shopping carts found in today's giant supermarkets. Simple: The bigger the cart the bigger the purchase.

"Pile it high, sell it low"[55] was the slogan of Michael J. Cullen, who is generally credited with opening the first large-scale supermarket, King Kullen, in August 1930 in Queens, NY.

Like the fast food restaurant, the supermarket offers similar expectations: predictability, consistency, familiarity, speed, low price, and minimum human interaction. Though the grocery market presents a seemingly wide variety of products, the assortment will be made up of branded and well-advertised products artfully displayed on the shelves according to well-researched marketing practices. If you've ever had to search for that one bottle (more likely a throw-away carton) of milk you came to buy, you will have found it in one of the far corners of the store, so placed to direct you to walk through various aisles, past the meat and deli sections and through the baked goods. If you've resisted any impulse purchases, congratulations, but, remember, you'll still be offered a tempting array of chocolate bars, candies, and magazines as you wait obediently at the checkout lineup.

Shopping at a supermarket is now orchestrated and managed. Every move of the customer has been carefully studied so that the store can be laid out and arranged to take full advantage of the shopper's habits. According to standard product placement practice, the fresh produce will be first in your line of sight as you enter. The highly polished apples, oranges, and other fruits will be your introduction to the glistening and theatrically lighted vegetables, many of which will come pre-packaged in amounts just a bit greater than you had intended to buy. If the store has a flower display, it will be right there up front. The impression is intended to be one of wholesome freshness, abundance, and enticing colour that will set the tone for your "shopping experience."

Along the supermarket aisles, high-markup, best sellers, and name brands will be in view in what marketers call the bull's-eye zone, second and third shelves, at eye and easy-reach level. Lower-priced goods are placed lower down, requiring an effort on your part to reach them. At the same time, anything that kids will be likely to urge parents to buy will be at the right level to meet young eyes. Another significant location is the *end cap*, found at the ends of aisles. Here you are encouraged to pause and view— and buy—seasonal specialties, new products, or featured sale items. All this time the canned music wafting from an invisible source will massage your mood and the pace at which you sashay happily along, assured that all is right with the world. This can only work if the customers feel powerless and do not question the treatment they're getting. They must be trained to believe that all this is for their own good. Training that is dutifully supplied by school.

Environmental psychologist Paco Underhill, in *Why We Buy, The Science of Shopping*,[56] says, "Two-thirds of what we buy in the supermarket we had no intention of buying," In other words, the plan is working. School delivers the well-trained unquestioning consumers.

Self-Checkout

As more and more profit became the sole goal of corporations, the *Semi-attended customer-activated terminal* (SACAT) or "self-service checkout" was introduced in the 1990s. It was immediately recognized that by having customers do the work of cashiers, fewer employees would be needed, costs could be reduced, and profits increased. So, another self-serve system was introduced to grocery stores, hardware stores, drug stores, and even libraries. Though a few human-operated checkout lines were provided for the obstinate, it was possible for one supervisor to oversee the operation of any number of terminals, hence "*semi-attended* customer-activated." Well, OK, some kinks had to be ironed out because a few wily customers figured out how to cheat by simply removing or exchanging bar-code stickers on expensive items for those of cheaper items. A weigh-out system was soon devised with the idea of matching the weight of bagged purchases with the amounts recorded by the system. This was only partially successful, but, as with shoplifting or *stock shrinkage*, losses were more than covered by savings in wages, staff training, and floor space. Bar-code stickers already meant that cashiers did not need to know the prices of canned, bottled, and packaged items, and now the stickers could be read by the SACAT. Though produce, when in quantities chosen by the customer and sold by weight, had to be dealt with separately, this problem is solved by prepackaged and coded lettuces, oranges, green beans, and other produce. Another advantage to prepackaging is that the customer can be enticed to buy more than he or she intended. Then, too, packaged fruits and vegetables tend to look brighter, fresher, cleaner, and more attractive than those in open display, and you can be persuaded to believe that no other human hand has touched them.

33

Tom Durrie

Soon to come is the automated shopping cart which will read barcodes and ring up your purchases as you go along. All you'll have to do is pop your card in a machine on your way out. Of course you'll package up your groceries yourself and carry them out to your car. No human contact required.

While there has been some backlash to self-serve checkout, we can be sure that big store corporations are not going to give up the economic advantages. All that is required is well-trained unquestioning customers who are willing to believe that they are somehow getting a "good deal."

Did I say backlash? The sole cashier at a Canadian Tire Store told me that many people prefer the automatic checkout because they don't want to talk to anyone.

Popular Music

There was a time not so long ago when popular songs were written and performed by grownups for a grownup audience. That meant that the music could be interesting and varied in harmony, melody, and instrumentation. Lyrics to the songs could be poetic or humorously clever. People like Cole Porter, George Gershwin, Jerome Kern, and Irving Berlin were composing songs that were heard on the radio, on jukeboxes, at high school dances, and on home record players everywhere. The songs were performed by trained and experienced musicians like Benny Goodman, Glen Miller, the Dorsey brothers, and Duke Ellington. Yes, the songs were popular with young people, too. But the content was adult. The teenage market had not yet been discovered.

Most of the popular music of today is aimed at teenage, and younger, fans, but the adult audience is also buying it—and buying into it. They know of nothing else. Sophisticated studies, as reported by *Scientific American*, looked at the elements of today's popular hits.[57] They tell us what even a casual listener can easily discern: the music is simpler, more repetitive, and much much louder. Persistent loudness is a result of the compression of dynamic range resulting in near-zero contrast. The music is always just plain loud. Electronic enhancement and auto-tune mean that you're unlikely ever to hear a vocalist's real voice, and computer-generated accompaniment is eliminating the need for actual musicians. The electronic drummer has been around for a while now. It's a digital device that by insistent repetition of simple rhythmic patterns or preprogrammed variations does away with the creativity and the expense of a human but less predictable drummer.

If most popular songs of today sound the same, it's because they are. Most of the songs in the top 100 charts by such performers as Katie Perry, Adele, Miley Cyrus, Avril Lavigne, Justin Timberlake, Justin Bieber, and Celine Dion, are created and produced by Lukasz Gottwald or Max Martin. Gottwald, known professionally as Dr. Luke, is an American songwriter and singer, now in his mid-40s, with over 150 songs to his credit, many of which have been best sellers, depending of course on who has recorded them. Max Martin, real name Karl Martin Sandberg, operates his music-producing kingdom in Sweden. Small wonder then that:

> A Spanish study gathered data on a gigantic database of pop songs between 1955 and 2010 and concluded that the amount of diversity and variation in chords, melodies, and instrumentation has steadily diminished over this period—or, as lead researcher Joan Serra succinctly put it, "We found evidence of a progressive homogenization of the musical discourse."[58]

Popular songs are also getting shorter to accommodate commercial interests as well as shortened attention spans. The average pop song is now less than three and a half minutes long.[59] Compare that with the five-minute play time of the 78 rpm record of the 1940s.

And it is assumed, even if not generally proved, that many pop singers *lip-sync* to their pre-recorded voice at live concerts.

Given the glitz and glamour—and loudness—of such concerts lip-syncing would be a nearly unavoidable temptation. Besides, what's the difference? The voice will be electronically enhanced, sounding the same whatever the source. I note that amplification and voice enhancement are now used regularly in musical comedy, a far cry from the days of Ethel Merman and Howard Keel. The only place you'll hear the actual sound of voices and instruments is at a classical music concert or opera.

In 1906, the great march composer and bandmaster John Philip Sousa protested the advent of recorded music in an article titled *The Menace of Mechanical Music.* He warned that recorded music "was becoming a substitute for human skill, intelligence, and soul." [60] Even earlier, Sir Arthur Sullivan (of Gilbert and Sullivan fame) commented on an 1888-cylinder recording, "Dear Mr. Edison ... I can only say that I am astonished and somewhat terrified at the result of this evening's experiments, astonished at the wonderful power you have developed, and terrified at the thought that so much hideous and bad music may be put on record forever." [61] If he only knew!

YAY, TEAM!
The World of Sports

In 1925, the Spanish philosopher José Ortega y Gasset wrote, "In these last few years we have seen almost all caravels of seriousness founder on the tidal wave of sports that floods the newspaper pages." [62] One hundred years later, the philosopher's words seem truly prophetic because what he observed then has multiplied beyond what would have been his wildest imagination. The "caravels of seriousness" no longer merely founder, they have long ago sunk out of sight. Sunk out of sight, that is, along with the newspaper pages he mentions. Reports of sports victories and losses, along with the successes and failures of sports heroes, are now accorded equal importance with international political events on television, radio, and popular media, Players on big-name teams and solo Olympic athletes are lauded more and paid more than any artist, musician, writer, doctor, academic, or politician.

Intellectual pursuits are discounted as irrelevant beside the glamour of a winning team.

Sports not only dominate the media but they also dominate the public imagination. Anyone living in Canada would be hard-pressed to have missed the hoopla and furor over the 2019 performance of the Toronto Raptors, the only Canadian team on the roster of the National Basketball Association. It was inescapable to be informed that the Raptors won the NBA Tournament Finals, causing an enormous sensation across the country. Thousands, if not millions, of people were leaping about and cheering "We won! We won! We won!" There were parades and parties and, no doubt, drunken revelries. Sarah McLachlan even "sang" the national anthem. The official final word was "The north has spoken,"[63] as though some significant event had occurred or, as was said, the Raptors have united the country and inspired thousands of youngsters to want to become basketball heroes. Perhaps uniting the country could be the goal of aspiring youngsters, but the million-dollar salaries of top players like Kyle Lowry ($33,296,296 US in 2019-2020)[64] may contribute to the incentive. Incidentally, Lowry, like the other hired members of the Toronto team, does not come from Canada. They are the mercenaries in today's battle for sports supremacy.

Ortega y Gasset continued his comment on sport with, "Cult of the body is an infallible symptom of a leaning toward youth, for only the young body is lithe and beautiful. Whereas cult of the mind betrays the resolve to accept old age, for the mind reaches plenitude only when the body begins to decline. The triumph of sport marks the victory of the values of youth over the values of age."[65] A glance (or two) at the Olympic Games will confirm this statement.

Alternating between summer and winter sports, the games are held every two years, with countries vying for a chance to host the games and the millions of dollars in revenue promised from tourism and advertising. Such profits do not come without cost however. Ranging in recent years from a low of $15.4 billion

(2018 winter games PyeongChang) to $35.0 billion (2020 summer games Tokyo),[66] it's not hard to see that the Olympics do not come cheap. The fact is that the investment rarely pays off except in bragging rights. Every nation wants to "own the podium" and take great pride in their athletes winning various medals. Though the Olympic athletes are usually nationals of the countries they represent, the vicarious triumph they provide is akin to the "We won! We won!" of the Canadian basketball fans.

Above all, sports seem to offer an excitement and stimulation lacking in arid contemporary lives. The advantage of a passive audience, so well provided by school, to marketers and advertisers is obvious. In an article in *The New Yorker*, Louis Menard wrote "For everyone knows what the social role of sports is today. It is, via commercials and endorsements, to sell stuff. And everyone knows what makes that possible is television." [67]

The televised Super Bowl is an outstanding example; seconds of advertising time sell for millions of dollars. With viewers numbering well over 100 million, you can see why advertisers are eager to occupy even a second or two of the telecast. Advertising has as its purpose the selling of goods that we didn't know we needed or wanted. Need I mention that this is a lesson we are taught in school from the earliest age? After all, isn't it a whole lot easier just to do what you're told rather than to struggle with the mental gymnastics required for making informed choices? As Fran Lebowitz wrote: "What is truly chilling is that there are a lot of smart people interested in sports. That just gives you no hope at all for the human race."[68]

Fast Food

When I was four or five years old, I often accompanied my mother when she worked in a small flower shop in the Beaumont district of Portland, Oregon. On these occasions I might be treated to lunch at a nearby restaurant, the O-So-Good. To me it was the *osogood* and it was there that I had my first hamburger. This delightful confection of a hamburger patty, some lettuce, perhaps relish, mayonnaise, and the iconic round bun immediately became my food of choice, right next to my other favourite, Franco-American canned spaghetti. I hasten to add, though, that I could enjoy such treats on rare occasions. Pretty well all of the food we ate was prepared at home, where breakfasts and dinners were always eaten with the family together, seated at the kitchen table.

When I was a teenager, living in Portland, Oregon in the 1940s, there were many independent restaurants, large and small, serving hamburgers and other foods. Department stores and even some drug stores had lunch counters and soda fountains. We all had favourites. My friend George Ryan and I would occasionally make the trip to North East 41st to have hamburgers and cherry pie at Yaw's Top Notch. Yaw's was a popular hamburger restaurant, priding itself on high-quality, efficient and friendly service, and reasonable prices. Around that time they added a drive-in service so that customers could be served and eat without getting out of their cars. No one had yet thought of lining up to buy packaged food to take away.

What's important here is that each restaurant or lunch counter was different, independently owned and operated. It wasn't until 1954 that the McDonald brothers' restaurant in San Bernardino, California, drew the attention of Ray Kroc, a salesman for Prince Castle, a supplier of restaurant equipment. Kroc noticed that the McDonalds were buying close to a dozen milkshake machines, unlike the two or three needed by most restaurants. What was their secret?

Not exactly a secret, but the brothers, observing that hamburgers were their most popular item, rejigged the operation basing it on Henry Ford's mass production model. By 1948, they had converted to a walk-up and take-out service offering only hamburgers, French fries, milkshakes, coffee, and Coca-Cola, all served in paper disposable containers. Such efficiencies meant low prices, immediate service, and a standardized product. Ray Kroc knew a good thing when he saw it and, signing a franchise agreement with the McDonalds, opened similar restaurants, named McDonald's of course, in Illinois. The franchise spread and, by 1961, Kroc had bought out the brothers and formed the McDonald's Corporation. The rest, as they say, is history. Now, almost sixty years later, you can go to any McDonald's restaurant in the world and get pretty much the same Big Mac that you would get in America.

It didn't take long for other burger operations to latch onto McDonald's marketing and expansion systems. You now have a "choice" of similar outlets like Burger King, A & W, or Wendy's. The key to success in this field is a well-trained public that will be content with predictability, consistency, similarity, speed (no waiting), and low price. No surprises, no guesswork, no decisions, no questions—no thinking required.

Fill 'er Up

Starting around 1913, drive-in stations selling gasoline began to appear throughout the United States and Canada. Soon developed by brand-name oil companies these often competed with each other in selling price and services offered. These businesses were known as *filling* or, ironically in the present-day context, *service* stations. When my father drove his Model A Ford into any one of them, two or three young men would immediately attend to cleaning the windshield, checking the tire pressures, checking the oil level (followed by showing the dipstick to the driver, who had an option of adding oil if needed). All this, while the requested amount of gas was being pumped into the car. This would usually be accompanied by an exchange of pleasantries or enquiries about road or mechanical conditions. And one could always expect clean washrooms and drinking fountains. After paying his bill to the smiling attendant, my father would always say, "Much obliged." Such were the social and business interactions of the 1930s and 40s.

Nowadays, as everyone knows, you drive into a gas station—or; heaven help us, a *gas bar*—and do the work yourself, never questioning why or to whose benefit. There is no one to thank or with whom to exchange pleasantries. You have become the unquestioning servant of a corporation. No wonder the name "service station" has disappeared from the lexicon. Again, school has taught us not to question what is being done to us by those in authority, in this case big powerful oil corporations.

ATMs

Though the idea of a machine that would dispense cash first emerged in the early 1960s, it was the concept of the identity card with PIN (personal identification number) in 1965 that started the proliferation of the ATM (automated teller machine) worldwide, "The essence of this system was that it enabled the verification of the customer with the debited account **without human intervention.**"[69] (Emphasis added) All you need to do is to train people to use the machine so contact with a human bank teller would be unnecessary. Fewer employees, bigger profits. The Automated Teller Machine goes by many names, depending on which company is running it and where in the world it may be. The most cunningly ironic label yet devised is *Personal Touch Banking.*

Interactions with machines and avoidance of human interactions are becoming more and more widely accepted. The advent of the *personal* assistant, digitally personified by Alexa, Siri, Cortana, et al is creating an illusion of human contact. A friendly-sounding and soothing voice will answer your questions, tell you jokes, and offer all kinds of help. It might be easy to forget that all responses come out of computer algorithms, preplanned, predesigned, and standardized, with none of the complicated and often unpredictable dealings with real people. Again, no thinking required.

41

Tom Durrie

The Decline of Print

A similar decline in readership and advertising support may be seen in print magazines. In the same way that big-box stores and fast food outlets are dominating the market and edging out privately owned businesses, digital media are overtaking print-on-paper. As Justine Jordan commented in *The Fashion Spot*, "The digital age has not only managed to kill time but it's also on the verge of killing print."[70] With major advertisers moving to Facebook, Google, and other internet-dominated media, print magazine sales are losing revenue at a rapid rate. "The estimated aggregate revenue of U.S. based periodical publishers has fallen sharply in the past decade from 46 billion U.S. dollars in 2007 to around 28 billion in 2017. Americans spent an average of 24 minutes reading magazines on a daily basis in 2010. This figure is forecast to decline to 15 minutes by 2018."[71] Given shortened attention spans, it's likely that fifteen minutes is but a memory today.

At the same time, online magazines and information sites are gaining in popularity and usage. Time Inc., publishers of the once-mighty *Time Magazine*, has recently undergone changes in ownership and public exposure. In 2017 *Time* still had a subscriber base of over two million, though down from 3.3 million in 2012.[72] In 2018, *Time* was bought by billionaire Marc Benioff. While Benioff and his wife Lynne are clear about intending to continue producing the magazine in print, they are expanding the publication's reach into the digital world. Marc tweeted, "The power of *Time* is its unique storytelling of the people and issues that affect us all and connect us all." At the same time, *Time.com*, the magazine's digital site has a subscriber base that grew from 27.4 million in 2015 to 31.7 million in 2018.[73] Capitalizing on the attraction of popular videos, Time Inc. is also expanding to streaming television with items like *Paws and Claws*, a collection of cute cat videos and the like.

Other tech world giants are also buying into the magazine industry. "The print product is an afterthought, overshadowed by investments in live events, podcasts, video, and partnerships with outside brands."[74] The future is clearly digital. In 2013, Jeff Bezos

42

of Amazon.com, Inc. bought *The Washington Post*, while Laurene Powell Jobs bought a majority stake in *The Atlantic*.

But, so what? After all, people *are* reading magazines and newspapers, if not in print at least on line. But is reading on a computer screen or smartphone the same as reading print on paper? Not according to Maryanne Wolf, award-winning professor of reading and author of *Reader Come Home.*[75] Her book begins with a detailed analysis of how the brain functions while reading, how the required networks are formed, and how reading activates the vision, language, and cognition areas of the brain. She uses the term *deep reading* to refer to how reading can combine language, vision, cognition, and affect, leading to complex and profound changes in brain chemistry. "Together, you and the author construct images out of a set of carefully chosen, sensory details conveyed only by words."[76] *Deep reading* refers to reading print, that experience familiar to readers of being lost in connection with the words of an author. In fact, we are transported to different times and different lands, and in non-fiction we are transformed by the author's thought processes and ability to express complicated issues.[77]

There is considerable evidence that digital on-screen reading is more transitory and shallow than print-on-paper reading. A 2003 study by Ziming Liu of San Jose State University concluded that "The screen-based reading behavior is characterized by more time spent on browsing and scanning, keyword spotting, one-time reading, non-linear reading, and reading more selectively, while less time is spent on in-depth reading, and concentrated reading. Decreasing sustained attention is also noted."[78]

Another study, conducted in Norway in 2013 [79] involved seventy-two Grade Ten students who were tested and selected for equivalent reading comprehension and vocabulary. Half of them were given a text to read in print while the other half read the same text on screen. The test that followed showed that the students who read print understood and retained more than the on-screen readers. Among possible reasons for the discrepancy was the need for scrolling to access pages of text on a computer while readers of text-on-paper could perceive the text as a whole as well as easily refer back or ahead while reading. Anyone who works or plays on a computer also knows of the distraction ("increased cognitive load") of ads, links, and click-bait, offering such items as "Test Your IQ" or to show you "The One WD40 Trick Everyone Should Know About" or "Plastic Surgeon Says Doing This Every Morning Will Snap Back Sagging Skin." What is that saying about the internet offering lots of information but no knowledge?

Another study showed that computer readers were inferior "both in writing and reading comprehension." Computer readers also reported more feelings of stress and fatigue than those reading on paper. The researchers "concluded that reading and working with a computer results in higher cognition workload compared with paper."[80] Summarizing from a number of studies, Gemma Walsh concluded that "Many researchers also question the effect of electronic reading on deep reading skills, comprehension and the development of long-term knowledge and critical thinking."[81]

In his book *The Shallows,*[82] Nicholas Carr suggests that the brain is plastic, and any regular activity changes it. So using the internet changes the brain; and it changes it in such a way that the *linear, literary mind* is under assault. The suggestion is that as skimming becomes our dominant mode of reading, we gradually lose our ability to read books. As Maryanne Wolf in her first book on reading puts it, "We are experiencing a shift from the *reading brain* to the *digital brain.*"[83] This is more revolutionary than the changes in the social and personal psyche caused by the invention of printing and movable type. The inescapable reality, as interpreted by virtually all the research and every study done, is that the process of reading on screen is radically different from that of reading print on paper. Or, as stated by Barry Cull in *Reading Revolutions,* "Far from a small development, online digital text represents a revolution in human learning and communication that we are only beginning to understand."[84] The implications for society—and especially education—are profound. Are schools doing anything about this? Other than handing out computer tablets to kindergarten kids?

The small rural school in the community where I live boasts that it has a one-to-one ratio of students and electronic tablets. In other words, kids are handed these devices and expected to use them the way paper and pencil would have been used in previous years. However, a tablet is not merely a streamlined version of pencil and paper, it is a different animal altogether. A paper, no longer available, titled *School Growth Plan-Inquiry Model Boston Bar Elementary-Secondary School 2018/2019* stated, with a tone of empty pride and helpless pathos: "The presence of electronic devices at school, whether supplied by the school or student owned, has increased substantially this year. . . . Teachers use electronic devices in delivering curriculum and consequently students use electronic devices to support their learning. However, many students struggle to use their personal electronic devices responsibly for educational purposes in classroom settings. Teachers are trying to teach respectful use over banning devices as this relates to the real world." Isn't this, as Nicolas Carr suggests, the linear, literary mind under assault?

While the school tries to have some effect by banning students' hand-held devices, it is irresistible to conclude that it's losing the battle. Though, sidestepping the issue in a teacherly, almost ironic, manner,—"many students struggle to use the personal electronic devices responsibly for educational purposes"—I would suggest that the real struggle for the kids is to use the devices to surf the net, communicate with your pals, or watch YouTube videos without getting caught. Gum chewing used to present a similar problem to youngsters, or as Harvey Korman demonstrates so beautifully in *Blazing Saddles*: "Chewing gum on line, eh? I hope you brought enough for everybody."[85] So the argument rages, to allow or not allow cell phones in the classroom. Meanwhile the kids are busily working out ways to bypass regulations and prohibitions. At the same time, though schools have not, to my knowledge, yet supplied chewing gum, the rush to get all the latest school-approved technologies into the classroom is headlong. Meanwhile, there's increasing evidence that screen time and specifically the blue light emitted from screens interferes with sleep, meaning that many young people are now sleep-deprived, while being encouraged by the school to spend more time on screen as though they weren't already spending every possible moment on video games or social media.

Are You Paying Attention?

In a review of an exhibition of photography, Peter Schjeldahl, in *The New Yorker* wrote "The projections also go by at a clip—eight seconds apiece for horizontal pictures and thirteen seconds for interspersed verticals—that panders to present-day attention deficits." [86]

We saw earlier how popular songs are now decreasing in length, no one need pay attention for more than a few minutes. Even that hardly counts because who actually "listens" to a popular song? Yes, the regularly repeated catchphrase, usually eight bars, of a song will get stuck in your head, but the overall shape, form, and direction will be of no consequence. I like to ask the question, "How can people raised with nothing but three-minute popular songs be expected ever to pay attention to a twenty-minute symphony, let alone a five-hour opera?"

If people are not expected to look at art photographs or listen to music for more than a few seconds, you can be sure that advertisers and marketers are well on top of this game. The Halo Group, a New York marketing agency, lets us know that "Snackable content is a key element to your marketing strategy. As **attention spans decrease,** consuming media in bite-sized pieces becomes more favorable." [87] (emphasis added.) Indeed, the term *Snackable content* seems to have caught on. Another group of advertising specialists informs us that "All of them [memes, gifs, videos] considered the fact that attention spans decrease, which is why consuming media in bite-sized pieces becomes more favorable and makes snackable content attractive for any kind of marketing strategy." [88]

Attention can be difficult to measure, though numerous attempts have been made. An article by Kevin McSpadden, in *Time Magazine* proclaimed, with the sensational headline, "You Now Have a Shorter Attention Span Than a Goldfish." The goldfish in question supposedly had an attention span of nine seconds whereas a study from Microsoft Corp. demonstrated that "people now generally lose concentration after eight seconds." This was seen as a reduction from the span of twelve seconds that was presumed to be common in the year 2000. The reduction is attributed to the distractions of multiple streams of media or "the effects of an increasingly digitalized lifestyle on the brain." [89] The study, done in Canada, also claimed that half the people studied will automatically reach for their phones when nothing else is occupying their attention, and two-thirds use social media for news, while fifty-nine per cent would feel lost "without the devices they use every day." [90] It is also noted that digital lifestyles are "decreasing the ability for prolonged attention and increasing appetites for more stimuli." Advertisers, take note, and teachers, wring your hands.

A less sensational study, reported by Neil A. Bradbury of the Chicago Medical School, concerned itself with college students' attention during lectures, specifically lectures about physiology. It seems that general trends in curriculum reform have moved toward a lecture-length of fifteen minutes "based upon the 'common knowledge' and 'consensus' that there is a decline in students' attention 10-15 minutes into lectures." At the same time, it is noted that the main determinant of attention may well be the presentation itself. In other words, a dull and dry lecturer will cause attention to wander and instructors should "enhance their teaching skills to provide not only rich content but also a *satisfying lecture experience* for the students." [91] (italics added) What about intellectual content? The risk I see here is that some lecturers will attempt to be entertaining rather than knowledgeable and informative about their topic. I'm sure we can all remember teachers or professors who fired our interest and attention by their own commitment and enthusiasm for their subject. They were not necessarily entertaining—or brief.

TED

Touching on lecturing as entertainment, it's worth noting the enormously popular TED Talks. The original idea of TED came when Richard Saul Wurman noticed the confluence of ideas in technology, entertainment, and design (hence TED), and, along with Harry Marks, sponsored a conference, in 1984, with demonstrations of then-cutting edge technology like compact discs and e-books, accompanied by talks about 3D graphics from Lucasfilm, and a demonstration by mathematician Benoit Mandelbrot of how to map coastlines using his developing theory of fractal geometry. Early on, the basic format was established and continues to be *de rigueur* today. Considering that college-student attention at lectures is in the ten- to fifteen-minute range, the TED talk limit of seventeen minutes seems on the mark with just a modest push on the boundary. Wurman's idea was that seventeen minutes would not only be right to engage an audience but would also force the speakers, known experts in their field, to condense their thoughts into manageable bites. In other words, the aim is for a cogent, immediately comprehensible statement of ideas and opinions without exhaustive argument or, as Pooh-Bah called it "corroborative detail, intended to give artistic verisimilitude to an otherwise bald and unconvincing narrative."[92] Above all, we must not bore anybody!

The first conference had little impact and was considered a failure. However, Wurman and Marks held on to the idea. They believed in possibilities, and started, in 1990, with the first TED Conference that took fire. Though the first conferences were by invitation only, it didn't take long before it was admission to all, simply by registration. Well, not so simply. Many people will be totally flummoxed and put off by the lengthy application form, and if that doesn't do it, the $10,000 admission fee probably will.[93] That's *many* people, but far from all. Admission to TED Talks is in high demand, and the events are usually sold out. Presumably, attendance offers opportunities to network with other successful applicants and even includes participation in a Q & A with the speakers. Like most conferences, the purpose is to spread ideas and inspire participants to "go out and do something."

In 2001, businessman and publisher Chris Anderson took charge of TED and placed it under the aegis of his non-profit Sapling Foundation. He expanded the subject range of the talks to include science, culture, education, business, and key global issues. He also established the TED Prize, which grants recipients $1 million to support their "one wish to change the world." Most important perhaps was the start, in 2006, of posting talks on line and free to view. The immediate success of the YouTube videos inspired Anderson to develop the organization as a global media initiative devoted to "ideas worth spreading." In 2009, Anderson introduced the TEDx initiative which offers licensing organizers to create their own TED-type events ($75-$100 admission fee). His bestselling 2016 book *TED Talks: The Official TED Guide to Public Speaking*[94] offers advice to those who would like to emulate TED talk speakers.

With 57,828,525 views and counting, the most popular TED talk of all time is the late Sir Ken Robinson on "Do schools kill creativity?"[95] Within the 17-minute limit, Sir Ken is guaranteed not to bore anyone. He has the audience laughing much of the time with his witty asides and amusing anecdotes. Could it be that it is his entertaining manner rather than the content of his talk that has attracted so much attention? Since the talk has been around since 2006 you'd think that schools would have changed radically by now if anyone took his message seriously. Neil Bradbury's advice to university lecturers to "enhance their teaching skills to provide not only rich content but also a satisfying lecture experience for the students" seems especially pertinent. Can a "satisfying lecture experience" be provocative, radical, disturbing, or maddening? Or profound?

Once Upon a Time

By way of contrast... On January 10th of 1776, Thomas Paine published a pamphlet titled *Common Sense* with a lengthy subtitle reading: *Addressed to the Inhabitants of America, on the following interesting subjects: namely: I. Of the origin and design of government in general; with concise remarks on the English constitution. II. Of monarchy and hereditary succession. III. Thoughts on the present state of American affairs. IV. Of the present ability of America; with some miscellaneous reflections.* (He would have lost the digital-brain reader already.) Coming at a time when the people of the American colonies were grumbling and complaining about the rule, and especially taxation, of the English monarchy, Paine's concise and passionate arguments against British rule and in favour of independence caused a furor. We can only imagine how statements like "Of more worth is one honest man to society and in the sight of God, than all the crowned ruffians that ever lived" would rouse a new and fervent patriotism in a people that were feeling more and more oppressed. While there was already fighting by way of protest, there were few or no thoughts of independence. It took *Common Sense* to inflame thoughts of rebellion and of a democratic republic governed by the people. But how was the word spread to the 2.5 million people then living in the thirteen American colonies? It was estimated by Neil Postman that by the end of 1776 half the American population had read Thomas Paine's *Common Sense*.[96] Upwards of 500,000 copies of this book were printed, meaning that every sixth American would have bought a copy, and each copy was probably read by at least three people. In fact, the pamphlet was read aloud in taverns, barbershops, and at public gatherings, while numerous hand-copied versions of parts or even the entire pamphlet were also circulated. This suggests that the rate of literacy was very high.

If you're thinking that a pamphlet is composed of two or three folded pages, guess again. Thomas Paine's *pamphlet* was some fifty pages in length and contained such sentences as,

> Government, like dress, is the badge of lost inno-
> cence; the palaces of kings are built on the ruins
> of the bowers of paradise. For were the impulses
> of conscience clear, uniform, and irresistibly
> obeyed, man would need no other lawgiver; but
> that not being the case, he finds it necessary to
> surrender up a part of his property to furnish
> means for the protection of the rest; and this he is
> induced to do by the same prudence which in eve-
> ry other case advises him out of two evils to
> choose the least.

At 410 characters, not including spaces, Paine would have had a hard time reducing such utterances to the 280 character limit of a Tweet. People who grew up reading the *King James Bible* would have had no trouble with Paine's writing.

In 1812, Pierre Samuel Du Pont de Nemours, a French economist and government official who had emigrated to the United States, could say, "The United States are more advanced in their educational facilities than most countries. . . . Most young Americans, therefore, can read, write and cipher. Not more than four in a thousand are unable to write legibly—even neatly;" . . . and "In America, a great number of people read the Bible, and all the people read a newspaper. The fathers read aloud to their children, while breakfast is being prepared—a task which occupies the mothers for three-quarters of an hour every morning. And as the newspapers of the United States are filled with all sorts of narratives . . . they disseminate an enormous amount of information."[97] Looks like a far cry from the sugar-coated-cereal-eating, TV-watching, texting, Twittering, and Instagram viewing of today's breakfast eaters. Does it go without saying that a semi-literate public is more likely to accept the claims of advertisers without question, believe conspiracy theories, admire boasting and prevaricating politicians, and regard with suspicion the word of scientists and literate social critics who tend to write long sentences using a large vocabulary? Concomitant with the decline of literacy and intelligent public discourse is the dominance of public school with its stranglehold on children and youth.

But how did people learn to read before there was school to teach them how to read? In most rural communities, reading was as much a part of life as talking. As the family sat around while mother, father, or an older sibling read aloud from the Bible or, say, *Pilgrim's Progress*, the children would learn that the marks on the pages stood for words and conveyed meaning, and in the same way that children, on their own, make sense of spoken language and teach themselves to talk, they will make sense of printed language, and teach themselves to read. Since the rate of literacy was so high, there were books and newspapers every-where. Literacy breeds literacy. It was only when school came along to *teach* how to read that reading became an intimidating chore and literacy declined accordingly.

In *Reading Without Nonsense*, Frank Smith explains, "We begin learning to read the first time we make any kind of sense of print, even just a one-word sign, and we learn something about reading every time we read."[98] When a child, or anyone, is unable to read on their own, they need someone else to read for them— and to them. In the same way that we help a child get dressed un-til, pretty soon, they're doing it all by themselves—without in-struction. No one will learn to read from "instructional" cartoons or *Sesame Street*. "You learn to read by reading"[99] in the same way that you learned to talk by talking.

And So—

In an article in *The New Yorker* about non-violent protest, Erica Chenoweth is quoted as saying, "The norms and institutions can grow weaker over years, or decades, without people notic-ing."[100] The social and intellectual life of a couple of past decades slips away to be replaced by modern "conveniences" with but a few older people saying "remember when." Innovations, however isolating and inconvenient, become accepted without question by the public because old-fashioned ways seem just that. A grocery chain may reduce personal service until people see self-service and automated checkout as convenient innovations. An automated teller machine may seem like a godsend if the bank has cut service by laying off most of its tellers. And we grudgingly accept automated phone answering—"listen for the following twenty options"—as unavoidable because "Your call is important to us." But there's no one there to answer the phone and engage in a polite and human response. In her hit song *Big Yellow Taxi*,[101] Joni Mitchell sings, "Don't it always seem to go/That you don't know what you've got 'til it's gone?" Or maybe you never knew it was there.

The Readymade Teenage Market

As the twentieth century wore on, market and corporate forces grew in power, so did the need for more consumers. And what better place to find those consumers than in school? The discovery, or rather the invention, of the teenage market[102] made a whole new segment of society, separate from adults as well as younger kids. There they were, already sorted out into grades and classes. Why, teenagers were even in separate institutions known as high schools.

While the loveable, zany, and exasperating teenager was well-known through books, radio programs, comic strips, and television,[103] he was not seen as a consumer until the 1940s. It turned out that girls were far easier to target as a market than were boys. So, new lines of specialized products were created to tap into the spending money that postwar teenagers now had: cosmetics, hairdressings, popular music (on 78 and later 45 rpm discs), clothing, and magazines. A new and separate teenage culture was created. But wait, that's only the beginning because there was an entire platoon of kids, known as *'tweens* (the apostrophe has now been dropped) just waiting to become a target market.[104] *Tween* refers to kids from age eight to twelve or nine to thirteen—those *between* childhood and adolescence. Again, girls were the primary target, and the arrow hit the bull's eye with the Spice Girls, a music group created and sold (in 1994) with the tween market in mind. The creators and pushers of this group certainly knew what they were aiming at. New products, aimed, again at girls, include cosmetics (yes, moisturizers, perfumes, and bath products for twelve-year-olds!), shoes and clothing, cameras, and fashion dolls (Hello, Barbie!). Market forces soon learned that they had a powerful ally in the kids whose persuasive powers could coerce parents into buying whatever products they were pushing.

And with the hypnotic assistance of television in mid-century, people no longer looked at each other or engaged in conversation as they sat, eyes fixed on the flickering screen, with TV tray set up in front of them and the frozen TV Dinner waiting to be popped into the microwave, no one had to interrupt their viewing. Since the purpose of television programming is to deliver an audience for commercials, programs became more predictable (find out what they're watching and give them more of it) and commercials louder, more frequent, shorter, and, yes, more creative.

The youth movement of the 1960s, with its protests and rebellious music, flared up and died out, overcome by economic interests and political conservatism. The neoliberal economic policies of Ronald Reagan and Margaret Thatcher secured the supremacy of corporate profits over the welfare of the citizenry. Then along came the Internet promising ready availability of information and a paperless society. We all know how off-kilter that became. However, it wasn't until the arrival of social media, in the early twenty-first century, that young people became fully divorced from the influence of parents, teachers, and other adults. Other adults, that is, besides those who are recognized as the glamorous celebrities of the moment.

Social media are driving the wedge further between the grown-up world and the peer-oriented world of youth. Even the grown-up world is not so grown up anymore. Adults, now cut loose from the peer group of the eighties and nineties they grew up in, have little to fall back on. Looking—and acting—young are the ideals. It is not unusual to see grown men and women dressed in clothing previously deemed only appropriate for children at play.

The clothing that used to belong to childhood—jeans, running shoes, T-shirts, baseball caps—have become common dress for adults, no matter what the occasion. Fitness clubs, cosmetics, and clothing are marketed to middle-aged adults with the promise of eternal youth. Any sense of adult dignity or decorum is seen as out-of-date, old-fashioned, or absurd. At the same time, the youth of today are living in a world of their own, associating almost exclusively, especially on social media, with others of their own age.

Small wonder, then, that children are not looking to parents and teachers as role models and sources of knowledge and wisdom. And because school, daycare, and a myriad of child-oriented sports and activities force children by segregation into a separate peer-oriented social group, even dividing that group into smaller groups based on age and ability, a set of standards and mores have self-generated within those groups. Because children, however bright and perceptive they may be, lack experience upon which to judge the value of behaviour, the culture of young people is based upon power and status, as well as popularity and fashion as influenced by media. In short, conformity, forced or otherwise. Like the stake driven into Dracula's heart, peer-oriented culture and social media have driven the wedge between children and adults.

In his remarkably insightful book of 1998 Frank Smith points out that, "The classic view of learning is encapsulated in seven words familiar to every speaker of English: *You learn from the company you keep*," [105] and if the company you keep consists of "friends" on social media, personalities on YouTube video channels, other inexperienced young people, ad men, and adults whose main concern is control, you are left to put together a culture of your own—with dire results. Smith contrasts "two visions of learning: an 'official theory' that learning is work and a 'classic' view that we learn effortlessly every moment of our waking lives."[106] Spend several hours a day on social media, and you will become part of that world, unconsciously and unintentionally. Because we learn who we are and what our place in society is, again without thinking about it or questioning why, we willingly allow ourselves to be manipulated by mass marketing, self-serve, shoddy entertainment, and an absence of social, artistic, or political engagement. We have absorbed from school that learning (as defined by school) is arduous, must be taught, and will be graded. Though schools are desperately trying to turn their version of learning into fun, they cannot compete with social media and targeted advertising. Graduating from school, at whatever level, is like being liberated from jail, the hoopla of graduation ceremonies to the contrary notwithstanding. Most people will have lost all interest in academic or intellectual pursuits, while attendance at college or university is seen solely as a road to higher income. They are quite content to submit to the blandishment of the carefully orchestrated manipulations of marketing and the (also manipulated) addictive qualities of social media and video games. I repeat: School serves as a con duit of unexamined societal values.

PART THREE

The World of Fun and Games

A. Shoot To Kill

This Changes Everything

This Changes Everything, the title of a 2014 book by Naomi Klein,[107] refers to climate change, but today's mind-boggling multitude of video games suggests that it's more than climate change that is transforming the way people think, spend their time, and construct a view of the world. It might be said that gaming provides a potentially addictive distraction from the harsh realities and impending disasters that surround us. Instead of providing a thoughtful and critical approach to the world or to computers, schools have rushed to jump onto the digital bandwagon, thinking that if every kid learns, from age five, to use the latest technological wonders, they will be all-the-more-ready for a future job. First of all, what ten-year-old cannot grasp, with astonishing alacrity and without instruction, the use of a computer or smartphone? And second, 99 per cent of the technology being pushed in elementary schools today will be obsolete before these kids reach high school. While the teachers are imagining that their students are diligently devoted to their lessons, the lure of video games, social media, and internet surfing are ever there in the not-so-distant background, beckoning to be followed like the pied piper, luring children away from adult influence.

The best I can do is to offer a description of a few of the most popular games as well as an introduction to the rapidly growing field of so-called educational games. You can be sure that new ones are being added every day. As profits soar and technology becomes increasingly sophisticated, games become increasingly realistic and immersive—and addictive. According to one report, by mid-2020 there were around 3.1 <u>billion</u> gamers worldwide; [108] the appeal of gaming is not to be underestimated. Look at it this way: with the world population rising toward eight billion in that same year, forty per cent of all men, women, and children will spend at least some of their time playing video games.

Does this suggest that individuals worldwide will spend many of their waking hours in front of a video screen, in solitude, without the need to communicate with other individuals either by voice or print? Or do the gaming "communities," sometimes consisting of millions of players, provide socialization and personal contact? I would say no for two reasons. One is that much interaction is online and with individuals identified only by an avatar name such as Gyemo, Lashoh, or Zizran. Often, there is no indication of location, age, or gender, which leads me to the second reason: the focus is entirely on the game. Whether playing cooperatively or competitively players do not discuss politics, literature, personal issues, music, or art; the concern is succeeding in the quest and aiming for the epic win. This is indeed bowling *alone*.

Real human interaction takes place face-to-face. From early childhood, we have learned to read another person's expression and meaning through eye contact, body and facial cues, and voice tone: all that is missing from online, text, or even video (e.g. Zoom) communication.

October 2019 saw the release of a video-game-based movie titled *Doom Annihilation*,[109] described as "a direct to video action horror film." *Doom* is a franchise specializing in "first-person shooter video games," in which an anonymous space marine fights a variety of demons and zombies. In case you don't know, a first-person shooter game is one in which the player is the protagonist who goes about shooting, usually in the head, threatening characters of all stripes. Interestingly, or alarmingly, enough, *Doom Annihilation* is distributed by the cozily domestic-sounding *Universal Pictures Home Entertainment* which admits the movie is rated R "for bloody violence and language throughout."[110]

The *Doom* franchise[111] has been notably successful in introducing first-person shooter games enhanced with 3D graphics, networked gameplay, and numerous profitable spinoffs such as comics, board games, novels, and movies. Since the title's launch, in 1993, more than ten million copies of *Doom* games have been sold.

In spite of the longer history of *Doom* and others, by far the most popular video game of 2019 was *Fortnite Battle Royale*, boasting more than 250 million players worldwide.[112] The popularity of the game has, as predicted (see below), grown exponentially. In January 2022 there were three to four million concurrent players with 350 million registered players.[113]

A major attraction of the game is that it is an online multiplayer game involving hundreds, thousands, or even millions of players worldwide at any given moment. Sitting at their computers, Game Boxes. or smartphones, participants strive, singly or in small groups, to be the last character "alive" at the end of the game. The illusion—or is it delusion?—is that this is some kind of happy community, engaged in a co-operative fun activity.

The Fortnite brand, developed and launched in 2017 by Epic Games Inc. of North Carolina, comprises three distinct game modes. Modes include the innocent-sounding "Fortnite: Save the World," described as a co-operative shooter-survival game in which up to four players fight off zombie-like creatures, and "Fortnite Creative," where players create worlds and battle arenas. But the runaway favourite, "Battle Royale," is a blazingly rapid interaction of player and computer images involving the building of protective structures and the fighting off of an array of mutant invaders. The player is armed with plenty of firepower, usually in the form of assault rifles. A how-to-play *Fortnight* website offers this helpful advice to the novice player:

> As a general rule, stick to assault rifles or SMGs [submachine guns] when you're first figuring out how to play Fortnite. Sniper rifles are useless under 75 metres, so although you'll want to keep one handy do *not* use it in close quarters combat unless you absolutely have to. Another thing to bear in mind when you're figuring out how to play Fortnite is if/when you're shooting someone up close and personal, you'll want to prioritize your shotgun. Shotguns - surprise surprise - do a *ton* of damage and are good for one-hit kills, so keep one

in your hands when you're exploring houses, basements, or any other small spaces.[114]

If you find "shooting someone up close and personal" somewhat disturbing, you won't be surprised to know that many parents have expressed concern. These games, after all, can be played by anyone anywhere with a computer, tablet, smartphone, or Game Box. There are no enforceable age restrictions. Or, as Common Sense Media puts it:

> And now many parents are taking notice of this rollicking game where players fight to the death. … On one hand, it's getting major points with kids and parents alike for building teamwork and thoughtful collaboration. On the other hand, it's a combat-based game with tons of guns and violence.[115]

"Teamwork and thoughtful collaboration" are among the oft-cited advantages of playing video games. The proponents claim that the games are vital to the enhancement of co-ordination, quick problem solving, and concentrated attention, all developed in a digital world that emphasizes rapid action and unceasing stimulation and excitement. The focus is on the game, so you don't wander off into discussions of personal interest or concerns. Thoughtful collaboration? The fast action and ever-changing images and challenges of the game hardly lead to much time for thought, conversation, teamwork—or collaboration.

Another popular video game, with ninety one million players logging in every month, is *Minecraft*. This is a "sandbox game," the type in which a player is free to roam a virtual world instead progressing from level to level. Unlike *Fortnite*, the purpose of *Minecraft* is "simply to build and explore (and survive)."[116] The action centres on odd block-like creatures who make tools and build things. The off-the-top object of the game is to build a shelter before sunset to protect yourself from the coming attack of monsters like Zombies or Creepers. In the Survival Mode (the default and most popular mode), players are confronted with a growing number of such alien attackers as the shooter aspect of the game grows in importance—and excitement. Putting a positive spin on the game, Elissa Strauss of CNN states, "Sure, there is a lot of moving around and killing bad guys, but that's far from the whole point. The bigger goal is survival, and creation and destruction are both key to that survival."[117] What is missing is the notion that acquiring real tools, learning how to use them, and then digging a mine or building a castle are difficult, time-consuming enterprises, not objects of instant gratification and "survival" as the game suggests. But that hasn't stopped schools from using the computer game as a fun way of learning: "Would you be shocked if your teacher assigned you to play Minecraft at school? . . . The Lego-like building game has become a popular tool for classroom lessons as well as life lessons."[118] Why, even "life lessons" can be a barrel of fun, violent or otherwise.

Standing out from the crowd of popular shoot-'em-up games is *Grand Theft Auto*, one of the most popular, controversial, and most highly praised of all games. Since its introduction in 2013, sales of *Grand Theft Auto V* had, by 2018, exceeded $6 billion, outstripping all other games as well as all other forms of entertainment, including movies, books, and music.[119] Keith Stuart in *The Guardian* described GTA V as "a sprawling tale of criminal maniacs self-destructing on a blood-splattered career trajectory to hell."[120] Apparently just what the contemporary game player is looking for. Called, by Tom Hoggins, a "bona fide cultural behemoth,"[121] *Grand Theft Auto* makes a strong statement about trends in contemporary society.

In these games, the player, by now inured to violence, takes on the role of one of three characters, all male (need I say?[122]), whose purpose is to advance in the hierarchy of organized crime. This is to be accomplished by carrying out various missions ordered by high-ranking members of the criminal world. Missions include assassinations, relentlessly fast and dangerous driving (remember it's *only* a game), gang associations, and high-level theft, along with the torture and obliteration of opponents. Characters may also visit strip clubs, movie houses, and even improve their appearance with a haircut, a new outfit, or a tattoo. Strip clubs will of course involve women, who are portrayed as prostitutes, nags, or sexy provocatrices, much cleavage in evidence. Tom Hoggins again: "Grand Theft Auto V is relentlessly misanthropic . . . women are shallow and sidelined, and the men front-and-center are heartless, psychotic, money-obsessed, philandering bastards . . . Grand Theft Auto V's treatment of women aims to make its audience uncomfortable. But do enough of my fellow male players feel that way?"[123] Remember, this is the most popular video game of them all.[124]

If you are one of those parents who worry about the effects that games like *Fortnite* or *Grand Theft Auto* might be having on your kids, Amazon has any number of soothing child-friendly suggestions. *Super Mario 3D World*, for example, "might be the best child-friendly game ever made" and "If you're looking for a game to play as a family, this is the one."[125] The series of more than twenty games began in 1985 with the launching, by the game giant Nintendo, of *Super Mario Bros.* (note the abbreviation, now the established and recognizable cognomen). The overarching object of the games is for the plumber Mario and his brother Luigi to rescue the Princess Toadstool (Toadstool?), who later became the more delicately titled Princess Peach, from Bowser, the leader of the cartoonish turtle-like characters of the Koopa Troopa. Bowser and the Koopas are, as you might guess, the enemies who are to be demolished by Mario, who jumps on and squashes them or throws and "fires" various implements, all the while leaping about and jumping with ease over obstacles. The archenemy Bowser retaliates by changing size and breathing fire. Numerous complications are introduced throughout the series but the basic plot of the game is the same: rescue the damsel in distress from the lascivious lovelorn villain, different from more "grown up" shoot-and-kill games in appearance only.

And On The Other Hand

Just think, by playing video games, you and your kids will improve co-ordination and problem-solving skills, enhance your concentration and memory, and improve your attention. Not to mention that multitasking, brain speed, and social skills are going to get better. Besides, you'll also learn a lot. These are only a few of the advantages cited by the proponents of video game playing, especially for children.

The "brain scientist" Daphne Bavelier has found many positive results, even from games like Call of Duty: Black Ops. Well, she does have some reservations: "But I'm going to argue that in **reasonable doses**, . . . those action-packed shooter games have quite powerful effects and positive effects on many different aspects of our behavior."[126] (Emphasis added.) It's not clear what "reasonable doses" would be. She also claims that—tests prove—playing action video games will improve your eyesight. You'll be able to read the small print on the medicine bottle and see better in foggy driving conditions. And if you happen to be older, playing games, like drinking red wine, will even make you live longer. What could be better than that? Her hope is to create a game that combines all of the attractions of a regular shooter game (this, she says, would be like chocolate coating) with the brain-enhancing qualities that she finds so beneficial (this would be the broccoli hidden inside) In other words, hide the good stuff within an irresistible attraction and teach while entertaining.

As the song says, "A spoonful of sugar helps the medicine go down."[127] This will be accomplished by a co-operative effort from brain scientists and "people that work in the software industry." She assures us that "it's actually doable, and we are on the right track."[128]

Writing in *HuffPost* Drew Guarini informs us that "Video games aren't bad for you. They're actually making your life better."[129] To demonstrate, he lists various studies that show the nearly miraculous benefits of gaming. For example, after a study of the brains of two groups, one playing *Super Mario* for thirty minutes a day for two months and another playing no video games at all (he didn't say what that group was doing instead of playing), German researchers examined the brains of the two groups with an MRI machine and reported the following:

> They found that the gaming group had a rise in gray matter in the right hippocampus, right pre-frontal cortex and the cerebellum -- areas of the brain responsible for spatial navigation, memory formation, strategic planning and fine motor skills in the hands. "While previous studies have shown differences in brain structure of video gamers, the present study can demonstrate the direct causal link between video gaming and a volumetric brain increase," study leader Simone Kühn said. "This proves that specific brain regions can be trained by means of video games." [130]

Indeed, Professor Bavelier cites similar results from her studies:

> So one part is the parietal cortex which is very well known to control the orientation of attention. The other one is the frontal lobe, which controls how we sustain attention, and another one is the anterior cingulate, which controls how we allocate and regulate attention and resolve conflict. Now, when we do brain imaging, we find that all three of these networks are actually much more efficient in people that play action games. [131]

Continuing with Guarini's article, each claim is backed up by cited research and capitalized for emphasis by Guarini himself:

> "Starcraft" May Make You Smarter
> Video Games May Slow The Aging Process
> They May Help Dyslexic Kids Read Better
> Video Games Can Be A Pain Reliever
> "Call Of Duty" Can Improve Your Eyesight

66

Video Games Can Be As Effective As One-On-One
Counseling
They Can Help Stroke Victims More Fully Recover[132]

Before you know it they'll be curing the common cold, but I can't help but notice that games "may" and "can" rather than "do" and "will."

Another game enthusiast, going by the name of *inf9YbR3* tells us, under a photo of three highly engaged six-year-olds, eyes focused and game controllers poised, that there are eight cognitive benefits of playing video games for kids—and—"Just as physical exercise helps in improving and strengthening your muscles, cognitive games help to indulge one's brain in constant stimulation, thus improving the brain's performance. The following are some of the cognitive benefits of playing video games." Therefore, constant stimulation:

1. Improves coordination
2. Improves problem-solving skills
3. Enhances memory
4. Improves attention and concentration
5. It is a great source of learning
6. Improves the brain's speed
7. Enhances multitasking skills
8. Improves social skills [133]

These, and the many other benefits proclaimed by the gaming industry and its acolytes, are attained by features like having to remember the rules of the game while playing, making split-second decisions to make the next move, and the need to coordinate vision, hearing, and physical movement. As often mentioned, gaming may be seen as a social activity, that is when individuals engage, online, to play a game together, either in cooperation or competition. It is suggested that this will create new friends, encourage working together, and generally be a great enhancement to players' social lives, even though they will never meet in real life or share any personal thoughts or information other than what concerns the game. Just think, if only Mozart or Einstein had played such games, what they could have accomplished! (Well, Mozart played billiards and Einstein played the violin in a string quartet. Same thing?)

Or is it simply that video games occupy time and provide stimulation in an otherwise arid society?

Reality is Broken

One of the smartest and most enthusiastic of the gamesters is Jane McGonigal. In 2006, at the age of twenty-eight and already a commercial game designer, she earned a PhD in performance studies from the University of California at Berkeley; she was the first in her department to study computer and video games. In 2009, while suffering from a severe concussion, she developed a game, ultimately titled *Superbetter*, that she believes aided her recovery dramatically. Her first book *Reality Is Broken,*[134] published in 2011, is a 400-page panegyric to the marvels of gaming and how games will transform society.

The high level of violence prevalent in shooter-type video games may cause concern. Though there seems to be no demonstrable correlation between game playing and heightened violence, the following description from an American Psychological Association report might give one pause. After first noting that the active role of the video game player makes educational games look promising, the writer, Craig Anderson, PhD, observes:

> Second, the arrival of a new generation of ultraviolent video games beginning in the early 1990s and continuing unabated to the present resulted in large numbers of children and youths actively participating in entertainment violence that went way beyond anything available to them on television or in movies. Recent video games reward players for killing innocent bystanders, police, and prostitutes, using a wide range of weapons including guns, knives, flame throwers, swords, baseball bats, cars, hands, and feet. Some include cut

scenes (i.e., brief movie clips supposedly designed to move the story forward) of strippers. In some, the player assumes the role of hero, whereas in others the player is a criminal.[135]

Does this seem like the road to solving "the world's most urgent problems" as Jane McGonigal would like us to believe?

In her view, gaming can nurture the problem-solving abilities to deal with the world's gravest problems like climate change and inequality. (My gosh, Thomas Piketty should have played *Minecraft* instead of writing two massive books on economics.) In her 2010 TED talk [136] McGonigal says that we are now spending three billion hours playing online games, and she would like to see that increase: "Three billion hours a week is not nearly enough game play to solve the world's most urgent problems." Her idea is that all those intense gamers will apply the smarts they have gained in the virtual world to solving the problems of the real world. She does acknowledge that there might be a hitch: "Now, the problem with collaborative online environments like World of Warcraft is that it's so satisfying to be on the verge of an epic win all the time, we decide to spend all our time in these game worlds. It's just better than reality."[137] She goes on to offer some historical evidence that gameplay will overcome all obstacles. But will it?

A key part of gaming is that the player is regularly rewarded and kept engaged by points and rewards. By slaying monsters or succeeding at heroic "quests" one may "level up," or go from Level 1 to higher levels, like advancing through grades in school. The reward of points, bells, and whistles signifying a winning move is not unlike getting an A on your report card. The ultimate prize of an "epic win" is now known to "incentivize" or create a motive for moving along in a game or, the game enthusiasts hope, in real life. Quoting McGonigal again: "We have to start making the real world work more like a game." And, indeed, if we consider how gaming is invading the classroom, she may see her dream come true.

Nothing is worth doing unless it's *fun*. If children must be lured into learning something by making it fun, even if that fun is shooting and killing people, then whatever that learning might be, it would not be worth doing for its own sake. Anything that isn't *fun* must be boring.

What You See Is What You Get

The addictive qualities of screen watching have been largely ignored—or exploited—by makers of children's television and videos. Dr. Dimitri Christakis of the University of Washington in Seattle said, "Prolonged exposure to rapid image change during [a] critical period of brain development [will] precondition the mind to expect high levels of stimulation [leading to] inattention in later life."[138] So it's hardly surprising that the hyperactivity of a brain engaged in assembling a TV image combined with brightly-coloured and jerky cartoon characters and puppets will be the perfect setting for the development of Attention Deficit. As indicated earlier, diagnosis of children with ADHD (Attention Deficit Hyperactivity Disorder) has grown dramatically over the past twenty years. With over twenty-three million children with this diagnosis,[139] we can be sure that the spread of this "affliction" will continue to grow, mostly in developed countries where almost all children, especially those in school, have screen devices. Might as well be dosing them with crystal meth or cocaine as with screen time, videos, or social media. Can anything that someone would spend ten hours a day or more on be anything other than addictive? And, as I said before, schools are eager participants in drugging children.

B. Learning As Fun or The Erosion of Childhood

Edutainment for Preschoolers and Babies

A thoughtful lady who was said to be a friend of the great physicist Albert Einstein once asked him how best to prepare her

70

young son to become a scientist. What kinds of books should she read to him? Einstein's reply was *Fairy Tales*.

"Of course," replied the woman, "but then what?"

"More fairy tales," was the reply.

Now, somewhat confused, the woman asked, "And after that?"

"Even more fairy tales."

This anecdote has been told many times and in various forms. Perhaps it is apocryphal, perhaps the great man was being contrary or provocative, we'll never know. What is clear, however, is that the meaning of the legend, if that's what it is, is to declare that a lively imagination must be the first and foremost requirement for the development of an active mind.

The name "Einstein" has come to be used to denote anyone of remarkable intelligence and learning or even the very notion of intelligence itself. *The Urban Dictionary* humorously defines the word as meaning "A really, really smart guy," and gives examples of the ironic use of the name: "Well he's bright but he's no *Einstein.*" and "Smart move, *Einstein.*" In other words, the name of the great physicist is used ironically as a "derogatory term for persons who proclaim something obvious or who do something especially stupid."[140]

At the same time, the celebrated genius of Albert Einstein has spawned any number of bizarre, and often profitable, enterprises, the best known of which is *Baby Einstein*, a collection of videos and recordings that, if played repeatedly to your infant offspring, were supposed to stimulate the tiny brain into spawning a mathematical genius. And thus the highly profitable industry of videos for babies and toddlers was born.

Baby Einstein was the creation of a Colorado mother, Julie Aigner-Clark, who, in 1996, felt a lack of educational material for her ten-month-old(!) daughter. She proceeded to create low-cost videos, in her basement, using borrowed equipment and a few puppets. It was believed that babies watching her videos would develop super brains, just like, you guessed it, that of Albert Einstein. The assumption being that small children will never learn anything if not prodded and stimulated into activity.

It didn't take long for Aigner-Clark to realize that she was onto something, so she actively promoted her videos at various toy trade shows until The Right Start, a major toy retailer, took on a few of her videos and sales were immediately brisk. As success grew, more products were created: books, toys, and flash cards. The runaway success of the first Baby Einstein videos obviously called for expansion of the original concept, leading to—hold on to your hat—Baby Mozart, Baby Van Gogh, Baby Galileo, Baby Newton, Baby Bach, and even Baby Shakespeare. These remarkable videos purport to introduce babies to poetry, science, art, and classical music. They all consist of animated toys and puppets accompanied, in most cases, by bits of poetry and synthesized music. The videos were designed to engage a baby's attention by showing brief rapidly changing scenes, minimal dialogue, and mesmerizing images—and they certainly did that.

Well, the success was immediate, and the rest, as they say, is history. The icing on the cake came when Baby Einstein Co. was purchased, in 2001, by The Walt Disney Company for a reported $25 million. With Julie Aigner-Clark and her husband William Clark as consultants, the Disney Company promised "products that expose babies to various forms of human expression—language, poetry, music, art and science, through ways that are nurturing and fun." The couple received all kinds of accolades for both their contribution to child development and their business acumen. Aigner-Clark appeared on Oprah Winfrey's show, and even President George W. Bush, in 2007, praised her as representing "the great enterprising spirit of America."[141]

It was all looking great until later in 2007 when various pediatricians and specialists in pediatrics demonstrated through studies that children who were raised on Baby Einstein or equivalent actually knew fewer words than those who weren't. The major study which delivered the news was that done by Dr. Dimitri Christakis, who was Director of the Center for Child Health, Behavior and Development, in Seattle, Washington, along with his colleague Frederick Zimmerman.[142] They surveyed one thousand parents in Minnesota and Washington, finding that thirty-two per cent of their babies had been shown Baby Einstein or Brainy Baby videos and that as many as 17 per cent of those had seen them for more than one hour per day. Their study revealed that with every hour per day spent watching baby DVDs and videos, infants learned six to eight fewer new vocabulary words than babies who never watched the videos. As Dr. Christakis said, "The more videos they watched, the fewer words they knew. These babies scored about 10 per cent lower on language skills than infants who had not watched these videos." The strongest effects were seen on babies eight to sixteen months old, the critical age at which language skills are beginning to form. All of these studies as well as a report by Dr. Jay L. Hoecker, M.D. [143] of the Mayo Clinic emphasize that regularly reading to young children boosts language ability for both babies and toddlers. After all, Einstein did say *read* fairy tales.

Responding to these studies and to pressure from various groups like the Campaign for a Commercial-Free Childhood[144] and the American Academy of Pediatrics,[145] Disney offered a refund to parents who had bought the videos. The offer was good only for DVDs purchased between June 5, 2004 and September 4, 2009. To soften the blow for those who were still believers, the company provided alternatives of discounts or exchanges on other Baby Einstein products.[146] Not to be intimidated, Baby Einstein fought back. Lashing out at what she called "Susan Linn's [Susan Linn was founding director of Campaign for a Commercial-Free Childhood] stunt," Susan McLain, general manager of the Baby Einstein Company, then a subsidiary of Disney, said, "For the past several years, Baby Einstein has been under attack by propaganda groups taking extreme positions that try to dictate what parents should do, say and buy. . . . Linn's obvious dislike for Baby Einstein has now turned into a sensational, headline-grabbing publicity campaign that seeks to twist and spin a simple, customer satisfaction action into a false admission of guilt." And then accusing Linn of conspiracy, "Linn's moves are carefully crafted to prey on parental guilt and uncertainty."[147] Remember, we're talking over $400 million in revenues.[148]

But the damage had been done. As a last-ditch attempt, William Clark, husband of Julie Aigner-Clark and co-founder of Baby Einstein, initiated a lawsuit against the University of Washington, asking for "The basis for what the university has represented to be ground-breaking research. Given that other research studies have not shown the same outcomes, we would like the raw data and analytical methods from the Washington studies so we can audit their methodology, and perhaps duplicate the studies, to see if the outcomes are the same."[149] Of course, whatever answers the university could supply were not enough to make a case that would assure the public. That is, any members of the public that were paying attention. Some were, because the refunds cost Disney an estimated $100 million.[150] Disney sold the Baby Einstein brand to Kids II, Inc.[151] (doing business as Kids2) on October 14, 2013. The price was, reportedly, considerably lower than that paid to the Clarks.

Kids2[152] ("Making parenthood a little bit easier, one tiny win at a time.") have switched the focus from videos to a multitude of Baby Einstein Toys & Gear,[153] all claiming to make your baby smarter. Products range from the Bendy Ball Rattle Toy at $5.99 U.S.: ("Your little one will light up with excitement with every bend and squeeze. The sensory ball helps with handling skills, and little fingers can explore all the colorful textures and shapes."[154]) to the Neighborhood Friends Activity Jumper ($99.99 US), a frightening array of bizarre and brightly coloured plastic "multi-sensory activities" promising "that this award-winning Baby Einstein jumper turns the idea of a baby bouncer into an imaginative world of discovery." Not only that, but among other things, it "Captivates & cultivates your baby's curiosity through twelve interactive activities with lights, songs, and sounds" with "Five easily-adjustable height positions to grow with baby." It "Introduces new languages (English, Spanish & French) and promotes language development."[155] How did baby ever learn anything without it? At least the level of stimulation, ("activities with lights, songs, and sounds") will prepare baby to enter the ever-exciting world of video games, sports, and social media.

If Baby Einstein's equipment turns out to be not enough, you can turn to Baby Prodigy[156] ("Raising smarter, happier children") which produces a wild array of CDs and DVDs, spinoffs on the old Baby Einstein model. The videos, as you might expect, are made up of short clips of cartoon-like animated puppets and plastic toy animals cavorting to computer-generated tinkly music. Since school readiness seems to be a concern of parents, we are offered Baby Prodigy Dookie and Dottie's Preschool DVD presented by Baby Genius. Dookie and Dottie (gender is clearly identified by Dottie's pink outfit, pink hair ribbon, and false eyelashes.) are two remarkably stupid-looking duck-like puppets that are there to lead the unsuspecting child through a bunch of "educational" episodes introducing shapes, colours, and other undescribed animations, all of which are intended to, and probably will, mesmerize any baby or preschooler who is plopped in front of them.

A strange and more recent manifestation of computer-animated videos for little kids is ChuChu TV, a YouTube channel featuring childlike creatures with alarmingly large eyes. They cavort, play, and sing along with traditional or sometimes invented nursery rhymes. The messages are homey and cozy, often showing parent figures interacting with the "children" in comforting ways. It started, in 2011, when software engineer Vinoth Chandar created a nursery rhyme video as an entertainment for his daughter whose nickname was Chu Chu. The video featured Chu Chu herself, looking not unlike the 1930s cartoon character Betty Boop, who was described as combining "in appearance the childish with the sophisticated—a large round baby face with big eyes and a nose like a button, framed in a somewhat careful coiffure, with a very small body."[157] As I suggested, this could well be the video Chu Chu herself. The description of Betty Boop continues with: "of which perhaps the leading characteristic is the most self-confident little bust imaginable." This may not be there yet, but I'm sure it's coming.

Tom Durrie

Now for the rhyme itself on which the video is based:
Chubby cheeks, dimple chin, rosy
lips, teeth within.
Curly hair, very fair, eyes are blue,
lovely too.
Teacher's pet, is that you?
Yes! Yes! Yes![158]

What this sexist and revolting little ditty has to do with traditional nursery rhymes is beyond my comprehension. The message is that little girls (this is Chu Chu after all) better be adorably cute and pleasing to authority.

We are given three repetitions of the song, each with different actions by the character. Between each iteration of the song there is a pretty landscape with at least ten different action figures carrying on. The video combines terminal cuteness with constant colourful action that would mesmerize and confuse any three-year-old. Not to worry though because each video also contains an educational or socially relevant message as reassurance for doubtful parents.

ChuChu TV became an overnight success after it was placed on YouTube with more videos of the same kind being constantly added. According to Alexis C. Madrigal in *The Atlantic*[159] ChuChu was already beating out the competition in 2018, with nineteen billion views and nineteen million subscribers as opposed to *Sesame Street's* five million views and six million subscribers. As of 2022, the ever-popular channel has over sixty million subscribers, growing by thirty thousand daily, having accumulated over forty-two billion views since its beginning.[160]

"There's gold in them thar hills," as the saying goes, and sure enough, ChuChu is rolling in dough. A conservative estimate from Net Worth Spot[161] suggests that earnings could be as much as $46.76 million per year. As you might guess, the "gold" comes from advertising and any number of the usual spin-off products: toys, dolls, clothing, books, etc.

One could see ChuChu TV as the evolutionary offspring of Baby Einstein, now with superior animation and just the right rhymes and tunes to captivate parents, who will happily let their kids watch it, though I doubt that they could stand it for more than thirty seconds. The important matter here is that parents must be trained to believe that the well-marketed experts and authorities are sure to know what is best for your kids.

After all, since the purpose of television is to deaden the mind and sell things, it's profitable to get kids hooked early.

The Mozart Effect

A curious offshoot of all this was The Mozart Effect, popularized by a 1997 book: *The Mozart Effect: Tapping the Power of Music to Heal the Body, Strengthen the Mind, and Unlock the Creative Spirit* by Don Campbell.[162] The title says it all. The book claims that listening to certain pieces of Mozart's music (the piano concertos in particular) will enhance intelligence and learning. No doubt seeing a marketing opportunity here, Campbell followed up with *The Mozart Effect for Children*.[163] Along with the book, available for purchase is a set of eight CDs of Mozart's music,[164] including the four-volume *The Mozart Effect for Babies*.

There is no suggestion that the grownups around may have been listening to or playing Mozart's music simply for their own pleasure or because they liked it. That didn't stop Campbell from creating Mozart CDs for adults. Enough to make any composer cringe is CD No. 5 "Relax and Unwind—Music for Deep Rest & Rejuvenation." *The New Yorker* music critic Alex Ross called it "Listening to Prozac."[165] The music historian Nicholas Till wrote, "The very freedom Mozart himself sought brings alienation and doubt to the individual in modern society, and his own life demonstrates the painful process which he himself underwent in his search for identity as a man and artist."[166] I think it's safe to say that any serious composer wants her or his music to be deeply engaging, life-changing, even disturbing. Experiencing great music is not like taking a warm bath—or watching a cartoon.

Of course, not to be outdone, Baby Einstein's collection now includes "Baby Mozart, Music to Stimulate Your Baby's Brain,"[167] a synthesized-sound performance accompanied by strange animated mechanical-looking objects and the usual idiotic puppets. As if any baby's brain *needed* stimulating! You can also

> Introduce baby to the splendor of classical music with Baby Mozart Music Festival--one of the original (and most beloved) Baby Einstein videos! Baby Mozart Music Festival also captivates baby with stimulating, colorful images. Babies are naturally drawn to the Baby Einstein videos – with puppets, sounds, and rhythm. Both you and your child will love these enchanting versions of classic compositions by Wolfgang Amadeus Mozart.[168]

I dare you! (Baby Einstein, Baby Mozart Music Festival, Classical Music for Toddlers, Full Episode)

All of the numerous music-as-edutainment videos and CDs are now available on YouTube. No need to buy any hardware since every baby, toddler, and preschooler would surely have their own tablet or smartphone. That gives them the advantage of skipping around and surfing rather than having to listen to or watch any complete video or piece of music. Perfect for the jangled inattentive brain ready to enter the digital world as well as the bland and tedious world of school.

The Mozart fad started with a French researcher named Alfred A. Tomatis, who in his 1991 book *Pourquoi Mozart?*[169] claimed that listening to Mozart's music could promote healing and increase intelligence. This notion was subjected to further study by a team headed by Dr. Frances Rauscher, a professor at the University of Wisconsin.[170] They discovered that there was a small and temporary improvement in spatial reasoning after hearing a recording of, for some reason, the Two-Piano Sonata K. 448. Spatial reasoning was measured by paper cutting and folding or pencil and paper maze tasks. Though Rauscher never claimed that listening to Mozart would lead to an increase in general intelligence, a public eager to find an effortless road to intellectual achievement was ready to believe otherwise. In enthusiastic response, Zell Miller, governor of Georgia, announced in 1996 that his proposed state budget would include $105,000 a year to provide every child born in Georgia with a tape or CD of classical music. He even said, "No one questions that listening to music at a very early age affects the spatial-temporal reasoning that underlies math and engineering and even chess."[171] Huh? Campbell's books not only offered confirmation of this notion but also created a promising new area of marketing.

Why All This Stuff?

But what's going on here, and what is all this stuff about? There is no reason whatever to believe that brightly coloured plastic gear, odd semi-human cartoon characters, or even Mozart's music, will contribute to brain development or to the creation of intelligent human beings. It has to start long before the gaudy playthings and videos come out.

But what's the point of all the stuff, other than selling more merchandise? First, it relieves parents of involvement in child care while reassuring them that their baby is "learning" something. In the process, the child is deprived of what really matters: physical and verbal contact with other human beings. Second, all this stuff reflects societal attitudes about babies and children. If children need to be taught (even by stupid puppets) and coerced into learning or discovering anything, the implication is that children won't learn or discover anything on their own so we'd better provide them with plenty of toys, games, and videos to activate their brains and to introduce them into a society that prizes constant stimulation over curiosity, self-directed discovery, and thoughtful experience. All of this gear also relieves parents of the time and effort of talking and reading to their babies and toddlers, while supposedly guiding little brains and getting them ready for school. Learning is thereby trivialized, free self-directed play is discouraged, and future consumers are being groomed for their role.

I remember watching my first son at around one year or slightly more sitting in his highchair with a collection of jar and container lids that had somehow ended up on the tray in front of him. He was intently concentrating on fitting these items together and trying various combinations to see what would work. This was a young brain growing and forming new synapses that would develop into intelligence and curiosity. It was serious work, no plastic gewgaws or videos required.

The jar lids are fine examples of the sort of playthings that are not only readily available but are also the interesting items of everyday life. My interests at age four were the pots and pans that were in the lower kitchen cupboards. These were items of interest because I had watched my mother doing all kinds of things with them, and I, like any small child, wanted to see what I could do with them. My mother was very tolerant of my activities, so I was allowed to remove what I wanted from the cupboard, try stacking them together, arranging them in various ways, and thus working to satisfy my curiosity which could then move on to what I would find in the greater world around me.

Simple playthings are the best because they permit and encourage imagination and creativity. As the venerable Dr. Spock said, "Children usually love simple toys best and play with them longest. This isn't because children are simple—it's because they have so much imagination."[172] And more recently, the National Association for the Education of Young Children has this to say, "Many safe and appropriate play materials are free items typically found at home. Cardboard boxes, plastic bowls and lids, collections of plastic bottle caps, and other 'treasures' can be used in more than one way by children of different ages."[173] Parents need not succumb to promotions for elaborate and expensive "educational" toys and videos. It's the plain and simple that develop curiosity and, hence, intelligence.

Bringing Up Baby

In October of 2017, Mattel was just about to release Aristotle, a remarkable device that would virtually eliminate the need for parents in a child's life. For example, "Aristotle is designed to comfort, entertain, teach, and assist during each development state—evolving with a child as their needs change from infancy to adolescence." And if that's not enough, Aristotle will "soothe a crying baby, reinforce good manners in kids, and even help kids learn a foreign language." Golly, you would hardly even need to know the kid's name! Extolling the new device, Jim Mitchell, vice president and general manager of Mattel's *nabi* brand said, "Raising kids can be hectic and we saw a need for an IoT [Internet of Things] system that simplifies the complex and dynamic lives of families, while providing them with peace of mind." Just about anything that was once learned in the arms of parents and grandparents can now be found on an electronic device.

Let's not forget marketing possibilities: Aristotle can "purchase diapers or find online deals." And, incredibly, "Aristotle's AI [artificial intelligence] will also have a unique personality that will appeal to parents and kids and will be presented as the great descendent of Aristotle himself."[174] *Poetics* be damned!

Alas, the glory was short-lived. A campaign led by Campaign for a Commercial-Free Childhood—you'll remember them from pressure applied to Baby Einstein—resulted in Mattel pulling Aristotle off the market before it even hit the shelves. Citing privacy concerns, a petition with over 15,000 signatures was submitted to Mattel, noting that "Aristotle also attempts to replace the care, judgment, and companionship of loving family members with faux nurturing and conversation from a robot designed to sell products and build brand loyalty."[175] If you think that was the end of it, guess again; the technology and the market are just too promising. As Rachel Peachman wrote in *The New York Times*, "Aristotle wasn't the first electronic device to come under fire—Mattel also was criticized when it released the Wi-Fi interactive Hello Barbie[176] in 2015—and it very likely won't be the last." In a similar vein, Peachman quotes Dr. Christakis as warning, "I'm glad that there was sufficient uproar and that this product went away, but it's not the last time we'll see such things." [177]

And indeed there is already a plentiful array of "such things" on the market. Amazon, via Amazon Kids+, has a special version of the well-known Alexa called Echo Dot Kids that will "Help kids learn and grow. Kids can ask Alexa questions, set alarms, and get help with their homework." It will "Unlock a world of kid-friendly content. Amazon Kids+ gives them access to thousands of hours of kid-friendly audible books, interactive games, and educational skills." [178] If that isn't enough, there are virtual babysitters that offer a real person—well, virtually real—to read, tell stories and talk, all in a manner tailored to your child's age. The performers are often out-of-work actors trying to make a buck in their spare time. Websites such as Care.com or Sittercity offer numerous possibilities. A slicker version of the digital sitter is Caribu, a video-based app where kids can "Read, draw, and play games in an interactive video-call." [179] When bedtime comes, a soothing presence will sing a lullaby to carry the kids off to dreamland. Parental presence not required.

No doubt, virtual nannies can be a great assistance to parents who are working at home. At least they do require that a person be around to offer some time-to-time connection with the child. Parents who have to work out of the house have a different set of problems to cope with. While governments following the neoliberal agenda are subsidizing corporate businesses with tax breaks and financial incentives, parents and the unemployed are left to fend for themselves. As profits soar, so do prices of housing and groceries; a single income cannot support children and a parent at home. Instead of providing reasonable income assistance and maternity leave, governments prefer to support daycare and preschool programs that get the kids out of the house and into school-like institutions, making the two-income family possible. The results of what I can only describe as alienation of children from parental care and contact are leading to a radical reorganization of society and of interpersonal relations. School then reinforces the social divide and promotes competition and striving for meaningless grades and rewards.

Following all the digital and virtual child-rearing devices, there is daycare. Government-supported daycare centres are available to look after children from birth to school age. We are assured that the daycare centres will be staffed by "certified early childhood educators." Early childhood is defined as birth to age five. While my experience with Early Childhood Educators has been limited, the two or three I've seen in action were marked by a saccharine and patronizing attitude. If you want to know what I mean, and if you're feeling brave and have a sound stomach, I dare you to view this video which is supposed to help your baby or toddler learn to talk[180]. You might ask yourself, as I did, what is it really teaching? What assumptions about adulthood and even about speech would a small child derive from this display?

Following daycare will be Head Start or Strong Start preschool programs that will get the kids psyched up for kindergarten or grade one. Then, with any luck, school will keep them at the grindstone for the next twelve years. By the time they emerge, we can count on a digitized, homogenized, addle-brained generation of ready-made consumers.

Television for Children

Television for children, especially *Sesame Street*, had already promoted the idea that learning can be administered as entertainment to a passive audience. It was *Sesame Street*, first seen in November of 1969, that transformed the content and rhythm of television for children. Television had already become the ready-made babysitter, but now parents could feel completely justified in parking babies and toddlers in front of the TV because they were being "educated." Presumably, your preschooler would be geared up to succeed at the chores of kindergarten and beyond. All with little or no effort on your part.

According to Malcolm Gladwell in *The Tipping Point,* "Sesame Street was built around a single, breakthrough insight: that if you can hold the attention of children, you can educate them." [181] And indeed, that concept was thoroughly researched and developed by the Children's Television Workshop (now known as the Sesame Workshop) with the idea of creating a show that would "master the addictive qualities of television and do something good with them." [182] The program, with its nutty and engaging puppets and celebrated guests, consisted of commercial-like scenarios introducing young viewers to verbal and behavioural concepts while entertaining them, even generating a new word: *edutainment.* A guiding principle was that every child should be acquainted with the alphabet and with numerals from one to ten before entering school. There is little question that Sesame Street did just that. [183] But it also did some other things.

"As a television show, and a good one, *Sesame Street* does not encourage children to love school, or anything about school. It encourages them to love television." [184] Since Neil Postman wrote this in 1985, schools have ramped up their efforts to make children love school by turning the classroom into a place of amusement and entertainment—a kind of extension of the Sesame Street ethic. A website offering tips for teachers leads off with "Prioritize fun and the learning will come." And "If you are having a good time, chances are your students are too." To have a good time just "Be goofy; show you care." [185] Sounds like a laugh riot! And let's not forget the gamified classroom and numerous other clever means to attract the attention of children who have become accustomed to being passive recipients of highly stimulating media. If education was once conveyed by speech and the printed word, requiring attention and participation, it is now conveyed by cartoon-like characters, goofy dialogue, and rapidly changing pictures. Participation is impossible and attention is optional.

During the 1960s, television was in transition. Moving away from something that was like radio-with-pictures or a televised stage show, the medium was developing a more attention-getting style of its own: fast cutting with shots of a few seconds or less, more frequent commercial breaks, and focus on images and personalities. The move was away from "talking heads" and stage-like performances like those seen on *The Ed Sullivan Show* (1948-1971). *Sesame Street* was right on the money, reflecting the style of popular programming of the time like Rowan and Martin's *Laugh-In* (1968-1973) whose predecessors included Olsen and Johnson's Broadway show and 1941 film *Hellzapoppin'*, offshoots of vaudeville and burlesque, with fast-moving series of short satirical gags and blackouts. It wouldn't be long before school had to catch up. Programs like *Sesame Street* led the way.

Sesame Street was a remarkably creative response to President Lyndon Johnson's "War on Poverty," declared in his 1964 State of the Union speech.[186] Heavily funded by the U.S. government, the Carnegie Foundation, and the Ford Foundation, *Sesame Street* promised to kick start little kids into good behaviour and readiness for the rigours of kindergarten and grade one. And once government and foundation funding dried up it provided substantial marketing opportunities in the way of videos, toys, clothes, books, etc.[187] The Tickle Me Elmo[188] craze of Christmas 1996 provided inspiration for numerous knockoff imitators just as *Sesame Street* inspired dozens of so-called "learning" TV shows and videos, all based on carefully researched curricula. The pay-TV cable channel Nickelodeon offered a day-long menu of edutainment shows for kids, including the wildly successful *Dora the Explorer* and *Blue's Clues*, both of which were aimed at preschoolers. On public TV, babies were encouraged to watch *Barney and Friends* and *Teletubbies*. As inane as these programs may seem to adults, they were precisely crafted to capture the attention of very small children. And that usually meant promoting products that the kids would badger their parents into buying for them. According to Dade Hayes, in *Anytime Playdate*, Dora alone generated over $1 billion in annual revenue from an array of more than two hundred branded products.[189]

However, changes were in the air as more and more children became tuned in to new electronic media: computers, tablets, and smartphones. While there has been a drop in TV-watching hours across all age groups, the most dramatic changes are among the young. According to the 2020 Nielson report the twelve to seventeen age group has been watching less than an hour a day of traditional television, slightly over six hours per week, a drop of more than 37 per cent over the past three years.[190] That doesn't mean, however, that kids aren't engaged in screen watching as much or more than ever. According to a survey in the UK, 63 per cent of children own a mobile phone by the age of seven. That number increases to 90 per cent by age eleven, and by secondary school, phone ownership is "almost universal."[191] And don't be surprised to learn that even little kids as young as one year old are using mobile devices for at least an hour a day. "Of children **younger than one year**, 52 per cent had watched television shows, 36 per cent had touched or scrolled a screen, 24 per cent had phoned someone, 15 per cent used apps, and 12 per cent played video games."[192] (emphasis added)

Subscription services such as the giant Netflix are providing an increasing number of movies and entertainment programs aimed at the family or children's market. An article by Brent Lang in Variety reported that

> Netflix hopes to popularize the concept of "must-binge" entertainment among the pre-adolescent set, much as it previously encouraged their parents to consume whole seasons of 'The Crown' and 'House of Cards' in a single sitting."--and sure enough—"Cobb [Melissa Cobb, head of the company's kids and family division] says that Netflix is dipping its toe into the consumer products realm, launching a line of toys and Halloween costumes tied to its show 'Super Monsters,' for instance . . . After all, as Disney, Illumination and other companies have learned, animated fare can inspire everything from T-shirts to theme park rides.[193]

And not to be left behind, Disney Plus launched its streaming service in 2019.

According to the Guinness Book of World Records, as reported on the *KIDS* website, the most in-demand and popular children's program is Nickelodeon's *SpongeBob SquarePants*[194]

SpongeBob SquarePants presents a rapid-fire quick-cutting series of episodes involving a group of bizarre non-human-looking characters, or what one might call caricatures of human types. SpongeBob himself is an animated square sponge, more kitchen-like than sea-like, who dashes through various conflict-full situations with gleeful and mindless optimism. Cartoon violence is pervasive amongst a dazzling array of brightly-coloured characters. Dialogue is both rapid and vapid, but the main impression is of a brain-addling race of machinegun-fired images and rat-tat-tat dialogue. The show is a brilliant representation of the twenty-first-century notion of entertainment for children. Most episodes even have a vaguely "educational" theme, addressing, for example, global warming (see "Endless Summer" or "The Bully"). The suggestion, though, is not to take these issues seriously, because, after all, life is just a stupid joke anyway.

Like every successful program of kids' entertainment, *SpongeBob SquarePants* has generated an enormously profitable array of products, bringing in upwards of a reported $13 billion revenue for Nickelodeon as of 2017.[195] The products range from T-shirts and posters to board games, amusement park rides, and a feature-length movie. Most successful of all is the video game Bikini Bottom. Bikini Bottom is the wink-wink-nudge-nudge suggestive title of the main character's undersea domain.

The evolution of children's television from such low-key programs as *Engineer Bill* (1954-1966) in which kids helped run model trains and engaged in various activities, *The Friendly Giant* (1953-1984), and the universally revered *Mister Rogers' Neighborhood* (1968-2001) through *Sesame Street* (1969-present) and *Barney &Friends* (1991-2004) right up to *SpongeBob SquarePants* is a progress from real adult people calmly speaking to children as though they were intelligent beings to the present wild array of idiotic computer generated cartoon-character programs. Simply enough, it was found that highly-coloured fast-action video kept young eyes on the screen longer than person-to-person conversation. Keep 'em stupid was working—and while they're there you might as well sell them something. Thank you, Baby Einstein.

The American Academy of Pediatrics discourages media use by children younger than eighteen to twenty-four months. Though their 1999 study concluded that children under two years old should not be allowed *any* screen time, seventeen years later, recommendations have relaxed, now caving to the ubiquity of screen media; video chatting—hello grandma on Skype—said to be OK for children under eighteen months. Up to twenty-four months, parents are advised to "choose high-quality programming [if you can find any] and watch it with their children to help them understand what they're seeing."[196] Once your kids are two years old, their screen time should be limited to one hour per day—with parental guidance and participation. After that, well, the sky's the limit, as long as parents set limits and guidelines. (Lotsa luck!)

It hardly seems necessary to mention that activities such as talking, playing, singing, smiling, and reading to babies and small children are more natural and far better than anything a video screen could offer. Even if a baby doesn't understand the words or the plot of a story, he or she, cuddled on your lap, will absorb the love and sense of communication that this brings. These activities are the foundations of speech and thought as well as emotional health. Seems obvious, doesn't it? Before the age of television, connections between children and grownups were the foundations of childrearing, but now that many parents themselves are already spending several hours a day watching television it didn't take long to discover that even a baby parked in front of the TV would be entranced (literally) by the flickering screen. And in many houses, there is at least one TV set on all the time. The video or computer screen has taken the place of parent and child interaction.

In his book *Four Arguments for the Elimination of Television,* author Jerry Mander explains, in a chapter titled "How Television Dims the Mind," how television images are created and assembled by the viewer. The process involves ". . . dots that are lighted one at a time according to a scanning system that starts behind the screen. Proceeding along a line from the upper-right portion of your screen across the top to the left, the scan lights some dots and skips others, depending upon the image to be conveyed."[197] (Computer screens operate in the same way.) This scanning process is repeated over and over at a speed of thirty times per second. Since the human brain processes this information at only about ten times per second, you think you are watching a steadily moving image, but your brain is busily engaged in creating that image. Mander goes on to say, "The first effect of this is to create a passive mental attitude. Since there is no way to stop the images, one merely gives over to them. More than this, one has to clear all channels of reception to allow them in more cleanly. Thinking only gets in the way."[198]

Concern over children's television-watching habits started early on. Dorothy and Jerome Singer, who were professors and researchers at Yale University, published *Television, Imagination, and Aggression: A Study of Preschoolers in 1981*. "Children are growing up today in an environment that includes an element of daily visual stimulation never before a part of human experience. Three- and four-year-olds get up at 6:30 a.m. and go over to a little box on which they watch cartoon figures bouncing around or pounding each other into pieces, soon magically revived; by 8:30 a.m., when bundled off to day care center or nursery school, they have already watched for at least an hour." Evenings are similarly occupied, only now with shows aimed at an adult audience. "Often well into 9:00 or 10:00 p.m. they continue to watch the movements on the box, usually only vaguely grasping the plots or the meaning of words used or distinguishing between commercials and program content. But the moving figures hold their attention!"[199] Well, that *was* television, which would now seem slow and boring to the ever-changing worlds of YouTube videos, Snapchat, Instagram, and TikTok. The television set had its place in the

living room, viewers seated in front. The latest handheld tech gizmos go anywhere and everywhere, ready to hold attention twenty-
four hours a day.

Learning As Fun

So much for entertainment. The latest wrinkle promoted
by game designers, aficionados, and, yes, education experts, is the
video game as a tool for learning—or edutainment, or the more
serious-sounding "gamified education." The driving idea is that if
you can make learning fun, you can make the kids learn almost
anything. Hence you'll find video games designed to teach mathematics, spelling, reading, history, foreign languages, science, you
name it. It's called "gamification." Why even *Grand Theft Auto*
can have its positive sides, at least according to James Gee, an education professor at the University of Wisconsin, Madison:

> Even violent games have a positive side, Gee
> says. "*Grand Theft Auto 3* does not exist to get off
> on shooting people. When the game begins, your
> character has just been released from jail. You
> need to figure out how to make a living, but the
> only people you know are criminals. Along the
> way, you might end up fighting or killing people,
> but you don't have to. . . . The game offers you a
> palette of choices. Players must confront moral di-
> lemmas, develop social relationships, and solve
> challenging problems that might apply to real life.
> How compelling would a game be if you only had
> good choices?[200]

All I can say is that I hope I never have to face "and solve
challenging problems that might apply to real life" as interpreted
by *Grand Theft Auto*. If the game isn't entirely about fighting or
killing people, I must have missed the point.

The real stars of edutainment are the games specifically
designed for what passes as learning. As blogger and avowed

90

gamer Kira Leigh writes on the Gamer Sensei video-game-coaching website: "We're about to see the most radical shift in education since the invention of writing, and I absolutely can't wait."[201] What she absolutely can't wait for must be something like the games listed as "10 Educational Video Games Your Kids Will Love."[202] There, you'll find such gems as *Dora the Explorer*, a TV show spinoff in which kids will "Follow maps, solve problems, learn new words and facts and have lots of silly fun along the way." Or your pre-schooler might be lured into filling in some blanks with *Reader Rabbit*,[203] which spins an elaborate tale involving various, cheaply animated cartoon animals. *Reader Rabbit* even offers a phonics-based version in case you're still a fan of Rudolph Flesch.[204]

While there are numerous websites listing the "best" learning games for kids of all ages, you'll find the same ones turning up again and again. What you'll also find is that most, by far, of these games are simply take-offs on familiar school chores like matching words and pictures, finding spots on a game board, choosing right answers, and filling in the blanks, now accompanied by idiotic looking cartoon creatures and cheap fabricated computer music. With new versions of this and that coming along, there is a plenitude of choices, though most of them are remarkably similar.

Speaking of rabbits who are assigned with teaching tasks, the content and action of educational games were accurately described by Frank Smith in his 1986 book *Insult to Intelligence*: "The teachers [at a convention introducing new concepts in teaching] were ... gazing at a cartoon representation of a desert scene on the screen of a small desktop computer. There was a bright blue sky above, a yellow landscape below, a few cacti, and in the center of it all a rabbit with large floppy ears and a mischievous look. In large print on the side of the screen were the letters r-bbit." After responding to a request to enter the player's name, the rabbit asks, "Can you fill in the missing letter in r-bbit?" When the correct letter was entered, " . . . bells rang and lights flashed, but now the rabbit's ears perked up and it began munching on a carrot that magically appeared from off-screen." [205] The player is then complimented on supplying a correct answer, and a running score of "progress" registers achievement. Except for the relentless promises of fun, such games bear a striking resemblance to what teachers call "seat work" or pencil and paper worksheets of similar mind-numbing fill-in-the-blanks and match-the-numbers exercises.

The Oregon Trail

No discussion of educational video games can be considered complete without mention of *The Oregon Trail*, which, since its creation in1971 to its most recent iteration in 2011, has been hailed as the *sine qua non* of educational games, though of questionable historical accuracy according to the website *9 myths you learned from playing Oregon Trail*.[206] On a harsher note, Bill Bigelow, writing in *Rethinking Our Classrooms, Volume 2*,[207] has little good to say about *The Oregon Trail*: "But as much as the game teaches, it mis-teaches more. In fundamental respects, '*Oregon Trail II*' is sexist, racist, culturally insensitive, and contemptuous of the earth. It imparts bad values and wrong history."[208]

Nevertheless, the game became wildly popular in U.S. elementary schools, selling more than sixty-five million copies and even coming bundled with many school computers. American games journalist Colin Campbell praised the game as "a cultural icon."[209]

Nostalgic adults seek online versions of the game they can play while reliving their childhoods. All the usual profitable spinoffs in the form of card games, board games, and T-shirts were, and still are, readily available. The Oregon Trail Card Game, while asking "How will you die on the Oregon Trail?" promises that "All sorts of gruesome deaths await you and the rest of your wagon party in this official multi-player card game version of the classic computer game." [210] Suitable for ages twelve and up!

Invented by three student teachers who wanted a *fun* way of teaching kids about the westward movement of the mid-1800s, *The Oregon Trail* places the player as leader of a party of pioneers travelling by covered wagon leaving Independence, Missouri, and heading for the Willamette Valley in Oregon. After choosing, or buying with what financial resources your chosen character may have, an array of supplies: food, ammunition, wagons, oxen, etc., the wagons head out on the trail. Along the way, various hazards will be encountered, including rivers to be crossed, broken wagon wheels and axles, accidents, diseases, and shortages of food and other supplies. Such hazards will turn up in the same unpredictable way that a Go to Jail card will turn up in Monopoly. And since it is, after all, a video game, there are various opportunities for shooting guns—at bison, deer, rabbits, and other assorted animals, supposedly to be used for food. The expectation might be that one hundred pounds of game would be plenty for one person to handle after butchering and being divided into manageable portions, but "in this gem of a game,"[211] players who are having so much fun shooting and killing are driven to bagging as much as two thousand pounds at a time. Well, *The Oregon Trail* never did claim to be conflict free. But the high-flown phrases of the MECC (Minnesota Educational Computing Corporation) reassure us that "*The Oregon Trail* stimulates your imagination as you develop your problem-solving skills and learn about an important phase of American history. Persistence and determination lead to greater success as you pursue your goal."[212]

Like the majority of games, including those claiming to be educational, some form of death[213] is an expected and welcome feature. In shooting games, it's generally blasting the head off some hapless opponent whose spewing blood and gore will provide a gratifying demonstration of the player's accuracy. Aside from the playful slaughter of buffalo and other wild game, human death in *The Oregon Trail* comes in the form of diseases—dysentery, cholera, typhoid, measles—or accidents like snakebite, drowning, or accidental shooting. The player of games like *Grand Theft Auto* will be rewarded for each opponent knocked off with scores and points that can be compared to those of other players, whereas in *The Oregon Trail* when someone dies, the player is rewarded by being able to create an amusing tombstone, such as "Here lies Dummy—rest in dumb pieces" or "Here lies Otis. With friends like Shane, who needs enemies."[214] In other words, death (violent or otherwise) is presented as an amusing aspect of an entertaining pastime. Those whose nostalgia extends to fond memories of playing *The Oregon Trail* in school can acquire T-shirts emblazoned with "You have died of dysentery" under an iconic image from the game.[215] How much fun is that?

Now Let's Get Serious

For a more recent and more technologically advanced experience with superb animation and graphics, turn to *Assassin's Creed Odyssey*, released by Ubisoft in 2018 as the eleventh in a series of so-called RPG games in which a peace-loving assassin (the player) fights with Templars, the bad guys, who want control. RPG, by the way, stands for Role-Playing Game, a game in which the single player "becomes" a character in plot-based action. Becoming a character in this type of game is very enticing: all characters, scenery, and action are about as realistic as computer animation can create in the early twenty-first century. Thus we are involved in action, well, fighting, taking place in an extravagant landscape of "restored" classical civilization. In fact:

> ANCIENT GREECE AWAITS
> Explore an entire country full of untamed environments and cities at the peak of Greece's Golden Age. Visit Sparta and witness Athens in its full glory, tread in the footsteps of legends like Odysseus and Hercules[216] and uncover the secrets of Greece. Unexpected encounters will breathe life into your story as you meet colorful characters, battle formidable foes, and more. [217]

Within this dramatic and ever-so-historical environment you can "Write your own epic odyssey and become a legendary Spartan hero, . . . an inspiring adventure where you must forge your destiny and define your own path in a world on the brink of tearing itself apart." You are encouraged to "Show off your extraordinary warrior abilities and shift the tides of battle during one of the deadliest conflicts of the time, the Peloponnesian War. Charge into epic clashes between Sparta and Athens in big battles pitting 150 vs. 150 soldiers against each other." In addition, "Unexpected encounters will breathe life into your story as you meet colorful characters, battle formidable foes, and more." Thucydides and Herodotus be damned! You now "Influence how history unfolds as you experience a rich and ever-changing world shaped by your decisions."[218] If you thought that ancient Greece was about Plato, Socrates, Aeschylus, Euripides, Homer, and Sappho, you will be briskly corrected by Louise Blain (aka Shiny Demon) who, in her review of the best single player games to play in 2019, informs us that: "Ancient Greece is a sprawling beautiful playground of murderous fun."[219]

For the more academically inclined, Ubisoft also offers the conflict-free *Assassin's Creed Discovery Tour*, which is "really meant for people wanting to learn through **the fun medium** of a video game"[220] (Emphasis added) Here, one can choose to tour "Famous Cities; Daily Life; Battles & War; Politics & Philosophy; Art, Religion & Myths."[221] Though not focused on fights and battles, each discovery results in a reward, like a *Pegasus* for travel or "avatars you can play with." As the player's character moves—along a line—from site to site, a soothing female voice describes details of what is being witnessed. It might be the Parthenon, various temples, or people at work. The mini-lecture is followed by a print sidebar containing more information, historical and otherwise. It is as the Ubisoft promotional material puts it: "A cross between the world of museums, archeology, and video games."[222] I couldn't help but notice how extremely attractive the young female guide and the (silent) bare-chested male-tourist-as-student are. They fit so perfectly into the lovely computer-generated landscape with its magnificent temples and assorted buildings. Indeed, how much fun can it be to identify with these superbly handsome characters while learning interesting tidbits about daily life in ancient Greece? Whatever serious scholars may think of the content, the visuals are spectacular examples of what can be done with computer animation. And, after all, scholarship is not the object here because we are *having fun*. The whole concept of learning as fun is nicely summed up by Colin Campbell in his 2019 review of *Assassin's Creed Discovery Tour*:

> Education is often, unfortunately, a bit of a chore. Books (a format that I revere) must work very hard to grab the attention of today's reader. But games like Discovery Tour aren't merely picturesque diversions about the ways of people who are long dead. They are joyful journeys into useful knowledge.

Not only that, but:

> What might our children become, if we encouraged them (and ourselves) to spend time deep inside the lessons of history, science, ethics and humanity, instead of skating above them aboard textbooks?

Though I'm not sure what "useful knowledge" might be, it's comforting to know that Mr. Campbell does not entirely disdain books; apparently, he regards them (from a distance?) with reverence. He goes on to inform us that "My guide for a tour of the Acropolis is Aspasia, the wily partner of Athenian leader Pericles."

What he doesn't bother to tell us is that the historical Aspasia was not only the "wily partner of Pericles," but also a whore, a madam, and a procurer, no doubt earning a bit of extra cash as one of Pericles's concubines. But, no matter, we're here to have fun. Let's go on:

After an introduction, Aspasia invites me to follow a pathway, with various stops along the way, where I gaze up at statues and buildings, as they likely looked 23 centuries ago. These stops trigger short vignettes that explain the thing I'm looking at. I'm also offered optional extra information in the form of text and images. At the end of the tour, Aspasia greets me again. I can ask her to quiz me on the information I've learned. The quizzes are appropriately straightforward, aimed at students of all ages. [223]

PC Gamer reassures anyone who might be suspicious of tests, quizzes, or exams: "These quizzes are fun and light-hearted, and if you get an answer wrong they'll explain why it was wrong, rather than just scolding you for not paying attention." [224] Whew!

Finally, here's a real clincher: "I can hang out with Socrates and get a primer on his grand philosophies." Grand philosophies? Well, that takes care of Socrates, and so much more chummy than having to absorb the thought, humour, and subtle sexual jokes of the *Phaedrus* or the *Symposium*. Never mind that, but if you're a teenage boy, watch your ass!

And Now, The Gamified Classroom

Given the enormous success of the video game industry, why not turn work, school, and life itself into a game? As Jane McGonigal says: "We have to start making the real world work more like a game." Or, as the three little maids from school in Gilbert and Sullivan's *The Mikado* so charmingly sing, "Life is a joke that's just begun." [225]

Since educational games like *The Oregon Trail* have been wildly popular, let's infuse school itself with a game-like atmosphere. Teachers are encouraged to "gamify" the classroom by using routines derived from video games as a way of *incentivizing* and engaging students in learning. Now, instead of grades, students are rewarded with points and badges—similar to the way the progress of players is tracked and rewarded in video games—as they move along a *quest* through the curriculum. Of course, competition is encouraged, and failure is OK as long as the student will try, try again, "and when students buy in, they make school a game worth playing."[226]

As with Skinner's Teaching Box, which I shall describe later, and other forms of programmed learning, each step successfully attained is reinforced with some kind of reward. Teachers are instructed to let their students know that they are starting at level zero and must make their way up the ladder, level by level if they hope for a good grade. And as they are constantly reminded, good grades are the hallmark of success in school and in later life.

To enhance the game of school, all kinds of clever and humorous tactics may be employed. The TeachThought staff suggests "students get sunglasses to wear until the period is over at 5 points, the privilege to take off their shoes at 10 points, a positive text to their parents at 15, and if the high score is over 15, whoever has it may 'steal' the teacher's chair."[227] Though Skinner would surely approve, it's hard to believe that grown-up people are dreaming up schemes like this. If you've read Mordecai Richler's 1968 novel *Cocksure*,[228] you may get a good laugh about such innovative positive reinforcements.

But some kids may not "buy in" to making "school a game worth playing." Such recalcitrant types have not been forgotten. We are told that "Competitive students will race to have the highest level in their class and grade which can be leveraged by creating quests which require them to recruit *lower level students* in quests which require both to practice [sic] target skills."[229][italics added] So, set the smart kids to getting the dumb kids to shape up. Alternatively, a revival of the dunce cap may not be far off.

As with any game—Monopoly, Chinese Checkers, or *Kill Zone: Shadow Fall*—the object of gamified learning is to win— and winning involves competition. The winner gains some kind of prize or reward, even if it's only the thought of being superior to others. As in video games, "levelling up" tracks success or failure at each stage of the "quest." In the school setting, it may be an A, the teacher's approval, the envy of one's classmates, or even one of the ever-so-cute reinforcements suggested by TeachThought. Unfortunately for the enthusiasts, though they're not to be stopped by contrary points of view, some critics have pointed out, using such methods in school is not at all the same as playing a video game. Gamers play because the game itself is exciting, dramatic, challenging, and fun; the gameplay itself is the reward. But the gamified classroom is using game tactics to get kids to do stuff they would not usually choose to do. The "experts" who design the curriculum decide what kids are supposed to know and what they are supposed to be learning. Then it's up to the school and the teachers to figure out how to make that learning happen. Regular standardized testing will show whether they are doing their job or not. The gamified classroom is just the latest wrinkle in the search for ways to make the kids do what they are told. And in this case without their knowing it—maybe.

In a paper titled *Gamification in Education* the researchers suggest that the game is really a cover-up for the serious underlying purposes:

> Serious games are games designed for a specific purpose related to training, not just for fun. They possess all game elements, they look like games, but their objective is to achieve something that is predetermined.[230]

As Daphne Bevalier suggests, you can get the kids to eat broccoli if you coat it in chocolate.[231]

There Will Be No Escape

Now that computer technology is well established in schools, and the gamified classroom is open for play, creative marketers are inventing and promoting all kinds of apps that will enhance learning and guarantee your child's success in school as well as extend surveillance of children from school to home. By the way, an *app* is what we used to call an "application," or a "computer program," words involving too many keystrokes for the convenience of texters. Of the many class management computer programs that are now available Class Dojo, frequently described as "awesome," is right up there on the top of the heap, claiming participation in 95 per cent of U.S. schools and 25 per cent of primary school teachers in ten countries. Its makers claim that one in six U.S. families with a child under fourteen is using the app daily.[232]

Since its launch in 2011, by founders Liam Don and Sam Chaudhary, the San Francisco-based company has raised over $65 million in venture capital funds, guaranteeing that they can live up to their promise that Class Dojo is free and will stay that way. Since it's obvious, however, that venture capitalists will expect some return on their investments, the program is now offering a subscription-for-pay called ClassDojo Beyond School. It is aimed at parents who are looking for ways to improve their children's behaviour through reflection, meditation, and mindfulness exercises. And, as one might expect, there are digital points to reward approved habits and behaviours at home. As Chaudhary says about the new program, "Kids spend half their days at home, where there are pockets of opportunities for less formal, less obvious learning opportunities, we want to help parents turn these opportunities into learning experiences." In other words, if the kids are going to learn anything, we'd better take charge and turn every experience into a *learning* experience—and ClassDojo Beyond School is just the ticket to make that happen.[233]

The free and basic ClassDojo also offers extensive means for teachers to communicate instantly with students and parents, tracking moment-by-moment behaviour while adding or subtracting points along the way. So while Mary may get reward-type points for sitting up straight, Jake may lose a few points by talking in class. Such incidents may then be simultaneously communicated to parents, who are expected to be dealing out reinforcements at home as well as making sure that homework assignments are done. While teachers can send messages, photos or videos to parents and to students, the kids cannot reply, comment, or send messages back. This is a one-way street with restricted access.

In addition to monitoring behaviour, the teacher may assign homework and in-school projects, all with ongoing comments to individuals or groups. Comments and remarks are accompanied by cheerful cartoon monsters, while cartoon-monster avatars are chosen and decorated by each kid. Given the cartoon format of the so-called learning games as well as trends in children's entertainment, it would seem that life itself, as well as personal identity, is a cartoon, and not much more.

Of course, it is assumed that every child, from kindergarten and before to grade twelve and after will have an iPad or similar computer tablet. A boon for the manufacturers of these devices if ever there was one! Schools are now spending millions of dollars on bringing computer technology into classrooms. According to a 2018 study from *Cambridge Assessment International Education*:

> In our survey, almost half (48 per cent) of students globally said they use a desktop computer during lessons at school, while 42 per cent use a smartphone, a third (33 per cent) say smartboards are used and one in five (20 per cent) use a tablet.[234]

The appeal of management programs like ClassDojo cannot be underestimated, and in spite of controversy surrounding student tablets, the proclaimed advantages for controlling classrooms full of kids are irresistible. Discipline and control have always been major issues in schools. Even the song "School Days" reminds us that discipline and teaching have always gone together:

School days, school days
Dear old Golden Rule days
'Reading and 'riting and 'rithmetic
Taught to the tune of the hick'ry stick[235]

Teachers are faced with dealing with disruptive and disre-spectful behaviours, demands from parents and school authorities, the distractions offered by cell phones, and students' lack of inter-est and attention. At the same time, they find themselves under threat of lawsuits whenever parents consider their children mis-treated. This can even be verbal abuse or harassment of one kind or another. Teachers, therefore, are forced to walk a narrow line, exerting control without risking offending anyone. Small wonder then that computerized management programs look so attractive. If child control can be extended from the school to the home, so much the better. The TeachThought website offers twelve com-puter and tablet programs to get parents on board.[236]

Many of these—thank you, Dr. Skinner—offer reward systems and competition as ways of controlling children.

Now Wait a Minute

Here's another list of marvellous benefits:

> 1. Enriches connections between the left and right brain
> 2. Boosts executive brain function
> 3. Strengthens speech processing
> 4. Magnifies memory
> 5. Promotes empathy
> 6. Slows brain aging
> 7. Fosters math and science ability
> 8. Improves motor skills
> 9. Elevates mental health
> 10. Sharpens self-esteem[237]

But this list isn't about playing video games. It's about playing a musical instrument.

Now virtually absent from school is anything about music, whether learning to play or learning to listen. It's an aspect of hu-man expression that schools have chosen to ignore. After all, even John Locke, in 1683, thought that music and art were a waste of time, especially for a gentleman. Well, music is OK for girls, but boys have to concentrate on more important matters, like sports or getting a job when they're out of school. Of course, this is contradictory to everything we know about music and how it makes thinking and feeling possible. Don't forget that Albert Einstein was an accomplished violinist and played regularly in a string quartet.

Probably the most famous example of the transformative power of music is *El Sistema*, a program that brings classical music instruction and performance to the children of the drug- and violence-ridden barrios in Venezuelan cities[238] and similar locations around the world. Founded in 1975 by Venezuelan economist and musician José Antonio Abreu (1939-2018) as an after-school music program for street kids in Caracas, it was primarily a social action project—how to solve a problem of lawlessness and aimlessness among youth—but it was also about encouraging a love of music for its own sake:

> Music has to be recognized as an agent of social development, in the highest sense because it transmits the highest values—solidarity, harmony, mutual compassion. And it has the ability to unite an entire community, and to express sublime feelings.—José Antonio Abreu[239]

He's talking about *classical* music.

The observable effects of *El Sistema* were studied and reported in 2016 by the journal of *Prevention Science*. The researchers concluded: "We find that the program improved self-control and reduced behavioral difficulties, with the effects concentrated among subgroups of vulnerable children." and "in boys, especially those exposed to violence at baseline . . . we find lower levels of aggressive behavior."[240]

Another study, published by *The International Journal of Music Education*, found that:

Benefits included high levels of musical achievement, increased learning opportunities, perceived benefits of discipline, perseverance, positive attitude, and hard work. Instructional challenges included low attendance, curricular balance, and teacher collaboration. The intensity and frequency of instruction were found to be the source of most benefits and challenges reported by the participants.[241]

The undeniable benefits of playing music have led to the creation of El Sistema programs around the world. *Friends of El Sistema Worldwide* lists 287 such programs in fifty-five different countries.[242]

The game-loving experts, like Daphne Bavelier and Drew Guarini, have specified what's happening in the brains of game players. Both claim an increase in grey matter and connectivity; the same brain regions are affected when playing music. Like most such studies, however, they don't tell us very much that we can't simply observe. Slice and dice brains all you like, perform all kinds of experiments and document them in endless scientific journals, but you'll never be able to measure mind or consciousness. Sure, various parts of the brain will light up, but they won't say "howdy," nor will you ever learn, in the lab, how someone could create "Shoo fly pie and apple pan dowdy makes your eyes light and your tummy say howdy,"[243] or *The Well-Tempered Clavier*. In other words, laboratory experiments on brain activity don't tell us much of anything about the person whose head that brain occupies.

The rapturous video game researchers love to report the wondrous happenings in the brains of players, but they don't talk about the emotional and social effects of having a third of the people (mostly males in their 30s) in the world glued to video screens and game controllers going on "quests" to shoot and kill monsters or people. Will game-playing lead them to a better understanding of literature, music, or art? Weary of *Grand Theft Auto*, will they turn to *Ulysses*? Will they become more sensitive to the needs and cares of other people? Empathy, for example, is not a feature common to game players, even if they join the multitudes out to vanquish the betrayers in *World of Warcraft*. It's not the same thing as, say, a thousand people in a concert hall being moved to tears by the Adagio from Mahler's Ninth Symphony.

The studies and comments I'm quoting are all about learning, playing, and listening to classical music, not popular music. There's a big difference.

A 2016 study done in China set out to show differences in brain reaction to popular vs. classical music. Though the test itself may be lacking in sufficient data, again demonstrating how little laboratory experiments actually prove, the researchers concluded that classical (they called it "artistic") music lit up the cognitive areas of the brain, while popular music evoked a more physical response, or, to quote the report:

> This study applied fMRI technology to explore the disparate neural activations in appreciation of popular and artistic music. Both sub-cortical (e.g., VS) and cortical (e.g., vmPFC) reward regions engaged in artistic and popular music aesthetic appreciation, while the sub-cortical reward region (e.g., putamen) was more sensitive to popular music while the cortical region (e.g., mPFC) was more sensitive to artistic music. In addition, the cognitive empathy regions, including PCC/PC, TPJp and arMFC, were more responsive to artistic music than popular music and control notes, implying more social cognition involved artistic music aesthetic appreciation. In conclusion, this study gives clear neuronal evidences supporting the view that **artistic music is of intelligence while the popular music is of physiology**. [244] Emphasis added.

If you've ever been to a rock concert you'll be aware of the visceral response. People can't help but wave their arms, jump up and down, beat their feet, and clap their hands—*popular music is of physiology*. An audience at a symphony concert or opera will sit quietly and attentively, applauding and cheering <u>after</u> the music has stopped—*artistic [music] is of intelligence*.

How is it that society has come to regard the exercise of intelligence as wearisome? Television and radio programs of classical music, serious drama, and sophisticated comedy have been replaced by rock stars, sit-coms, and rah rah sports reporting. These have become the dominant elements of culture. Remembering that school does not educate but promotes ignorance and the disdain of anything intellectual, you'll see how the deadening influence of school is pervasive in society. If a person has grown up hearing only three-minute songs, it's unlikely that they would readily attend to a twenty-minute symphony let alone a five-hour opera. This would suggest that the cortical region that lit up as the subject heard an operatic selection is simply underdeveloped in the inexperienced listener. The product of schooling will not be just an inexperienced listener, he will not even know that symphonies and operas exist.

In his book on the history of music and humankind *The Musical Human*, Michael Spitzer writes:

> I will argue that listening to a sonata or a symphony is akin to "walking" through a virtual landscape whose pathways are musical processes. The breadth of musical landscapes is particular to the Western classical tradition, and is certainly not shared by the three-minute culture of pop songs. . . . I believe that the consciousness-raising experience of "walking" through a classical "landscape"—whose breadth can stretch from twenty minutes to several hours—represents one of the pinnacles of Western culture."[245]

Why are there no programs in public schools that deal with classical music—or any music at all? Maybe it *was* John Locke who set the tone that the music and the arts are effeminate and suspect. Ah yes, they are the "frills" that are the first to fall to budget cuts. Or maybe it is that music is of intelligence, the last thing school wants to deal with.

So What?

"Music," Ludwig van Beethoven argued, "is a higher revelation than all wisdom and philosophy." The assertion seems reasonable enough if you consider his late string quartets, but it's absurd if your reference point is the collected works of Justin Bieber.—Tom Jacobs, in Pacific Standard.[246]

In his entertaining 2008 TED talk, Benjamin Zander uses the *Prelude Op. 28, No. 4 in e minor* (Chopin) to entrance an audience with its slow and steady movement toward a final harmonic resolution. It's a very simple and brief piece of music that is profoundly moving. A silence falls over the audience as he plays the piece. Zander uses this to show the emotional and transformative power of classical music.[247]

As one of the highest forms of human expression, shouldn't such music be a major part of any educational endeavour? The answer is easy: school is not an "educational endeavour," it is there to impede education, to maintain ignorance and gullibility.

C. Social Media

Even Better Than TV or Games

What with the ever-growing popularity, especially among kids, of social media, we are seeing pro and con arguments galore. Though you can find more comprehensive listings of benefits, here are a mere five from a website called Atlanta Parent:

1. Invites creative expression
2. Fosters purposeful mindfulness
3. Connects kids with friends
4. Promotes awareness
5. Raises critical thinkers

Of course, that's not all. You'll also find such praiseworthy benefits as: Socialization, even for the most introverted among us; Support for personal growth; Sets you on your path as a life-long learner; Spreads positivity. And perhaps the most significant of all: Allows you to have *fun*. [248]

However, there is a dark side to social media that is rarely acknowledged by its proponents.

Facebook and Friends

The granddaddy of social networking, *Facebook*, founded in 2004 (a long, long time ago by contemporary standards) is leading the pack with 2.6 billion users, or people that log in at least once a month. From what was expected to be a modest beginning as a way to connect students at Harvard, *Facebook* exploded into the most used and most influential of social media, now with one-third of the people in the world posting, viewing, and "friending." What are they posting and viewing though? Even a cursory perusal of *Facebook* pages will reveal a plethora of trivia, banal aphorisms, adorable cats and dogs, and what is assumed to be humour. Some people post links to political or medical articles (Here's where conspiracy theories abound.), reports about family incidents, and ever-frequent birthday greetings. (*Facebook* records your birthdate and tells everyone about it.) And, oh yes, there are those people who love posting photos of what they're having for lunch or dinner and other such bits of stimulating information. It's no wonder that *Facebook* is declining in popularity among young people, though still maintaining its overall leadership by a wide margin.

Omnicore reports some interesting statistics about *Facebook* users. As of January 2021, the major users were between the ages of twenty-five and thirty-four (19.3 per cent male; 13.2 per cent female) with a diminishing follow-up of ages eighteen to twenty-four (23.8 per cent). The curve levels out as the user group ages, with the sixty-five-and-over group being nearly gender equal. As might be expected, though, that particular age is the smallest of all user groups, representing less than 5 per cent of total users.[249] This is in spite of what is said about seniors using media to keep in touch with their grandchildren.

A website named *tom's guide*[250] tells us that the three main uses of *Facebook* are "Keep In Touch With Faraway Family and Friends, Share Photos and Information, and Get Your News."[251] Most of the other websites about *Facebook* reveal what it's really about and how Mark Zuckerberg's empire makes billions of dollars per year: through advertising. By the way, the "empire" includes several other social media sites like *Instagram*, *Facebook Messenger*, and *WhatsApp*. If social media are about inter-connectedness, they provide marketers with a simple and effective way of finding and hitting their target. Every move you make, every link you click, every picture you look at, and every bit of music you access will be tracked, monitored, and recorded. This information will then be transmitted and sold to marketing companies who will be glad to hit you with "relevant" ads. Considering that *Facebook* revenue for a twelve-month period ending March 2021 was nearly $95 billion,[252] things aren't looking too bad.

Since advertising is the reason for social media in the first place, there's a helpful run-down to help admen find their target audience. Here are the five sites that are most popular with youth:

> 1. Instagram. One of the most popular social media platforms for teens and young adults . . . well over 1 billion monthly users.
> 2. YouTube. A must for reaching their more than 2 billion monthly users ... with a heavy concentration in the age range of 15 to 34 years olds [sic].
> 3. Facebook. With nearly 2.5 billion monthly users, Facebook is hands down the largest social media site in the world. It's developed a somewhat negative reputation amongst younger users that are increasingly turning to alternative sites.
> 4. TikTok, Over 800 million monthly users . . . concentrated amongst those between the ages of 16 to 24.
> 5. Snapchat. Young adults between the ages of 18 and 24 make up a massive 78 per cent of active users who partake in the platform's over 14 billion daily video views. [253]

With almost the entire world attached, just find the right demographic, and you have a marketer's dream!

All About Instagram

Zuckerberg knew a good thing when he saw it; he bought Instagram for $1 billion in 2012. Within two months of its launch, in October 2010, Instagram had over one million followers, growing to one billion by 2020, attesting to its widespread appeal, especially to teenagers—and most are now in possession of a smartphone. In fact, the application, or app, was designed for the display of photos and short videos on the phone's small screen, but by 2014 it was adapted for use on desktop computers using Windows 10, meaning that a webcam can readily be used to transmit videos and selfies. Among its many features, Instagram provides filters for enhancement of uploaded media, thus assuring that users can show themselves in the best possible light. Posts, which can include comments and messages, may be shared publicly or restricted to pre-chosen followers. But who wants to be restricted, considering that the whole point is to amass as many followers and "likes" as possible?

Users click *like* or *follow* to show their admiration or approval of what they see. And what they may see includes just about everything. As with Facebook, the site's operators have been plagued with obscene or objectionable content, ever problematic and hard to control. Many users will object to being censored, while others will be drawn to pornographic imagery and abusive commentary. There are always ways around any restrictions that may be applied by websites or parents. Such apps as Lipsi, Tellonym, Holla, and Houseparty offer virtually unrestricted text and image content which can lead to risky behaviour involving strangers, cyberbullies, or presumed friends. It's true that most of these sites, including Instagram, ask for birthdates and set age limits, but there is no way to verify claims of being thirteen, eighteen, or whatever. For example, on my Facebook page I entered January 1, 1905 as my birthdate. This has never been questioned. There is nothing stopping a savvy six-year-old from signing on to Instagram. In an October 2018 article in *The New York Times*, Judi Ketteler wrote, "In his first weekend on Instagram, my 9-year-old posted 20 times in 24 hours. He put up a video of himself doing a front flip wearing only his boxer shorts, followed back every single user who followed him, and went 'live' in a friend's basement without the parents knowing."[254] So when Omnicore tells us that 67 per cent of U.S. adults and 72 per cent of U.S. teens are using Instagram what does that actually mean?[255]

It means that anyone of any age can access these websites by simply lying. So let's accept that Instagram is readily available to anyone of any age, and once they have a homepage they will have access to millions, well, actually billions, of photographs and comments. And not all of these are pictures of flowers, celebrities, and cute cats. By entering the Search & Explore feature—just click on the magnifying glass at the bottom of the page—you can, as Instagram tells us, "find photos and videos that you might like from accounts you don't yet follow. You may also see curated topics we think the Instagram community will enjoy."[256] Curated topics—or advertising—means that Instagram notes every choice made and every interest shown by users and hangs related pages and links onto the homepage. Getting a product onto the Search & Explore page gives access to the teenage market, a merchandiser's dream. Of course, there's more to it than that. The Search allows you to enter any word, name, category, or title, and the results will be instantly available. For example, a hashtag combined with certain code words or "emojis" will reveal hundreds of pornographic and semi-pornographic sites: "Users are flooding Instagram with pornography. Amongst all the images of cute puppies, donuts, and holiday snaps, people can find endless pornographic images and links to find even more on other platforms."[257] *Emojis*, by the way, are those cute little images, like the ubiquitous smiley face, that provide shortcuts for verbal expression. Instagram offers lists of hundreds of them.[258]

Yes, posting pornographic or abusive images is contrary to Instagram's "Community Guidelines"[259] but any images that are taken down can be, and are, instantly replaced. As Nicole Harris and Anna Halkidis wrote on the website Parents: "Due to the nature of the app, kids might stumble upon people participating in dangerous stunts and challenges, prejudiced or racist viewpoints, substance use, violent photographs, sexual videos, and other inappropriate content. Kids can view these public posts even if their own account is set to private." [260] If I remember correctly from my own youth, teenagers are endlessly curious about sex and comparative anatomy, so, for better or worse, technology now supplies abundant resources for satisfying that curiosity. If, as a parent, you think you can have the talk about the birds and the bees or control your kid's use of social media, forget it, you are living in a pre-internet world. Parents are advised to have serious discussions with their kids about dangers of internet use—and abuse—and to install parental controls and keep a watchful eye on what they're doing. Lotsa luck, because the kids are sharing what they find with each other, and as with Instagram and others trying to take down porno sites, there are ways around everything. In June of 2020 **verywell**family reported that "The average teen spends about nine hours per day using media for their enjoyment. Frighteningly, those same teens spend less than an average of 10 minutes a day talking to their parents." [261] The kids are living in a peer-oriented digital culture of their own and have little time for adult interference.

Are We Having Fun Yet?

There is another dark side of social media, especially for young people and especially for girls. Photographs posted on *Instagram* are created to make the subjects appear as glamorous as possible, often by means of makeup, Photoshop, and Instagram filters. As a result, kids are encouraged to compare themselves to images of "perfect" individuals, either models, celebrities, or other kids who are posting selfies. Every selfie posted invites comparison and comment. Reporting in Time on a British study, Amanda MacMillan wrote:

> Social media posts can also set unrealistic expectations and create feelings of inadequacy and low self-esteem, the authors wrote. This may explain why Instagram, where personal photos take center stage, received the worst scores for body image and anxiety. As one survey respondent wrote, "Instagram easily makes girls and women feel as if their bodies aren't good enough as people add filters and edit their pictures in order for them to look 'perfect'." [262]

> Another study found that "53 per cent of 13-year-old American girls are unhappy with their bodies. This number grows to 78 per cent by the time girls reach 17." [263]

A Canadian study shows similar results.[264]

There was further comment on the report from Shirley Cramer of the Royal Society for Public Health, who said:

> Social media has been described as more addictive than cigarettes and alcohol, and is now so entrenched in the lives of young people that it is no longer possible to ignore it when talking about young people's mental health issues. Through our Young Health Movement, young people have told us that social media has had both a positive and negative impact on their mental health. It's interesting to see Instagram and Snapchat ranking as the worst for mental health and wellbeing – both platforms are very image-focused and it appears they may be driving feelings of inadequacy and anxiety in young people. [265]

All you have to do is look at the pictures that kids are posting. Everyone must be smiling, be good-looking, sexy, and appearing to be having fun, especially with a group of equally good-looking, smiling, and laughing friends. And this is the standard with which comparisons will be made. As if that isn't enough, there are those who will make negative and hurtful comments about anyone who doesn't make the grade. Remember, the goal is to get as many *likes*, followers, and favourable comments as possible. The competition is high, and if you don't succeed, you're a loser. Alex Hearn, in a *Guardian* article, put it this way: "If Facebook demonstrates that everyone is boring and Twitter proves that everyone is awful, Instagram makes you worry that everyone is perfect—except you."[266]

FOMO or Fear of Missing Out is another phenomenon that keeps kids hooked and on line. Missing Out means not being part of the in-crowd, or not having fun while everyone else is. If you find yourself checking your e-mail or Facebook page constantly throughout the day, you know what FOMO is. It's a driving compulsion; not doing it can make you feel as if you might miss something, or "a pervasive apprehension that others might be having rewarding experiences from which one is absent."[267] Here's how *not* to get left out: According to a 2019 study of American kids by *Common Sense Media*[268] teenagers are spending an average of seven hours and twenty-two minutes per day, not including at school or for homework, on screen media entertainment, while 'tweens (eight to twelve years old) follow up with close to five hours per day. Most of this "entertainment" is accessed via the hand-held smartphone. The 2018 Pew Research Study noted that "95 per cent of teens now report they have a smartphone or access to one. These mobile connections are in turn fueling more-persistent online activities: 45 per cent of teens now say they are online on a near-constant basis." [269]

The term "social" media may well be misleading because teens who spend hours a day on a smartphone are less likely to have a face-to-face social life. "They don't need to leave home to spend time with their friends." The screen is the replacement for human contact. In the same article in *The Atlantic,* Jean Twenge explains that teenagers of what she refers to as the "iGen" are spending less time on homework, dating, working for pay, or just hanging out than the previous generation. That spare time is now spent, smartphone in hand, on social media.

> Social-networking sites like Facebook promise to connect us to friends. But the portrait of iGen teens emerging from the data is one of a lonely, dislocated generation. Teens who visit social-networking sites every day but see their friends in person less frequently are the most likely to agree with the statements "A lot of times I feel lonely," "I often feel left out of things," and "I often wish I had more good friends." [270]

We have already noted the increase in youth suicide as a result of depression, anxiety, and despair directly related to what we should rename *Antisocial Media.*

Remembering that Instagram and similar apps are driven by *likes*, it's not hard to imagine it becoming a popularity contest, driving kids to go all out to make themselves look attractive and impressive. This can lead to dangerous behaviour like taking on challenges or posing in revealing outfits. A quick internet search will reveal any number of sites offering "sexy" pose suggestions for girls.[271] And boys.[272] You'll notice, however, that the emphasis is on revealing and provocative poses for young women.

Such posts may not only be unsuccessful at acquiring *likes* but may also result in negative and hurtful comments. If a user has a public account, and most teenagers do, anyone on Instagram will have access, meaning that anyone can view and comment on what's there. It's easy to imagine that there are people out there, even "friends," who will enjoy posting mean and critical remarks. Kids are also going to be comparing themselves with the glamorous airbrushed and photo-edited pictures they see of celebrities and models, leading to depleted self-esteem and a desire for unattainable perfection.

One curious feature of "perfection" is *thigh gap*. A picture of a girl or young woman posing feet together and bare-legged is supposed to show a gap between her upper thighs. As put by Wikipedia, "Beginning around 2011, women in the West began to consider the thigh gap a special feature of female physical attractiveness. The thigh gap has been associated with femininity and fragility."[273] Though physically impossible for the majority of women, the thigh gap mania leads to obsession with extreme thinness, which in turn leads to excessive dieting. And there are plenty of dubious diet schemes and advertised guaranteed weight loss products to be found on the internet and via Instagram hashtags like #thighgap or #skinnyinspiration, all glorifying the unattainable, or dangerously attainable, ideal of being extremely skinny. The sources of information on health and nutrition that media users may find are often motivated less by scientific evidence than by fad trends and financial incentives. Again from the website Parents: "A study from *Association for Psychological Science* found teens who spend more time on their screens are more likely to report depressive symptoms and suicidal behaviors. Instagram has also been linked to anxiety, loneliness, and a "fear of missing out"

(FOMO). If your kids don't have content filtering, they could potentially come across photos or videos that are highly personal or sensitive—even ones that glorify self-harm or eating disorders."[274]

Let's not forget that Instagram is but one of dozens of social media sites that offer communication, pictures, and access to anything you—or your kids—can think of. You'll find that teenagers are very clever at hiding what they're doing, and most of the time they are alone, day or night, in their bedroom. You'll never know what they are into. This is the new world that we are living in. It's a new world that is well supported by the schools that are supposed to be encouraging thoughtful behaviour and what they like to call "critical thinking." Massing kids together, segregated by age, exacerbates the divide between grownups and children and intensifies the formation of peer culture.

Sextortion

In late 2012 the well-publicized story of Amanda Todd brought the issue of teenage suicide to public attention. Amanda was fifteen when she hanged herself at her home in Port Coquitlam, a suburb of Vancouver in British Columbia. Creating online videos came naturally to her; she was posting videos of herself singing as early as age nine. In her early teens she became involved, like most kids her age, in Facebook and other social media. With her username "cutielover," (Remember, she was nine years old!) she attracted many favourable compliments from her singing and performance videos, but at age thirteen she was also attracting comments about her looks. She corresponded with a flirtatious and flattering young (as far as she knew) man. He eventually cajoled her into "flashing," that is, showing her bare breasts. He then kept asking for a "show," meaning she was to perform sexual acts on webcam. Whoever the "admiring male" was (he was later caught and convicted) then told her that he would expose her image to all her Facebook friends unless she "performed" for him. This kind of extortion has become so common that it boasts a new name "sextortion." When she refused to perform, in retaliation, the picture of her nude bosom was posted all over the internet. As the image went viral, a barrage of insults, hate messages, threats, and demeaning comments were aimed at her. She tried changing schools to find a new group of friends but found no relief. The pervasive internet followed her everywhere. In a downward spiral, she attempted suicide twice, only bringing on more ridicule. By this time, no one would befriend her or offer support. Criticism from others quickly became internalized into self-criticism and self-torture—external reinforcement no longer required. Since she was now rejected by her all-encompassing peer group, she did not have recourse to adult support, thus driven to depression and self-harm. The teachers and other adults in school maintain their distance as authorities, hardly people for kids to trust or confide in. Because the peer culture is the only source of comfort and support, rejection can be devastating.

The sad result is shown in a now-famous YouTube video that she made just five weeks before her death. Rather than speaking, she holds up hand-written cards, one by one, beginning with "I've decided to tell you about my never ending story." The touching pathos of this video reveals the loneliness of a young person driven to despair by bullying from peers and an absence of adult support. The absence of that support, resulting from the alienation of school, drives kids to seek support from their peer group. When that becomes hostile, the result can be tragic. The final card reads: "I have nobody I need someone" and then: "My name is Amanda Todd."

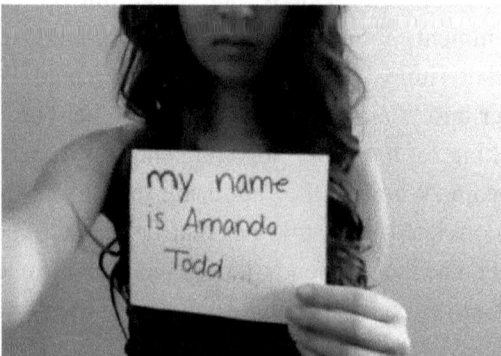

If Amanda's case were but one sad tale of a lonely teenager, we could shed a tear or two and let it go at that. A Wikipedia article[275] lists forty-seven suicides between 1997 and 2019 of victims of bullying, ages eight to seventeen. Each listing is accompanied by a story of relentless abuse, criticism, and mistreatment by peers or parents and teachers. Some kids were harassed for their appearance, some for personality traits, others for simply being different—characteristics that brought out the hate and disdain of their classmates. They were spit upon, called names, jeered at, pushed around, or had their belongings stolen or destroyed. Reports to school authorities were usually dismissed with comments like "boys will be boys" or "just be tough and ignore it." Few or no offers of help or support were forthcoming. The *Insider* reports that the suicide rate for ages ten to twenty-four in the U.S. rose by 57.4 per cent from 2007 to 2018.[276] That means that 6,807 young Americans took their own lives for all reasons in 2018. There is every reason to believe that similar numbers would apply world wide and that the suicide rate will continue to climb.

The Dutch man, age thirty-eight, who pushed Amanda Todd into suicide was arrested in January of 2014. He was accused of harassing thirty-four young women and five gay men from countries as far away as Britain, Canada, Norway, and the United States. He had abused dozens of young girls by gaining their trust through speaking with them on the internet. He then abused that trust by forcing them to perform sexual acts before their webcams. If they refused to do it more than once, he threatened to send their images to their relatives or to publish them on pornography sites. He was convicted and sentenced to eleven years in prison. In addition, in 2022, he was convicted, in British Columbia, and sentenced to thirteen additional years in prison.

There is no reason to believe that this was a unique case. Such are the "friends" of children on social media.

A Peer-Oriented Culture

How does it happen that kids are spending so much time on social media, playing video games, watching YouTube videos, and vying with glamourized images for popularity within their peer group? How does it happen that kids today seem distant, easily bored, sexually precocious, indifferent or defiant to parents and teachers, uninterested in anything beyond what's readily available on a smartphone, either bullies or victims of bullying, and on a downward spiral into depression and self-harm? As children progress through school they become more and more oriented toward their peers, exclusive of all else.

Compulsory attendance at school guarantees that this will happen. Once a child commits the crime of being six years old, she will be confined for six hours per day in a bureaucratic, authoritarian institution that will place her in a segregated group of others of her age and ability. Contrary to her natural impulses, she will have to sit still and be quiet. Going to the washroom, eating and drinking, asking questions, daydreaming, socializing, playing, and sleeping will all be strictly controlled and regulated according to the school's agenda. Her days will be structured by a single adult stranger known as a teacher, and she has no say whatsoever as to who that adult will be. This is the situation a child will have to cope with for the next twelve years. Is there any question that a child's spirit will be crushed by such a regime? Well, almost. Oppression leads to resentment and, wherever possible, rebellion. And when open rebellion is impossible, more subtle means will be found.

There are plenty of the oppressed around who will gravitate together because they are all in the same boat. As the years pass this peer group—and the school makes sure that age groups do not mix—will solidify into a culture of its own, with its own standards and deviant means of resisting authority. It's no surprise that you'll find the same kind of group mentality among penitentiary inmates. Prisoners do not look up to the guards for guidance and protection. Is it any different with kids in school? Just substitute *teachers* for *guards*, *principal* for *warden*.

In their 2004 book *Hold On To Your Kids*.[277] Gordon Neufeld and Gabor Maté describe what they call "vertical" as opposed to "horizontal" transmission of culture. In a society in which children identify with parents, grandparents, older siblings, uncles, aunties, other adults, and sometimes even teachers, they learn about the manners, customs, and beliefs of a broad and mature culture. Out of this, they develop a personality and culture that become who they are and how they will become part of the world around them. Of course, they will also associate with other kids and engage in play and kid-oriented activities, but the dominant influence in their lives will be coming from adults—vertically, from top down.

If, on the other hand, children are dissociated from the grown-up world, driven to association with those of their own age by segregation or rebellion, and, lacking experience of the world other than that which they learn from commercial media, they will make up a set of standards and beliefs of their own. Neufeld and Maté explain:

> The problem is not that children have friends their own age or that they form connections with other children—such ties are only natural and can serve a healthy purpose. In cultures that are adult oriented, in which the guiding principles and values are those of the more mature generations, children attach to other children without losing their bearings or without having to reject parental influences. In our society that is no longer the case, peer bonds have come to replace relationships with adults as children's primary sources of orientation.[278]

In addition to peer influence, however, there is a new and irresistible authority in the form of social media. An article in *The Guardian* reported on a talk given by Sean Parker, founding president of Facebook.[279] In a 2017 talk about cancer research[280] at an event hosted by the American news website Axios, Parker digressed to express some thoughts about the social media giant. His revealing comments apply to all social media:

> He explained that when Facebook was being developed the objective was: "How do we consume as much of your time and conscious attention as possible?" It was this mindset that led to the creation of features such as the "like" button that would give users "a little dopamine hit" to encourage them to upload more content.
>
> "It's a social-validation feedback loop ... exactly the kind of thing that a hacker like myself would come up with, because you're exploiting a vulnerability in human psychology."
>
> "It literally changes your relationship with society, with each other. It probably interferes with productivity in weird ways. God only knows what it's doing to our children's brains," he said."[281]

His statements have been confirmed by numerous studies. An article in *Time* confirms that:

> Research has linked social media and other phone-based activities with an uptick in feel-good neurochemicals like dopamine, which could drive compulsive device use and promote feelings of distraction, fatigue, or irritability when kids are separated from their phones.
>
> Even if smartphones aren't the root cause of a teen's anxiety or other issues, . . . they may turn out to be an accelerant—the gasoline that turns a flicker of adolescent angst into a blaze.[282]

Depression, loneliness, suicide, fragmented attention, lack of sleep, increased risk of ADHD, low attachment to parents, obsession with appearance, crash dieting—the list goes on.

How have we allowed this to happen to our children?

PART FOUR

How Did We End Up With School?
And Why

A: How and Why It All Started

The Fredericks

From 1688 to 1840—Frederick William I to Frederick William III—the kings of Prussia entertained notions of schooling for the masses as means of maintaining civil order and securing military prowess. When it comes to schooling, they are "the grand old masters, /Whose distant footsteps echo/Through the corridors of Time."[283] Today's thoughts about the purposes of public education are not much different from theirs of 400 years ago. It's what we have come to call "education."

The first more or less organized and purposeful school system was spelled out when, in 1763, Frederick II (1712-1786), r.1740-1786), known as "the Great," issued the General Education Regulations (*General-Landschul-Reglement*). Though not very successful due to a lack of funding resources and suitable teachers, the elements of a universal compulsory school system were set for more than two hundred and fifty years. Speaking of suitable teachers, around the 1720s those considered "suitable" to be teachers were tailors, linen weavers, smiths, wheelwrights, and carpenters. (As we'll see later, not much different from the class of people who are teachers today.) Pay was so poor that an occupation other than teaching was considered necessary. Though a regulation of 1738 restricted the teaching profession to tailors, Frederick II, after ascending the

Frederick II, The Great

throne in 1740, could express his dissatisfaction with the teaching profession, recommending that disabled soldiers replace the tailors. A lasting association of artisanal labour with teaching—the school teacher as craftsman—was established and persists to this day.

There had been attempts to establish some form of universal schooling in eighteenth-century Prussia. As early as 1717 Frederick William I, thinking that some education might keep the peasantry under control and might produce better, more obedient soldiers, made a half-hearted attempt at setting up primary schools, but money and co-operation were reluctantly and meagrely supplied by local councils. And the peasants were not easy to corral. At that time, and well into the nineteenth century, there was a fear that education might make the peasants uppity. This fear was well-expressed by Frederick II in 1779: "In country places, a little reading and writing should be enough, for if they know too much . . . [they] will run off to the cities and become clerks or some such thing."[284] Education, after all, had always been the purview of the nobility. Why would the lower classes need to know how to read or write? But, as we shall see, reading and writing were not the issue. Social control, moral improvement, and obedience were—and still are.

The idea of the 1763 regulations, however unrealized, was to maintain state-funded schools, trained teachers, and compulsory attendance from age five to fourteen. Frederick's principal advisor and creator of the education regulations was Johann Julius Hecker (1707-1768),[285] an educator and proponent of teacher training and universal education with an already established relationship with the monarchy. Johann Hecker's educational panache was first discovered by Frederick II's father and predecessor Frederick William I (1688-1740, r.1713-1740) who appointed him, in 1739, as the first pastor of the Trinity Church in Berlin. As early as 1749, he had established a school for young working-class people to prepare them for work in the growing industries of the time. He followed that with a school for the training of teachers, the first of its kind. The curriculum included training in architecture, building, manufacturing, commerce, and trade with a heavy emphasis on Calvinist ideals of hard work, godliness, and obedience, principles that also formed the foundation of the 1763 education rules. Presaging Pestalozzi's ideals of education through practical experience, Hecker started a garden near his school. In addition to vegetables, herbs, and fruit trees, the garden included a mulberry plantation for silk production. It is important to remember that this school, and others of its kind, were still serving the young of the wage-earning and well-off classes. The peasantry was still lurking, dangerously, in the background awaiting the "enlightenment" of state-promoted compulsory schooling.

As the enlightened monarch—this was, after all, the Age of Enlightenment—that he was, Frederick II re-established, in 1744, the Prussian Academy of Sciences that had been axed, as a cost-cutting measure, by Frederick's despotic father, Frederick William. This enabled him to assemble around him some of the best thinkers, artists, and musicians of the time. This, by the way, resulted in the famous visit of Johann Sebastian Bach to the King's court in 1748. Frederick, who was an accomplished flutist, played a theme of his own devising and asked Bach to improvise various fugues and canons on it. This resulted in the composition of The Musical Offering, completed by Bach upon his return to Leipzig. He was 63 at the time and died two years later. The visit of Bach illustrates the King's lively interest in and support of music, literature, and art. Theatrical, musical, operatic, and artistic performances were held frequently at *Sans Souci*, the King's elegant rococo palace, where he could relax, away from the pomp and ceremony of the Berlin court. If this description makes him sound effete, it is incorrect because he proved himself a military genius, expanding and consolidating his kingdom, and more than doubling (to 196,000 men) the size of the army left by his father. Frederick was no wimp, personally leading his armies into battle inspiring courage among the soldiers he led. On at least six occasions, the very horse he was riding was shot out from under him. No wonder he became known as "the Great."

Probably the most famous visitor and sometime resident of Frederick's palace at Potsdam was the French philosopher and writer Voltaire (François-Marie Arouet 1694-1778), who, like Frederick, was a champion of Enlightenment ideals of freedom of speech, religious freedom, and humanitarian tolerance. Though cordiality between the two men did not last, Voltaire never-the-less left a lasting impression of progressive Enlightenment thought.

An interesting member of the Academy of Sciences appointed by Frederick was Johann Georg Sulzer (1720-1779). Sulzer was a Swiss mathematician, philosopher, and scientist whose primary interest was in the arts, especially music, which he considered to be the highest of art forms. His encyclopedic *General Theory of the Fine Arts* was widely consulted among musical theorists of the late Eighteenth and early Nineteenth Centuries. However, as a member of the Academy, he held the directorship of the "class of speculative philosophy" from 1775 until his death in 1779. His essay of 1748 *An Essay on the Education and Instruction of Children* was no doubt highly influential in the creation of the *General Regulations* of 1763. One writer on education, Stephen Hicks,[286] places Sulzer along with Locke and Rousseau as a powerful influencer of thought on childhood and learning, especially in German schools. Just read between lines in the following, bypassing the eighteenth-century rhetoric, and his essay will reveal a trend of thought about childhood and education that underlies much of the teaching and child-rearing methods of today. Take for example:

> Willfulness:
> As far as willfulness is concerned, this expresses itself as a natural recourse in tenderest childhood. [*i.e. children are likely to create a ruckus when they don't get what they want—the terrible twos?*] … If willfulness and wickedness are not driven out, it is impossible to give a child a good education.

Orderliness:

The order one insists upon has an indisputable influence on their minds, and if children become accustomed to orderliness at a very early age, they will suppose thereafter that this is completely natural because they can no longer realize that it has been artfully instilled in them. [*see the BCTF tips for classroom management*]

Obedience:

Obedience is so important that all education is actually nothing other than learning how to obey. . Obedience requires children to (1) **willingly** do as they are told, (2) **willingly** refrain from doing what they are forbidden, and (3) accept rules made for their own sake.[287]

Sound familiar? (The parenthetical comments and the bold on "willingly" are mine.)

The way *Willfulness, Orderliness,* and *Obedience* are to be handled has slowly morphed over the centuries from direct and open top-down management to a more subtle form of psychological manipulation. *Willfulness* is now called "acting out;" *Orderliness* is "every child **needs** structure," though always "artfully instilled in them;" *Obedience* is known as "classroom management." The kids are expected to accept willingly the demands of school by *co-operating* with the teacher—for their own good and for the benefit of all involved. Older and openly authoritarian styles of discipline (Do as you're told or get punished.) are replaced with more subtle means of coercion. Like advertising, you learn to buy something because you are told that you need it or that it will be good for you.

Paul Verhaeghe describes how the notion of "agreement" is used in school:

Think of a conversation between a school teacher and her student: "We agree that you will..." The odd switch from the first person plural to the second person singular, from 'we' to 'you,' reveals the underlying message. I want you to do this. If you don't do it, you will be punished." This has little to do with a real agreement, in which both sides have a say and reach a settlement.[288]

Now getting back to Frederick the Great, it's amazing that he survived his childhood to become the benevolent and intelligent monarch that he was. His father was a harsh disciplinarian and passionate militarist, so much so that he became known as "The Soldier King." Through conscription of peasants and hiring of mercenaries, he increased the size of the Prussian army from 38,000 men to 83,000, engaging the military strategist Prince Leopold of Anhalt-Dessau (1676-1747) to help turn the army into a formidable fighting machine. He introduced such innovations as the iron ramrod to replace the wooden one then in use, relentless drill in loading and firing of muskets, severe punishment for misbehaviour, and the slow march, or goose step, chillingly familiar from films of the World War II German army. With increased firepower (each soldier was expected to fire six times per minute, or three times faster than other armies), bayonets fixed on their rifles, and lock-step uniformity, the Prussians struck fear in the hearts of other fighting forces. As we have seen, son Frederick took full advantage of these military advances, and added his brilliant strategy, courage, and prowess to the mix, establishing the ascendency of Prussia in Europe, leading right up to World War II.

The rigid training of soldiers under Frederick William's command is sometimes cited by critics of schooling as the origin of the learning methods applied to school curricula. However, as we'll see, this is not what Horace Mann and others observed in Prussian schools of the nineteenth century. The military style of methodical teaching and learning didn't become "the way it is done" until the rise of Taylorism and the efficiency movement in the early twentieth century

As a curious sideline, Frederick William had a bizarre fixation on tall men. He scoured the countryside for men over six feet tall and with them formed a special non-fighting regiment for his own pleasure. Under his personal supervision he would stretch some men on the rack, also practising a form of eugenics, pairing up tall men and women in order to produce tall offspring, perhaps presaging the Nazi's efforts to breed a blond Arian race.

As a sideline more distressing than curious, Frederick William detested what he thought of as his son's effeminacy. Any wavering, like playing the flute or loving music, from a rigidly "masculine" deportment resulted in severe punishment. Two stories provide harrowing examples: At age sixteen Frederick had formed an attachment to a seventeen-year-old page, Peter Keith, of his father's court. When this was discovered, Keith was sent away to a distant regiment and young Frederick was banished to his father's hunting lodge. After his return, he became close friends with Hans Hermann von Katte, a Prussian officer a few years older than the prince. Together with a few junior army officers they plotted fleeing to England. When the plot was discovered and the friendship between Frederick and Katte revealed for what it was, Frederick was jailed and Katte sentenced to death by beheading. The king then forced Frederick to watch the execution. After release, Frederick was stripped of military rank and sent to Küstrin, a small town on the Dutch border, where he was to receive two years of rigorous schooling in statecraft and administration. After that, he was allowed to return to Berlin. He was to become king eight years later.

There is something important to be said about the relationship between these two men, father and son, king and prince. The father's rigid moral, military and intellectual views are exemplified by his distaste for anything French—he considered the French decadent and frivolous—and his elimination of music, art, science, and philosophy—he considered those to be threatening to religious and manly virtue—from his court. The defunding of the Academy of Sciences (cost-cutting measures, sound familiar?) and the relentless drilling of the military are prime examples of his rule. His son, the Crown Prince, engendered his father's wrath, by showing a keen devotion to the French language and culture, learning to play the flute, pursuing music and the other arts as essential parts of culture. How much do these two streams still flow in the twenty-first century? Do we not favour discipline over permissiveness, and sports over arts? Don't discipline and sports represent manly pursuits, while music, art, and thought fall into the feminine domain? Real men don't play the flute!

Following the death of Frederick II, his half-brother ascended the throne, reigning as Frederick William II (1744-1797) from 1786 until his death. In contrast to his predecessors, he "was of an easy-going and pleasure-loving disposition, averse from sustained effort of any kind, and sensual by nature."[289] Under the influence of one Johann Christoph von Wöllner (1732-1800), whom Frederick II had described as a "treacherous and intriguing priest," the new king dabbled in Rosicrucianism and Freemasonry while openly professing a reactionary and anti-Enlightenment support for religion and German culture. His spending habits decimated the treasury and he had little interest in the military; when he died, he left the state in bankruptcy and confusion, the army decayed, and the monarchy discredited. As for education, he realized that schools and universities could provide reinforcement of his religious views, training the public to adapt to religious orthodoxy. Further steps were taken to ensure compulsory attendance and training of teachers—leave nothing to chance. Incompetence and self-indulgence led to senseless political strategies leaving "Prussia morally isolated in Europe on the eve of the titanic struggle between the monarchical principle and the new political creed of the Revolution."[290]

His successor, King Frederick William III (1770-1840, r.1797-1840), though lacking in both confidence and competence, did what he could to beef up the economy and restore moral credibility to the monarchy. Trying to steer clear of the Napoleonic wars (1803-1815) that followed the French revolution, he maintained neutrality until yielding to the influence of the queen (Frederica Louisa of Hesse-Darmstadt) and leader of the pro-war Prussian party, he made an unprovoked attack against Napoleon's troops at the double battle of Jena-Auerstedt. In a crushing and humiliating defeat, the Prussian army, which had outnumbered the French 250,000 to 160,000, sustained 65,000 dead, including two of the royal family, 160,000 taken prisoner, and multiple losses of artillery. Moreover, they then had to endure the occupation of Berlin by the French and had to bow to Napoleon's heavy financial demands. The pride in Prussian military power and the hope of unification of certain German duchies had been brought to the ground. Whatever happened to the fearsome fighting forces of Frederick William I and the glory of the Prussian nation? Clearly, something had to be done.

Now What Do We Do?

What went wrong? was the question addressed by thinkers of the time, including Johann Gottlieb Fichte (1762-1814). In 1807-1808 Fichte delivered fourteen *Addresses to the German Nation (Reden an die deutsche Nation),*[291] laying out a theory of nationalistic universal education (to include boys and girls on an equal basis) designed to strengthen and unify German identity and loyalty to the state. Education was to be intrinsic in building a national character. "An absolutely new system of German national education . . . must be able surely and infallibly to mould and determine, according to rules, the real vital impulses and actions of its pupils."[292]

Presaging modern views on stimulating a child's interest in curricular topics, Fichte urges the creation in the mind of images of "the good, simply as such and for its own sake."[293] And "The reason for demanding self-activity in regard to that image is this: only on that condition can the image created engage the active pleasure of the pupil."[294] But the pupil is not to be relied upon to create such a vision on his or her own:

> Now, this pleasure will be kindled only by the pupil's self-activity being stimulated at the same time and becoming manifest to him in the given object, so that this object pleases not only in itself, but also as an object of the manifestation of mental power. [However] This creative mental activity

> which is to be developed in the pupil is undoubt-
> edly an activity according to rules, which become
> known to the active pupil until he sees from his
> direct experience that they alone are possible.[295]

In other words, the pupil must be led to believe that what
is taught is all there is. There is no education outside of school,
and school will produce the ideal moral and disciplined citizen.

> The new education must consist essentially in this,
> that it completely destroys freedom of will in the
> soil which it undertakes to cultivate, and produces
> on the contrary strict necessity in the decisions of
> the will, the opposite being impossible. Such a
> will can henceforth be relied on with confidence
> and certainty.[296]

Fichte poo-poos traditional education because it did not attempt to bring everyone into line. The good guys did not become
good because of education; they were already good by their nature; education had nothing to do with it. And therefore, the bad
guys would stay bad, and education failed to change them. The
new education would be different.

> Those who in the past became good did so thanks
> to their natural disposition, which outweighed the
> influence of their bad environment, and not be-
> cause of their education in any way, for otherwise
> all the pupils would have become good. . . . The
> education proposed by me, therefore, is to be a re-
> liable and deliberate art for fashioning in man a
> stable and infallible good will. That is its first
> characteristic. [297]

The result:

> On the other hand, the State which introduced
> universally the national education proposed by us,
> from the moment that a new generation of youths
> had passed through it, would need no special army

at all, but would have in them an army such as no age has seen. . . . The State can summon them and put them under arms when it will, and can be sure that no enemy will defeat them.[298]

It's pretty clear that the "new" education was to concern itself not so much with reading and writing but with the development of a nationalistic and obedient populace, guaranteed to win the next war. The wording (change "army" to "consumers") may be different these days, but the basic ideas are the same.

Fichte's concept of education provided a philosophical enhancement to the Prussian system of 1763, which had pretty much the same objective. However, by the mid-nineteenth-century the strict rigour of a militaristic educational approach had been tempered, somewhat, by the philosophy and method of Johann Heinrich Pestalozzi, whose work with children was recognized, studied, praised, seen as a useful technique, and later dismissed. When emphasizing the importance of teacher training, Fichte had already recommended: "For the first establishment, capable teachers and educators above all are needed. Pestalozzi's school has trained such people, and is always ready to train more."[299]

Pestalozzi's ideas about education had already made a widespread impression. Opposed to methods of memorize-and-recite, he believed that instruction should follow the interests and abilities of the child based on real-life experience and observation. Radically humanistic for his time, Pestalozzi, under the influence of Rousseau, saw education as a drawing out rather than a pouring in. Teaching was to proceed from the simple to the complex in line with a child's development. Obviously, this method was to be adapted to Fichte's more authoritarian approach. Instruction will now *influence* "the interests and abilities of the child." Along the same lines, the British Columbia curriculum of 2017 "aims to personalize learning, making it more student-centered and flexible," with something called "deep, active learning."[300] The kids in school today have no more say about what goes on, how they are expected to behave, and what is supposed to *be good for them,* than did the Prussian kids of 1763. Our children are the peasants of today.

It was the Prussian/Pestalozzi model of education that so impressed people like Horace Mann and Egerton Ryerson. Following visits to Germany, they were inspired to introduce a similar system to American and Canadian schools, though not so much for the military as for the factories and offices. They saw an opportunity to transform the ragtag one-room schools that served a mostly rural population into an organized system that would produce a unified and predictable product: a manageable and well-trained citizenry. By 1852, in Massachusetts, attendance at school was made compulsory; Ontario followed suit in 1871. In both countries, a universal curriculum was created, larger schools built, pupils segregated into grades, and teachers trained and certified in approved methods. In line with Fichte's nationalistic biases, school is still the place where you'll find flag waving, anthem singing, and pledges of allegiance.

B. Visitors from North America

Horace Mann and Egerton Ryerson

Teaching methods, as reported by observers of Prussian schools, were based on observation and on leading questions posed by the teacher. Letters (reading) was not introduced in the early grades, instead; children describe sights they've seen and experiences they've had in great detail. Their descriptions are then expanded on and developed by the teacher. This method was recorded in 1844 by Horace Mann in the *Seventh Annual Report* [301] and quoted extensively three years later by Egerton Ryerson in his *Report on a System of Public Elementary Instruction for Upper Canada* [302]. Ryerson was not one to mince words when it came to compulsory education:

> The branches of knowledge which it is essential that all should understand, should be provided *for all*, and taught to all; should be brought within the reach of the most needy, and forced upon the attention of the most careless. [303]

On a more cheerful note, Horace Mann describes the positive and salutary nature of classroom instruction:

> In the case I am now to describe, I entered a classroom of sixty children, of about six years of age. The children were just taking their seats, all smiles and expectation. They had been at school but a few weeks, but long enough to have contracted a love for it. The teacher took his station before them, and after making a playful remark which excited a light titter around the room, and effectually arrested attention, he gave a signal for silence. After waiting a moment, during which every countenance was composed and every noise hushed, he made a prayer consisting of a single

sentence, asking that as they had come together to learn, they might be good and diligent. He then spoke to them of the beautiful day, asked what they knew about the seasons, referred to the different kinds of fruit trees then in bearing, and questioned them upon the uses of trees in constructing houses, furniture, &c. Frequently he threw in sportive remarks which enlivened the whole school, but without ever producing the slightest symptom of disorder.[304]

A remarkable scene, considering it describes a class of sixty six-year-olds! One can only wonder how such ideal behaviour was obtained. Mann goes on to describe what might these days be called "a teachable moment."

It is obvious from the account I have given of these primary lessons, that there is no restriction as to the choice of subjects, and no limits to the extent of information that may be engrafted upon them. What more natural than that a kind teacher should attempt to gain the attention and win the good-will of an active, eager-minded boy just entering his school, by speaking to him about the domestic animals which he plays with, or tends at home, the dog, the cat, the sheep, the horse, the cow. Yet, without any interruption or overleaping of natural boundaries, this simple lesson may be expanded into a knowledge of all quadrupeds, their characteristics and habits of life, the uses of their flesh, skins, fur, bones, horns or ivory, the parts of the world where they live, &c. &c. . . . What more natural than that a benevolent teacher should ask a blushing little girl about the flowers in her vases or garden at home; and yet, this having been done, the door is opened that leads to all botanical knowledge, to the flowers of all the seasons and all the zones, to the trees cultivated by the hand of man, or the primeval forests that darken the face of continents.[305]

So here's a way to deaden curiosity by turning any experience into a lesson and providing answers to questions that have not been asked. We'll pass by the "blushing little girl" with her flowers and vases as a sexist attitude not unexpected in the mid-nineteenth-century. I can only wonder if such an attitude might still be found in society and in schools today.

Mann, who along with Ryerson was an ardent proponent of compulsory school attendance, had reason to query its wide acceptance in Prussia.

> I had frequent conversations with school teachers and school officers respecting this compulsory attendance of the children. . . . The children are so fond of the school, the benefits of public instruction are now so universally acknowledged, and the whole public sentiment has become so conformed to the practice, that I believe there is quite as little complaint under the rigorous system of Prussia as under our lax one. One school officer of whom I inquired, whether this enforced school attendance were acceptable and popular, replied, that the people did not know any other way, and that all the children were born with an innate idea of going to school.[306]

In the twenty-first-century world (remember that Mann was writing almost 200 years ago) the necessity of school attendance is so seldom questioned that parents assume that "children were born with an innate idea of going to school."

With his usual indignation and italic emphasis, Ryerson addressed the issue of compulsory attendance in Canada:

> I allude to the compulsory attendance of children at a School, as required by the laws of Prussia and several other States of Europe. The prevalent impression is, that such a law is arbitrary-despotic-inconsistent with the rights of parents and the liberties of the subject. But what is the principle on which this law is founded? The principle is this,

that every child in the end has a right to such an education as will fit him to be an honest and useful member of community, that if the parent or guardian *cannot* provide him with such an education, *the State is bound* to do so, and that if the parent *will* not do so, the State *will* protect *the child* against such a parent's cupidity and inhumanity, and the State will protect the community at large against any parent (if the term can be applied to such a character) sending forth into it, an uneducated savage, an idle vagabond, or an unprincipled thief.[307]

Clearly, Ryerson believed, as many people do today, that children have to be taken in hand, disciplined, and trained or, for sure, they'll become "an uneducated savage" or "an idle vagabond." Ryerson, after all, was one of the authors of the Canadian residential school system that was intended to "civilize" (and Christianize) the indigenous people of the country.

Such sentiments are echoed in the U.S. *No Child Left Behind Act* of 2002 aimed at bringing "disadvantaged" children up to snuff. As we shall see, that project lasted until 2015, when it was replaced by the similar *Every Student Succeeds Act*. Such misguided, expensive, and ineffective projects were supposed to reduce ignorance and poverty by inculcating middle-class standards into lower-class children. No one thought that measures to reduce poverty might be more effective.

Calvin Ellis Stowe

Another American visitor to the Prussian schools was Calvin Ellis Stowe (1802-1886). Besides being a Biblical scholar and advocate for public education, Stowe had the distinction of being the husband of Harriet Beecher Stowe (1811-1896), abolitionist and author of the influential best-seller *Uncle Tom's Cabin* (1852). In 1836, Calvin Stowe sailed for Europe with an official appointment from the Ohio State Legislature to visit, as agent, the public schools of Europe, particularly those of Prussia. Upon his return, he published *Report on Elementary Public Education in Europe*[308] emphasizing, as one might expect, the religious and moral aspects of Prussian schooling. Like the other visitors to Prussia, he was deeply impressed with how orderly and disciplined the schools were, with children deeply committed (subjugated?) to the control of the teacher: "The children must be given up implicitly to the discipline of the school. Nothing can be done unless the teacher has the entire control of his pupils in school hours, and out of school too, so far as the rules of the school are concerned."[309] Remember these words; they echo through the halls of public school right to the present day. For "and out of school too" read "homework." And then there is ClassDojo and similar surveillance techniques.

As an illustration of the orderly structure of the school day and of the curriculum, Stowe includes a reproduction of a "Weekly course of study" which would have been posted for all to see—and follow. Each day, Monday to Saturday, is divided into one-hour segments, 7:00 a.m. to 5:00 p.m., in which each teacher is assigned a class and subject. As in most public schools today, the day is divided into periods, usually of about one hour each, devoted to one subject at a time. The subjects being so taught in the Prussian school visited by Stowe included Religion, German, French, Arithmetic, Latin, History, Singing, Geography, Reading, Drawing, and Writing, each applied to a designated grade level and each given its one-hour slot in the day.[310]. Furthermore, the teacher was to "impress upon the mind of his class, that diligence, scrupulous fidelity and conscientious self-control, are the surest guarantees of success in life."[311] And, in this case, success in life could be guaranteed because "What topic in all that is necessary for a sound business education is here omitted?"[312] Finally, Stowe sees no shortcomings in the schooling that he observed:

> What faculty of mind is there that is not developed in the scheme of instruction sketched above? I know of none. The perceptive and reflective fac-

143

ulties, the memory and the judgment, the imagination and the taste, the moral and religious faculty, and even the various kinds of physical and manual dexterity, all have opportunity for development and exercise. Indeed, I think the system in its great outlines, as nearly complete as human ingenuity and skill can make it.[313]

Throughout, Stowe is impressed by the ever-present religious and moral training—each lesson, he observed, was ended with a reading from the Bible—impressing on every child that "God protects and rewards the good, and punishes the bad."[314] No doubt of great importance in improving the lives of the orphans (mostly war orphans) and peasants whose morals the schools were intended to elevate.

On Second Thought

Not everyone thought that the Prussian schools were all that great. The travel writer Samuel Laing (1780-1868) expressed an opposite opinion.[315] Speaking of the system of education in Prussia, Laing decries the necessity of government certification which underlies the drive for continuous universal schooling:

The generous feelings, impulses, and motives of youth, are smothered under the servile institutions of the governments, by which all means of living in any of the liberal professions, or even in the ordinary branches of industry, are to be obtained only by government licence, appointment, and favour, not by moral worth, merit, and exertion gaining the public estimation. Morally they are slaves of enslaved minds.[316]

I leave it up to the reader to decide how applicable his statements are to present day qualifications and certifications for professional or other employment.

Laing continues in a similar vein, having already stated that knowing how to read and write "are the means only, not the end, the tools, not the work, in the education of man."[317]

> Compulsory education, compulsory religion, compulsory military service, and the finger of government interfering in all action and opinion, and leaving nothing to free will and uncontrolled individual judgment, produce youths well educated, as it is called, because they can read, write, and sing, well dressed, well drilled, and able bodied.[318]

But Horace Mann saw so much good in the Prussian schools that he felt they should not be condemned simply because the system is sustained by arbitrary power. The "arbitrary power" he refers to is the monarchical government still in effect in Prussia. He seems to overlook the extension of that power into the classroom. Teaching methods must supersede any means of control required to exert them:

> In the first place the evils imputed to it, were easily and naturally separable from the good which it was not denied to possess. If the Prussian schoolmaster has better methods of teaching reading, writing, grammar, geography, arithmetic, &c., so that, in half the time, he produces greater and better results, surely, we may copy his modes of teaching these elements, without adopting his notions of passive obedience to government, or of blind adherence to the articles of a church. [319]

How else, except through passivity and obedience, could sixty small children "all smiles and expectation" be kept under control in the classroom he so enthusiastically described?

Also cited and dismissed by Horace Mann were the writings of Robert Vaughn (1795-1868), who wrote extensively on society, government, religion, and education.[320] Vaughn, like Laing, was highly critical of the Prussian system, finding that the hand of government in education was stifling to freedom of thought and religion:

> We do not scruple to say, that we look with much misgiving on the Prussian education system, and that we do so in part, on account of the relation in which it stands to a scheme of government which has superseded all liberty, civil and religious.[321]

In contrast to Mann's willingness to excuse despotic control, Vaughn questions whether or not it can be separated from what passes as education:

> But it has hitherto been too much the manner of despotic governments to make an abuse even of what is in itself good. . . . We venture to ask whether there be not some danger lest this new means of power over the popular mind should become only another instrument of arbitrary rule.[322]

By the time of Vaughn's second edition, the working class Chartist movement in England had been demanding voting rights for all men (women not yet included) since the early 1830s. When Vaughn talks about arbitrary rule, he must have seen that the Prussian populace was not agitating for reform, and he makes the point that the education system there managed to keep the lower classes under control. All that Mann and Ryerson could see, though, was that the lower classes were being somehow elevated by being forced to attend school. At least, they believed that the peasantry was receiving training in Christian morality, behaviour, and obedience to authority.

How would such training be different in American and Canadian democracies with popular notions of individual liberty? In actuality, it wasn't any different. The kind of organized and well-ordered school they envisioned was necessarily an autocratic system, with a predetermined curriculum, children sorted by age and grade, compliant behaviour enforced, and all with a hierarchical management consisting of government, school trustees, superintendents, principals, and teachers. In fact, a system virtually identical with that of today. School is the only institution in our society, aside from prison, that demands compulsory attendance, enforced occupation, and controlled behaviour by its inmates. Strange that in a democratic society proclaiming individual rights and freedoms, such an antidemocratic system should, for twelve years or more, have control and influence over its young.

C. Locke and Friends: The Philosophy of Education

John Locke

John Locke (1632-1704) was a leader of Enlightenment views of childhood and education. Having come from a well-off family (his father was a legal clerk and captain of civil military forces), he was educated in the best schools, the first of which would be at home under his father's tutelage. As a teenager he was sent to the prestigious Westminster School in London and later to Oxford, where he attained both bachelor's and master's degrees, completing his studies in 1658. As a young man of modern ideas, he found the classical Aristotelian philosophical studies of the university of little use, preferring to read Descartes, Spinoza, Francis Bacon, and Isaac Newton, forming his own views of man's relationship to society, government, and God. This was the age of the triumph of reason over authority: the Enlightenment.

After spending five years appointed as a lecturer in Greek and Rhetoric, Locke had to decide on a profession. The choices were the law, the church, or medicine. He chose medicine and went on to become a noted physician and surgeon. However, his main interests were in emerging thought about human nature, government, and religion. His writings had a profound influence on the political and populist movements of the day. His *Essay Concerning Human Understanding*, published in 1689, proposed that humans are born without innate ideas of right and wrong, the existence of God, of logic, or mathematical concepts. In other words, the human mind at birth is a blank slate, or *tabula rasa*.[323] This suggests that human nature is basically good and individuals are capable of defining the content of their character based on experience. At the same time, though, there are certain characteristics that come with being a member of the human species, and that there is such a thing as human nature that is immutable. Locke then proposed that there are basic natural rights that every person is entitled to. This is reflected in the American Declaration of Independence (1776): "We hold these truths to be self-evident, that all men are created equal, that they are endowed by their Creator with certain unalienable Rights, that among these are Life, Liberty and the pursuit of Happiness."

In his *Two Treatises of Government,* also published in 1689, though written earlier, Locke stated that government should be concerned with the protection of life, liberty, and property, and that these were inalienable human rights. Also of key importance is the idea that government derives its power, not from a divine inherited right, but by a consensual arrangement with the people. In other words: democracy. This also implies that the people have the right to remove, by force if necessary, any government that is not protecting human rights.

Locke's writings had a far-flung and powerful influence, leading to the American revolution of 1776 and the French revolution of 1789—and probably to the intense American commitment to the right to bear arms. So government derived its power, not from inherited authority but from contractual agreements with the people. He believed in separation of church and state—or religious freedom. No one was to be punished for what they believed. Human rights are innate rather than given by authority. It's easy to see that many of his ideas were adopted by the creators of the American Declaration of Independence, not to mention the French revolution of 1789. It could be said that revolution was in the air as people began to accept that they could challenge authority and demand their rights.

When it comes to thinking about school, it's worth re-membering Locke's principles of rule by consent and learning by experience and how contemporary school hierarchy has developed in ways contrary to Enlightenment thought. Children in school have no rights, inalienable or otherwise. They may only be al-lowed privileges, and those are strictly limited by authority.

Locke on Education

It was in 1684 that Locke's friends, Mary and Edward Clarke, asked him for advice in raising their son Edward Jr. He responded with a series of letters that eventually became the essay *Some Thoughts Concerning Education*. It was not until 1693, after considerable revision and addition, that the book was published. The very first sentences in the book let us know where this is go-ing:

> A sound mind in a sound body, is a short but full description of a happy state in the world: he that has these two, has little more to wish for, and he that wants either of them, will be but little the bet-ter for anything else. Men's happiness or misery is most part of their own making.[324]

When it comes to the "sound body" we can forgive Locke's dictatorial views on infant and early childhood care. After all, death at these ages was so common in the seventeenth century that it might be wise to "toughen them up" before it was too late. He suggests that children should be accustomed to being outside "even in winter." Such exposure, in all weathers, "Thus the body may be brought to bear almost anything."[325] Well in advance of Benjamin Spock,[326] Locke advised a vegetarian diet for children over two. At the same time, children were not to be treated too tenderly, but more as farmers ("the honest farmers") might treat theirs because ". . . most children's constitutions are either spoiled, or at least harmed, by cockering and tenderness."[327] Girls are rarely mentioned,—education was not to be for them—but being kept in the shade might be better for "beauty in the daughters, yet I will take the liberty to say, that the more they are in the air, without prejudice to their faces, the stronger and the healthier they will be"[328] As for children having all their needs and wants satisfied:

> It seems plain to me, that the principle of all virtue and excellency lies in a power of denying ourselves the satisfaction of our own desires, where reason does not authorize them. . . . If therefore I might be heard, I would advise, that, contrary to the ordinary way, children should be used to submit their desires, and go without their longings, even from their very cradles.[329]

Similar notions of baby and child care persisted into the 1920s, well into, we might say, the pre-Spock era with echoes even today of 1920s style "scientific" baby care and childrearing.[330] (More about this later.) Having laid the foundation, now let's get to training and discipline, and in this, I find Locke is often severe, though ambivalent about his recommendations:

> I have spoken so much of carrying a strict hand over children, that perhaps I shall be suspected of not considering enough what is due to their tender age and constitutions. But that opinion will vanish, when you have heard me a little farther. For I am very apt to think that great severity of punishment does but very little good: nay, great harm in education: and I believe it will be found *cæteris paribus*, those children who have been most chastised, seldom make the best men.[331]

And

> If the mind be curbed, and humbled too much in children; if their spirits be abased and broken much, by too strict an hand over them; they lose all their vigour and industry.[332]

But

> Remove hope and fear, and there is an end to all discipline.[333]

That being said, he is very concerned that obedience to parents' commands should be established at an early age. And, as a believer in the *tabula rasa*, he is dismissive of the negative effect physical punishment may have on a very small child because: "A compliance and suppleness of their wills, being by a steady hand introduced by parents, before children have memories to retain the beginnings of it, will seem natural to them and will work afterwards in them."[334] It seems that the "blank slate" is there to be written on, and *that* by a firm parental hand, especially the father, who should be held in awe, and even fear, by the child. We have to accept that in the pre-Freud seventeenth century no one would have considered the formation of the subconscious mind during infancy. While the message may be "Do what you're told," the infant is creating wordless images of the world in which he finds himself. Is it dark, cold, and threatening or loving, warm, and accepting?

Perhaps his lengthy discourse on punishment can best be summed up by saying that a little goes a long way, though a little or a long way is not clearly defined. But I still find his emphasis on the need for correction quite contrary to his stated belief that human nature is basically good. This is in contrast to the thinking of his predecessor Thomas Hobbes (1588-1679) who firmly believed that human nature was destructive, contrary, and self-interested, or as put in his most famous words: "The life of man, solitary, poor, nasty, brutish, and short."[335]

Though physical punishment is to be avoided except "on great occasions, and cases of extremity,"[336] Locke also warns against using rewards as inducements:

> On the other side, to flatter children by rewards of things that are pleasant to them, is as carefully to

> be avoided. He that will give to his son apples, or sugar-plums, or what else of this kind he is most delighted with, to make him learn his book, does but authorise his love of pleasure . . . [337]

In other words, the reward becomes the goal and diminishes the pleasure that might be taken in achievement for its own sake.[338]

When it comes to teaching and learning, Locke is in favour of encouraging the child's interest without undue coercion or application of too many rules. Don't try to make your pupils do what you want, but rather pay attention to their wants.

> They should seldom be put about doing even those things you have got an inclination in them to, but when they have a mind and disposition to it. He that loves reading, writing, music, etc. finds yet in himself certain seasons wherein those things have no relish to him: and, if at that time he forces himself to it, he only pothers and wearies himself to no purpose. So it is with children.[339]

Be that as it may, children are still to be led in one way or another to do what the grownups want them to do and to learn. This, he tells us, is best done through example:

> And if the things which they observe others do, be ordered so that they insinuate themselves into them, as the privilege of an age or condition above theirs; then ambition, and the desire still to get forward, and higher, and to be like those above them, will set them on work, and make them go on with vigour and pleasure; pleasure in what they have begun by their own desire.[340]

These thoughts are echoed in what Frank Smith, writing some 314 years later, calls the classic view of learning: "We learn from people around us with whom we identify."[341] Here we would understand that identifying with another person means thinking that I am just like so-and-so and will become as much like them as I can. However, each person can identify with any number of other people: parents, grandparents, uncles, aunts, siblings, friends, and any number of others. And, from these, we choose, without thinking about it, qualities to imitate and take on as our own. In Locke's case, this identification process is to be reinforced with subtle and not-so-subtle bits of coercion. Remembering that he was addressing his *Thoughts on Education* to the reasonably well-to-do and aiming to produce the perfect English gentleman (girls do not enter into this picture), the child will be best educated by a tutor:

> I am sure, he who is able to be at the charge of a tutor at home, may there give his son a more genteel carriage, more manly thoughts, and a sense of what is worthy and becoming, with a greater proficiency in learning into the bargain, and ripen him up sooner into a man, than any at school can do.[342]

Locke strongly warns against the influence of schoolfellows:

> And it is not the waggeries or cheats practised among schoolboys, it is not their roughness one to another, nor the well laid plots of robbing an orchard together, that makes an able man, but the principles of justice, generosity, and sobriety, joined with observation and industry, qualities which I judge schoolboys do not learn much of one another.[343]

Add to this his negative, though forgiving, comments about mass instruction in schools—"For, let the master's industry and skill be ever so great, it is impossible he should have 50 or 100 scholars under his eye . . . "[344]—proper gentlemanly conduct could hardly be taught. This begins to sound close to contemporary recommendations for homeschooling as well as warning of the dangers of peer culture.

We can thank Locke for at least playing down physical and verbal abuse of children. On an almost contemporary note, he cautions that parents who do not discipline their children physically are in for criticism: "I foresee here it will be objected to me: what then, will you have children never beaten, not chid, for any fault? This will be to let loose the reins to all kind of disorder."[345] This will not be a worry, he suggests, if awe of their parents has been already implanted. Beating is of little good because the lesson it was meant to implant is soon forgotten along with the pain of the punishment. "But yet there is one, and but one fault, for which, I think, children should be beaten and that is obstinacy or rebellion."[346]

Once the child is properly under control in mind and body, it is time to get on with education. But this is not to be an arduous process of many years "in fear of the schoolmaster's rod. . . . How else is it possible, that a child should be chained to the oar seven, eight, or ten of the best years of his life, to get a language or two [French and Latin], which I think might be had at a great deal cheaper rate of pains and time, and be learned almost in playing?"[347] *Almost* being the operative word here, but the implication that a child's interests and abilities should be taken into account was certainly radical for the time. But it is important to start early. "When he can talk, it is time he should begin to learn to read."[348] And we are again cautioned that this must not be looked on as a business or a task:

> I have always had a fancy that learning might be made a play and recreation to children; and that they might be brought to desire to be taught, if it is proposed to them as a thing of honour, credit, delight, and recreation, or as a reward for doing something else, and if they were never chid or corrected for the neglect of it.[349]

To accomplish this he suggests the use of playthings, like ivory balls or wooden blocks with letters of the alphabet written on them, so that play, under the guidance of a parent or tutor, will result in learning letters and then combining these into syllables. This will soon lead to reading of literature suitable for children, and for this Locke recommends *Aesop's Fables*, preferably in a book with pictures. Better blocks and balls than flogging, though, here we are, 300 years later with teachers still trying to turn learning into fun.[350]

Once reading is underway, the next step is writing, or, as we used to call it, penmanship. Tasteful and attractive handwriting would have been essential among the accomplishments of a young gentleman. Writing letters, also of great importance, comes later, while drawing is a skill that should go along with writing. Fair enough, because a travelling gentleman would have no other means of recording what he saw.

"As soon as he can speak English, it is time for him to learn some other language: this nobody doubts of when French is proposed."[351] Along with his other advanced ideas, Locke proposes that French, and later, Latin, is best learned through speech and conversation rather than through rules of grammar.

> But because French is a living language, and to be used more in speaking, that it should be first learned, that the yet pliant organs of speech might be accustomed to a due formation of those sounds, and he get the habit of pronouncing French well, which is harder to be done the longer it is delayed.[352]

Only after French is mastered—usually in a year or two—should the child move on to Latin. Latin was considered of importance to the educated person because most scholarly, scientific, and philosophical writing was done in that language. Latin should be learned in the same way as French, that is by talking and reading. However, we are cautioned "that he do not forget to read English, which may be preserved by his mother . . . hearing him read some chosen parts of the scripture, or other English book, every day."[353]

For what is to be learned in school, Locke's words have a particularly contemporary ring. Children who are forced to learn something will soon forget it, no matter how important it is deemed to be:

> Latin I look upon as absolutely necessary to a gentleman; and indeed custom, which prevails over every thing, has made it so much a part of education, that even those children who are whipped to it, and made spend many hours of their precious time uneasily in Latin, who, after they are gone from school, are never to have more to do with it, as long as they live.[354]

He goes on to say that it is foolish to waste children's time on matters that will be of no avail to them in future life. Yes, Latin may be "absolutely necessary" for a gentleman but is completely unnecessary for anyone destined for a trade. This is another one of Locke's pervasive ideas: that school should be about training for work or, in the case of the *country gentleman*, for intellectual endeavour that will enhance his social or political life.

Once reading, writing, drawing, and languages have been mastered, we can move on to other essentials in the curriculum. These would include geography, arithmetic, history, law, rhetoric, and morality. All these are to be taught in a planned sequence of easy to difficult:

> Great care must be taken with children, to begin with that which is plain and simple, and to teach them as little as can be at once, and settle that well in their heads, before you proceed to the next, or anything new. . . . Give them first one simple idea, and see that they take it right, and perfectly comprehend it, before you go any further; and then add some other simple idea, which lies next in your way to what you aim at; and so proceeding by gentle and insensible steps, children, without confusion and amazement, will have their under-

standings opened, and their thoughts extended, farther than could have been expected.[355]

This could well have been written, minus the elegant punctuation, by any contemporary curriculum maker.

Also in line with contemporary thought (viz. school budget cuts), Locke sees no use in poetry or music. After all, there is no money to be made through poetry:

> It is very seldom seen that any one discovers mines of gold or silver in Parnassus. It is a pleasant air, but a barren soil; and there are very few instances of those who have added to their patrimony by any thing they have reaped from thence. Poetry and gaming, which usually go together, are alike in this too, that they seldom bring any advantage, but to those who have nothing else to live on.[356]

Well, that takes care of that. We'll have to assume that Locke was such a dedicated student of science and other "serious" matters that he wouldn't have noticed the outpourings of Milton, Dryden, Marvell, Donne, Lovelace, Herrick, and other poets of his time. Among the arts, dancing may be OK because "being that which gives graceful motions all the life, and above all things, manliness and a becoming confidence to young children, I think it cannot be learned too early."[357] Music might be of some use for dancing but serves no other purpose:

> Music is thought to have some affinity with dancing, and a good hand, upon some instruments, is by many people mightily valued. But it wastes so much of a young man's time, to gain but a moderate skill in it, and engages often in such odd company, that many think it much better spared, and I have, amongst men of parts and business, so seldom heard any one commended or esteemed for having an excellency in music, that amongst all

157

those things, that ever came into the list of accomplishments, I think I may give it the last
place.[358]

So music is not only a waste of time but it brings one in
contact with "such odd company" that it is best avoided. Though
useless for "men of parts and business," a certain degree of skill,
especially on keyboard instruments, would have been a suitable
adornment for a young lady.[359] Reverse snobbery of this sort is not
unknown today.

Having settled the score on poetry and music, we are informed that "Fencing and riding the great horse, are looked upon
as so necessary parts of breeding, that it would be thought a great
omission to neglect them."[360] Riding, after all, will give "a man a
firm and graceful seat on horseback," but fencing, though also
considered a necessary qualification "in the breeding of a gentleman,"[361] may make "them more often touchy than needs, on points
of honour, and slight or no provocations."[362] Dueling over points
of honour was not uncommon, well into the eighteenth century, so
I suppose that any young man of consequence would be considered a wimp if he was not trained in fencing. Replace riding and
fencing with hockey and soccer, and you have the contemporary
equivalent.

Lest the young gentleman grow tired of these occupations,
plus the necessity of ongoing study, he is encouraged to take up
some kind of trade, strictly along the lines of a hobby. Though
painting might be desirable, it is too sedentary and would take too
much time to become any good at. Therefore, Locke recommends
such pastimes as "gardening or husbandry in general, and working
in wood, as a carpenter, joiner, or turner; these being fit and
healthy recreations for a man of study or business,"[363] while at the
same time warning against the lure of play, especially playing
cards and gambling. "Play, wherein persons of condition, especially ladies, waste so much of their time, is a plain instance to me,
that men cannot be perfectly idle, they must be doing some-

thing."[364] Therefore, recreational time is to be spent on some wholesome activity, not unlike the active do-it-yourselfer of today.

The Pervasive Influence of Locke

After reading this brief summary, it will likely become clear how much we are still influenced by Locke's thinking. Consider:

1. Government. It goes without saying that democratic governments are established by a contractual agreement with the electorate, a significant difference being that armed force is, or should be, replaced by voting.

2. Inalienable rights. Each person has guaranteed rights that may not be minimized or taken away. These are often spelled out in such human rights legislation as Canada's Charter of Rights and Freedoms.

3. Childrearing a) Being too permissive or demand-regulated can lead to "spoiled" children. They must learn early that they can't always get what they want.

4. Childrearing b) Many parents still believe that children must be *taught* proper behaviour from an early age, by means of disapproving comments or even some form of punishment. Note the popularity of "time-outs."

5. Sexism. Girls do not need education beyond the rudiments of reading and writing. Higher learning, especially, is for men only.

6. Real men do not play music. Nor do they paint or write poetry. The arts are a waste of time and of a suspicious social milieu.

7. A man who is comfortably off should have a manly hobby, like woodworking, landscaping, or gardening. Playing golf would suffice.

8. Education must have a pre-determined curriculum. The student must learn what is prescribed and in a set order.

9. Learning goes from easy to difficult. While this seems logical, it results in a step-by-step learning process, best illustrated by Skinner's teaching machines.

10. Physical development is important for boys. Schools emphasize sports teams and competition more for boys than girls, and the reputation of the school is often connected to performance in sports.

Jean-Jacques Rousseau

It could be said that Jean-Jacques Rousseau (1712-1778) was a true man of the Enlightenment. He was a musician, an engraver, a servant, a secretary, almost a priest, a fugitive, a novelist, a traveller, a music teacher, copyist and composer, a philosopher, a tutor, a business manager, a Catholic, a Calvinist, and all-around shit-disturber. His writings, most notably *Origins of Inequality* (1755), *The Social Contract* (1762), and *Emile; or On Education* (*Émile, ou De l'éducation*) (1762) were highly influential, often dangerously so. Some of these works were banned on religious or political grounds. Though they may have found his work contradictory, maddening, and yet brilliant, people like Voltaire, Diderot, Hume, and even Frederick the Great offered him protection and support. In 1762, as a refugee in Neuchâtel, Rousseau wrote to the king asking for his protection. Frederick's response, written to the governor of Neuchâtel, is amusing but at the same time shows the king's open-minded generosity, also giving us some insight into Rousseau's personality:

> We must succor this poor unfortunate. His only offense is to have strange opinions which he thinks are good ones. I will send a hundred crowns, from which you will be kind enough to give him as much as he needs. I think he will accept them in kind more readily than in cash. If we were not at war, if we were not ruined, I would build him a hermitage with a garden, where he could live as I believe our first fathers

did. . . . I think poor Rousseau has missed his vocation; he was obviously born to be a famous anchorite, a desert father, celebrated for his austerities and flagellations. . . . I conclude that the morals of your savage are as pure as his mind is illogical.[365]

Rousseau was born in Geneva where his father was a watchmaker with exaggerated opinions of his own importance. Left in his father's care—his mother died in childbirth—he had a lonely but happy early childhood. When he was ten years old, his father fled from Geneva to avoid arrest after an eccentric episode of sword waving. For the next six years, he was treated as a poor relation by the uncle and aunt in whose care he had been left. No doubt finding the situation intolerable, he left Geneva at sixteen to become an adventurer and Roman Catholic convert. He soon found a position as secretary—and lover in a ménage a trois—with the baroness Louise-Éléanore de Warens, a Catholic convert and inheritor of titled wealth. She was twelve years his senior. The Catholic religion was obviously to be interpreted rather liberally, with forgiveness of sins through confession an especially agreeable aspect. Her social circle, of which Rousseau was now a part, consisted of educated elite, introducing him to the world of letters, ideas, and music. He took up a serious study of music, later even devising a system of numerical notation that was to enable printing of music with typographical symbols. He maintained his study and practice of music for the rest of his life. A major musical success came with his one-act opera *Le devin du village* (The Village Soothsayer), first produced for the public in Paris in 1753. It was an immediate success, so much so that Rousseau was offered a life pension by Louis XV, who loved the work. Rousseau refused the pension; he was making plenty of money from the opera and didn't need to kowtow to royalty—yet. *Le devin du village* still

1A scene from *Le Devin du Village*

holds a great deal of charm and is presented on the stage from time to time.[366] But I digress. As an opera fan, I've always found this little work to be most delightful, but it's Rousseau's books and essays that are of greatest significance.

One more detail: his musical interests, not to mention his feisty nature, led him to become fully involved in the famous *Querelle des bouffons* (1752-1754), a public controversy over Italian versus French opera. Rousseau favoured the Italian side, roundly condemning French music as having no melody or emotion as well as lacking the public appeal that Italian opera was enjoying at the time. Music, however, was but one side of this fascinating man.

Between 1728 and 1742, with the salon of Mme. de Warens as a home base, he travelled to Turin, where worked briefly as a domestic servant, he then embarked on studies to become a Catholic priest but soon switched to being an itinerant musician and copyist. In 1740 he moved to Lyons to take up a position as a tutor. There he was introduced to a circle of leading proponents of the French Enlightenment. In 1742, in Paris, he had met Denis Diderot (1713-1784), who later engaged him to write articles on music for the *Encyclopédie*, a leading document of Enlightenment thought. After a brief stint as secretary to the French ambassador in Venice, (He was quickly fired from that position "for not having the ability to put up with a boss whom he viewed as stupid and arrogant" [367]), he moved, now permanently (at least permanently for a while), to Paris in 1744.

In Paris, he supported himself as a copyist and music teacher, meanwhile hobnobbing and making a name for himself with the leading radical thinkers of the day. In the hotel where he was living (near the Sorbonne) he met Thérèse Levasseur, a semi-literate seamstress, and stayed with her for the rest of his life. They married in 1768, but not before having five children. Rousseau was criticized, especially when writing about child care in *Émile*, for turning these children over to foundling homes instead of raising them himself, but there may have been extenuating circumstances. He claimed that they would be better off because he was in no position to give them a proper upbringing. Then, too, there is some doubt about paternity; they may not even have been his. (One of Thérèse's, perhaps many, affairs was with James Boswell.)

In 1754, returning, with Thérèse in tow, to Geneva, he re-adopted Calvinist religious principles in order to reclaim his heritage and citizenship. Let's just say that his religious views were flexible, as circumstances required. His insistence, in his writing, on the basic goodness of human nature did not endear him to many religious leaders. His radical views and his growing paranoia led to a falling out with many of his Parisian friends. It was about this time that he, and Thérèse, were offered a house on the estate of the Duke and Duchess of Luxembourg at Montmorency, north of Paris. It was there, over the next four years, that Rousseau completed some of his most famous writing, including *The Social Contract* and *Émile* (1762), as well as the widely read novel *The New Heloise*. No longer able to return to Geneva because of his religious beliefs, Rousseau sought retreat and haven in Berne, but he was unable to escape the public attention that came from his writings. He did not handle fame and criticism well.

In 1766, he was taken in by David Hume (1711-1776) in England. Hume was famous—and infamous—for his views on human nature. Both men were leaders in Enlightenment thought, representatives of the threat to public and religious complacency from revisionist views of human nature, politics, and the existence of God. That didn't mean that they agreed, however. Completely without foundation, Rousseau accused Hume of conspiring against him, leading to the breakup of the friendship and Rousseau's return, under an assumed name, to Paris. It wasn't until three years later that he could return openly, under the condition that he not publish any of his work. Under this restriction, he wrote his autobiography, *The Confessions*, and held private readings until they were banned by police upon the urging of Diderot and others who were wary of their inclusion in the book. *The Confessions* was not published until 1782, four years after Rousseau's death.

Now increasingly isolated, he continued writing, completing, before his death, ten meditations titled *Reveries of the Solitary Walker*. The book opens with this statement:

> BEHOLD me, then, as if alone upon the earth, having neither brother, relative, friend, or society, but my own thoughts; the most social and affectionate of men, proscribed, as it were, by unanimous consent. They have sought in the refinement of their hatred, what would be the most cruel torment to my susceptible soul, and have rent asunder every bond which attached me to them.[368]

On July 2nd of 1782, staying at Ermenonville, outside of Paris, while on his usual early morning walk, he died of a stroke. Even then, some former friends claimed that he had committed suicide. He was buried there on a small island, *Ile des Peupliers*. Later, in 1794, his remains were moved to the Panthéon in Paris, where he lies next to Voltaire and other key figures of the French revolution.

We can only marvel at the prolific output and original thought of this man, who maintained productivity in spite of criticism, ostracism, and growing paranoia. It was a time when traditional authoritarian views were being challenged by emerging humanism. It was the Age of Reason—man could figure things out for himself—and of burgeoning Romanticism. It was a time when such topics were widely discussed and acted upon. It was a time of revolution when the idea of democratic rule was toppling inherited monarchy.

After his tumultuous youth, Rousseau first achieved notoriety by winning a prize, in 1750, from the Académie de Dijon. The prize-winning essay was *Discours sur les sciences et les arts (Discourse on the arts and sciences),* a diatribe against the corrupting influence of arts and science on what he considered to be the basic goodness of man and nature. Outrage followed. In the Preface to the essay, Rousseau makes it clear that he knows exactly what he's doing, and probably relishing it:

> I foresee that I shall not readily be forgiven for having taken up the position I have adopted. Setting myself up against all that is nowadays most admired, I can expect no less than a universal outcry against me: nor is the approbation of a few sensible men enough to make me count on that of the public. But I have taken my stand, and I shall be at no pains to please either intellectuals or men of the world.[369]

Like Locke, Rousseau saw childhood as a time distinct and different from adulthood, requiring specialized treatment, with a degree, especially in Locke's case, of guidance and discipline. Rather than drum into the child what we think is good for him or what will be preparation for adulthood, let the child engage in childish activity and play; let the child be a child. Both Locke and Rousseau, though separated by more than sixty years, are reflecting changing views of childhood.

It was Rousseau's writing, in Book I of *Emile*, that brought about an end to swaddling—the practice of tightly wrapping infants and restricting their movements—and encouraged mothers to breast feed their children rather than farming them out to wet nurses. We should be guided by natural impulses, not those imposed by society.

In all of Rousseau's writing, he holds firm to the belief that mankind is basically good, but is corrupted by the influences of society. "Man is born free; and everywhere he is in chains"—the famous opening line of *The Social Contract*. Even in the *Discourse on the arts and sciences,* he deplores the kind of education young people are getting: "Even from our infancy an absurd system of education serves to adorn our wit and corrupt our judgment." True education should be about virtue, not academic abilities:

> We see, on every side, huge institutions, where our youth are educated at great expense, and instructed in everything but their duty. . . . They will

> be able to compose verses which they can hardly understand; and without being capable of distinguishing truth from error, they will possess the art of making them unrecognisable by specious arguments. But magnanimity, equity, temperance, humanity and courage will be words of which they know not the meaning.[370]

These thoughts form the theme of his major work on education.

Infancy, childhood, adolescence, and education are the subjects of *Emile, or On Education*, published in 1762, then banned and publicly burned in Paris and Geneva,[371] is Rousseau's major work on the nature of education and of human growth and development. In contrast to the Calvinist view that we are born evil and into sin, Rousseau firmly believed in the basic goodness of human nature. (This is what raised the dander of Protestant forces.) The issue is how to reconcile the free individual with the corrupting demands of society. This is laid out in the famous opening sentence of the book: "Everything is good as it leaves the hands of the Author of things; everything degenerates in the hands of man." Education, then, must be devoted to producing the ideal human who can live a moral and productive life without succumbing to the attractions of wealth, prestige, and fashion. This is to be accomplished by nurturing and following the natural inclinations and abilities of the child, definitely in a natural setting outside of village or city. These can be influenced to a certain extent by what is presented to the young child by his parents or tutors, but the emphasis is to be on nature and the out-of-doors. Needless to say, Emile is not to be saddled with lessons and a set course of studies. No need for age six to be the time when a child must learn to read:

> In thus taking away all duties from children, [the duty of studying the fables of La Fontaine] I take away the instruments of their greatest misery— that is, books. Reading is the plague of childhood and almost the only occupation we know how to give it. At twelve Emile will hardly know what a book is. But, it will be said, he certainly must at

least know how to read. I agree. He must know
how to read when reading is useful to him; up to
then it is only good for boring him.

If one ought to demand nothing of children
through obedience, it follows that they can learn
nothing of which they do not feel the real and present advantage in either pleasure or utility. Otherwise, what motive would bring them to learn it?[372]

The idea of a twelve-year-old who cannot read is a matter
to arouse consternation if not outrage in those who put stock in
training in "literacy," as they like to put it, starting no later than
age six. This is what school is expected to do. And school has all
the graded primers and readers to put the kids through their paces.
After all, it's all been worked out scientifically—by experts. There
are even parents who are trying to teach their kids to read before
they can walk. They'll find plenty of toys and videos to help them
on their way.[373] We've seen from the statistics just how successful
this is.

Rousseau has this to say about the teaching of reading:

A great business is made of seeking the best
methods of teaching reading. Desks and cards are
invented; a child's room is made into a printing
shop. Locke wants him to learn to read with dice.
Now is that not a clever invention? What a pity! A
means surer than all these, and the one always
forgotten, is the desire to learn. Give your child
this desire, then let your desks and your dice go.
Any method will be good for him.[374]

See A. S. Neill (below) on "Any method will be good for
him." Rousseau lives on!

The urgency about reading—if a child isn't learning to
read, there is something wrong—arises from the notion that success in school means success in later life. Children must not live in
the moment; they must not waste time in play; they must be guided by some *future* that they can barely comprehend.

What, then, must be thought of that barbarous education which sacrifices the present to an uncertain future, which burdens a child with chains of every sort and begins by making him miserable in order to prepare him from afar for I know not what pretended happiness which it is to be believed he will never enjoy? Even if I were to suppose this education reasonable in its object, how can one without indignation see poor unfortunates submitted to an unbearable yoke and condemned to continual labor like galley slaves, without any assurance that so many efforts will ever be useful to them?[375]

If we pervert the natural inclinations of childhood by insisting on obedience—how could school operate without obedience?—we encourage a false personality kowtowing to authority:

What results from this? [trying to persuade your pupils of the duty of obedience] Firstly, by imposing on them a duty they do not feel, you set them against your tyranny and turn them away from loving you. Secondly, you teach them to become dissemblers, fakers, and liars in order to extort rewards or escape punishments. Finally, by accustoming them always to cover a secret motive with an apparent motive, you yourselves give them the means of deceiving you ceaselessly, of depriving you of the knowledge of their true character, and of fobbing you and others off with vain words when the occasion serves.[376]

No wonder Rousseau inspired the wrath of the Calvinists and others who believed in original sin and the innate wickedness of the child. Where they saw evil, he saw only goodness. Where they demanded discipline and obedience, he wanted freedom. The free person has no need to seek permission, "from which it follows that the first of all goods is not authority but freedom. The truly free man wants only what he can do and does what he pleases.

That is my fundamental maxim. It need only be applied to child-hood for all the rules of education to flow from it."[377] Dangerous words! As dangerous today as they were two hundred and sixty years ago!

Rousseau's entire approach to education is based upon freedom of the child to discover his own interests and abilities. Such discoveries can only happen in a rich and loving environment in which children are free to "be active, run, yell, always be in motion. Let him be a man in his vigor, and soon he will be one in his reason."[378] A belief in the natural drive to grow and learn without direction, largely ignored in schools today, but espoused, following in Rousseau's footsteps, by Pestalozzi and later by John Dewey and A.S. Neill.

I agree with Rousseau when he cites use or enjoyment as motives for learning. I suppose you could say that reading is of *use* as a motive when it comes to making it through school, but that is a contrived use and certainly not an enjoyable one. The point that I will come back to again and again is that which Frank Smith makes: "You learn from the company you keep." If your family and the people you know are not readers, why would you bother? I contend that children are highly motivated to be a part of the particular social circle in which they find themselves, in other words, the company they keep. In early childhood it's family, and then peers on social media. Since pretty well everyone walks and talks, uses spoons and forks, and wears clothes, little kids will make every effort to acquire those skills, and if everyone around them reads, they will want to do that too. Remember that children, especially very young ones, are keenly perceptive. They take in and register everything they see and hear, and don't think you can fool them into practising what *you* don't practise. If your kids see that you are always genuinely polite, you would never have to remind them (usually said rudely) "What do you say?" *You learn from the company you keep.* Once in school, however, your kids will be thrown into the maelstrom of their peer group, and that is the influence that will take over completely. *The company you keep* now takes on a more sinister meaning. For better or worse:

> The lessons pupils get from one another in the schoolyard are a hundred times more useful to them than everything they will ever be told in class.[379]

"Useful" as Rousseau meant it means something very different today. Children, when thrown together on the school playground, will learn more from each other than they ever will from any teacher.

As Emile grows into adolescence he has been given every opportunity to learn from nature and through his own experience. Above all, he knows how to learn:

> Among the small number of things he knows and knows well, the most important is that there are many things of which he is ignorant and which he can know one day; there are many more that other men know that he will never know in his life; and there are an infinite number of others that no man will ever know. Emile has a mind that is universal not by its learning but by its faculty to acquire learning; a mind that is open, intelligent and ready for everything . . . if not instructed, at least able to be instructed. . . . Once again, my object is not to give him science but to teach him to acquire science when needed.[380]

In other words, he is, like Albert Einstein, "passionately curious."[381] The grades, certificates, and degrees that mark off stages of schooling are meaningless.

Reading *Emile or On Education*, one is struck by the deep humanity of the man. He has a penetrating understanding of infancy and childhood. The influence of Rousseau comes across loud and clear to anyone whose thinking challenges the standard, government-approved forms of education.

Johann Heinrich Deweu

Johann Heinrich Pestalozzi (1746-1827) was the most in-fluential pedagogue of the eighteenth century and, arguably, of all time. Influence may be viewed in different ways. Even today some educationists will claim that his methods are still being used in schools. It's true that the now passé theories of John Dewey de-scended from Pestalozzi, and many teachers think of themselves as providing child-centred education. The truth is that the kind of schooling and teaching that Pestalozzi had in mind is simply not applicable to anything that goes on in a present-day public school.

The man was an interesting and unusual character, and from all reports a bit of a wild man: unkempt, hyperactive, and driven. Consider this interesting description from John Alfred Green's 1900 book *The Educational Ideas of Pestalozzi:*

> The man who had never been able to spell correct-ly, and who always readily owned to his friends that he spoiled whatever he put his hands to, had become the prophet of instruction and of educa-tion; the man who lived always in the present, and whose intellectual life . . . had no history, was the inspiring personality of a movement of vast sig-nificance in the history of culture. The man who had scarcely been outside his own country had drawn to himself the astonished attention of the whole world, and the man who always com-plained of his absolute unfitness for a position of authority was the dominating force in a great movement and the object of a devotion which for his sake sought to make the "impossible possi-ble."[382]

Though his every venture seemed to end in failure, he held to his firm belief in the goodness of humans and the possibility of intellectual development in the most downtrodden. Like Rousseau, he believed in the essential goodness of human nature however it might be corrupted by civilization:

> Friend, man is good, and desires what is good; at
> the same time he desires his own welfare with it.
> If he is bad, certainly the way is blocked up along
> which he would be good. Oh! this blocking up is a
> terrible thing; and it is so common, and man is
> therefore so seldom good. Yet I believe every-
> where and always in the human heart. In this faith
> I now go on in my untrodden way, as if it were on
> a paved Roman road.[383]

And in the goodness of nature, especially when it comes to children's learning:

> Nature only does us good; she alone leads us un-
> corrupted and unshaken to truth and wisdom. The
> more I followed her track, the more I sought to
> unite my deeds to hers and strained my powers to
> keep pace with her footsteps, the more infinite this
> step appeared to me. But the power of children to
> follow her is just as infinite.[384]

Though his life may look like a series of starts, stops, and
blunders, he was driven by his love for the poor and his vision of a
better life for the downtrodden.

Pestalozzi spent his childhood in Zurich with his mother
and a housemaid, following the death of his father, a surgeon,
when he was five. At the age of fifteen, he attended the *gymnasium* (high school) where he studied politics, history, Hebrew, and,
of course, Greek. It was during this time that holiday visits to his
grandfather, a clergyman, awakened him to the plight of the poor.
Together they would travel to the schools and houses of parishion-
ers, and there he saw the results of the grinding poverty of the
peasants whose ignorance left them helpless. He saw the results of
children put to work in the factories and the little help provided by
the religious schools that taught nothing but memorization of the
catechism.

Following an early venture into the clergy, he tried politics and the law, both of which proved unsuited to his humanitarian nature. In 1769, he made an attempt at farming after working for a year with the successful agronomist Johann Rudolf Tschiffeli (1716-1780). He acquired, with a crushing mortgage, a plot of barren land, idealistically hoping to better the lives of the poor through improved methods of agriculture. He even named the place *Neuhof* (a rather grandiose term meaning something a bit bigger than *New Farm.*) This turned out to be far from successful, but his life in the farming community (Birr, Switzerland) once again brought the plight of peasant children to his attention. He was deeply moved by the poverty and suffering of children, many of whom were war orphans reduced to begging or working long hours on farms or in factories. Around 1773, he opened his house to poor children, clothing, feeding them, and educating them in trades at which they might achieve some independence. By 1778, he was housing some thirty-seven children.

While the children were engaged in spinning and weaving under trained craftsmen, Pestalozzi was teaching them how to read and write, all the while developing his theories of education based on the interests of the child in a permissive atmosphere of love and care. Unlike the standard educational methods of the time: memorization, recitation, and discipline (stand and deliver—or else), Pestalozzi was favouring group co-operation, physical exercise, music, drawing, collecting, and model making. Allowances were made for individual differences, and children were grouped by ability rather than by age. It became clear, though, that financial management was not Pestalozzi's strong point, and by 1779 the venture was deeply in debt and had to be closed down. With help from a few friends, he was able to save the house but was otherwise reduced to penury.

Not one to be easily defeated, Pestalozzi turned to writing to save himself, his wife, and their young son. He spent the next eighteen years barely surviving but producing some six volumes putting forth his ideas about child-rearing and education. The first of these, *The Evening Hours of a Hermit* (*Die Abendstunde eines Linsiedlers*) was published, in 1780, by Isaac Iselin (1728-1782)[385] in his *Ephemeriden*[386] of Humanity, (*Ephemeriden der Menschheit*) a magazine of political and social tracts. Pestalozzi's article is a more or less random collection of aphoristic statements about humanity, education, family, nature, duties of rulers, and belief in God. Among these he didn't hesitate to take a shot at conventional education:

> Vain desire for the mere phantom of truth, the kind of desire that exhausts people without purpose, the desire for the voice, sound or words about truth that have no interest to attract people at all nor are applicable for practical service; to subject a growing human with all his power to the stiff and one-sided opinion of a schoolmaster, or exchange of words that are the basis of human education as well as thousands of technics in education that are in fashion—all over-laborious and leading a human away from the Way of Nature.[387]

The importance of learning through direct experience of Nature (always capitalized) is more important than books or lessons, especially those of the schools of the time:

> This artificial method adopted by schooling, which forces the order of words everywhere without waiting for free, calm and mild advance of Nature, trains a human in such a manner that the lack of his essential inner faculty be covered, by which a human becomes artificial and vain, as befits the shallow and superficial mode of living of this century.[388]

If at this time his ideas were still in a formative stage, he was able to present them more clearly in the novel *Leonard and Gertrude* (*Lienhard und Gertrud*) which was published in a series of revisions and editions from 1781 to 1787. This is a moralistic novel, a portrayal of German rural life, almost a premonition of

Dickens, illustrating that the poor will show hearts of gold and a love of honest labour if given half a chance. The tale circles around an ideal wife and mother, Gertrude, who teaches her children spinning, model behaviour, and arithmetic at home. As the novel develops, the local peasants and the aspiring young schoolmaster are shown how domestic industry supported by parental love and guidance can form the basis of a school and of a reformed society. Evil-doers see the errors of their ways, the benevolent ruler sees to the well-being of his subjects, however poor, while motherly love triumphs over all.

The new school, in Pestalozzi's view, must spring from an ideal home, with a loving mother and masterful father. This is what will create the society of the future, based on a larger concept of the family. As with Rousseau, and similar to Locke, the mother is the source of love and learning, while the father provides benevolent control and support. Gender roles were clearly defined.

> We can do very little with the people, unless the next generation is to have a very different training from that our schools furnish. The school ought really to stand in the closest connection with the life of the home, instead of, as now, in strong contradiction to it.[389]

Gertrude's form of teaching and learning is based on direct experience, not with books and lectures, but with real hands-on work. As seen in Horace Mann's report of the Prussian schools, each piece of learning arises from the child's observations, prompted and enlarged upon by the teacher. Presumably, the child's interest has been aroused, and he or she will eagerly engage in the next step:

> While they were spinning and sewing, she taught them to count and cipher, for she regarded arithmetic as the foundation of all intellectual order. Her method was to let the children count their threads or stitches both forwards and backwards, and add and subtract, multiply and divide the result by different numbers. The children vied with

> each other in this game, trying to see who could be quickest and surest in the exercise. When they were tired, they sang songs, and night and morning Gertrude prayed with them.[390]

Learning comes from direct experience:

> The instruction she gave them in the rudiments of arithmetic was intimately connected with the realities of life. She taught them to count the number of steps from one end of the room to the other, and two of the rows of five panes each, in one of the windows, gave her an opportunity to unfold the decimal relations of numbers. . . . Above all, in every occupation of life she taught them an accurate and intelligent observation of common objects and the forces of nature.[391]

Children also learn from each other; the age of Gertrude's children ranges from very young to adolescent. Boys and girls live, work, and play together. As in the one-room school, the older kids help teach the younger ones:

> All that Gertrude's children knew, they knew so thoroughly that they were able to teach it to the younger ones; and this they often begged permission to do.[392]

These first books achieved a certain degree of attention and a growing interest in the author's ideas about education. Between 1781 and 1797 he barely sustained his family with various articles and books, ending with *My Enquiries into the Course of Nature in the development of the Human Race* (*Meine Nachforschungen über den Gang der Natur in der Entwicklung des Menschengeschlechts*) that had been suggested by the famous philosopher Johann Gottlieb Fichte. Pestalozzi met him in 1794 while returning from a trip to Leipzig to visit his sister. Fichte saw in Pestalozzi's ideas the key to solving the growing problem of education in Prussia. In *Addresses to the German Nation* (*Reden an die deutsche Nation*) of 1808, Fichte recommended that teachers receive training from Pestalozzi's school at Yverdon. It should be clear from this that the Prussian school system of the later eighteenth and early nineteenth centuries was based on developing humanitarian views of education, not, as sometimes claimed, on the training routines of the military.

When serfdom was abolished in Switzerland in 1798, Pestalozzi was inspired to submit a proposal to the government for the establishment of a school. His ideas were accepted, but the school did not happen until January of 1799 when, following the French invasion and virtual destruction of the mid-Switzerland town of Stans, an Ursuline convent there was to become an orphanage for children left parentless and destitute by the war. In spite of near-insurmountable difficulties Pestalozzi seized upon this as the perfect fit for the development of his plans for a school:

> I went gladly, for I hoped to offer these innocent little ones some compensation for the loss they had sustained, and to find in their wretchedness a basis for their gratitude. In my zeal to put my hands to the task which had been the great dream of my life, I should have been ready to begin even in the highest Alps and without fire and water, so to speak, had I only been allowed.[393]

The orphan's school was ousted, after a few months, in favour of a military hospital, but the experience solidified Pestalozzi's determination to have a school under his own direction. Also at this time, Philipp Albert Stapfer (1766-1840), who became Minister of Arts and Sciences under the new French-led Helvetic Republic, favoured Pestalozzi's ideas and had in mind the establishment of a school for the training of teachers.

Pestalozzi's dream was realized, more or less, when he was assigned by Stapfer to a teaching position in Burgdorf, a Swiss city located between Bern and Zurich. He was assigned to a lower school that was under the control of a local shoemaker who did not approve of Pestalozzi's methods. And, as reported by

Green in his biographical treatment, the parents were suspicious of Pestalozzi's educational ideas:

> Instead of learning the catechism, the children were repeating some ABC rubbish after their new teacher, and were frivolously wasting time over drawing. If this man was to experiment with the children, let him do it in the burghers' school. The parents could not fail to be attracted by this last argument, and they declined to allow their little ones to be experimented upon.[394]

This was only a temporary setback as some of Pestalozzi's friends obtained a position for him at one of the lower schools in town. The children in his charge were five to eight years old, and he set about teaching and developing his ideas with tireless zeal. Instead of expected criticism, his pupils made extraordinary progress,[395] so much so that he was soon promoted to a position in one of the "better" schools in town. Meanwhile, war in the eastern part of Switzerland managed to produce a large number of orphaned children. Some thirty of these were sent to Burgdorf under the charge of one Hermann Krüzi (1775-1844) who soon became an ally and devoted assistant to Pestalozzi.

Pestalozzi was convinced that growth and learning took place in an orderly fashion, and he was determined to map this progress and develop teaching methods in accordance with it. However, as part of a larger school, he was criticized by doubtful parents and subjected to the expected school discipline. This was in spite of very favourable reviews he had received from the education authorities. Consequently, he determined to set up his own independent school. Again with the help of Stapfer, who not only created the Friends of Education, a society for fund-raising and promotion of Pestalozzi's ideas but also obtained approval for the Educational Institute for the Children of the Middle Classes (October, 1800). This enabled Pestalozzi the freedom he needed to pursue refining his theories of teaching and learning. But because the Educational Institute was dependent upon tuition payments,

Pestalozzi's dream of educating the poor was difficult to realize. Though he took in as many children of the poor as he could, he believed it was through the training of teachers that the masses of poor could be reached. Therefore, he called upon a government commission to examine and report on his work, hoping to establish the credibility necessary to expand to teacher training. Accordingly, a committee of three was duly appointed and arrived to examine the school. The report, which was mostly positive, gave a detailed description of Pestalozzi's method at work:

> There is no trace of memory drill. Everything which the child learns is the result of his own observation, of his own experience. He learns nothing which he does not understand, he understands everything which he learns. In the lower classes the chief exercises deal with observation and naming. The boys are led to notice first the objects in the room, then they go over the whole house, observing and naming everything. When this source is exhausted they are taken into the garden, into the fields, and the woods, gradually accumulating a large stock of mental pictures and names. The children are then led to notice the objects in greater detail, their situation and the relations of their parts, their permanent and changeable qualities, the qualities that are general and those that are peculiar to them, their influence, their function, and their destiny. Thus they pass from simple to complex ideas, from mental images and names to judgments, descriptions, conclusions—in one word, to the definite and intelligent use of language. They understand what they say, and they say what they understand.[396]

The report was widely read and led the more enlightened departments of the government to provide financial support, thus guaranteeing regular pay for the staff, training in the method for a number of teachers, and the publication of Pestalozzi's ABC-type teaching books. The moral and religious training of the students

179

Tom Durrie

was praised, but criticism was levelled at the lack of cleanliness in the school.[397]

During all this, having by now formulated his ideas, he wrote *How Gertrude Teaches Her Children* (*Gertrud ihre Kinder lehrt*) (October 1801), his most influential and widely read book. His work in Burgdorf and the publication of this book brought widespread recognition and even fame. This meant a constant parade of curious visitors eager to see all these radical notions in action.[398] Nevertheless, the authorities in Paris, especially Napoleon, were neither impressed nor interested. Once again, as at Stans, the French-led Swiss government decided that the buildings at Burgdorf were needed for official purposes. As a gesture to avoid public criticism, Pestalozzi was offered the use of an old monastery at Münchenbuchsee.[399] Though there were other offers, he accepted, and his tenure in Burgdorf ended in June of 1804. Attempts to collaborate with an existing school in the new location were short-lived, and when offers to set up with two of his former teachers came in October, he packed up and left for Yverdon.

Yverdon, on the western side of Switzerland, was an ideal setting, located on Lake Neuchâtel in a plain surrounded by the Jura Mountains and hills formed by the Broye River. For the first nine months, supported by a generous gift from the King of Denmark, Pestalozzi had the luxury of being able to spend his time writing, resulting in *Views and Experiences Relating to the Idea of Elementary Education (Ein Blick auf meine Erziehungszwecke und Erziehungswversuch)*.

The Institute at Yverdon was opened in July 1805, attracting students from all over Europe. Students, that is, of parents wealthy and adventurous enough to trust their kids to the methods employed there; governments, interested in adopting the new ideas, were sending teachers there to study how it was done. As we shall see from the reports of Mann and Ryerson, the methods were adopted by the Prussian school system which they observed in the 1800s. And, as recommended by Fichte, the teachers in those schools had been trained in Pestalozzian methods. However, as

180

with most programs and organizations started by an idealistic individual, differences of opinion arose.

In 1803, while still at Burgdorf, Pestalozzi had taken on two new staff members: Johannes Niederer (1779-1843) and Johann Joseph Schmid (1785-1851). Niederer, who was well-educated, had been a clergyman before joining Pestalozzi in 1803, while Schmid, who started as a poor pupil at Burgdorf, was invited to the staff because he showed outstanding abilities as a scholar and teacher. Niederer publicized the school at Burgdorf and then at Yverdon through various magazine articles, which were, not unexpectedly, based on his interpretations of Pestalozzi's vision. While this resulted in fame and numerous visitors, it was the foundation of disagreement about methods and practices at the school. As put by Green, "Even the visitors who came from all parts of Europe, and who were the outward and visible sign of the glory of the Institution, were a source of difficulty. They took up valuable time and exposed the teachers to the temptation to work primarily for show."[400]

Under Niederer's influence, and to appeal to a higher class of parents, classics such as Latin and Greek were purported to be taught, though no teacher there was qualified in those subjects, and surely, classical education was at odds with Pestalozzi's dream of educating the poor. After growing disagreement, termed the "canker of disunion," Niederer finally broke ranks and left in 1817.

Meanwhile, Schmid, always at odds with Niederer's ambitious plans, had become a skilled teacher of mathematics and an acute man of business. The rocky finances of the Institute were a constant source of emotional distress and conflict, and there was the ever-present but vain hope that the school might come under government sponsorship. Back in 1810, upon Niederer's urging, opposed by Schmid, another government commission was called in. The report, which damned with faint praise, assured that the Institute would not receive official support. Schmid submitted his (short-lived) resignation. The near financial collapse of the Institute followed.

As Horatio says, "When sorrows come, they come not single spies but in battalions."[401] Pestalozzi's wife died, in 1815, and a parade of staff resignations included that of the long-standing and devoted Krüsi. It appeared that collapse was imminent, but when Schmid returned, in the same year, he attempted a vigorous reorganization of the school's finances and successfully arranged for the publication of a collection of Pestalozzi's writing. This yielded enough money to encourage the ever-optimistic Pestalozzi, against Schmid's wishes, to establish a special school at Clendy for children of the poor. Again, Pestalozzi caved to the interests of others and added the teaching of English, French, and Latin, not exactly what the poor children were calling for. Within a year, and under Schmid's direction, the children of the Clendy school were brought to Yverdon, uniting the two institutions. Now arose criticism from the town authorities, who said, in effect, "We don't want our rich kids mixing with the riff-raff." During this difficult time, Pestalozzi never left off writing, producing two biographical works (not published until 1826) and a piece defending his dedication to the education of the poor. The latter is summarized by Green:

> He complains bitterly that Switzerland is lagging behind Prussia in this matter. The foundations of national welfare are everywhere alike; salvation lies only in the education of the children, but the children belong to the parents and not to the state.... "May all the noble and the good unite against this tendency to forget that the home is the chief agency in the education of the moral, intellectual, and physical power."[402]

The "tendency to forget" refers to the state control of schools. Pestalozzi always believed that schools should be locally organized and controlled, assuring that the educational needs of children, not of the state, would be served. A very interesting point, since the establishment, by governments, of schools, especially with compulsory and universal attendance, was intended to bring the lower classes, i.e. peasants, under control. Remember that wealthy-class parents could, and still can, pay to send their kids to private schools or to hire private tutors, thereby avoiding mixing their offspring with the lower classes. In other words, most developments in schooling ran contrary to Pestalozzi's ideals. Doesn't the very concept of "state-run compulsory school" imply and insist upon a group of students being given instruction, from the top down, by a teacher who promotes a universal curriculum set down by state-employed "experts"? Pestalozzi's method, like that of Dewey, dangerously suggests flexibility and responding to individual needs and interests.

A perhaps romanticized image of Pestalozzi is portrayed in an 1879 painting *Pestalozzi with the orphans at Stans* (*Pestalozzi bei den Waisen von Stans*)[403] by Konrad Grob (1828-1904). A benevolent-looking Pestalozzi is surrounded by children, some

clinging to his back while he holds the hand of a small, perhaps ill, child who is in the arms of an older boy. It is a scene of comfortable disarray, one of happy adoring children of all ages with their beloved school master seated at the centre. Hardly the image of a teacher that could be associated with any regular school we know of.

Statues in Zurich and Yverdon also show Pestalozzi in tender and informal contact with children. Compare this with the disciplined classrooms expected in most schools. Pestalozzi did not hesitate to express his contempt for the constraints of standard schooling:

> We leave children, up to their fifth year, in the full enjoyment of nature; we let every impression of nature work upon them; they feel their power; they already know full well the joy of unrestrained liberty and all its charms. The free natural bent which the sensuous happy wild thing takes in his development, has in them already taken its most decided direction. And after they have enjoyed this happiness of sensuous life for five whole years, we make all nature round them vanish from before their eyes; tyrannically stop the delightful course of their unrestrained freedom, pen them up like sheep, whole flocks huddled together, in stinking rooms; pitilessly chain them for hours, days, weeks, months, years, to the contemplation of unattractive and monotonous letters (and, contrasted with their former condition), to a maddening course of life.[404]

Back at Yverdon, trouble was brewing. In spite of, or because of, Pestalozzi's polemical writings, his profound desire to bring his brand of education to the poor, and the increasing influence of, or at least curiosity about, his ideas, the Yverdon school was doomed by disagreements and financial woes. It closed in 1825. With shattered hopes, he returned to his home at Neuhof to devote himself to writing. In the two short years that remained for him, he published *Swan Song (Schwanengesang)*, revisions of earlier works, in which he not only reviews his life's work but also his experiences at Yverdon. It was the latter that aroused the indignation and mockery of former followers and Yverdon staff. Again Green: "The old man suffered terribly from these attacks, not so much on his own account, but because men were pouring scorn upon his work, upon things which to him were holy."[405] Pestalozzi died in February of 1827.

The Pestalozzian Method has been described many times and in many ways, but it's safe to say that, inspired by his work with children of the poor, it developed from a deep compassion for the young and an idealistic dream of improving their lives for the future. He also strongly believed that education began in the home and with the mother:

> From the moment that a mother takes a child upon her lap, she teaches him. She brings nearer to his senses what nature has scattered afar off over large areas and in confusion, and makes the action of receiving sense-impressions and the knowledge derived from them, easy, pleasant, and delightful to him.[406]

Presumably, to assist mothers in the early education of their children, Pestalozzi published, in 1803, *The Mother's Book, or A Guide for Mothers in Teaching their children to observe and to talk* (*Buch der Mutter, oder Anleitung für Mutter ihre Kinder bemerken und reden zu lehren*). The book was largely the work of the (almost) ever-faithful Hermann Krüzi, though we can assume that Pestalozzi approved. We can also assume that the idea that a mother should be this involved in teaching her children was radical for its time. From the very beginning, parents are advised to pronounce the basic sounds of language (ba, ba, ba, da, da, da, ma, ma, ma, la, la, la, etc.[407]) to the infant. This will progress to naming objects that the child observes, and indeed there was also a book of woodcut illustrations to be used in teaching names and numbers. Always, the mother is the one who with care and attention leads the child to more complicated concepts:

> Here also I prepare the children for the first step by a very simple but psychological instruction in speech. Without letting fall a word about forms and rules, let the mother first repeat before the child simple sentences only, as exercises. These should be imitated, as much for the sake of exercising the organs of speech, as for the sake of the

sentences themselves. We must clearly distinguish
between these two objects: exercise in pronunciation and learning words as language; and practise
the first by itself, independently of the second.
When the meaning and pronunciation are understood, the mother should repeat the following
kinds of sentences:

Father is kind.
The butterfly has gay wings.
The cow eats grass.
The fir has a straight stem.[408]

Other, similar books followed. Here, in line with the
thinking of Locke and Rousseau, learning is to start at the simplest
level and progress to the more complicated but always based upon
"sense impression"[409] or observation-based learning (as opposed to
book learning). This is the concept of *Anschauung*, from the German verb *anschauen*, meaning to look at or to examine. According
to Pestalozzi, all learning was the result of *Anschauung* or direct
experience with nature, and this experience was to be enhanced, or
guided, by a perceptive and loving grownup who would pose appropriate questions and encourage conversation, thereby leading
the child from simple naming of objects into more complex
thoughts and concepts. He explained this in his report anticipating
the visit of a deputation from Stapfer's Society for the Friends of
Education:

I wish always to let sense impression precede the
word, and definite knowledge the judgment I
wish to make words and talk unimportant on the
human mind, and to secure that preponderance
due to the actual impressions of physical objects
(*Anschauung*), that forms such a remarkable protection against mere noise and empty sound. From
his very first development I wish to lead my child
into the whole circle of Nature surrounding him; I
would organize his learning to talk by a collection
of natural products; I would teach him early to abstract all physical generalizations from separate

physical facts, and teach him to express them in words; and I would everywhere substitute physical generalizations for those metaphysical generalizations with which we begin the instruction of our race. Not till after the foundation of human, knowledge, (sense impressions of Nature,) has been fairly laid and secure would I begin the dull, abstract work of studying from books.[410]

It's pretty clear, though, that this is not a process that could work easily with a large group of children, but it was large-group instruction that so impressed Horace Mann on his visit to the Prussian schools. Contrary to the essence of Pestalozzi's method, applying it to an organized classroom full of kids with one teacher in charge would require some kind of formula—do this, do that, say this, say that—thus obviating the informality and the individual and personal touch and, yes, love, essential to Pestalozzi's way of dealing with kids. The books that provided just such a formula were, as far as we know (Pestalozzi was too busy with his theoretical work), written by staff members like Krüsi. This was, no doubt, a well-intentioned effort to bring fame and money to the school, but probably contributed much to the disagreements that led to the end of the Yverdon institute as well as the dilution and interpretation of Pestalozzi's ideals to conform to a rigid and regulated style of education.

Pestalozzi's notion of education sprang from Rousseau's *Emile*. "Directly Rousseau's Emile appeared," Pestalozzi says, "my visionary and highly speculative mind was enthusiastically seized by this visionary and highly speculative book."[411]

Pestalozzi was so under the influence of Rousseau that he named his only child, born in 1770, Jean-Jacques. With *Emile* as a model, Pestalozzi developed his methods of child-centred education around handicrafts, farming, and outdoor activities, always building on the child's natural interests. Rousseau's promotion of the goodness of nature along with the idealization of rural and peasant life had far-ranging effects, all the way from ladies of the French court dressing as shepherdesses to the 1960s youthful

dreams of back-to-nature. Along the way, freedom from the tram-
mels of civilized life was romanticized in novels like *The Swiss
Family Robinson (Der Schweizerische Robinson)* by Johann David
Wyss in 1812. The stage had been set by the enormously popular
Robinson Crusoe (Daniel Defoe, 1719) and the many imitations
that followed. A genre of desert island castaway tales that came to
be known as *Robinsonade*, emerged from the success of Defoe's
novel. The corrupting influence of civilized life, especially urban
life, on the "natural" man has been explored in countless novels,
fictional histories, and life experiences. Among these are found
Thomas More's *Utopia* (1516), Voltaire's *Candide (Candide, ou
l'Optimisme,* 1759), and Henry David Thoreau's *Walden* (1854), to
name but a few. It's no surprise then that the ideal Free School,
like Neill's Summerhill, would be found in a rustic rural setting
where children can climb trees, build forts, and run and play to
their heart's content. [412]

John Dewey

John Dewey (1859-1952) was in many ways a visionary
and reformer along the lines of Pestalozzi, and was subject to the
same fate. Both men placed the interests of the child ahead of subject matter, Pestalozzi gradually introducing topics of interest
while he and the child worked together, and Dewey creating a
workshop of crafts and arts that he believed would inspire learning
that would grow out of the child's interests. Dewey foresaw that
there would be distrust of his methods if the goal of intellectual
development through experience was misinterpreted as chaotic
and undirected. "Failure to give constant attention to development
of the intellectual content of experiences and to obtain ever-
increasing organization of facts and ideas may in the end merely
strengthen the tendency toward a reactionary return to intellectual
and moral authoritarianism."[413] We have seen how Pestalozzi's
ideals were undermined by notions of a required curriculum. In

other words, children were not to be trusted in directing, even with guidance, their own learning. Dewey's ideas were somewhat observed in pre-Sputnik California, but even then many parents and educators thought going in that direction was too soft. Such doubters were soon assuaged by the pushers of top-down instruction in science and mathematics, and let all that other stuff, like language, art, and history, take care of itself.

In his writing, Dewey was consistently critical of the traditional school as having little or no connection with a child's real life:

> From the standpoint of the child, the great waste in the school comes from his inability to utilize the experiences he gets outside of the school in any complete and free way within the school itself; while, on the other hand, he is unable to apply in daily life what he is learning at school. That is the isolation of the school—its isolation from life. When the child gets into the schoolroom, he has to put out of his mind a large part of the ideas, interests, and activities that predominate in his home and neighborhood. So the school, being unable to utilize this everyday experience, sets painfully to work, on another tack and by a variety of means, to arouse in the child an interest in school studies.[414]

And very significantly, I think, Dewey observes that school as we know it is an institution unlike any other:

> Finally, the general pattern of school organization (by which I mean the relations of pupils to one another and to the teachers) constitutes a kind of institution sharply marked off from other social institutions. Call up to imagination the ordinary schoolroom, its time-schedules, schemes of classification, of examination and promotion, of rules of order, and I think you will grasp what is meant by "patterns of organization." If you then contrast this

> scene with what goes on in the family, for example,
> you will appreciate what is meant by the school be-
> ing a kind of institution sharply marked off from
> any other form of social organization.[415]

I would add that there is one institution remarkably similar to school: prison.

Dewey's ideals of education suggest that any meaningful learning must spring from experience and that it is the job of the school to provide opportunities for such experience. Therefore, a school should be set up along the lines of a workshop. There should be looms, carpentry tools and materials, gardens, cooking equipment, paints, crayons and pencils for artwork, and opportunities for creative play of all kinds. At the same time, every experience is seen as a starting point for learning and developing understanding. Children's play is to be seen as the starting point for deeper learning: "What are we to do with this interest—are we to ignore it, or just excite and draw it out? Or shall we get hold of it and direct it to something ahead, something better?"[416] This is where the teacher comes in, directing and guiding experience "toward something better." In such a school, for example, a visitor may observe "boys as well as girls of ten, twelve, and thirteen years of age engaged in sewing and weaving." But if this activity is solely of utilitarian value ("sewing on buttons and making patches"), it could hardly be seen as educative. Of striking similarity to the *teachable moments* described by Horace Mann (the boy learning from a discussion of domestic animals about quadrupeds and the various uses to which they may be put, and the "blushing little girl" whose pleasure in flowers leads to a study of botany), Dewey describes sewing and weaving as potentials for expanded learning:

> We find that this work gives the point of departure
> from which the child can trace and follow the
> progress of mankind in history, getting an insight
> also into the materials used and the mechanical
> principles involved. In connection with these oc-

cupations the historic development of man is re-capitulated. For example, the children are first given the raw material—the flax, the cotton plant, the wool as it comes from the back of the sheep (if we could take them to the place where the sheep are sheared, so much the better). Then a study is made of these materials from the standpoint of their adaptation to the uses to which they may be put. For instance a comparison of the cotton fiber with wool fiber is made.[417]

If flowers can lead to botany and sheep shearing to the study of textiles, working with a spinning wheel (Remember, this was written in 1902, although it's hard to imagine that spinning wheels were still all that common.) will lead to physics, through working out "diagrams of the direction of forces concerned in treadle and wheel, and the ratio of velocities between wheel and spindle."[418]

There is no question but what Dewey's understanding of how children learn and his ideal of how a school should be orga-nized are more humane and more encompassing of a child's inter-ests than top-down instruction based on a curriculum laid on by the powers above. The old-style school with "its passivity of atti-tude, its mechanical massing of children, its uniformity of curricu-lum and method" means that "the center of gravity is outside the child. It is in the teacher, the textbook, anywhere and everywhere you please except in the immediate instincts and activities of the child . . . the school is not the place where the child lives."[419] But changing the school to a "place where the child lives" means an entirely different style of teaching—even a different style of teacher. The teacher must now be responsive to the interests and pursuits of children—and not just responsive but following as well as guiding. This means that the teacher must be sensitive to the individuality of each child, engaging children in whatever activi-ties they find appealing, accepting a wide range of individual dif-ferences, becoming a participant in the learning process, and en-gaging in "intelligent exploration and exploitation of the potentialities inherent in experience." Dewey recognizes the problem in this approach:

> Failure to give constant attention to development of the intellectual content of experiences and to obtain ever-increasing organization of facts and ideas may in the end merely strengthen the tendency toward a reactionary return to intellectual and moral authoritarianism.[420]

Simply enough, if anticipated learning outcomes are not forthcoming, (e.g. a child is not learning to read at age six) the tendency is to accede to the lament: "I knew it all along, this method does not work." Never mind that authoritarian systems don't work either, but they have a more clearly defined structure that may provide some reassurance to nervous teachers and parents.

It now becomes obvious why so-called progressive methods were discredited by Sputnik's beeping in 1957, resulting in the panicky demand for hard-nosed teaching and testing in science and mathematics. Well, this didn't work either, causing regular revisions, especially in the United States, to programs like the National Defence Act (1958); A Nation at Risk (1983); Unlocking Our Future (1998); and the ever-popular STEM. The reluctance to accept the child's natural drive toward discovery and learning is clearly illustrated by the undermining of the theories and practices of Locke, Rousseau, Pestalozzi, Froebel, Dewey, Montessori, and many other progressives. It boils down to whether or not we begin with the natural learning instincts of the child or start with preconceived notions of how the child should behave and what he should turn into. If the former, we will accept and allow; if the latter we will control and dictate.

Lev Vygotsky

One of the most important, and least known, researchers and thinkers about child development and learning was Lev Semyonovitch Vygotsky (1896-1934). Least known because much of his research remains untranslated from Russian, and even that which has been translated can be difficult to comprehend. He simply did not live long enough to polish and complete his work. Furthermore, instead of clear-cut processes and directives, Vygotsky offers a view of infancy and childhood that may seem lacking in the step-by-step development, requiring strict guidance, made popular by the likes of John B. Watson, B. F. Skinner, and even John Locke.

There are only three books of Vygotsky's now available in English: *Thought and Language, The Psychology of Art,* and *Mind in Society.* The last and most useful of these, actually a selection of essays, has been carefully edited by a group of Vygotsky scholars.[421] Numerous other books proclaim explanation and application of Vygotsky's theories of learning and development. You'll also find numerous articles and YouTube talks on the internet. What is startling about Vygotsky's views is that, if taken seriously, they are completely contrary to common child-rearing practices in twentieth- and twenty-first-century society, including the whole unexamined philosophical foundation of school. We tend to believe that our child-rearing and educational practices are only natural and proper, that there are no valid alternatives. Vygotsky suggests otherwise.

Lev Vygotsky was born November 5, 1896 to a well-off art- and literature-loving family in the Bylorussian town of Orsha; he was then raised in the city of Gomel. Significantly perhaps, he was homeschooled until 1911 when he entered the *gymnasium* (high school), completing studies there—with honours—in two years. In 1913, he entered Moscow University to pursue his interests in humanities and social sciences but switching, at his parents' request, to medicine. After but one semester he turned to the study of law. This may give some idea of his broad range of interests, which included history, linguistics, sociology, literature, theatre, psychology, and philosophy.

Following the Bolshevik revolution of 1917, Vygotsky returned to his hometown of Gomel, where, until 1923, he taught literature and psychology, while also directing the theatre section of the adult education centre. His lectures and journalistic articles of the time reflected his growing interest in psychology and pedagogy. By 1925 he had completed his dissertation, *The Psychology of Art* (not published until 1960) as well as a book titled *Pedagogical Psychiatry*. He was finally awarded a scholarly degree, though he was suffering from a severe episode of tuberculosis, the disease which ended his short life in 1934.

In 1924, following an apparently brilliant lecture at the Second All-Russian Psychoneurological Congress, he was invited to become a research fellow at the Psychological Institute in Moscow. While there, his interests became dedicated to the study of the processes of learning and the role of language in cognitive development. The period 1926 to 1930 marked the emergence of his major theories and studies regarding the development of higher cognitive functions and language.

At the same time as Vygotsky was doing his research, developments in psychological theory were flourishing in Europe and in America. Among these was Wilhelm Wundt (1832-1920), often known as the "father of experimental psychology," who, as the epithet suggests, established psychology as a branch of science, determining that conscious mental states could be studied scientifically by planned experimentation. There was Ivan Pavlov (1849-1936), whose well-known experiments with salivation and dogs promoted notions of stimulus and response, while in the United States, John B. Watson (1878-1928) took Pavlov's theory of conditioned response to the next level with the development of behaviourism, reducing all human behaviour to positive versus negative stimuli. Another version of psychology, perhaps in reaction to Wundt's detailed analyses, was Gestalt Psychology, which suggested that human experience cannot be broken down into its various parts but should be seen in its totality, that is as a whole picture or *Gestalt*. The principal initiator of Gestalt was Max Wertheimer (1880-1943), but anyone around in the 1960s will remember Fritz Perls and the trendy Gestalt Psychotherapy.

Perhaps most important and most often compared with Vygotsky is his contemporary Jean Piaget (1896-1980). As opposed to the earlier notion that the young mind was simply a blank slate upon which experience would leave its mark, Piaget developed the idea that the child is actively involved in his or her own development. Thus, at even the earliest stages of growth, reflex responses, such as sucking and grasping, initiate and direct the infant's exploration of the environment. These and other actions then become refined and perfected as the infant grows and "works on" them. This would be what Piaget called the Sensorimotor Stage, happening roughly from birth to two years. Similar processes continue as the brain develops and the child's movements expand into its environment.

And so cognitive development proceeds stage by stage as the brain becomes ready to take on new skills and information. Following the first level, comes the Preoperational Stage (age two to seven) with the rudimentary use of language and symbol, limited by the child's inability to perceive the world from any perspective but his own. This stage evolves into the Concrete Operational Stage (age seven to eleven) in which the young person begins to see that there are experiences of the world other than her own, though abstract and hypothetical concepts may yet be illusive. At last, we arrive at the Formal Operational Stage (twelve and up), which, I suppose, would include me and anyone reading, this far at least, this book.

The conclusion is that these stages are universal, predictable, and observable. All children, regardless of social or cultural setting, will go through these stages more or less at the same ages. You can see that school grades and curricula are based on this theory. Thus, at age seven in the Concrete Operational Stage, children are expected to learn to read, observe school discipline, perform arithmetical processes, etc. Nevertheless, throughout the stages, Piaget and his followers assert that the child is actively involved through a kind of trial and error process: "Let's throw this glass of milk on the floor and see what happens."

Vygotsky's central concept, in contrast, is that cognitive development is advanced through interaction with other people; community plays a central role in the process of making sense of the world. The brain does not proceed along step by step, preparing itself for the next learning challenge, but grows and shapes itself in response to experience with others. Looked at this way, cognitive development is a creative process, the young mind is actively engaged in creating itself in response to social interaction, especially involving speech. Therefore, each child's development will be different and will proceed at a different pace.

For Vygotsky, speech is the critical element. The very grammar and syntax of language determine the manner in which we describe and define our world. I would add, though, that speech is not the only means by which the child creates a view of his or her place in society. Speech is reinforced by gesture, facial expression, tone of voice, touch, emotion, and the placement of the child in the family constellation. This means that the relationship between mother, or primary caregiver, and child is of crucial importance.

Vygotsky did not emphasize stages of development, he saw mental growth as a continuum that progressed by the use of language and by association with other people. Or, to quote Vygotsky, "learning awakens a variety of internal developmental processes that are able to operate only when the child is interacting with people in his environment and in cooperation with his peers."[422] The implications are more profound than one might guess.

Consider Vygotsky's view of development and compare it with our more traditional cultural beliefs:

> Our [Vygotsky's] concept of development implies a rejection of the frequently held view that cognitive development results from the gradual accumulation of separate changes. We believe that child development is a complex dialectical pro-

cess characterized by periodicity, unevenness in the development of different functions, metamorphosis or qualitative transformation of one form into another, intertwining of external and internal factors, and adaptive processes which overcome impediments that the child encounters.[423]

Vygotsky tells us that the child is an intelligent being, inevitably learning all the time by what she experiences around her. Growth and cognitive development happen as a result of the child's interpretation of experience. If the child's experience is one of a harsh and restrictive world, cognitive development will be detoured by anxiety. A rich, loving, varied, and welcoming world will result in confidence, curiosity, and intelligence.

I have already mentioned the oft-repeated trope from Frank Smith, "You learn from the company you keep."[424] The adults and peers in the child's life are the models by which experience is interpreted. With language, we must think not only of *what* is said but also of *how* it is said. I will come later to how contemporary technology and so-called educational toys and videos are creating images of a non-existent world that leaves the young person ill-equipped to deal with the real world of flesh and blood.

It seems to me that the other aspects of Vygotsky's teachings spring from the basic concept of social interaction. What is called the Zone of Proximal Development (ZPD) suggests that a child, or any learner, can benefit from help from others. There are three areas of learning; the ZPD sits in the middle. The first, or inner, zone consists of what the child (learner) can learn on his own. The outer zone represents that area beyond immediate ability. The middle zone is where learning takes place with the help or example of another, known as "The More Knowledgeable Other," Take, as an example, learning to play the piano. Assuming the availability of a piano, a child may experiment with notes and combinations of notes. Without instruction, the young musician may pick out tunes and a few basic harmonies. Then, in the Zone of Proximal Development, a teacher, an advanced learner, or even seeing and hearing accomplished pianists, will lead to the development of technique and musical understanding, though the *Hammerklavier* will lie in waiting on the outer edges of zone three. At the same time, any real learning or development can only result from interest and a desire to learn. This, as I think every school teacher knows, cannot be artificially created, no matter how hard you might try.

You can imagine that educationists have seized upon Vygotsky as a way of improving what goes on in school. Given the Zone of Proximal Development, teachers could pair up more accomplished kids with the less accomplished so they could presumably learn from each other. The teacher could tune in to each child's ZPD to present the next learning "challenge," as determined, that is, by the school and its curriculum. It is immediately obvious that this would be impossible in a class of twenty-five or more kids, all, if we take Vygotsky seriously, at different individual stages of development.

"Scaffolding" is often listed as one of Vygotsky's concepts, but the term was coined by the American educational psychologist Jerome Bruner (1915-2016), who promoted the importance of support and direction in the zone of proximal development. Like most thinkers in education, he was searching for ways to push learning in the direction determined by school. He saw "scaffolding as a temporary adaptive support in a historically congruent way by the idea of teacher/student or adult/child functional system that is constituted in an accomplishment of some task, thus bridging current state of the student's abilities with an anticipated future state."[425]

"Anticipated future state" are the key words here. Who is doing the anticipating? The school wants me to learn the multiplication tables which are meaningless and irrelevant to me, though, in Zone One, I certainly have a rudimentary idea of what multiplication is all about, but I have no use for it. But if someone believes that all ten-year-olds should know that "7 times 8 is 56" and so on, they will, if savvy to Vygotsky, determine how much I already know and build the "scaffold" around that. So the "knowledgeable other" provides (whether I want it or not) the support, or scaffold, to urge me on to the next level. This is what happens when Vygotsky goes to school.

In a revealing study by Jerome Bruner, David Wood, and Gail Ross, in 1976[426], thirty children, ages three to five, were subjected to a scaffolding type of instruction by a group of tutors. The tasks presented to the kids involved sets of blocks that could be fit together in various ways. The toys were designed to be "fun" and "interesting."

First of all, the tutors observed each child to see what he or she would do, not exactly instructing but offering little suggestions from time to time. Soon, the Zone of Proximal Development was determined and the tutor would demonstrate or instruct with the idea of moving the child toward Zone Three. However, "They did not always enjoy giving up imaginative play for the more constrained task of building a pyramid with due regard for geometric constraints. Imaginative work during free play was often followed by a rather uninspired performance of the presented task."[427] What does this say, given Vygotsky's notion that higher mental processes originate from social processes? What is the "social process" here? Quoting again from the study: "The tutor has the role of keeping them in pursuit of a particular objective. Partly it involves keeping the child 'in the field,' and partly a deployment of zest and sympathy to keep him motivated."[428] I can only interpret this as a discount of the child's imagination and interest by a perhaps well-meaning but controlling and directing "knowledgeable other." A predetermined goal has been set and the child must be pushed along by whatever means possible. Those means could be "zest and sympathy" or rewards and punishments.

It is startling to realize that, if we take Vygotsky seriously, we're doing everything wrong. Much of parenthood and all of school are based upon the theories of Jean Piaget and John B. Watson, [429] not to mention John Locke. Vygotsky invites us to examine and question our relationships with children and the interpretation of the world and of themselves that we are promoting.

Tom Durrie

A. S. Neill

*Before prejudices and human institutions have corrupt-
ed our natural inclinations, the happiness of children,
like that of men, consists in the use of their freedom.—*
Emile[430]

An outstanding example of the accept-and-allow approach
may be found in Alexander Sutherland Neill (1883-1973) whose
Summerhill School, opened in 1921, is still running today. Summerhill is a democratic community in which children and adults
are equal participants. Neill was opposed to any kind of coercion
or direction other than the basic rule of "you are free to do whatever you like as long as you do not interfere with the freedom of
someone else." He defined this as "freedom not licence." Summerhill School offers traditional classes in school subjects, but
attendance is optional. Also provided for use at any time are all
kinds of art supplies, as well as pottery and building materials. The
school is governed by weekly (or more frequent) meetings at
which each child and each adult has but one vote. A chairman[431] is
elected at the first meeting of the term; that person appoints the
chairman for the following meeting, that one for the next, and so
on. According to Neill's description of meetings, they are usually
concerned with social matters, minor thieving, or other forms of
misbehaviour. Punishments are handed out and are almost always
accepted. In any case, appeal is always possible.

> An oft-heard objection to children acting as judg-
> es is that they punish too harshly. I find it not so.
> On the contrary, they are very lenient. On no oc-
> casion has there been a harsh sentence at Sum-
> merhill. And invariably the punishment has some
> relation to the crime.[432]

It should go without saying that physical punishments of
any kind are simply not a part of the Summerhill ethic.

The philosophy of Summerhill is best described by Neill himself:

> Well, we set out to make a school in which we should allow children freedom to be themselves. In order to do this, we had to renounce all discipline, all direction, all suggestion, all moral training, and all religious instruction. We have been called brave, but it did not require courage. All it required was what we had—a complete belief in the child as a good, not an evil, being. For almost forty years, this belief in the goodness of the child has never wavered; it rather has become a final faith.
>
> My view is that a child is innately wise and realistic. If left to himself without adult suggestion of any kind, he will develop as far as he is capable of developing. Logically, Summerhill is a place in which people who have the innate ability and wish to be scholars will be scholars; while those who are only fit to sweep the streets will sweep the streets. But we have not produced a street cleaner so far. Nor do I write this snobbishly, for I would rather see a school produce a happy street cleaner than a neurotic scholar.
>
> What is Summerhill like? Well, for one thing, lessons are optional. Children can go to them or stay away from them—for years if they want to. There is a timetable—but only for the teachers.
>
> The children have classes usually according to their age, but sometimes according to their interests. We have no new methods of teaching, because we do not consider that teaching in itself matters very much.[433] Whether a school has or has not a special method for teaching long division is of no significance, for long division is of no importance except to those who want to learn it. And the child who wants to learn long division will learn it no matter how it is taught. [434]

A. S. Neill

In contrast to other theories of education and teaching, Summerhill, as Neill says above, has "no new methods of teaching." The implication is that methods of teaching, however innovative, are designed to induce children into following what is thought to be good for them. Learning, in the school sense of the word, will take place when the child's interest develops without suggestion, urging, or coercion. As we have seen, the theories and practices of education discussed so far have been ways in which to get children to learn something, perhaps by expanding on a child's expressed interests, through coercion with threats of failure or promises of reward, or turning the whole process into fun. Neill has no truck with this or any of the other forms of teaching. Mentioning a book by Caldwell Cook titled *The Play Way*,[435] he writes:

> I think it was only a new way of bolstering the theory that learning is of the utmost importance. Cook held that learning was so important that the pill should be sugared with play. This notion that unless a child is learning something he is wasting his time is nothing less than a curse—a curse that blinds thousands of teachers and most school inspectors. Fifty years ago the watchword was "Learn through doing." Today the watchword is "Learn through playing." Play is thus used only as

a means to an end, but to what good end I do not really know.[436]

One can only imagine his reaction to the gamified classroom of today.

At Summerhill, children are free to play as much as they like. "Summerhill might be defined as a school in which play is of the greatest importance."[437] Since all lessons are optional, many children will spend all their days in play with full acceptance and approval. Play is considered vital and essential. "At Summerhill the six-year-olds play the whole day long—play with fantasy. . . . Small children live a life of fantasy and they carry this fantasy over into action."[438] Contemporary society disdains play as a waste of time unless it is somehow justified with some kind of learning apparatus. Thus we have such abominations as *Playskool Learning Toys*, educational computer games, *Baby Einstein*, and, yes, *Sesame Street*. I would suggest that all such "learning" implements are there to kill imagination and fantasy resulting in the deadening of curiosity and any natural impulse toward learning and discovery. Forbid or direct play and you forbid curiosity. If Summerhill is more therapeutic than educational, Neill always saw the world's problems, like war, crime, addiction, and misery of all kinds, as results of the oppression of children through discipline, training, guidance, and, above all, the absence of unconditional love and approval.

Of course, people who hear about so-called free schools, like Summerhill, doubt that any kids attending would ever be successful in later life. You know, if they play all day, how will they ever learn to work? The fact is that many Summerhill students have passed the GCSE (General Certificate of Secondary Education) exam, often after less than a year's study. When kids are motivated by their own interests and goals, there is no shortage of application to the tasks at hand.

The children take GCSEs at 16 (A-levels are not offered) and, according to official figures, 46 per cent get five or more at A*-C including English and maths, against 58.6 per cent nationally.[439]

Ofsted (Office for Standards in Education, UK Government) was mostly favourable in its 2019 report on Summerhill, for example:

> This is a good school.
> Pupils currently at the school make good progress across year groups and in the different subjects.
> The progress that pupils with special educational needs and/or disabilities (SEND) make is improving strongly. Leaders are successfully making sure that teachers are well trained to meet the needs of these pupils.
> The quality of teaching is good, particularly in English. Teachers know their pupils well and they plan learning that is well matched to the different learning needs of pupils.
> Behaviour is good. Pupils are polite, well-mannered and courteous.
> Bullying is rare. As a result, pupils feel safe at school.[440]

The fact that the children are "polite, well-mannered and courteous" is worth noting since there is no training, direction, or coercion toward good manners. This is an attribute that is of great advantage in the grown-up world of work. We can breathe a sigh of relief when it comes to "bullying is rare" since, in public schools, bullying is a plague that no one seems to be able to cure. The National Bullying Prevention Center of Minneapolis, founded in 2006, "actively leads social change to prevent childhood bullying" and yet reports that one out of every five students report being bullied in school.[441] Why is it that anti-bullying programs like pink shirt days, constant supervision, and even in-school guards have done little or nothing to change the bully/victim configuration among kids? Summerhill, I remind you, has no such programs.

Numerous stories from Summerhill graduates can be found on the internet,[442] mostly telling of a happy time of growth and development leading to a successful adult life. If there is a lesson to be learned from Summerhill, it is that love and freedom are the bases of healthy growth and development. "If the emotions are free, the intellect will look after itself"[443] Or, as I'm sure that I heard or read Neill say, "Take care of the heart and the gizzard, and the brain will look after itself."

If you detect a certain bias in my description of Summerhill, you're on the right track. However, I shall quickly point out that I am not the only one. Let's go back to 1762 with Jean Jacques Rousseau, one of the first if not *the* first to extoll the instinctual goodness of children and to advise freedom without the constraints of instruction:

> Nature has, for strengthening the body and making it grow, means that ought never be opposed. A child must not be constrained to stay when he wants to go nor to go when he wants to stay. When children's wills are not spoiled by our fault, children want nothing uselessly. They have to jump, run, and shout when they wish. All their movements are needs of their constitution seeking to strengthen itself.[444]

Prescient of Neill's "freedom not licence," Rousseau suggests that "All the instruments have been tried save one, the only one precisely that can succeed: well-regulated freedom."[445]

As we have seen, Rousseau also had no truck with traditional educational methods:

> Always sermonizers, always moralists, always pedants, for one idea you give them, believing it to be good, you give them at the same time twenty that are worthless. Full of what is going on in your head, you do not see the effect you are producing in theirs.[446]

Tom Durrie

In school as we know it, children are granted a few privileges, but they have no rights.

> It is one of the mistakes of ordinary educations that, speaking at first to children of their duties, never of their rights, one begins by telling them the opposite of what is necessary, what they cannot understand, and what cannot interest them.[447]

Plus ça change! Rousseau was writing about children's rights more than two hundred fifty years ago. Has our attitude toward children changed much since then? I remind the reader of the tips for discipline supplied by the British Columbia Teachers Federation (below). Even the word *rights* is accompanied by a warning: "Discipline and good behaviour are learned, and they must be constantly reinforced. Guide your students to know what to do in all situations rather than punish misdeeds. Help your students understand that with rights come responsibilities."[448] Just what *rights* are they talking about?

The Lord of the Flies

While we're at it, we might as well deal with *Lord of the Flies*,[449] often cited as "Well, just see what happens when you turn a bunch of kids loose. It ain't nice." But it has been pointed out that the boys in the novel were all products of strict moralistic English public (private) schools. The assumption we can draw from this book is that human nature is destructive and unsympathetic, as opposed to the assumptions of Neill, Dewey, Rousseau, and Pestalozzi, that human nature is good. "Destructive and unsympathetic" is what happens when disciplinary constraints are removed and youngsters, well, people, cut loose, try every trick in the book to create mischief, and drive everyone crazy. This is the craziness period, usually up to two months, that happens before a disciplined kid will settle down and figure out that no one is impressed and that you might as well relax and join into the community. The boys in *Lord of the Flies* haven't got there yet. Rousseau explained this phenomenon more than 200 years ago:

> The perpetual constraint under which you keep your pupils exacerbates their vivacity. The more they are held in check under your eyes, the more they are turbulent the moment they get away. . . . Two schoolboys from the city will do more damage in a place than the young of an entire village. Close up a little gentleman and a little peasant in a room. The former will have turned everything upside down, broken everything, before the latter has left his place. Why is this, if it is not because the one hastens to abuse a moment of license, while the other, always sure of his freedom, is never in a hurry to make use of it?[450]

Neill describes this phenomenon like this:

> I see the results of bondage in new pupils coming from prep schools and convents. They are bundles of insincerity, with an unreal politeness and phony manners.
>
> Their reaction to freedom is rapid and tiresome. For the first week or two, they open doors for the teachers, call me "Sir," and wash carefully. They glance at me with "respect," which is easily recognized as fear. After a few weeks of freedom, they show what they really are. They become impudent, unmannerly, unwashed. They do all the things they have been forbidden to do in the past: they swear, they smoke, they break things. And all the time, they have a polite and insincere expression in their eyes and in their voices.
>
> It takes at least six months for them to lose their insincerity. After that, they also lose their deference to what they regarded as authority. In just about six months, they are natural, healthy kids who say what they think without fluster or hate.[451]

A more recent account comes from Alfie Kohn:

Some who support more coercive strategies assume that children will run wild if they are not controlled. However, the children for whom this is true typically turn out to be those accustomed to being controlled—those who are not trusted, given explanations, encouraged to think for themselves, helped to develop and internalize good values, and so on. Control breeds the need for more control, which then is used to justify the use of control.[452]

A somewhat fictionalized but accurate and beautiful made-for-TV movie: *Summerhill*,[453] directed by Jon East, provides a view of the *adjustment period* as well as a moving portrayal of the school and what goes on there.

A Question of Freedom

Following various decrees aimed at educating the peasantry and inculcating patriotism, a system of compulsory school attendance had been established in Prussia in the late eighteenth and early nineteenth centuries. Meanwhile, England lagged behind, tangled in arguments about liberty and the freedom of individual citizens. As in most other countries, education had been the exclusive purview of the aristocracy with the church providing moral instruction for the lower classes, but growing industrialization and increased voting rights cast dark shadows over the privileges of the educated upper classes. Uh oh, we'd better do something about this!

In October of 1833, John Arthur Roebuck (1802-1879) spoke to a resolution of his for Parliament "to consider the means of establishing a system of National Education."

He explained that education is not the mere acquisition of the ability to read and write, or perhaps do some arithmetic, but "means not merely the conferring these necessary means or instruments for the acquiring of knowledge, but it means also the so training or fashioning the intellectual and moral qualities of the individual, that he may be able and willing to acquire knowledge, and to turn it to its right use. It means the so framing the mind of the individual, that he may become a useful and virtuous member of society in the various relations of life." [454]

Education, therefore, was to be seen as the means of creating an enlightened and moral citizenry by "framing the mind." After all, England was as much plagued by mischievous, unruly, and rebellious lower classes as any other country of the time. Roebuck, who, incidentally, grew up in Canada, was a close friend of Jeremy Bentham (1748-1832), John Stuart Mill, (1806-1873), and his father James Mill, all of whom were proponents of Utilitarianism, an ethic which proposed that happiness was the greatest good to which humans could strive, or, as put by Bentham, *utility* is "that property in any object, whereby it tends to produce benefit, advantage, pleasure, good, or happiness . . . [or] to prevent the happening of mischief, pain, evil, or unhappiness to the party whose interest is considered."[455] So, Roebuck argues that education will produce wide-spread good and subsequent happiness. However, enforcing education on the masses may well create unhappiness for those who would prefer a life of ignorance and indigence. Is it OK to cause unhappiness to a few in order to benefit the many, or at least benefit the many in the eyes of a few? This is only one dilemma of utilitarianism and of requiring by law that all children attend school. For whose benefit is that? Well, compulsory school attendance is now so widely accepted that such a question is rarely, if ever, asked. Perhaps Roebuck had the answer when he said, "The people at present are far too ignorant to render themselves happy."[456] Instead, let's just say that the common belief is that **children do not know what is good for them.**

In England, the first compulsory education act did not appear until 1870.

In *On Liberty* (1859), John Stuart Mill, often called the greatest English language philosopher, presents a concise definition of freedom that lines up nicely with Neill's freedom-not-licence: "The liberty of the individual must be thus far limited; he must not make himself a nuisance to other people."[457] Mill also favours freedom of expression and freedom of the press. However, though he would support an opinion expressed in print that "corn dealers are starvers of the poor," he draws the line at such an opinion "delivered orally to an excited mob assembled before the house of a corn dealer, or when handed out among the same mob in the form of a placard." Such actions "may justly incur punishment."[458] In the present day, would we, for example, allow the Holocaust denier to rant in print, but punish anyone who scrawls swastikas on the synagogue? It's a simple concept that asks for the intelligent tolerance and judgment of diverse opinions, however ill-conceived. Would we then permit the dispersal of hatred directed at ethnic or other groups, or even individuals, whether in print, in social media, or in public speeches? I don't think so because such denigrating statements can be seen to be harmful to another person's self-esteem and well-being. The question to ask is *why*; why should a person feel hatred toward any other person, no matter what ethnicity, religion, or economic status. Where does such hatred come from? It doesn't seem to come from small children, at least not until they've been to school.

There is evidence to show that small children, under seven, do not judge or even notice ethnic differences among their playmates. Of course, this is going to depend upon whether or not kids are playing with kids outside of their own ethnic or language group. An article by Tom Jacobs reviewing a recent study says, "They found both black and white kids were less likely to see certain abilities or attitudes as determined by race if they lived in a more racially diverse area."[459] This suggests to me that kids playing together in the kind of freedom described by J. S. Mill and A. S. Neill are not influenced by, in fact hardly notice, differences in skin colour, accent, or language spoken. A young woman I know was describing how she learned Spanish. At four or five she played in a sandbox with a Spanish-speaking neighbour kid; she said that she just accepted what she called "sandbox talk" and soon learned to communicate. I'm sure the same was true of her playmate. The crucial issue here is playing together, which does not imply a disciplined classroom setting or lessons about diversity. Mr. Jacobs concludes his article with, "So it appears we don't come out of the womb predisposed to categorizing people by race. That encouraging news makes the task of determining how and when it takes root in young minds that much more urgent."

John Stuart Mill's understanding of liberty suggests that a person may not be forced to do something just because it is thought to be for his or her own good. This is also true when it comes to stopping someone from doing something that might be seen as harmful to themselves:

> That the only purpose for which power can be rightfully exercised over any member of a civilized community, against his will, is to prevent harm to others. His own good, either physical or moral, is not a sufficient warrant. He cannot rightfully be compelled to do or forbear because it will be better for him to do so, because it will make him happier, because, in the opinions of others, to do so would be wise or even right.[460]

On the other hand, he asserts the importance of education for all to the point that it should be legally required and enforced by the state: "Is it not almost a self-evident axiom that the State should require and compel the education, up to a certain standard, of every human being who is born its citizen?"[461] In this case, his own good *is* "a sufficient warrant . . . because, in the opinions of others, to do so would be wise or even right." Doesn't this imply that an individual, especially a child, cannot determine what is his own good? I'm sure that the devisers of public school curricula and the teachers that deliver them are certain that they know what is good for children. Though Mill believes that everyone must be educated, he also says that the State itself should not be determining or controlling education:

> The objections which are urged with reason against State education do not apply to the en-

forcement of education by the State, but to the State's taking upon itself to direct that education, which is a totally different thing. That the whole or any large part of the education of the people should be in State hands, I go as far as anyone in deprecating. All that has been said of the importance of individuality of character, and diversity in opinions and modes of conduct, involves, as of the same unspeakable importance, diversity of education.[462]

Protecting Children—Sort Of

At the time when *On Liberty* was written (1859) providing nurture and care to children was not required by law. It wasn't until thirty years later that Parliament enacted the Children's Charter or *The Prevention of Cruelty to, and Protection of, Children Act 1889*, enabling police to enter any place where a child, defined as a boy under fourteen or a girl under sixteen, "has been or is being ill-treated or neglected . . . in a manner likely to cause the child unnecessary suffering or to be injurious to its health."[463] The act included guidelines for the employment of children and the elimination of begging. Suitable sanctions for infringement were defined; they included fines or imprisonment. However: "Nothing in this Act contained shall be construed to take or affect the right of any parent, teacher, or other person having the lawful control or charge of a child to administer punishment to such a child."[464] Just what kind of punishment is not defined. As we shall see, punishment, including paddling, strapping, or spanking, of children is still permitted in many jurisdictions. (e.g. Australia, South Korea, some states in the U.S., India, and parts of Africa) This is not to say that verbal abuse and threats are not common—and permitted. In many countries, Canada included. Parents are allowed to spank their children as long as it doesn't leave a bruise or similar physical trauma. In other words, in Canada, you can beat your kids all you like as long as it doesn't show. The assumption is that children have to be disciplined and that physical abuse is an acceptable way to do it. And if physical abuse is not available, criticism and humiliation will have to do.

If Mill can be seen to approve of enforcing education of children, he is wary of state control.

> A general state education is a mere contrivance for molding people to be exactly like one another; and as the mold in which it casts them is that which pleases the predominant power in the government—whether this be a monarch, a priesthood, an aristocracy, of the majority of the existing generation—in proportion as it is efficient and successful, it establishes a despotism over the mind, leading by natural tendency to one over the body.[465]

His words are worth pondering.

Let's add *a compulsory curriculum* to the "that which pleases the predominant power in the government."

D. The Denial of Freedom

Control and Educate

If the reader has any doubts about the importance of discipline and obedience in school in the twenty-first century, I invite you to read these excerpts from "tips" for classroom management from the British Columbia Teachers Federation:

Under the general heading "Classroom Management," we are told that

> Discipline and good behaviour are learned, and they must be constantly reinforced. Guide your

students to know what to do in all situations rather than punish misdeeds. Help your students understand that with rights come responsibilities. Encourage your students to be responsible for their learning and behaviour. When students make choices, they learn new skills and gain social awareness from the outcome of those decisions.

<u>What works</u>
- Involve students in forming rules and consequences.
- Tell students what you expect, provide a model for good behaviour, check for understanding, and allow for practice and follow-up. Don't assume that students know how to act appropriately.
- They need to be taught and coached to manage their behaviour.
- Create a classroom environment that provides structure and support and reinforces positive behaviour. Set your standards high; be clear and realistic in your expectations.

<u>Tips for rules</u>
- keep rules short, precise, and succinct to focus on specific behaviour
- limit yourself to six rules
- post rules with consequences, and send a copy home
- state rules in positive terms whenever possible
- teach rules
- add a new rule if a misbehaviour is repetitive
- when enforcing rules, preserve student dignity.

<u>Tips for consequences</u>
- be logical, clear, and specific

- have a range of alternatives
- use consequences, not punishment
- post consequence with the rule.

Children are not to be trusted, so teachers are advised to keep an ever-watchful eye out for misbehaviour and to respond quickly with consequences, i.e. punishment. A list of "strategies" to be employed by the teacher is then provided. These include moving "about the room, pausing near potential 'trouble spots,'" Here's a tip for handling troublesome students: "Sometimes having the student respond to a question or become involved in an activity can eliminate the undesired behaviour. Asking for a show of hands, having students perform a physical activity, or having each student write a quick answer to a question can make all students accountable for an immediate response." All the while, remember that "Your objective is to instill inner self-control in students, not merely to exert your control over them. Set the tone of your classroom from the start by being firm and fair, friendly yet professional." [466] Most of the advice provided in this document could just as easily be directed at an ad writer, or, like a Harlequin Romance, writing a curriculum requires a special style, all its own.

Though corporal punishment has been illegal throughout Canada since 2004 (Austria banned such punishment in 1870; there was a complete ban in Britain in 1998.), there are still nineteen American states in which children may be punished by paddling (striking on the buttocks three [at least three times?] or more times with a paddle one half-inch thick and over two feet long! Black students are paddled at two-and-a-half times the rate of white students.)[467] More than 128 countries throughout the world now have total bans on the brutalization of children by corporal punishment.[468] Nevertheless, school reflects a prevailing attitude that children must be corrected and taught, by whatever means, acceptable behaviour. *Whatever means* these days would include detention, withdrawal of privileges, writing lines (rote discipline), threats of failure, time out (solitary confinement), expulsion, counselling, and medication. The use of counselling, implying that a non-compliant youngster has mental problems, fits well into the current notions of "classroom management," and if worse comes to worst, exceptionally difficult children, especially boys, can be diagnosed with Attention Deficit Disorder and prescribed medication. For such recalcitrant individuals the DSM-V even has a convenient description of something known as Oppositional Defiant Disorder.[469] The assumption is that obedience is required because students are there to be taught and to learn something, and for that to happen, they must pay attention, do as they are told, and they'd better not talk back. How could it be, though, that in any collection of arbitrarily selected children or adults, constrained to engage in specific tasks and exhibit approved behaviour, there would not be some who would be rebellious and a nuisance to those in charge? No surprise that you'd find this in prisons as well as in classrooms. And finally, there are always those kids who will accept the demands of school and do their best to make the most of it at whatever cost to their self-esteem and education. The smart ones will carry on as Mark Twain stated the case: "I never let my schooling interfere with my education."[470]

What's the Point of It All?

Once we have the kids in school, well disciplined, duly segregated by age, grade, and classroom, we'd better decide what we expect them to do. Enter the Curriculum. The curriculum lays out, usually in mind-numbing detail, what results are expected after a youngster has spent nine-or-so months per year in his predetermined grade and up to thirteen years in the school system. Since the establishment of compulsory school attendance, 1852 in Massachusetts, 1871 in Ontario, a tremendous amount of work and verbiage has been spent figuring out what should be going on in public schools. At first, it was all about hard knowledge, memorization, obedience, and patriotic loyalty; we now have today's more liberal-sounding definition of "learning outcomes," strongly suggestive of the cost-benefit-analysis so popular with neoliberal economics. However, there is a striking similarity regarding the purpose and ultimately the content of schooling across a century.

British Columbia's new curriculum had this to say, in 2016:

> Today we live in a state of constant change. It is a technology-rich world, where communication is instant and information is immediately accessible. The way we interact with each other personally, socially, and at work has changed forever. Knowledge is growing and information is changing extremely quickly, creating new possibilities. This is the world our students are entering.
>
> British Columbia's curriculum is being modernized to respond to this demanding world. To develop new models, the Ministry consulted with education experts both locally and internationally. They agree that to prepare students for the future, the curriculum must be student-centred and flexible, and maintain a focus on literacy and numeracy, while supporting deeper learning.[471]

What "student-centred" means is not defined, and it's probably safe to say that "maintain a focus on literacy and numeracy" was included to reassure nervous parents that schools were not slipping back into the questionable new math and whole-word reading of previous decades.

The Curriculum as Recipe

Every ten years or so departments of education release a redesigned curriculum for schools. Created by "experts" in childhood and education, the curriculum is intended to set out so-called "learning outcomes" for every grade from kindergarten to grade twelve. In true assembly line fashion, step-by-step subject areas are spelled out. The steps are designed in such a way that student progress may be tested along the way just to be sure that the *product* is shaping up as prescribed. The curriculum is like a recipe: put these ingredients together one by one, mix thoroughly, place in a mold, test frequently, and bake in a cheerless atmosphere for twelve years, and behold! a certified product, a high school graduate, will emerge. Perhaps Colonel Calverly says it best in Gilbert and Sullivan's *Patience,* just substitute *School Kid* for *Heavy Dragoon*:

> *Take of these elements all that is fusible,*
> *Melt them all down in a pipkin or crucible,*
> *Set them to simmer and take off the scum,*
> *And a Heavy Dragoon is the residuum!*[472]

In Canada, unlike in the U.S., the federal government has no say in curriculum structure or development. Consequently, each province develops its own programs and expected outcomes, though as one might expect, there are not vast differences from province to province in what goes on in schools nor are there great differences between what you would find in schools to the south. Dipping into various contemporary curricula one finds vague and imaginary goals for childhood learning. In Saskatchewan, for example, kindergarten kids are supposed to be "Experiencing a Sense of Wonder, Awe, and Joy,"[473] while school in Ontario will "set children on a path of lifelong learning and nurture competencies that they will need to thrive in the world of today and tomorrow." Continuing with such lofty objectives, we find that grade six students in Alberta "learn to think for themselves, revise their ideas and dig to find answers to questions that challenge them,"[474] and kids of the same age in Nova Scotia will be wondering "How and why do authors use foreshadowing/flashbacks/story structure to organize the plot of the story?"[475] Strangely perhaps, I have yet to meet the eleven- or twelve-year-old who is preoccupied with such notions, and doesn't school seem an unlikely place to encounter "Wonder, Awe and Joy?"

For a more detailed example, take a look at the very up-to-the-minute new curriculum from the British Columbia Ministry of Education. Described as "Concept based, competency driven," the updated curriculum, "informed by research and global trends,"[476] was "rolled out" starting in 2016 with kindergarten through grade nine, completing the process to grade twelve by 2019. The Ministry's website contains various colourful graphs and illustrations revealing the "Know-Do-Understand Model," which is based on "the generalizations, principles, key concepts and other important ideas in an area of learning,"[477] now known as the *Big Ideas*. (Anyone interested in seeing the graphics without having to read the text can find a dazzling array of them on a convenient website.)[478]

To quote from the actual curriculum:

> These big ideas are what students should understand by the completion of the curriculum for their grade, but they are intended to persist beyond a single grade and aid in future understanding. These are the concepts or principles that you want students to fully understand beyond anything else in the course, class or subject.[479]

Accordingly, each subject area has its age- and grade-appropriate Big Ideas. For example, in the field of English Language Arts, kindergarten to grade nine kids will be happy to know that "Language and story can be a source of creativity and joy."[480] For reasons unexplained, "story" becomes "text" from grade four on. In the field of mathematics, we find among other Big Ideas that grade seven youngsters will absorb the notion that "The constant ratio between the circumference and diameter of circles can be used to describe, measure, and compare spatial relationships,"[481] while any budding young scientist in grade one will find that "Matter is useful because of its properties."[482] Then advancing by grade nine to know that "The biosphere, geosphere, hydrosphere, and atmosphere are interconnected, as matter cycles and energy flows through them."[483] But let's not forget about the arts, where, throughout the grades, it will be hammered home that "Dance, drama, music, and visual arts are each unique languages for creating and communicating,"[484] though the details of these "unique languages" will be mostly ignored. These are but a few examples of the bewildering array of the Big Ideas that a friend of mine described as "like cotton candy."

To be more specific, here are what are described as "curricular competencies" to be mastered by grade six students:[485]

- Exchange ideas and viewpoints to build shared understanding and extend thinking
- Use writing and design processes to plan, develop, and create engaging and meaningful literary and informational texts for a variety of purposes and audiences
- Assess and refine texts to improve their clarity, effectiveness, and impact according to purpose, audience, and message
- Use an increasing repertoire of conventions of Canadian spelling, grammar, and punctuation
- Use and experiment with oral storytelling processes
- Select and use appropriate features, forms, and genres according to audience, purpose, and message
- Transform ideas and information to create original texts
- Express an opinion and support it with credible evidence

The language used allows for a great deal of flexibility. "Exchange ideas," "plan, develop and create," "an increasing repertoire," "Use and experiment," "Transform ideas," "express and support" are all terms that allow for a wide range of interpretations, but if you're a teacher, you'd better be sure that your kids will show evidence of having absorbed at least some of this gobbledygook ("cotton candy") by scoring well on the standardized test.

In spite of, or because of, the elaborate and professional-sounding lingo, the curriculum *limits* what the school is expected to teach and what the students are expected to learn. School then divides learning into "subjects" and each subject is allotted a "period" of time. Students are then kept busy with assignments, tests, and homework; individual interests and pursuits are discouraged. The goal of a "good grade" is paramount.

E. And Then What Happened?

The School Before School

Now consider the one-room school common to American and Canadian rural life of the nineteenth century. Here, all ages and grades were gathered into one school room where very young kids were given instruction together with older kids, all grades and all subjects taught by one teacher. Everyone in the schoolroom could listen to the lessons and recitations of all grade levels, though the concept of grade levels was not introduced until the mid-nineteenth century. Before that, students were sorted more or less by age and achievement. Sitting there at your desk or bench you would know what lessons were coming and which you had already covered. One former one-room school student recalled:

> In my early school years, I could always listen to the older students as they read new stories in reading class, often tales I had not heard before. They used new words that I didn't know or understand. Their history and geography classes opened my eyes to more new worlds. I was often fascinated by the poems my older schoolmates had memorized to recite in class. Time after time, those upper grade classes caught and held my attention. Again and again, they stretched my young imagination.[486]

Everyone played together and studied together, with the older kids expected to help the younger kids with their lessons and playground games. This system of instruction, similar to that employed by Pestalozzi's Gertrude, had been given various names, take your pick: "mutual instruction," "monitorial system," or "Bell-Lancaster method."[487] Older children would teach younger ones, and the abler pupils in these schools became helpers to the teacher, teaching other students what they had already learned. Method and a large part of content were left up to individual teachers. The quality of education was tied largely to a teacher's ability to function as a member of the community and to pass on skill and knowledge to a room full of youngsters. Much of what was taught would depend on the talents and interests of the teacher. If he or she knew music, dancing, or poetry, the children would learn music, dancing, or poetry, though reading, accompanied by spelling and penmanship, was always of prime importance. The textbooks of the time also offered generous servings of moralistic and patriotic guidance. Because the schoolhouse was also a centre of community activity, (It was the place where community meetings and socials were held.) parents were welcome and were often involved in day-to-day school activities, providing needed assistance to a busy and overworked teacher.

Before teachers were trained and prepared for teaching by attending normal school, there were few requirements for taking over a one-room school. The teacher could well be a young woman from a local family or a man or woman imported from elsewhere. Discipline might sometimes be harsh since there were few laws governing treatment of children. Nevertheless, the teacher's close involvement in the community and with families would have had a moderating effect.

> As an amusing and perhaps instructive excursion into one-room school discipline may I recommend a scene in which Mae West takes over a class of disruptive young men in *My Little Chickadee* (Universal Pictures 1940)[488]

Since attendance was voluntary, children entered school at whatever age, usually seven or eight, was felt appropriate by their parents. Work at home or on the farm would take precedence over school. As late as 1870, students attended only 53 per cent of school days, and little over half of students attended daily.[489] School was usually in session for only 132 days a year (compared with around 180 now.)[490] Summer holidays—still universally enjoyed by young people everywhere—were necessitated by planting and harvesting. Another former student

> Started kindergarten with two boys who were not as interested in reading as she was, so her teacher let her do the first-grade work, and the next year she moved into second grade. George Brassow (Lodi Plains, 1934-1943) was the only one in his eighth-grade class, so he moved at his own speed and finished all the work by February. (He stayed home the rest of the term, working on his family's farm.)[491]

What's important here is that the helter-skelter mixture of ages, abilities, and accomplishments meant that all children had to get along with each other and be part of a larger group. The teacher, usually a young woman, was also a part of the community, living there, often billeted by a local family. She would be well-known to everyone, joining into clubs and local events. Outside of school, boys worked with their fathers and brothers on the farm or in a local trade, and girls learned womanly activities like sewing, cooking, and child care at home. As mentioned before, many children were taught to read by their parents or older siblings, often from the *King James Bible*. It was expected that all ages would engage in political discussion and religious practice. Children were introduced into the dominant culture by the blending of family, school, and community life. Morality, manners, political thought, diet, religious belief, and worldview were passed down from adults to children.

Until the late nineteenth and early twentieth centuries, there was no such thing as evaluating students' performance by tests and grades. After all, the teacher knew each child and his or her family intimately and progress in learning could simply be discussed. The success of the student was the measure of the success of the teacher. If your kid was doing poorly in school, it was considered the teacher's problem, not some fault of the kid's. In those blessed days, there was no such thing as the standardized testing and grading that has now become an impediment to learning and pedagogy. As in all classical forms of education, there was a relationship between master and student.

Divide and Conquer

This began to change with Horace Mann's school reforms of the 1850s. Instead of having a mixture of ages and abilities as in the one-room school, he advocated segregating and separating students by age into grades through which they were to progress year by year. With the introduction of compulsory schooling, beginning in 1852 in Massachusetts, 1871 in Canada, more and more children were attending school, necessitating either larger schools or transporting kids by bus to a school in a nearby city. Separating kids by age into grades was a way of dealing with the growing school population. The days of the one-room school were numbered.

Admiral Seymoour School, Vancouver, BC
Built in 1904

Especially as people moved to cities, larger schools were needed and the grade system was a perfect fit for a big building divided into classrooms. Also promoted by Mann was the systematic training of teachers. State-supported Normal Schools, teaching "how to teach," didn't take hold in the U.S. and Canada until the mid-nineteenth century. Training meant that individual teachers would specialize in whatever grade they chose to work in. Thus, the primary grades teacher would have some special training in how very young children were believed to learn, and the upper grades teacher would know how to keep the class under control and doing what they were supposed to do.

The nineteenth-century egg-crate-model city school building drove wedges between ages of children and between adults and children. No longer would the older kids be helping the younger kids; no longer would kids of all ages be playing together, no longer would the kids be learning from their parents, grandparents, and aunts and uncles. The only adults that young people would know in school were teachers, who were now professionals, assuming a role of aloof authority, guiding and controlling. They were no longer members of the outside-of-school community. Parents rarely knew any teachers personally; the only time they might meet would be on a designated parent day or if summoned for consultation over a problem child.

The Efficiency Revolution

The August 1912 edition of *The Ladies Home Journal* opened with an editorial entitled "The Case of Seventeen Million Children—Is Our Public School System Proving an Utter Failure?" Perhaps the answer is right there in the question, but the author continues with a scathing condemnation of the school system of the day:

> Can you imagine a more grossly stupid, a more genuinely asinine system tenaciously persisted in to the fearful detriment of over seventeen million children and at a cost to you of over four hundred and three million dollars each year—a system that not only is absolutely ineffective in its results, but also actually harmful in that it throws every year ninety-three out of every one hundred children into the world of action absolutely unfitted for even the simplest tasks in life? Can you wonder that we have so many inefficient men and women; that in so many families there are so many failures; that our boys and girls can make so little money that in the one case they are driven into the saloons from discouragement, and in the other into the brothels to save themselves from starvation? Yet that is exactly what the public-school system is today doing, and has been doing. [492]

Though not the only opening salvo, the article is indicative of the kind of criticism that was being levelled at schools in the popular press, especially in magazines like *The Ladies Home Journal, McClure's, Atlantic Monthly, Educational Review,* and *Saturday Evening Post.* "which not only had circulations in the millions but were journals which catered to and were read by those middle-class groups who had led the progressive movement and had become reform-conscious in the preceding decade."[493] It was during the preceding decade that Frederick Taylor's notions of efficiency and scientific management had a firm grip on factory and machine shop labour, spreading to all aspects of daily life, including household activities, grocery shopping, and, of course, education. As early as 1902, no less a personage than Andrew Carnegie decried higher education in *The Empire of Business.* "In my own experience I can say that I have known few young men intended for business who were not injured by a collegiate education. . . . The fire and energy have been stamped out of them, and how to so manage as to live a life of idleness and not a life of usefulness has become the chief question with them."[494] In other words, the purpose of education was simply to prepare young people for a life of work, either as managers or labourers. The thinking was that anything else that schools might teach was considered impractical and useless. The emphasis was on making money, and education was to be the training toward that end.

In my experience, neither before nor since have schools come under such public criticism. And it was criticism that had profound implications, implications which still influence the way schools operate and the way education is defined. As Raymond Callahan in *The Cult of Efficiency* points out: "A less tangible but more important corollary of the practical movement was a strong current of anti-intellectualism which, when it was given expression, generally appeared in such phrases as 'mere scholastic education' or 'mere book learning.'"[495] We're all familiar with the "ivory tower" as a pejorative for intellectual or artistic achievement. In the November 2020 election, seventy-one million Americans voted to keep in office a president who was a supreme example of a populist (I'm just as dumb as you are.), ill-mannered, inar-

ticulate, sexist, racist boob, who is nevertheless praised as "telling
it the way it is." In 1980, Isaac Asimov, in *Newsweek,* wrote:

> There is a cult of ignorance in the United States,
> and there always has been. Anti-intellectualism
> has been a constant thread winding its way
> through our political and cultural life, nurtured by
> the false notion that democracy means that my ig-
> norance is just as good as your knowledge.[496]

As I've already pointed out and will continue to do so,
schools in the U.S. and Canada are trivializing education by trying
to make it *fun* as they focus more and more on job training rather
than scholarship, and ignorance rather than curiosity. STEM (Science, Technology, Engineering, Mathematics) is the latest wrinkle
in the fabric woven to create uniformity for schools and universities doing the work of corporations by training workers and executives while also producing a line of ready-made consumers.

The Latest Wrinkle: Taylorism

Frederick Winslow Taylor (1856-1915) was what today
we would call a "control freak." He was born to a well-to-do
Quaker family in a German Quaker and Mennonite suburb of Philadelphia. His father, Franklin Taylor, was educated at Princeton
and, as a lawyer, amassed a fortune dealing in mortgages. The
family had strong roots in the republic, going back to 1677 when
the Taylor ancestors settled in New Jersey. Frederick's mother,
Emily Anette Taylor (née Winslow), was a Mayflower descendent
and an ardent abolitionist. She provided Frederick's education until, as a teenager, he spent three years completing his education in
France and Germany and travelling throughout Europe. Upon return to the United States, he entered Phillips Exeter Academy in
New Hampshire, where he proved himself to be an outstanding
student. Though he later passed the entrance examination to Harvard, his plans to attend were cancelled due to poor eyesight. At

nineteen, upon his doctor's recommendation, he was apprenticed as a patternmaker and machinist at the Enterprise Hydraulic Works in Philadelphia. After completing his apprenticeship, he went to the Midvale Steel Company, where he advanced rapidly through the ranks, eventually becoming chief engineer.

This began his lifelong dedication to improving efficiency and production through what he later termed "scientific management." Using stopwatches and slide rules he analyzed the movements of workers in meticulous detail, with the aim of eliminating any unnecessary movements or pauses. He was particularly dismayed by the practice of what was then called "soldiering," which he described in *The Principles of Scientific Management*, blaming labour unions for telling their members that they were overworked and that "Under this fallacious idea a large proportion of the workmen . . . each day deliberately work slowly so as to curtail the output." [497] Highly skilled workers would be encouraged to slow down so as not to outdo their less-skilled co-workers.

Scientific Management in Action

Before Taylor came along, men in shops and factories each produced a product by fashioning the part, or sometimes the whole, of whatever they were working on. This meant that each worker was a craftsman skilled in his job. It also meant that work could be slow and uneven. In *Clockwork*,[498] a short film by Eric Breitbart, the parts of a machine under construction are shown piling up as work in one department was slower than that in another. We can imagine Taylor being driven to distraction by the sight of such inefficiency. He called this kind of work "rule of thumb" or "piece work," and determined to create a method and approach eliminating control of productivity by individual workers. This meant that management was to take control of all parts of the manufacturing process. After studying how each product was made and breaking that process down into a sequence of small steps (Here's where his slide rule and stopwatch came into play.), a manager would assign each worker a particular repetitive task, a task that would not require the kind of skill that was necessary for piece work. Without a need for skilled machinists and other knowledgeable employees, lower wages could be paid to workers who would simply repeat the same, usually simple, operation over and over. Though Taylor decried what he called the old "incentive and initiative" method of encouraging each man to perfect his particular job as best he could, he was not above offering an incentive of higher wages to the man who performed his assigned job most swiftly and efficiently. From many of his statements, it becomes obvious that Taylor didn't think much of the ordinary labourer. He wrote of "the development of each man to his state of maximum efficiency, so that he may be able to do, generally speaking, the highest grade of work for which his natural abilities fit him."[499] In the now famous study of pig iron carriers (See Breitbart's film for an illustration of Taylor's "scientific" plan of the work.) Taylor talks with a fictitious workman he calls Schmidt. In a few steps of inducement he convinces Schmidt that he can earn a higher wage if he will follow detailed instructions: "When this man [the manager] tells you to walk, you walk; when he tells you to sit down, you sit down, and you don't talk back at him."[500] He goes on to say, "With a man of the mentally sluggish type of Schmidt it is appropriate and not unkind, since it is effective in fixing his attention on the high wages which he wants and away from what, if it were called to his attention, he probably would consider impossibly hard work." Then, after describing the process of working out the "fraction of a horse-power a man was able to exert, that is, how many foot-pounds of work a man could do in a day,"[501] he describes the ideal pig iron handler as a man who "shall be so stupid and so phlegmatic that he more nearly resembles in his mental make-up the ox than any other type."[502] He does generously acknowledge that this kind of hard physical labour would not be suitable for a person of intelligence. As for a "person of intelligence," the new duties of management are grouped under four headings, the second of which tells us that managers "scientifically select and then train, teach, and develop the workman, whereas in the past he chose his own work and trained himself as best he could" and "they heartily cooperate with the men so as to insure all of the work [is] being done in accordance with the principles of the science."[503]

Scientific Management Goes to School

One of the most influential writers on education in the early twentieth century was Elwood P. Cubberley (1868-1941).[504] Cubberley was a professor of education at Stanford University and served as Dean of the School of Education from 1917 until his retirement in 1933. His *Public Education in the United States*,[505] though primarily created as a textbook for teacher training, is a detailed and meticulous accounting of the history of education and public school. Carefully reviewing many different theories of education he finally arrives at the latest developments of the twentieth century.

Unlike some current critics of the school system, like John Taylor Gatto, who say that the American school system was based on the Prussian military,[506] Cubberley says otherwise. He found that Horace Mann saw more of the influence of Pestalozzi than of Prussian military precision:

> The schools of the German States, with their Pestalozzian methods and subject-matter, trained and well-informed teachers, oral instruction, mild discipline, class organization, normal schools for teachers, and intelligent supervision, particularly won his [Horace Mann's] enthusiastic approval.[507]

He then makes it clear that Prussian education methods were not assimilated willy-nilly by American schools:

> That we at this time adopted the German *Volks-chule*, as has recently been asserted, an examination of the evidence will show was hardly the

231

> case. Not only did we not adopt its curriculum, or
> spirit, or method of instruction, but we did not
> adopt even its graded system. . . . The great thing
> we got from the study of Prussian schools was not
> a borrowing or imitation of any part or feature—
> our own development had been proceeding natu-
> rally and steadily toward the lines we eventually
> followed, long before we knew of Prussian
> work—but rather a marked stimulus to a further
> and faster development along lines which were al-
> ready well under way.[508]

As can be seen from Mann's description of the classroom,
quoted earlier, the teacher instructed by asking leading questions,
engaging the child's interest and curiosity, while encouraging observation of everyday surroundings. This was the Prussian version
of Pestalozzi's Rousseau-inspired ideas of child-directed education. Going back to Horace Mann's description of the German
classroom, the influence of Pestalozzi is obvious. His influence
extends all the way to John Dewey and even to A. S. Neill, who
would likely have agreed with Pestalozzi.

Cubberley appreciated Pestalozzi for his abiding belief in
human nature and the power of gentle and loving guidance:

> His elaboration of the thought of Rousseau that
> education was an individual development, a draw-
> ing out and not a pouring in; that the basis of all
> education exists in the nature of man; and that the
> method of education is to be sought and not con-
> structed, were his great contributions.[509]

> "What Pestalozzi tried most of all to do was to get
> children to use their senses and their minds, to
> look carefully, to count, to observe forms, to get,
> by means of their five senses, clear impressions
> and ideas as to objects and life in the world about
> them, and then to think over what they had seen
> and be able to answer his questions, because they
> had observed carefully and reasoned clearly."[510]

Though touched by Pestalozzi's ideas and work, and noting that "[He] had done a work of the greatest importance in reorganizing and redirecting the education of children," but at the same time, "all his work had been based wholly on observation and experimentation, and without attempting to measure it up with any guiding scientific principle." [511] But, fortunately for the sake of efficiency, those scientific principles were now (1919) available to schools.

> Within the past quarter of a century a number of new educational conceptions have come to the front which have already deeply modified our educational thinking and practices, and which promise to do more than any previous impulses to reorganize our educational work after a rational plan and to give scientific direction to our educational procedure. Within this period of time entirely new means of attacking educational problems have been developed through the application of statistical procedures, the use of standardized tests, and the devising of scales for the measurement of the intelligence of school children. [512]

With an unacknowledged nod to Frederick Taylor, we are told that

> The scientific purpose of the new movements has been to enable us to determine educational results quantitatively, and to make it possible for us to evolve, by the careful measurement of schools and children, a series of standards of measurement (measuring sticks for school work) and units of accomplishment (time and effort evaluations of instruction) which can be applied to schools anywhere to determine, scientifically, the economy or wastefulness and the efficiency or inefficiency of the work being done. [513]

Having read this, you will not be surprised to read:

233

Our schools are, in a sense, factories in which the raw products (children) are to be shaped and fashioned into products to meet the various demands of life. The specifications for manufacturing come from the demands of twentieth-century civilization, and it is the business of the school to build its pupils according to the specifications laid down.[514]

How far is this from Taylor's obsessive use of stopwatches and slide rules? And how would it apply to schools today? But, at the time, there was a new breeze blowing in the air of educational research, and Cubberley gives full credit to "The leader in this new movement [who] has been Professor Edward L. Thorndike, of Teachers College, Columbia University." This leads us directly to the behaviourism of B. F. Skinner and John B. Watson.

Edward L. Thorndike (1874-1949) was the first to perform so-called learning experiments on animals. This he did with puzzle boxes. This was a box rigged up in such a way that an animal (usually a cat) placed therein could only escape if a certain lever that would open a door were pushed. At first, as might be expected, the cat would try aimlessly to get out of the box, eventually contacting the all-important lever accidentally. After having achieved a few moments of freedom, the cat was placed back in the box where it would once again attempt to get out. After a number of tries, the cat would eventually associate pressing the lever with opening the cage. Like Taylor before him, Thorndike timed the cat's actions with a stopwatch and made graphs for how long it took the animal to repeat the action leading to escape—and to a reward of food. Thus a connection between a reward and a certain action was established. The cat's learning was not a result of observation or calculation but a simple connection between one action and another. This was Thorndike's *Law of Effect* which asserted that any behaviour that is followed by pleasant consequences will be repeated. And the opposite is also true: any behaviour followed by unpleasant consequences will be avoided. It's not a huge leap to see how this would lead to the idea of "operant conditioning," positive reinforcement as a means to get people, kids in school for example, to do what was considered good for them. We will see how Skinner's Teaching Machine broke learning down into incremental steps, a la Taylorism in the factory, rewarding each successful move along the way. Schools hand out incentive rewards like As and Bs on your report card or prizes for doing what you're told.

Taylor used initiative and incentive (higher pay) to motivate the drudge Schmidt mentioned above. After convincing Schmidt that he could be a "high-priced" man, that is he could earn $1.85 per day rather than the $1.12 he was now earning if he would work harder, he concludes with this bit of reinforcement:

> Now, Schmidt, you are a first-class pig-iron handler and know your business well. You have been handling at the rate of 12½ tons per day. I have given considerable study to handling pig iron, and feel sure that you could do a much larger day's work than you have been doing. Now don't you think that if you really tried you could handle 47 tons of pig iron per day, instead of 12½ tons?[515]

Though the idea of rewards and punishments as means of controlling behaviour has long been debunked (see Alphie Kohn and Daniel Pink) schools and some businesses continue along the fault lines, more of this later. For now, let's see how the ideas of B. F. Skinner are still reinforcing the use of rewards and punishments.

B. F. Skinner Is Alive and Well!

When I was a school teacher (1957-1967) I observed that much of what teachers talked about in the staff room was student behaviour, especially misbehaviour, and how to fix it. The actions of certain intractable youngsters were a special cause for dismay. The remedies proposed and used were usually some form of punishment, such as a good dressing down, after-school detention, threats of bad marks, and, in those days, the strap. One day, I proposed a "humane" solution to all these problems, and I offered my proposal in all seriousness—well, semi-seriousness. My idea was that every child's desk or seat should be wired in such a way that an electric shock of varied intensity could be administered by the teacher from a control panel on his or her desk. That way inattention or misbehaviour could be immediately punished and corrected. Would this not be more humane and more effective than the means currently in use? You will remember that these were days the operant conditioning of B. F. Skinner held out hope for longed-for improvements in learning and behaviour in schools. The teachers were horrified by my plan; they considered it inhumane and cruel, and so continued with the respected traditional methods, including physical punishment, that had been in use for generations.

The method that I suggested would be considered a form of classical, associative, respondent, or Pavlovian conditioning. In the electrified classroom that I proposed, misbehaviour and electrical shock were to become associated: stop one to avoid the other. It's safe to say that everyone has heard of Pavlov's dogs. (Does the name Pavlov ring a bell?) Ivan Pavlov (1849-1936) noticed that dogs that were brought food by their keepers would begin to salivate the moment they saw the keeper, even if no food was forthcoming. He then carried out various experiments, the most famous of which was getting the unsuspecting dogs to associate the ringing of a bell with the presentation of food. Pretty soon, the dogs would salivate when they heard the bell, food or no food. This is known as associative or classical conditioning. That is, a certain response is associated with a simultaneous unrelated stimulus until the stimulus alone will create the response. Imagine that I play a certain piece of music every time I give you pie and ice cream. Pretty soon you will practically taste the yummy dessert every time you hear that music. Or, the taste of pie will be music to your ears. (Remember *Shoofly pie and apple pan dowdy*? See above.)

John B. Watson (1878-1958) figured that psychology as a science was getting nowhere. Since scientific research meant measuring, weighing, and calculating things, he asked how can you measure and weigh love, hate, or fear. In a 1913 paper *Psychology as the Behaviorist Views It,* Watson laid out his theory that the only way to understand—and control—the human psyche was through the observation of behaviour. He dismissed all forms of introspection or other cognitive processes as being impossible to access and therefore irrelevant. As he wrote in his 1913 paper:

> The time seems to have come when psychology must discard all reference to consciousness; when it need no longer delude itself into thinking that it is making mental states the object of observation. We have become so enmeshed in speculative questions concerning the elements of mind, the nature of conscious content . . . that I, as an experimental student, feel that something is wrong with our premises and the types of problems which develop from them. [516]

Based on Pavlov's experiments, he deduced that all behaviour is a result of some kind of stimulus and that humans are born with a blank brain (Locke's *tabula rasa*) ready to be programmed by whatever might impact that brain.

In an appallingly heartless experiment, Watson showed that a small child could be trained to be terrified of something he was previously attracted to. This was the famous *Little Albert* experiment. The child, a nine-month-old boy, was presented with a white rat toward which he showed interest and no fear. Then, every time the rat was brought out, a loud clanging noise was made. It wasn't long before Albert associated the very unpleasant noise with the presence of the white rat, then becoming terrified of the rat whether there was a loud noise or not. This response was soon extended toward any white furry object, proving Watson's assertions of the nature of what he labelled behaviourism. In his popular advice-to-parents book *Behaviorism,* he goes so far as to say:

> Give me a dozen healthy infants, well-formed,
> and my own specified world to bring them up in
> and I'll guarantee to take any one at random and
> train him to become any type of specialist I might
> select—doctor, lawyer, artist, merchant-chief and,
> yes, even beggar-man and thief, regardless of his
> talents, penchants, tendencies, abilities, vocations,
> and race of his ancestors.[517]

Significantly, J. B. Watson followed his years promoting behaviourism with a successful career in advertising.

B. F. Skinner (Burrhus Frederic Skinner, 1904-1990) turned to what he called "operant conditioning." The difference being that instead of having stimulus and response happen at the same time, the stimulus, reward, or punishment, follows the behaviour. When the dog sits and stays as told, it is given a treat and, before long, sitting and staying follow the command, no treats required. Since behaviourism sees no difference between animals and humans, the same methods are applied to each, reminiscent of Taylor's view of the brutish workman. For the child who sits still at the dinner table or does her homework, praise or a promised treat is given. "Now, Johnny, as soon as you've cleaned your room you may watch TV." Undesirable behaviours are followed with a crisp punishment. "Suzie, if you don't stop whining you'll have to go to your room." It's easy to see how operant conditioning is still a favourite tactic of school teachers and, sadly, many parents. If you have doubts, look again at the "tips for classroom control," *ClassDojo*, and the gamified classroom.

One of Skinner's most celebrated achievements involved pigeons and ping pong balls. He did this by selectively rewarding, with a seed or two, random behaviours until the pigeons learned that every time they accidentally batted a ball with their beaks, they would get a bit to eat. Sure enough, it didn't take long for them to repeat the action that brought the treat. Behold, pigeons were playing ping pong! Well, they *appeared* to be playing ping pong. Of course, the birds weren't having fun, were not competing, and had no concept of playing a game, but in the minds of many people this demonstrated an effective method for teaching and learning. According to Skinner's 1954 paper *The Science of Learning and the Art of Teaching*:

> Once we have arranged the particular type of consequence called a reinforcement, our techniques permit us to shape up the behavior of an organism almost at will. It has become a routine exercise to demonstrate this in classes in elementary psychology by conditioning such an organism as a pigeon.[518]

Recall that behaviourists saw no difference between lab animals and humans.

Skinner's contribution to education was the Teaching Box and what became programmed learning. The idea was to break down every subject into small incremental steps and then—this was the innovation—reinforce each step with a reward. This idea was not entirely original with Skinner. Frederick W. Taylor and Edward Thorndike had pushed for incremental steps in factory production and teaching, each step to be analyzed and rated according to success or failure. Skinner's Box was a teaching machine that would not allow the student to progress to the next increment until the present one had been mastered. In the school setting, individualized learning was possible because each child would have his or her own box and could progress at their own pace. The units of learning were small, and success at each step was rewarded—or reinforced—with words of praise or the delights of being able to move to the next step. Blogger Audrey Watters calls it "Pigeon training with a snazzier interface."[519]

After considering the how ineffective existing methods of instruction that depend mostly upon adverse reinforcement, he concluded that

> The whole process of becoming competent in any field must be divided into a very large number of very small steps, and reinforcement must be contingent upon the accomplishment of each step.

239

And:

> Mechanical and electrical devices must be used. . .
> . We have every reason to expect, therefore, that
> the most effective control of human learning will
> require instrumental aid. The simple fact is that, as
> a mere reinforcing mechanism, the teacher is out
> of date.[520]

Skinner machine in action

The costly *Teaching Box* was soon supplemented or replaced by printed programmed learning textbooks or boxes of colourful cards all arranged so that the student would progress in the
prescribed orderly fashion. It's easy to see how the print and paper
method has become outmoded by flashy and stimulating "educational" computer games because, however flashy they are, games
encourage the player to stay engaged with, mostly, positive reinforcements. As usual, the whole idea is to get the kids in school to
do what they're told. But what's missing here? Frank Smith, in *The
Book of Learning and Forgetting*, reminds us that, "When psychology's grotesque convictions about learning came into classrooms out went any possibility that students might learn anything
about ethics, respect, loyalty, morality, honesty, charity, collaboration, compassion or care." [521] These are the matters of human existence that are learned from the arts, from music, from poetry, and
from drama.

PART FIVE

The Next Big Thing

STEM Invades the U.S.A.

STEM (Science, Technology, Engineering, Mathematics.) has crept into schools like a malignant tumour. It all started in 1957 when the U.S. panicked because the Russians had launched Sputnik, whose constant beeping from outer space reminded them that they had lost the race to get there first. Schools were blamed for not producing enough scientists and for drifting away from the efficiency principles so popular in the first part of the century. And the blame was levelled squarely at John Dewey. The application to schools of his ideas had become labelled Progressive Education. "Child-centred learning," "Experiential Learning," and "Teach the Whole Child" had become the watchwords of the 1940s and 1950s. Or, as put by Christopher Dawson in *The Crisis of Western Civilization*, "In his [Dewey's] views our purpose for education is not the communication of knowledge but the sharing of social experience, so that the child shall become integrated into the democratic community." [522] As citizens—or future citizens—of a democracy, children were to be considered individuals, each with their own interests and their own style of learning. The school was to offer materials that would stimulate interest and personal development. These were ideas that, post-Sputnik, were considered too soft. Progressive education was getting a bad rep.

In the late 1950s, when I was teaching grade five in California, the curriculum emphasized the westward expansion of the United States in the early nineteenth century. When the children first entered the classroom, they were to encounter various "realia," like a candle mold, a flint-lock rifle, log-cabin-building tools, period clothing, and pictures of pioneers, covered wagons, and the like. These items were expected to stimulate questions that would lead to further investigation. Once curiosity was aroused, learning could then happen through experimentation, reading, or whatever else might be on hand. The kids might try making candles out of tallow or building something with toy logs; they might sing songs and learn dances from the early days. It's not hard to imagine how

245

these experiences might lead to learning everything from reading and writing to arithmetic, although these would not occur in an orderly or planned, easy-to-measure, sequence. To facilitate learning the students would be organized into groups in which they would develop social and democratic skills. Music and art were important parts of every day in school. In such a child-centred classroom, top-down instruction was discouraged in favour of discovery. The child was to be seen as a free individual with his or her own aptitudes and interests, actively involved in learning.

Just as progressive education was a reaction against the rigid authoritarian teaching and testing of the efficiency movement, the back-to-basics Sputnik revolution of the 1960s discarded the flexibility and unpredictability of Deweyism. The emerging youth hippie culture and the failure of the United States to win the space race were blamed on everything from child-centred learning to Dr. Benjamin Spock's methods of infant care and child-rearing.[523]

In a speedy reply to Sputnik's beeping, in September of 1958, and just in time for the beginning of the school year, the U.S. Congress, with President Dwight Eisenhower, had passed the *National Defence Education Act*, which was intended to boost learning in science and technology in schools and universities by offering grants and fellowships to promising students and prospective teachers as well as giving financial support to state education systems developing a new hard-learning curriculum. No more mollycoddling with vague undefinable learning goals!

Riding the crest of the new wave was Rudolph Flesch with *Why Johnny Can't Read,*[524] dismissing whole-word reading in favour of phonics drill (champ, chop, chow, chip, chess . . .), and B. F. Skinner's step-by-step learning (with reinforcements), top-down instruction, competition, and regular testing. After all, if the brain starts as an empty vessel, as viewed by Watson and Skinner (thank you, John Locke), why not simply pour in the wanted contents and, *voilà*, a mathematician or scientist will be ready to go to work? So proclaimed Watson as far back as 1925.

However, not so fast! The 1960s had other things to think about: the Vietnam War, Martin Luther King, Rosa Parks, Alan Ginsberg, Timothy Leary, and all they stood for. The U.S. was too busy sending its young men off to be slaughtered, integrating schools, and dealing with a bunch of unruly kids to pay a lot of attention to teaching science. Nevertheless, the successful moon landing of 1969 and the ongoing Cold War between the U.S. and The Soviet Union created an uneasy feeling that American students were falling behind in science and mathematics.

In March of 1970, President Richard Nixon addressed the U.S. Congress on education. He began his speech by saying, "American education is in serious need of reform," urging a "searching re-examination of our entire approach to learning." To do just that, the *National Institute of Education* was created, in 1972, with a fund of $250 million U.S. dollars. But after carrying out a few rather ineffective studies, the institute was finally terminated in 1983. Hard on its heels came *A Nation at Risk*,[525] a report with more lasting impact, from Ronald Reagan's National Commission on Excellence in Education. *A Nation at Risk* deplored the state of education in the United States, citing dreary statistics on literacy (23 million Americans were functionally illiterate), an unbroken decline, from 1963 to 1980, in Scholastic Aptitude Tests (SAT), and a similar decline in science achievement tests taken by seventeen-year-olds in 1969, 1973, and 1977. Consequently, "The average graduate of our schools and colleges today is not as well-educated as the average graduate of 25 or 35 years ago, when a much smaller proportion of our population completed high school and college. The negative impact of this fact likewise cannot be overstated."[526] But overstated it was.

As one might expect, the commission concluded its report with a set of recommendations that amounted to the usual "It's not working so let's do more of it." Included was the set of Five New Basics: English, Mathematics, Science, Social Studies, and Computer Science. "Whatever the student's educational or work objectives, knowledge of the New Basics is the foundation of success for the after-school years and, therefore, forms the core of the modern curriculum." While the emphasis was on the high school years, education in elementary school ("effective study and work skills . . . should be introduced in the early grades . . .") was presumed to lay the foundation for the demands that lie ahead. And the demands were considerable: more homework, firm codes of student conduct (including segregating disruptive students), upgraded textbooks with "rigorous and challenging material," standardized achievement tests, and, if that weren't enough, school districts "should strongly consider seven-hour school days, as well as a 200- to 220-day school year." [527]

It turned out that more was less, because in 1998 came the next major step in this "strange eventful history,"[528] a report from the Committee on Science, titled *Unlocking Our Future, Toward a New National Science Policy.*[529] In the section on education at the K-12 level, the report states hopefully, "We depend on our schools, colleges, and universities not only to turn out scientists and engineers, but also to turn out the people who play the myriad other roles in the scientific enterprise that are equally important, if less visible." Once again, it is the responsibility of schools to crank out a workforce, a workforce that, in the nineteenth and early twentieth centuries was to fill offices and factories, but now laboratories and industrial plants. Well and good, one might suppose, but the situation turns out to be less than promising: "There are, however, growing indications that science and math education in too many of our Nation's schools is letting down our students." Sound familiar? Here, the committee cites some dire information from the Third International Math and Science Study:

> For the U.S., TIMSS revealed some serious problems. Although U.S. fourth graders did relatively well in both math and science, eighth graders sunk to the middle of the pack. By twelfth grade, the last year of mandatory schooling, U.S. students were among the very worst in the world, and in some areas, such as physics, were dead last.

So, the more schooling they got the worse they were. As usual, the solution is simply to toughen up and do more of the same:

> Curricula for all elementary and secondary years that are rigorous in content, emphasize the mastery of fundamental scientific and mathematical concepts as well as the modes of scientific inquiry, and encourage the natural curiosity of children by conveying the excitement of science and math must be developed and implemented.[530]

Around the same time, there appeared a similar report from the Committee on Equal Opportunities in Science and Engineering.

I believe that it was here that the acronym STEM found its origin, although the committee got it slightly wrong by declaring that "The National Science Foundation (NSF) has a key role in creating and maintaining the science, mathematics, engineering, and technology (SMET) capacity in this nation."[531] The rather unfortunate sounding SMET was rearranged, in 2001, by biologist Judith Ramaley to the more euphonious STEM.[532] (Now there's an acronym that teachers and administrators can get behind!) This report echoes much that is found in the Committee on Science report, letting us know that "America's awareness of the need for student achievement in mathematics and science has never been keener" and at the same time noting that the assessment of the Third International Math and Science Study "is a cause for concern." *La plus ça change, plus c'est la même chose.*

A more serious and ongoing issue about women, minorities, and persons with disabilities was pointed out in this report: "That minorities and women, who make up the large majority of the population, are underrepresented in science, mathematics, and engineering professions does not bode well for the country's future economic prosperity." The answer is "a number of programs undertaken by the National Science Foundation that focus on increasing higher level course taking, enrollment in science, mathematics, and engineering majors at the undergraduate level, and graduation from baccalaureate, master's and PhD programs in science, mathematics and engineering fields." The purpose being to increase higher-level course taking by the under-represented demographic.

We all know how girls are expected to be weak in mathematics and sciences in spite of modern Barbie's many career choices, but ethnic minorities and the disabled often end up in inner-city schools where, we are told by the report, that "students in high minority enrollment schools are much more likely to be taught mathematics and science by a teacher who does not have either a major or certification in the content area being taught." Thus, the prophecy is self-fulfilled.

An article in *The Guardian* reports on a study from the OECD (Organization for Economic Co-operation and Development). It's worth including a larger quote from this article about the difference between expectations and performance of girls vs. boys in school:

> The OECD's research found that girls do worse than boys in maths, and that boys come out top even among high-performing students, in countries that took part in the OECD's assessments of 15-year-olds.
>
> The OECD said: "What emerges from these analyses is particularly worrying. Even many high-achieving girls have low levels of confidence in their ability to solve science and mathematics problems and express high levels of anxiety towards mathematics."
>
> Yet girls were also found to have more positive attitudes to school in general, did more homework, more often read for pleasure and were less likely to play video games—so that far fewer girls than boys were among underachieving school pupils. [533]

The solution? "OECD study suggests school performance could be boosted by parents encouraging girls to consider careers involving subjects such as engineering." Do you think the situation has changed much or at all since this study was done in 2015? Even though Barbie appears in scientific garb she is still the supra-feminine model female, an unattainable ideal.

On a more encouraging note, you can read just about anywhere that STEM jobs pay a lot more than non-STEM jobs. According to the U.S. Bureau of Labor Statistics, the median salary (in 2019) in a STEM job was $86,980 whereas the non-STEM worker would have to make do with a mere $38,160.[534] But, according to the Smithsonian Science Education Center, there will be a multitude of openings in STEM-type jobs. Despite enticements, many of these jobs will remain unfilled:

> STEM-related jobs grew at three times the rate of non-STEM jobs between 2000 and 2010. By 2018, it is projected that 2.4 million STEM jobs will go unfilled.

The perplexing problem of minorities still exists:

> At the same time, minorities are deeply underrepresented in STEM fields—just 2.2% of Latinos, 2.7% of African Americans, and 3.3% of Native Americans and Alaska Natives have earned a university degree in STEM fields. This underrepresentation means that minorities lack qualifications to access STEM-related jobs, which, in addition to being more plentiful, are also better paid than many other jobs.

And it comes as no surprise that schools are, again, falling down on the job:

> Seventy-eight per cent of high school graduates don't meet benchmark readiness for one or more college courses in mathematics, science, reading, or English. [535]

And here's more bad news:

The Junior Achievement USA and Ernst & Young survey of 13-to-17-year-old students highlights how teens' career choices, educational priorities and economic outlook shifted over a year and how they vary by gender. According to the survey, while boys' interest in STEM dropped by 12 percentage points, girls' interest remained unchanged at 11 per cent both years.[536]

According to an article that asked "Why Is STEM Education Important?" *Stem Village* mentions that "Fifty-five per cent of students are struggling to meet the basic skills requirements in math and most students choose not to take electives or advanced courses that are required to continue on in a STEM-related field."[537] So, those 2.4 million jobs will continue to go unfilled.

But things are getting worse. The website ID Tech informs us that "it's estimated that 3.5 million jobs will need to be filled by 2025." But will those jobs be filled? The answer seems to be NO, "because people just aren't fit to fill such openings." Why?

Only 20 per cent of US high school graduates are prepared for college-level coursework in STEM majors.
Seventy-four per cent of middle school girls express an interest in engineering, science, and math. . . . But only 0.4 per cent choose computer science as a major when they get to college.
Two out of three US women say they were not encouraged to pursue a career in STEM.
Forty per cent of black students switch out of STEM majors before earning a degree.

And here's the usual answer:

The Department of Education recently invested $540 million in STEM education.[538]

As usual, the schools are called upon to beef up teaching, requirements, and testing in maths and sciences even though results have steadily declined and have not improved since 1958. It would seem that school does a good job of turning kids off learning of any kind, and the long-range lure of a hefty income and the prestige of being on the cutting edge are not enough to replace an intrinsic and individual interest in these areas of human endeavour, or whatever might be left of intrinsic interest and enthusiasm once school has done its work.

"Insanity is doing the same thing over and over and expecting different results."[539]

Which Child Gets Left Behind?

Then came the most colossal showing of bureaucratic blundering yet, or at least you would have thought that the recognized failure of schools to produce expected results over the past sixty years would have given someone second thoughts. On January 8, 2002, U.S. President George W. Bush signed the *No Child Left Behind Act*, dramatically increasing federal influence in education and requiring schools throughout the nation to demonstrate improvements in learning, known as "Adequate Yearly Progress"—or else!--the *or else* being accessibility to federal funding. The focus was to single out underachieving students, the usual suspects being immigrants (ESL learners), poor and minority children, and students in co-called special classes. These, along with any other stragglers, were to be brought up to a state-determined proficiency level. Of course, the upshot of the process was "Many A Child Left Behind." States could adjust what was meant by proficiency by creating curriculum content, especially in Maths and Reading (the subjects that were to be measured), in line with the median performers. Nevertheless, state-determined curricula had to have approval by a federal board, asserting federal control over education, and giving the president a higher approval rating by those who still believed that school was the answer to shortcomings in education.

Adequate Yearly Progress (AYP) was to be measured by standardized assessments, i.e. tests, administered annually to grades three through eight and once in high school. State education departments had to report overall test results and single out the sub-groups mentioned above for reporting. Any state that didn't meet the grade had to set aside funds for special individual tutoring and to permit students to move to a "better" school if they chose to. Some temptations are hard to resist, and state education departments could simply ease off standards of proficiency to make the AYP look better. Teachers were also on the hook to show how well their students were doing, so why not aim most instruction on what you figure will be on the test? Since maths and reading were big on the agenda, why not downplay other subjects like social studies, languages, music, art, and sciences that, after all, wouldn't count for much anyway?

Because, in 2014, it looked like at least 80 per cent of schools were not going to meet their AYP, President Obama introduced legislation easing some of the requirements of NCLB.

Nevertheless, the NCLB Waiver Plan gave responsibility for university entrance standards and teacher evaluation to the federal Secretary of Education. In a familiar-sounding trope, Obama said, "If we are serious about building an economy that lasts, . . . we have to get serious about education."[540] The result of all this "getting serious about education" was that standardized testing was to dominate the purpose of what went on in schools.

Testing for Profit

Creators, publishers, and scorers must have been rubbing their hands in glee because the dramatic rise in the demand for such tests would mean an equally dramatic rise in profits. Students were to be tested regularly throughout their school years, and big publishing companies like McGraw-Hill, Houghton Mifflin Har-

court, and Pearson Education stood poised to make massive profits. They were already publishing the textbooks on which the tests
would be based, so what could be better? A study done by the
Council of Great City Schools in 2015 found that pre-kindergarten
to grade twelve students took an average of 112.3 mandated standardized tests over those years. That's as many as eight tests per
student per year.[541] With the overall spending on tests being upwards of $4 billion per year, the profit window was looking wide
open. In fact, Pearson Education, which is a division of the Lon-
don-based conglomerate Pearson PLC and owner of the textbook
wing of Simon & Schuster, saw profits rise 175 per cent in the
years following *No Child Left Behind.* Peter Jovanovich, chief executive of Pearson Education, addressing a group of Wall Street
investment analysts, said (of NCLB). "This almost reads like our
business plan."[542]

Despite widespread criticism of testing and its value in
education, the U.S. government continues to require it, and
schools must keep the kids sharpening their pencils and scratching
in the little boxes on the multiple-choice tests. These tests have the
advantage of being easily machine graded, and you can be sure
there is money being made by companies that specialize in doing
just that.

There is also money to be made by tutors who will help
prepare your child to take and presumably succeed at the test.
Though these operations are aimed mainly at high-stakes university entrance exams, you can be sure that well-to-do parents will be
signing their elementary and secondary school kids for after-
school tutoring. After all, if "College Begins in Kindergarten,"
("No it doesn't!" says Sir Ken Robinson in his popular TED Talk,
Bring on the Learning Revolution.[543]) you'd better be sure those
kids are passing their tests and getting good grades from age five
and on. The test preparation industry, as it is now known, is a
market predicted to reach a staggering revenue of more than $30
billion by 2021.[544]

Though there are numerous companies, individuals, and
organizations offering *testprep* tutoring, the gold star for success

in this industry goes to *Sylvan Learning Inc.*,[545] a tutoring program with franchised centres throughout the U.S. and Canada. From between $40 and $100 per hour, you can have your child tutored, sometimes with up to two other students, at a Sylvan Center near you, but if you're on the STEM bandwagon, it will cost as much as $99 per hour.[546] The latest wrinkle is *SylvanSync*,[547] a digital learning system which provides lessons on tablets with instructor oversight. Apparently, they've got something that regular public schools don't have. Or, if the parents are paying for it the pressure is on?

A competing company, the *Kumon Math and Reading Program*[548] places more emphasis on drills and worksheets but is not as costly as Sylvan. In any case, the message of school is loud and clear: Fail at school, fail at life! So, if you really care about your children's future, you'd better make sure that they get good grades, from kindergarten on. Well, if you can afford it that is. Even Walmart is luring teenagers to stock shelves and bag groceries at sub-minimum wage by offering free prep courses for SAT and ACT tests. Who could resist?

Standardized Teaching and Standardized Learning

I've already mentioned the obvious pitfalls of standardized or high-stakes testing. And the stakes are indeed high when teachers are rated, and even paid, based on the performance of their students. Who wouldn't do everything in their power to see that their class scored well when the chips were down? It's not exactly cheating to play down those subjects that are unlikely to appear on a test and to drill on what will more than likely show up.

But there are many more shortcomings to these tests than any teacher could deal with. The very nature of a multiple choice or true-false exam is that there is no place for questions or ambiguity, nor is a test-taker able to find out and discuss why such and such an answer was considered correct or incorrect. Every question must have only one correct answer and choosing that answer has become the goal of teaching and learning. Maybe even worse is that the test questions were devised by an unidentifiable committee working for a major publisher specializing in test printing and distribution.

The problem is right there in the name *standardized*. This assumes that there are standards to which every school child should conform, which also suggests that there is such a thing as a standard school kid who will dutifully choose from A, B, C, or D and that the results will somehow be meaningful. Well, the results are meaningful, but only within the school setting. There is nothing in real life that resembles a multiple choice test any more than we write book reports on every book we read or ask for permission to use the washroom. School people talk a lot about how they are preparing our kids to be successful in the grownup world, but writing tests and studying for tests are far removed from the choices and trials that the grownup world has to offer.

Administering a test calls for an artificial manufactured environment. Desks are placed far enough apart so there's no chance of peeking at what anyone else is doing, there will probably be a severe monitor strolling up and down the aisles making sure that no one is dallying; the test will be strictly timed so you'd better not stop to think or daydream, no chance of responding to the call of nature, and above all, there is to be no talking, no asking questions, and no moving about of any kind. It's a structured situation guaranteed to produce anxiety in all but those who can be indifferent to the outcome. Anything similar to this environment can only be found in prisons.

In a *Huff Post* article, poet Sara Holbrook writes "I can't answer these Texas standardized test questions about my own poems." Indeed, her experience should tell us that understanding a poem cannot be reduced to a couple of questions to be answered by choosing A, B, C, or D. In her frustration, she writes, "These test questions were just made up and tragically, incomprehensibly; kids' futures and the evaluations of their teachers will be based on their ability to guess the so-called correct answers to made up questions."[549]

An article in *The New York Times* pointed out subtle and misleading inaccuracies in a test administered by *The Texas Education Agency*, the state department responsible for education in that state. Dr. Mark Loewe, a Dallas physicist, found that a question about the proximity of planets to the earth, while aimed at a typical ten-year-old, "Ignores the physical world woven into the question, and that might trip up brighter fifth graders." Other scientists and mathematicians pouring over tests found numerous ambiguities and misleading questions. Professor James A. Middleton of Arizona State University estimated that a quarter of the questions he analyzed had mistakes in content or context.[550] Though tests may be constantly vetted and improved by the committees making them up, errors are bound to creep in.

Speaking of the "ability to guess the so-called correct answer," it is possible to pass such a test using a fair amount of guesswork. In fact, it was reported in 2009 that New York sixth graders could, by guessing alone, score high enough on an English exam to avoid being held back a grade.[551]

With "15 secret strategies" offered by Complete Test Preparation, you can "Pass with the least amount of studying"[552] Admittedly, the standards are low, but what the hell! It helps to remember that the A to D or A to E choices are distributed in roughly equal amounts throughout the test so that if you marked every answer as B, you'd get at least 20 to 25 per cent of them right. Don't forget that those sneaky test-makers are out to get you because, in just about every set of possible answers, there is one distractor, an incorrect answer made to appeal to a student's naïve intuition. Knowing this will help you to choose answers that are less obvious. A more sophisticated approach, which we'll call "informed guessing," can be found on numerous websites offering helpful advice. *The Insider* offers four helpful tips to "outsmart any multiple choice test."[553] If you've seen Todd Solondz's 2001 film *Storytelling*, you'll recall the scene in which the teenage character Scoobie sits for the SAT. We see him filling in the spots on the test to spell out the words FUCK YOU, and we later find out that he has been admitted to Princeton. It's a fictitious joke that reminds us what a non-fictitious joke such tests are. But it's a joke with very high stakes for students of all ages. What it has to do with education is anybody's guess.

The game of testing has dire consequences. One is that only testable subjects, like reading and mathematics, can be tested. As mentioned before, this has led schools to emphasize those subjects while downplaying or eliminating everything else. This represents a serious shift in thought about the meaning of education. Learning must be reduced to a matter of questions and answers, and those only about prescribed subjects. The result has to be a tendency to slide away from ambiguity, asking questions, and following one's own interests. Test questions have to be concrete and specific. For example, one set of questions about Sara Holbrook's poem was:

> Dividing the poem into two stanzas allows the poet to— A) compare the speaker's schedule with the train's schedule; B) ask questions to keep the reader guessing about what will happen; C) contrast the speaker's feelings about weekends and Mondays; D) incorporate reminders for the reader about where the action takes place.

Aside from having little or nothing to do with the meaning of the poem, there is nothing—there can't be anything—about the reader's emotional or intellectual response to the poem. Emotion and feeling, therefore, don't count. Think of this: you can analyze a Beethoven symphony by parsing its key changes, formal structure, dynamic range, orchestration, etc., and you still will know nothing about how the players or the listeners feel about the music and why people go on playing and listening to it. Individual emotional response is impossible to explain in anything other than poetic or musical terms. And how do you measure that? Well, some researchers have measured physical responses to music by hooking up listeners to devices that would record their temperature, heart rate, blood pressure, and skin moisture (did they sweat or not?). Measurable responses, yes, but they don't explain the listener's or viewer's feelings and emotions any more than a standardized test can measure a student's interest or personal involvement in the matter being tested. What if every test also included the question: Were you interested in this problem, poem, or subject? Or: Did you learn this because it would be on this test?

Let's look at some other damages caused by standardized testing. Such tests are designed to make comparisons: school to school, teacher to teacher, student to student, and even student present to student past. The *Fraser Institute* publishes an annual ranking of elementary and secondary schools in British Columbia, Alberta, and Ontario, as well as a ranking of secondary schools in Quebec.[554] These rankings are based on standardized tests. The better the kids perform on the test, the higher the ranking of their school. It's not exactly a surprise that private schools and schools in the tonier parts of town rank highest. As we have seen, kids in inner-city schools generally do poorly on tests. Again, not exactly a surprise, considering that immigrant kids and kids from impoverished backgrounds may be ill at ease with the language of tests as well as the highly controlled conditions under which tests are administered.

As we know, the right-wing *Fraser Institute* favours private schools, because, as they are fond of telling us, private schools offer parents a *choice*.[555] Of course that's a choice that few can afford, meaning that parents with the means will move their kids from the rough and tumble of public school to the more refined air of a private school or a school on the "better" side of town. Starting with right-wing neoliberal governments, private schools have been receiving public funding, as such governments quietly push for privatization of schools along with just about everything else. The vicious absurdity of the *Fraser Institute's* school rankings and the intent of demeaning immigrants and the disadvantaged are all too obvious.

Comparing a child's performance on a current test with the results of an earlier test sends signals to parents and teachers. Supposing your daughter shows a steady decline in mathematics (as measured by the test), uh oh, we'd better do something. The prescription, as usual, is to do more of the same: teach and drill her more assiduously to improve her performance. In other words, apply the pressure. Placing singular emphasis on the demands of school ignores the interests, worries, and attention of the child. Imagine if Mozart had been given such a test, for sure he would have failed miserably because his mind would have been completely occupied by thoughts of music and, well, as we know from his letters, other less lofty matters. Having to sit for a test would have been an annoyance and a complete waste of his time, as it is for all children. Standardized tests serve the purposes of school, not of kids or parents.

The present and future achievement of any individual child or young person is going to be judged by a comparison with some kind of predetermined national standard. A great amount of effort is put into creating test questions that can be answered correctly by about 50 per cent of students. This is like setting the standard for the tippy top of the bell curve. Those who provide fewer correct answers slip off toward the left and the more skillful test takers occupy the right side. To put it bluntly, each test-taker is measured against a level of mediocrity, the kind of mediocrity that is prized by schools. If you end up too far on the left you'll be put into the dumb class or, maybe worse, be given some remedial teaching; fall too far on the right and you end up risking being classified and segregated as "gifted." Tests that are there to measure and judge school performance ignore the information and knowledge that kids have picked up from experiences outside of school. Can they really be said to measure learning or ability?

So what are the questions that kids are supposed to answer? Any number of websites offer help for test preparation and even give your kids a preview of typical test questions. The website of the formidable STAAR (State of Texas Assessments of Academic Readiness) offers dozens of previously-administered tests that reveal hundreds of mind-numbing questions aimed at kids from grade three through high school.[556] Try taking any one of these tests and you'll find yourself becoming impatient and irritated. If it can have this effect on an adult, imagine what it is like for an eight-year-old. Here are three examples of questions from the 2019 STAAR test for grade three mathematics:

> Serafina put a total of 42 cupcakes into packages. She put 6 cupcakes into each package.
> What is the total number of packages Serafina used for these cupcakes?
> Record your answer and fill in the bubbles on your answer document. Be sure to use the correct place value.

> Samantha, Gordon, and Diego each brought an ice chest to a picnic.
> • The weight of Samantha's ice chest was 83 pounds. • The weight of Gordon's ice chest was 28 pounds. • The weight of Diego's ice chest was 37 pounds.
> What was the difference in pounds between the weight of Samantha's ice chest and the combined weight of Gordon's and Diego's ice chests?
> Record your answer and fill in the bubbles on your answer document. Be sure to use the correct place value

> There are 18 spoons in a drawer. This expression represents the number of forks in the same drawer.
> 2×18
> Which statement is true?
> F There are 2 more spoons than forks in the drawer.
> G There are 2 more forks than spoons in the drawer.

> H There are 2 times as many forks as spoons in the drawer.
>
> J There are 2 times as many spoons as forks in the drawer.

My eyes glaze over and I want to run away screaming. Now imagine that you are eight years old and confronted with thirty-two similar questions. And you are expected to concentrate on such a test for four hours! Children are the only individuals in our society that are regularly subjected to such cruel and unusual punishment!

To rank a child or a school in, say, mathematics, test makers must create some kind of measurement of a child's understanding of numbers and basic calculations at what is thought to be appropriate for a given age. They must necessarily consider social, cultural, and economic backgrounds, assuming that the level and standard of instruction will be at least roughly the same wherever the test is given. A dicey assumption at best. This is a daunting task and test makers are but moderately successful. Given the questions above, can we assume that every child knows what a cupcake is, or an ice chest? And note "Record your answer and fill in the bubbles on your answer document. Be sure to use the correct place value." Huh?

Speaking of cupcakes and ice chests, years ago in a small remote community school, I was to administer a standardized test to grades six and seven. On this test, there were questions about the use of a telephone. These kids had never seen a telephone other than the payphone in its booth at the general store. Not one of them would have ever used the payphone let alone the desk-style phone that was pictured. The point is that whatever the questions or the context, putting children to the test will create stress, anxiety, and confusion. How, then, dare we give so much importance to test results? Or is the purpose to crush the child's spirit and turn learning into a chore? Tests are doing an excellent job of that.

Now imagine high school graduates faced with the SAT, even more stressful because they are well aware of the high stakes consequences. As we have seen before, preparation for the SAT has become a major industry, and that includes test-prep for elementary school kids. Standardized tests have now become the stepping stones toward success or failure in school, turning the whole notion of education and learning into an elaborate set of questions and answers. Or, as bluntly stated by Monty Neill, executive director of *Fair Test, The National Center for Fair and Open Testing*:

> High-stakes testing has narrowed and dumbed down curricula; eliminated time spent on untested subjects like social studies, art, and even recess; turned classrooms into little more than test preparation centers; reduced high school graduation rates; and driven good teachers from the profession. [557]

It seems so obvious that this is precisely what is happening, why do schools continue testing and placing so much importance on test scores? No one seems to consider that all this may not be a very good idea after all. Or, I'll ask this again, can it be that tests help to accomplish what schools are really all about?

Here is H. L. Mencken's explanation in *The American Mercury* from 1924:

> [The] erroneous assumption is to the effect that the aim of public; education; is to fill the young of the species with knowledge and awaken their intelligence, and so make them fit to discharge the duties of citizenship in an enlightened and independent manner. Nothing could be further from the truth. The aim of public education is not to spread enlightenment at all; it is simply to reduce as many individuals as possible to the same safe level, to breed and train a standardized citizenry, to put down dissent and originality. [558]

STEMing the Tide in Canada

Education, in Canada, is completely and separately under the control of each of the ten provinces and three territories. There is no Minister of Education in the federal government, nor is there, as in the U.S., a department of education. That is not to say, however, that STEM has not infiltrated into Canadian schools and that the usual lamentations over the shortage of STEM graduates and the multitude of unfilled STEM jobs are not heard in Canada as well as in the United States. According to the Dutch international human resources consulting firm *Randstad*, tech jobs are already plentiful in Canada and numbers will increase in coming years, so much so that "STEM jobs generally pay well beyond the rate of inflation and continue to increase."[559] But as usual there is a problem with demographics: "Women, visible minorities, persons with disabilities, indigenous people and immigrants are still underrepresented in STEM positions." On the brighter side, however, are U.S. Trump-style immigration policies that are slowing down Canada's "brain drain" problem (highly trained Canadian technicians moving to higher-paying jobs in Silicon Valley). Canada also has the advantage of not feeling a need to be *first* in the space race.

This is not to say that the government of Canada has not been involved, at least peripherally, in the promotion of sciences. In addition to the usual aquariums, zoos, and science centres, the government has held the Canada-Wide Science Fair every year since 1962, "bringing together the country's top young scientists in Grades Seven to Twelve."[560] Students who have completed an acceptable science project are eligible, as judged by a regional coordinator, to attend the conference as delegates and to display their projects. Awards, medals, and prizes are to be had by the most promising. There are also grant programs supporting science education that are available through government agencies like the *Natural Sciences and Engineering Research Council of Canada*. Various organizations like the *Canadian Mathematical Society* promote scientific ventures through competitions and prizes supported by provincial governments, universities, and corporate and private donors.

There are business-supported organizations that are promoting STEM education in schools and universities. A major one of these is *Canada 2067*, describing itself as "a national initiative to shape the future of science, technology, engineering and math (STEM) learning, focusing on kindergarten to grade twelve."[561] Among the sponsors and supporters of this organization may be counted such corporations as Samsung, Toyota, Best Buy, Rio Tinto, Chevron, Dow, and, yes, the Government of Canada. The National Leadership Conference, a project of *Canada 2067* and *Let's Talk Science*, was mounted in Toronto in December 2017, a "unique event [that] brought together diverse stakeholders—youth, educators, industry, policy-makers, community partners and others—with the shared goal of preparing Canadian youth to thrive in a technology-driven world for generations to come."[562] The organization also held a number of Youth Summits around the country (Vancouver, Calgary, Montreal, Toronto, St. John's), in 2017-2018, at which motivational speakers addressed "approximately 200" grade nine and ten students on STEM-type careers.[563] As I watched some of these speakers I felt uneasy at what I heard as a condescending tone: *kidtalk*. Words like "cool" and "awesome" are frequently heard. Nevertheless, the whole scheme was to inform and excite these kids about studying the STEM subjects which would lead them to engaging and profitable careers.

Canada 2067 has also laid out a Learning Roadmap which addresses basic issues around STEM education: teaching, learning, industry, government involvement, and inclusivity (women, minorities, indigenous people). Of greater significance, perhaps, is *The Learning Framework*. Here's where you will find out that there are questions about the readiness of Canadian schools to take on the job of preparing students for the STEM future—or at least the future that is envisioned by the STEM promoters. While Canadian schools appear to be doing well by international standards, there are still doubts about just how effective they are, and, as usual, there is more than a hint that schools are not doing enough:

"Are the skills youth are being taught the ones they will need to be successful tomorrow? Is there enough focus on key disciplines such as science, technology, engineering, and mathematics (STEM), which are particularly important in a world being rapidly transformed by new technologies?" And "the long-term success of any strategy for growth and innovation ultimately depends on what happens inside school buildings and classrooms."[564] Even though it's clear that it doesn't work, we keep on believing that teaching something in school will somehow have a predictable impact on children and society. The uncredited authors of *The Learning Framework* see that the decentralized school system in Canada creates a problem of tracking and evaluating nationwide methods and achievements. Though they don't say so, the implication is that a U.S. system of federal government involvement in education would be preferable.

Since computer technology is considered to be essential to future entry into the technological workforce, teaching computer coding to children seemed like a good idea. As far back as 2017, British Columbia, New Brunswick, and Nova Scotia have made coding a part of the grades one to six curriculum, but there is disagreement about the value of teaching coding because it is likely that artificial intelligence will make coding as obsolete as a typewriter within twenty years. Nevertheless, it is seen as a valuable *entrée* into the STEM world which promises the delivery of "twenty-first century skills" such as problem-solving, decision-making, leadership, and the ever-popular critical thinking. Critical thinking is another one of those things, also promised by video-game playing, that children ought to be taught. It's not a surprise that similar declining interest in STEM is found in Canada as in the U.S., as observed in a study by the Ontario think tank *The Mowat Centre* in 2019.

> While children seem to naturally gravitate towards STEM in primary school, when they reach their teenage years a perception that STEM subjects are too difficult, boring, nerdy or otherwise unattractive, seems to take hold. This results in many stu-

dents self-selecting out of elective STEM courses in secondary school, often because they don't identify with the stereotypes that surround these subjects or lack the self-confidence to pursue what they see as more difficult subjects. [565]

As in the United States, Canadian schools are also thought to be foundering when it comes to STEM education, and, I might add, just about every other aspect of what schools are presumed to be doing.

I think Ivan Illich put it right when he said "School is an institution built on the axiom that learning is the result of teaching. And institutional wisdom continues to accept this axiom, despite overwhelming evidence to the contrary."[566]

Standardized Testing in Canada

Canada's decentralized approach to education has made it possible to avoid the relentless testing of school kids so common in the U.S. Since each province and territory has control over curricula and testing practices, there is considerable variety. Nevertheless, it is safe to say that testing is not the be-all and end-all of student assessment. Above all, standardized tests are not used by schools to rate and compare students with each other or even with past performance. With the exception of the *Fraser Institute*, tests are not used to compare and rate schools to one another. Generally, a student's grades will be based on marks given by teachers, sometimes blended with provincial test results. In most cases, however, provincial tests are used only as a guide to the general level of learning in schools throughout the province. The number of tests administered through the school years varies widely from five (grades three, five, six, nine, and eleven) in Prince Edward Island to the optional one (for students not in the regular school stream) in Saskatchewan or New Brunswick.

The only national organization concerned with education is *The Council of Ministers of Education, Canada*, a body that was formed in 1967 to provide discussion, research, and advocacy on behalf of provincial education ministries. The CMEC also assists in the delivery and administration of the PISA (Programme for International Student Assessment). The PISA was devised in 1997 by the *Organisation for Economic Co-operation and Development* (OECD) as a means of assessing the state of education around the world. The triennial test, which covers the so-called core subjects of Mathematics, Reading, and Science, emphasizing one of these subjects in rotation, is given to fifteen-year-old students just completing their first years of compulsory schooling. The test itself is not compulsory and is not used to compare schools or students within the country. In Canada, the most recent test (2022) was taken by some 30,000 students in the provinces and territories. The 2022 test included "creative thinking as the innovative domain."[567] Test-takers are chosen at random with the hope of providing a relatively accurate sample. In my opinion, such tests do not provide much useful information and can easily be used to demonstrate that the school systems of countries that consistently come out on top must be the best and that their methods should be adopted by others. In this light, it's interesting to note that, in 2018, China was ranked number one in all subject areas. Does that mean that Chinese students are better educated or simply better drilled on test-taking, memorization, and following orders? Canada and Finland can be found among the top ten or twenty while the U.S., in spite of, or because of, its rigorous testing, is found lagging far behind. Aside from providing the occasional pat on the back for the successful, of what conceivable value could the test results be when it comes to any individual youngster and their intellectual development? An anonymously quoted primary teacher put it this way: "A good test score does not make a good school—or a bad school, for that matter," she says. "It doesn't tell you what your child knows or doesn't know—just whether they can write a test and follow instructions. It doesn't mean anything else."[568] What makes testing doubly strange and irrelevant is that there is nothing like it in the grown-up world of work, any more than (as I wrote earlier) there is a requirement to submit a report on every book you read. High-stakes testing is reserved for the world of school children, setting them apart from society in general, generating anxiety, perverting the purpose of education, and wasting their time.

Another Kind of Test

Standardized testing in schools is based on the assumption that learning can be measured scientifically, in the same way that height and weight or temperature might be measured and charted. This is a mistake made in other areas like psychology, turning what should be a philosophical and introspective study into sets of charts and graphs illustrating various "scientific" experiments. Now in its fifth iteration the Diagnostic Statistical Manual, first published in 1952, lays out lists of symptoms of an ever-growing array of mental disorders. For example, here is the beginning list of symptoms of Attention Deficit/Hyperactivity Disorder:1) Inattention, persisting for at least six months, and not attributed to developmental phase, which is manifested by:

- Lack of attention to detail, or careless mistakes.
- Difficulty maintaining attention.
- Lack of attendance when directly addressed.
- Not following instructions.
- Avoidant of tasks that require sustained mental effort.
- Frequently losing things.
- Distractedness and forgetfulness.

Sound familiar? I don't know anyone, including me, who does not display these symptoms. Maybe not steadily for the required six months, but enough to qualify. Small wonder then that an estimated 11 per cent of school kids have been saddled with an Attention Deficit diagnosis.[569]

Of course, this is only the beginning, but lists like this allow the psychiatrist to tick off observable behaviours and conclude that the patient is suffering from such and such a mental illness.

This places the individual child into a category that can be dealt with, well, categorically. The diagnosis can then lead to treatment (i.e. prescription drugs). The underlying assumption is that a person's mental and emotional state can be treated in the same way that one might treat high blood pressure or diabetes. How would Joan of Arc, Beethoven, or Charles Darwin have fared on the psychiatric or educational achievement test? Did Albert Einstein ever have to take a Scholastic Achievement Test? If he had, he would have made a poor showing. We already know that he was not much of a success in school and that he failed the entrance exam to the Zurich Polytechnic School. Surely Joan of Arc would have been diagnosed as schizophrenic and institutionalized (Waddaya mean Jesus told you to lead the French to victory? You must be nuts or something.) Beethoven "needed" Ritalin and the latest in hearing aids, and Darwin would be a likely candidate for bipolar treatment. Mother Teresa surely should have been prescribed Ativan, and Francis of Assisi was a candidate for electroconvulsive therapy if ever there was one. There is no place for saints in a digital culture.

By trying to turn intangibles like psychology and education into sciences, using laboratory practices similar to those of physics or chemistry, the experts have missed the point of meaningful human experience. It's like trying to measure love, virtue, truth, or religious ecstasy. I was watching a dance performance once, and when it was over the person next to me said, what did that mean? I said, "If you could put that into words, you wouldn't have to do the dance." Isadora Duncan put it this way: "If I could tell you what it meant, there would be no point in dancing it."[570]

Like measuring galvanic responses to music, as mentioned above, data can tell us nothing about learning, feeling, or growing up.

Now, people will say, "Don't you want your doctor to pass a test of medical knowledge?" Of course I do, and there is no question that entering a profession requires a certain amount of hard knowledge. But every doctor, engineer, or carpenter will tell you that they learned most of what they know by experience, by working with accomplished and experienced workers in their field. If I were about to have brain surgery, I'd want the surgeon to be well experienced and highly skilled in doing what he or she had to do. How many tests he or she had passed, what courses they had taken, or what grades they were given would be irrelevant. And let's remember that eight-year-old kids are not applying to enter a profession.

PART SIX

The School and Its Agenda

Is School Necessary?

The people who believe that school is the only place where education happens would say *yes* to this question. Historically, the people who believed that compulsory schooling would guarantee an enlightened populace would also say *yes*, and so would those who create curricula, legislate school attendance, and participate daily in what goes on in schools.

Should there be any doubt, proponents have felt called upon to proclaim the meaning and necessity of compulsory public schooling. As we have seen, reasons for school have varied over the years, but the arguments in favour proclaim that school will prepare young people for the vagaries of society and work.

In 1915, John Franklin Bobbitt, a former teacher and professor at the University of Chicago, was a champion of curricula that traded classical subjects for subjects that corresponded to the social needs of industrial society. He believed that people should not be taught what they would never use. Reflecting the efficiency trend of the time, this is how he put it in his 1915 book *What Schools Teach and Might Teach*:

> Both school people and community should remember that since schools are to fit people for social conditions, and since these conditions are continually changing, the work of the schools must correspondingly change. Social growth is never complete; it is especially rapid in our generation. The work of education in preparing for these ever-new conditions can likewise never be complete, crystallized, perfected. It must grow and change as fast as social conditions make such changes necessary.[571]

From the beginning, advocates of public schooling proclaimed the need for an adaptive workforce. After his visit to Prussian schools in 1840, Egerton Ryerson published *his* views on education. He reported:

The changes and developements [sic] which have been made in the arts, modes of labour, methods of business, systems of commerce, administrations of the Government, and indeed every department of civilization, involve the necessity and importance of a corresponding character in our whole system of public instruction. The same amount of skill and knowledge which would have enabled an artizan [sic] or a tradesman, or merchant, or even a professional man, to have excelled in former years, would be by no means adequate to success in the present stage of mental developement [sic] and of keen and skilful competition.

The state of society then, no less than the wants of our country, requires that every youth of the land should be trained to industry and practice, whether that training be extensive or limited.

Now, education thus practical, includes religion and morality; secondly, the developement [sic] to a certain extent of all our faculties; thirdly, an acquaintance with several branches of elementary knowledge.[572]

At least Ryerson allows a nod to "elementary knowledge."

Horace Mann was more of an idealistic visionary of the possibilities of education, though viewed from within contemporary society, there is a strong element of irony in this statement:

Now, surely, nothing but Universal Education can counter-work this tendency to the domination of capital and the servility of labor. If one class possesses all the wealth and the education, while the residue of society is ignorant and poor, it matters not by what name the relation between them may be called; the latter, in fact and in truth, will be the servile dependants [sic] and subjects of the former. But if education be equably diffused, it will draw property after it, by the strongest of all attractions;

for such a thing never did happen, and never can happen, as that an intelligent and practical body of men should be permanently poor.

Education, then, beyond all other devices of human origin, is the great equalizer of the conditions of men--the balance-wheel of the social machinery. . . . It does better than to disarm the poor of their hostility towards the rich; it prevents being poor. . . .The spread of education, by enlarging the cultivated class or caste, will open a wider area over which the social feelings will expand; and, if this education should be universal and complete, it would do more than all things else to obliterate factitious distinctions in society.[573]

Again, it would appear that school has missed the mark. According to World Inequality Report 2022,[574] 50 per cent of the world's population holds 2 per cent of the world's wealth, 10 per cent holds 75 per cent, and 1 per cent enjoys 38 percent. Mann's ideal of school has done little "to obliterate factitious distinctions in society." What does school have to do with this? A lot, as I hope to point out in the following pages.

Closer to home, the British Columbia School Curriculum 2016, sounds very much like Franklin Bobbitt of one hundred years previous:

Today we live in a state of constant change. It is a technology-rich world, where communication is instant and information is immediately accessible. The way we interact with each other personally, socially, and at work has changed forever. Knowledge is growing and information is changing extremely quickly, creating new possibilities. This is the world our students are entering.[575]

What goes around comes around! Comparing these statements, we see that schools must always be preparing the young for an unpredictable and ever-changing future. How they go about doing this is another matter. School bears little resemblance to the social and commercial world outside of the classroom. In a democratic society such as ours, people are free to associate with whomever they choose; they are guaranteed freedom of expression, even if their views are contrary to established views. In a representative democracy, officials who reflect the wishes of the public are chosen by election. This is not what happens in school.

Democracy is, after all, just what Winston Churchill called it: [T]he worst form of government except for all the others that have been tried."[576] A democratic society calls for an involved and thoughtful electorate. Are young people confined to school learning about the ambiguities and responsibilities of participating in a democratic society? In Canada and the U.S., fewer than 70 per cent of the eligible populace actually vote, and this number seems to be on the decline. You might think that eighteen-year-olds who become eligible to vote would flock to the polls. Alas, that is far from true. Fewer than 50 percent of eligible youth (18-24) have turned out to vote in recent elections in the U.S. and Canada. In other words, high school graduates seem to have little interest in participating in a democratic society. Shouldn't we see this as an alarming trend?

Instead of civic involvement, the reasons for sending kids to school, often demanded by law, were historically religious or military. These were the ends that determined what was to be taught. In Sparta, it was relentless military training; in Athens, it was Plato's ideal of an enlightened citizenry; for Martin Luther, it was so people could read the Bible; for the Prussian kings it was to quell peasant uprisings and to create an obedient military; for over one hundred years to today, it has been about creating a disciplined workforce by upgrading the lower classes, first for the factories and now for technology. What has always been passed off as "education" is the hidden and unconscious curriculum of obedience, competition, and ignorance.

I encourage the reader to go back to the beginning of this book and tell me if school does what it says it does. And if you agree that school is a failure at its advertised mission, then just what is it doing? So what is the reality of school? If it fails so miserably, why do we keep sending our kids to it?

School as Corporation

In her book on reading, Diane McGuinness invites us to consider a fictitious company called XYZ Corporation. This company has been entirely funded by taxpayers for over one hundred years, yet its fail rate is as high as 60 to 75 per cent. Everyone is required, by law, to buy XYZ's products, like it or not. "Not only was there a high fail rate, but the manufacturing process itself was toxic. It destroyed millions of people's lives. They were unable to get or hold a job, to participate in higher education, to get off welfare, or to escape the inner city, and many were sucked into a life of crime."

The XYZ Corporation acknowledged that there were problems and called for more tax dollars to create what McGuiness calls "product-recall schemes." This meant the hiring of multitudes of specialists, experts, and administrators. When that didn't work they "shifted the focus on the raw material, claiming it was flawed." So school shifts the focus onto the children, the raw material. They probably have bad genes, brain disorders, or learning disabilities. Some may even have mental problems like ADHD. These can be controlled with drugs or by calling on experts in learning disabilities or remedial reading. All of which will cost more money. And so it goes.

To complete the comparison with school, the author gives us a list of XYZ Corporate advantages that would apply to public education. Here are a few of them:

- Customer required by law to purchase your product
- No competition
- Unending source of capital
- No product guarantee
- Not accountable to its customers

- Cannot be sued for product failure
- Twice as many administrators as workers
- Two-thirds of revenues allocated to administration
- Worker training has little or no relevance to on-the-job skills
- Fifty per cent worker attrition rate every five years
- The workers' union is part of corporate management[577]

This is the organization that has a monopoly on our children. And you have little or no say about what goes on there; the operation is veiled in a cloak of very expensive bureaucracy. What recourse do you have if your child is miserable at school or learning nothing except how to tolerate boredom? As it says above: Not accountable to its customers. What do you know about education? It's under the control of *experts* at the university who claim to know way more about children and learning than you ever could.

Corporate ambitions are not easily satisfied, and saturation of the market is the goal. The "corporation" we're talking about is now insinuating itself, to an ever greater extent, into the lives of its "customers". It is now convincing us that the usual twelve years (mostly required by government) are not enough and that we'd better add more at both ends. At least, you should send your kids to pre-school (in Canada sometimes known as StrongStart) to get them prepared for kindergarten.

But preschool is probably not enough, so we now have daycare to take over ever younger children. Why stop at five-year-olds when working parents are going to need daycare that can start in infancy? Governments are even promising to support daycare programs so parents need pay as little as $10 per day to have their children managed and trained by professional child-care *experts*, who, as usual, know way more about babies and toddlers than you.

. After five or so years in those institutions, they'll spend the next twelve years working through the grades, finally ending with a solemn graduation ceremony and probably a drunken party or two. But, as the graduation speaker will tell everyone, this is not the end, it's just the beginning. Since a high school diploma is not worth much these days, a university degree will be the ticket to entrance into a well-paying job. The university, once for the pursuit of higher learning in the liberal arts and sciences, has become the path to higher-paying jobs and professions.

By the time you are considered ready to seek a job—or a *position*—you will have spent around twenty-four years in the corporation's institutions, meaning that you'll be well-schooled in the routines and beliefs of the system.

Promises, Promises

As quoted by Horace Mann speaking of schools he visited in Germany: "The people did not know any other way, and that all the children were born with an innate idea of going to school." [578]

Most parents send their kids to school without asking why. They do this because they believe that it is a necessary and valuable part of every child's growing up. It is what they call "education." "You'll never get anywhere in life if you don't have an education. Fail at school, fail at life," so goes the standard platitude. School promises success.

"Promises" being the operative word, I did a search on "Why should I go to school?" I found any number of websites proclaiming all kinds of good stuff that school is supposed to do for kids. I can't resist quoting a few of the more choice reasons given: I especially like this one: "Moreover, one will inevitably learn something throughout their years in kindergarten and elementary, especially high school and college," [579] It's nice to know that in sixteen years of school one can't help but learn *something*. Then there's the inevitable, "Qualify for jobs." [580] Again, the cant is that you'll never get anywhere without certification and unless you've completed the required years of schooling. Children are often asked, "What are you going to be when you grow up?" as though childhood is nothing but a training ground for adulthood.

"Social skills" is another one that comes up frequently. I've heard parents say that they want their kids to learn social skills by hanging out with kids their own age.[581] Doesn't this mean becoming part of a peer group or joining a peer-oriented culture with its own standards of behaviour, not those of a civilized adult society? What that has to do with developing social skills is beyond me.

> The Promises (I collected these from various websites):
> 1. School helps you find your major or "What are you going to be when you grow up?'
> 2. School prepares you for the real world.
> 3. You will make new friends and gain social skills such as networking.
> 4. You will learn how to become a useful, law-abiding citizen of the world, co-operative and responsible.
> 5. You will learn how to qualify for jobs by learning arithmetic, spelling, grammar, and how to use computers, calculators, and tablets.
> 6. You may participate in extra-curricular, after-school, activities such as football, dance, chess, math club, martial arts, floor hockey, drama, and many others.

Now look at what really happens:

1. School institutionalizes young people, effectively keeping them out of touch with the real world of work and professions. Opportunity to associate with working grownups is limited to immediate family and teachers. While confined in school, they will learn an idealized fantasy of careers that lie before them.

2. Yet school is nothing like the *real* world. School is more like prison, in which inmates are confined and kept separate from everyday society. In school as in prison, attendance is compulsory, rules must be obeyed, and ordinary functions like eating, drinking, and use of the toilet are strictly regulated. Quiet obedience and compliance are demanded and enforced. Segregation,

known as "time out," is a common punishment in both prisons and schools.

3. School segregates children into age and achievement groups where association with anyone outside of the designated group is rarely possible. In addition to their classmates, they will experience but a small number of adults (teachers) who are trained to act as functions rather than humans. Like prison guards (see above) teachers are not to fraternize with students lest they lose the all-important power to control.

4. Unlike democratic society, school is an authoritarian dictatorship in which arbitrary rules and regulations are enforced by evaluations, judgments (grades), comparison with others, humiliating discipline, and the threat of failure. Children are rewarded for being docile and compliant instead of being active participants in their education. Notice that you are to be "co-operative and responsible," rather than informed and questioning. Small wonder that 40 per cent of the population doesn't vote.

A young student activist had this to say:

> Every election, young people get to hear all the latest platitudes about the power of the youth vote. It's true that we're the largest voting bloc in Canada. It's also true that, as it stands, we have little faith in democracy. Youth don't have much real experience with democracy in practice. As we navigate traditional family structures and our education system, we're often taught to obey authority without question. Consequently, when we come of age, many of us aren't used to having ownership over our lives and our communities,[582]

5. The nineteenth- and early twentieth-century city school with compulsory attendance was modelled on notions of scientific management as espoused by Frederick Taylor. Accordingly, and following the logic of the factory, school turns learning into a chore, dividing academic pursuits into subjects, and each subject into gradient steps to be assessed at regular intervals by standardized tests. The curriculum, which determines what goes on and

what doesn't go on in school, reads like a recipe book: combine these ingredients in this order to arrive at a predictable product.

6. Teachers are discouraged from spending out-of-school unpaid time on extracurricular activities. What is offered will depend upon the availability and willingness of volunteer parents and others from the community, consequently not many schools offer after-school activities.

Teachers: Good, Bad, and Indifferent

School is an institution built on the axiom that learning is the result of teaching. And institutional wisdom continues to accept this axiom, despite overwhelming evidence to the contrary.—Ivan Illich [583]

I will start with five stories drawn from my school experiences:

1. As a grade five teacher in California in the 1950s, I wanted to have beautiful things, especially art, in my classroom. Luckily, the regional school district had a supply of various instructional items (known as "realia") as well as a few framed art prints. I was a great fan of Picasso's Blue and Rose Periods, so when I saw that they had one, I ordered it. As I recall it was one of the melancholic harlequin paintings. When it arrived, I was showing it and raving about it to a group of teachers; the only comment was, "I don't see anything good about that." By the way, the kids loved it.

2. At a teachers' workshop (a "professional" day, no doubt), there was a talk by a man who had written about and studied folk tales that were passed down through generations in Appalachian America. He told of the many stories about Jack of *Jack and the Beanstalk* fame and his many adventures. He also mentioned a story about a king who had three daughters among whom

he was going to divide his kingdom. There was no response when he asked if anyone recognized this plot. Well, that is, until I piped up with *King Lear*. Seemed obvious to me, but the other teachers showed not even a nodding acquaintance with Shakespeare.

3. This is something that happened to me when I was around twelve years old. I loved music, and I was showing considerable promise as a piano student. I also hated arithmetic. I should say that due to lack of interest I was defeated by matters like long division. I imagined a man somewhere fiendishly devising long-division problems especially to torture *me*. One day after school, I had been summoned from the piano practice room to one of the classrooms. I was told to finish my arithmetic assignment, "But I have to practise," said I. The teacher said: "Arithmetic is far more EEssential." (emphasis on EE) These words were stinging, making arithmetic even more baffling and impossible. I even came to distrust anything that was labelled *eessential*.

4. During the 1970s, I was working as narrator in Vancouver Opera's *Opera-in-the-Schools* program. Along with four singers, a pianist, and several volunteers, we would set up and perform a one-hour English version of a popular opera. Throughout the season, we did this at two different elementary schools every day. The audience consisted of eighty or so youngsters, grades four to seven, seated on the gymnasium floor. Strategically arranged along the outer walls would be teachers seated on chairs, supposedly keeping a watchful eye on their charges. More than once, various teachers would be observed marking papers, occasionally glancing up to make sure that no one was misbehaving, but showing no interest whatsoever in our performance.

5. At these presentations, the school principal would often introduce us, usually including a stern directive to be quiet and pay attention. There was one principal, however, who took the cake. He said to the kids—and I'm not kidding—"You're not here to enjoy this, you're here to *learn*!" That was a hard act to follow.

In their book *What's Wrong With Our Schools—and How We Can Fix Them*,[584] the authors give us four qualities of effective teachers as laid out by James Stronge in *Qualities of Effective*

Teachers. Here, with brief summarizing quotes are the four headings:

> 1. Personal and Professional Attributes: "Notably, effective teachers demonstrate a strong dedication to teaching, actively seek professional growth, and possess positive attitudes about their lives and work."
> 2. Organizational Skills: "... arrangement of the classroom ... " "... high priority to sustain students' attention and managing students by establishing rules of discipline ..." "... limit disruptions in their teaching and learning activities."
> 3. Instructional Skills: "They carefully link learning objectives and students' activities." "... prize student engagement, and they lead, direct, and pace their students' learning activities."
> 4. Evaluation Procedures: " monitor the progress of their students carefully ..." "assign homework and tests that clearly relate to the knowledge and skills that have been taught ..."[585]

You'll notice that there is no mention of intellectual, artistic, or academic achievement. It may even be that a knowledge of and interest in the liberal arts are not desirable qualities for effective classroom teachers. Studies in the liberal arts tend to make people questioning rather than directive, thoughtful rather than decisive, and permissive rather than authoritarian. I have written elsewhere [586] about public disdain for "intellectual" politicians. Teachers, like politicians, should be "just folks," good at what we want them to do and not asking too many questions.

We have all had teachers, some good, some bad, most indifferent. When I make derogatory remarks about schools or teachers, someone will always say, "I had some wonderful teachers." But when I ask how many, the answer is usually one or two. This would be out of how many? Maybe around twenty, depending on how often you moved to different schools and how the schools were organized. If you can agree with my numbers, this suggests a 2:20 or one out of ten success rate, meaning that the vast majority of teachers are incompetent, objectionable, forgettable, or mediocre. Not a great recommendation for schools.

Personal assessments are, however, mere conjecture. Let's look at some harder evidence: The U.S. *National Center for Education Statistics* reported SAT (Scholastic Assessment Test) scores for university applicants in various disciplines.[587] Scores are shown in three areas: Critical Reading, Mathematics, and Writing. Using averages of the three scores for comparison purposes, we find that intended education majors rank only slightly above various trades and below more traditional academic majors. Here are some average scores from 2009-2010 (the latest available) for comparison:

564	English Literature and Letters
562	Physics
549	Humanities and Liberal Arts
506	Visual and Performing Arts
481	**Education**
475	Agriculture
460	Consumer Services
453	Culinary Services
422	Construction Trades

In an article titled *Educational Ineptitude*, Dr. Walter E. Williams, a Professor of Economics at George Mason University, refers to retired Indiana University (of Pennsylvania) physics professor Donald E. Simanek, who "has assembled considerable data on just who becomes a teacher," and continues:

> Freshman college students who choose education as a major "are on the average, one of the academically weakest groups. . . . Some of the more capable who initially chose teaching will find the teacher-preparation curriculum to be boring and intellectually empty, and shift to curricula that are academically more challenging and rewarding." Simanek adds: "On tests such as the Wesman Per-

sonnel Classification Test of verbal analogy and elementary arithmetical computations, the teachers scored, on average, only slightly better than clerical workers. A rather low score was enough to pass. Yet half the teachers failed."[588]

We can conclude that teachers belong to a service rather than an academic profession. Their training consists of courses about *how to teach* rather than containing intellectual content. Of course, it can be argued that the hard knowledge content required for teaching elementary school, or even high school, is minimal. It's all there in the textbooks anyway. What matters is the teacher's ability to control, regulate, and organize. By now, you know I'm saying that control-regulate-organize is, in fact, the main message and curriculum of school. Hence, acquaintance with the liberal arts, the traditional subjects of classic education, is not required.

School teaching, like nursing or house cleaning ("the cleaning lady"), is a standard career choice for women, and, to this day, teaching, especially in elementary school, has remained the purview of women. There is even evidence that the ratio of male to female teachers is steadily dropping. Of the 271,200 elementary and kindergarten teachers in Canada in 2011, 84 per cent were women and 16 per cent men.[589] By 2016 the number had changed to 96 per cent women and 4 per cent men, a substantial change.[590]

There are many reasons for this, but it is easy to see that our society regards the care and rearing of children, especially little children, as woman's work. In high school, the percentage of male teachers does increase, to around 41 per cent[591] because, it would seem, teaching hard subject matter to older kids is a more acceptable occupation for men. Or is it because teenagers are thought to be more "difficult to handle" than younger kids?

Moving up through the ranks, we see that upwardly mobile men are more likely to become principals, supervisors, or superintendents than are women. This is a reflection of the gender stereotyping still common in our society. Though there are observable changes, especially in the corporate world, school is doing little to alter the gender separation in administrative and curatorial roles.

Whether or not IQ matters as a measure of intelligence, it's interesting to see where teachers fall in that regard. Similar to the ranking using SAT scores, elementary school teachers will be found in the middle or slightly below the middle. Writing in *The Elementary School Journal* in 1932, Superintendent R. V. Jordan was less than complimentary. About prospective teachers in Wisconsin, he noted that they "had a median intelligence percentile of 52 and that they might be described as 'run of the mine.'" [592] Perhaps there has been some improvement over the ninety or so years since this was written, but a series of graphs in a paper presented at the 2002 meeting of the *American Psychological Association* indicates that the IQ scores[593] of elementary school teachers fall in the range of average. That is, from a low of around 86 to a high of 125,[594] average being 100. This lines them up nicely with the professions shown by SAT scores above. On a more positive note, John Gerndt, a former teacher, answering the question "What's the Average IQ of a school teacher?" on the website *Quora*, says:

> You don't necessarily want the very brightest people teaching average people. Second, it's an indicator of how desirable the job is. Let's call it: the job generally sucks. Its low pay, low prestige, high responsibilities and unstable nature means only some sort of highly motivated, high ideals kind of person would walk that road. So teachers are not, on the whole, the best and brightest, so what? They are often really fine people doing a really tough job. They deserve your respect.[595]

The suggestion is that a person of above average learning, thought, and intellectual endeavour is not suited for teaching "average" students. But is it *average* that we want to maintain? We've already noted the anti-intellectual trends in society: the distrust of the "egg-head" who dwells in the "ivory tower," and is somehow out of touch with the real world. Is this what schools should be supporting?

Whether any of this is pertinent at all depends upon what you believe education should be about. Do we want our young people to rise above average or to fall into line with everyone else? Do we want them to ask questions and pursue their own interests or to stay within the limits of what school teaches?

I am reminded of a conversation I overheard. Two boys who were faced with entering junior high school (starting at grade eight) were worried about how they were to fit in. One said, "Just act normal," to which the other replied, "But not too normal." I assume that would mean that the goal is to be average, just like everyone else, don't be different. School sets the standard of mediocrity, with the teacher as the model.

Though the following could be said about any number of professions, an article entitled "A Study of Teacher Personality" M. Tschechtelin reports:

> In her study of personality of teachers, Barker [no citation given] found that members of the teaching profession were subject to the usual types of varieties of personality adjustments. She says, "Despite long years of training and experience there are undoubtedly many teachers in responsible positions who are immature, poorly adjusted, or even actually unwholesome in their personalities.[596]

Not a pleasant thought. Things may have changed since 1951, though I doubt it.

The Training of Teachers

There wasn't much thought of training teachers until the early nineteenth century when Johann Fichte recommended that Pestalozzi's methods be adapted to Prussian schools. Before that, tradesmen like tailors and carpenters were considered fit to teach children in schools, but as compulsory public schooling became more widespread, teaching, as a specialized profession, would require training. By 1830, colleges for training and certification were established in Prussia, and, as salaries were set by regulation, teaching was more and more regarded as a unique profession.

The United States and Canada followed suit as public schools were established in cities. The first state-supported so-called "normal schools" for teacher training were established in 1839 in Massachusetts. Canada, being a much younger nation, did not have such schools until the early twentieth century.

These schools provided approximately nine months of instruction in basic curriculum content and *how to teach*. Reference books such as the following formed the basis of the courses of study:

> Sears, *Classroom Organization and Control* (New Edition).
> Thomas, *Principles and Technique of Teaching*.
> Bagley, *Classroom Management*.
> Leunes, *The Teaching of Arithmetic*.
> Overman, *A Course in Arithmetic for Teachers*.
> Osburn, *A Socialized Study of Corrective Arithmetic*.
> [597]

The emphasis is on *how to*, though it would seem that arithmetic is the subject that prospective teachers needed to learn about.

Requirements for teaching have "toughened up" since the days of the normal school, and in most jurisdictions, teacher certification comes after a Bachelor of Education or similar academic degree, followed by a year or so of training and practical experience in the classroom (practicum). Secondary-school teachers may be called upon to show some specialization in the subject they propose to teach.

The courses recommended for the bachelor of education degree include such weighty subjects as educational psychology, child development, teaching methods, research methods, and early

childhood and elementary education. It is probably because of
these that education majors are regarded with a certain disdain, the
assumption being that these are easy or "cake" courses, well beneath the more demanding academic pursuits. It's not surprising
then that Professor Williams, again quoting Simanek, has this to
say:

> One of the very best things that can be done for
> education is to eliminate schools of education.
> There's little in the curriculum that contributes di-
> rectly to the development of the mind. Simanek
> says that "most teachers have learned 'methods
> and skills' of teaching, but don't have a solid un-
> derstanding of the subject they teach. So they end
> up 'teaching' trivia, misinformation and intellec-
> tual garbage, but doing it with 'professional'
> polish. Most do not display love of learning, nor
> the ability to do intense intellectual activity of any
> kind. Lacking these qualities, they cannot possibly
> inspire and nourish these qualities in their stu-
> dents."

Duly certified, with practicum completed, the novice
teacher now is ready to go solo in front of a class of twenty or
more young children.

Paradigms of the Classroom

You may have noticed that one of the attributes found in *The Qualities of Effective Teachers, Organizational Skills*, is "arrangement of the classroom," and among the normal school reference books you'll find *Classroom Organization and Control*, suggesting that appearance and seating arrangement are key to the management and control of students. As in the early days, teachers are advised to pay careful attention to the classroom setup. To lend a hand to the beginning teacher, there are quite a few helpful videos and articles on classroom management and arrangement that suggest various seating plans to avoid trouble and maintain control.

The familiar old standard desks-in-rows arrangement will probably still be found in many classrooms, especially in high schools. There was a time (I remember it well.) when the desks were fastened to long boards on the floor so they could not be moved. This was the layout of the classroom and there was no changing it. Like a military platoon or marching formation, the rows are straight, the students are facing forward, and the teacher stands in front, lecture style, in a position of authority. The disadvantage of this setup is that those in front receive more attention and will be more involved than those sitting farther back. Unless the teacher keeps a watchful eye on the kids sitting toward the rear, there will be a risk of inattention and off-task behaviour.

Modern desks are designed to be moveable and somewhat more comfortable. With desks no longer bolted to the floor, a variety of arrangements is possible, with change always an option. The row-on-row setup might be softened somewhat with a fan-like stadium-style arrangement, depending on the amount of space available, but the rows are still there. In a college lecture hall, you may see a similar fan-like arrangement with the professor's lectern or podium in the middle as the focus of attention. We can assume that these students are there because they want to be and will be paying attention. Elementary and high school classes present a different set of problems.

Contemporary trends suggest a casual, less severe-looking classroom. Variations include placing desks side-by-side or in groups of three or four, facing one another, to aid students in working together. The teacher can now move about with ease because there is no clear distinction between front and back. But if the kids are in such small groups, they are likely to engage in off-the-lesson conversation, note-passing, or exchange of meaningful glances. Hence it is vital that the teacher choose carefully who gets to sit with whom. This is best done once the personalities of the students are known. A lax and inattentive student could be seated with two or three dedicated ones, who will then set a positive example, etc.

The dangers of paired or group seating are to be handled tactfully, because:

> Since students are in partners, it can be more difficult to stop talking or off-task behavior. You may find that 1-2 students need to be "islands" and sit separated from a partner to do their best learning and maintain focus. Depending on how you present this, it can be stigmatizing for a student to have to sit alone.
> I found that it was really important to explain why the student was becoming an island when I made

this move. I also made sure to explain what he or she needed to do to become part of a pair again.

When any child is made to sit separately, parents should be informed of the "benefits for their child and his or her learning rather than the idea of this being a punishment." [598]

Among other possibilities, you'll find the horseshoe and double horseshoe shape enabling the teacher to stand in the middle and students opposite one another to engage in debate or discussion. There's even the teacher-in-the-middle, theatre-in-the-round setting, still aimed at creating a more or less casual, less tradition-bound image of the classroom.

Probably the most trendy and modern classroom will have students in flexible groups seated around tables in a homey living-room kind of atmosphere. The teacher may even be found sitting among the students distributing attention from table to table.

In the modern classroom, colour is all-important, so the floor might be carpeted in an attractive shade of blue, while tables and chairs contrast in a bright yellow. The walls will be adorned with pictures, mottoes, and examples of students' work, all planned so the children will feel at home and unthreatened. Dress will surely be informal or casual, with the teacher, as a friendly and cheerful leader (iron fist in velvet glove?), there to help the kids learn whatever the curriculum has determined.

But every arrangement poses its risks: of inattention and off-task conversation. No matter what the classroom looks like, the teacher sets the design and maintains control. With a room of twenty or more youngsters, a teacher has little choice but to focus on keeping them quiet and appearing to pay attention.

What Teacher Wants, Teacher Gets

In a famous study done by Robert Rosenthal and Lenore Jacobsen[599] strong evidence is presented indicating that teachers have higher expectations of students with higher IQ scores, even when those scores are distributed randomly. As one might expect, pupils to whom higher scores were assigned (again at random) received more attention and were regarded more favourably than those who were thought to be less capable. Students that teachers expected to succeed were given more time to answer questions, more specific feedback, and more approval in the way of smiles, nods, and pats on the back. Interestingly enough, the students that were thought to be more intelligent and were treated accordingly actually showed improvement in IQ scores and academic achievement. Maybe being *teacher's pet* pays off.

But that is just one aspect of teacher favouritism. A study by Jere E. Brophy[600] suggests that perceived racial or economic minorities are expected to perform more poorly and, consequently, are treated accordingly. As explained in a Clearing House blog:

> Without realizing it, teachers reveal expectations in learning opportunities provided. A teacher might set lower standards for historically low-achieving students or he/she might perceive various students' behaviors differently. A delayed response from a non-minority, more affluent student might be perceived as thoughtful consideration, while the same delayed response from a minority, lower-income student might be considered as a lack of understanding. These dif-

ferences in teacher behavior convey expectations to students, which can significantly affect their own behavior in ways that impede academic achievement.[601]

Like the hidden curriculum, no one dare acknowledge this or even be aware that it's happening.

Neoliberal Economics in the Classroom

How did a virtually unknown economic theory penetrate schools and influence the thinking of teachers and other educators? And *unknown* only because the word *neoliberalism* is rarely spoken. As George Monbiot, author of *How Did We Get into This Mess?*,[602] points out in an article in *The Guardian*, "Imagine if the people of the Soviet Union had never heard of communism. The ideology that dominates our lives, has, for most of us, no name."[603]

In 1938, at a meeting in Paris, the term *neoliberalism* was given to an economic and social movement that was created to counter the social democratic measures introduced in the United States by President Franklin D. Roosevelt (1882-1945). It will be remembered that Roosevelt brought the country out of the devastating effects of the depression by supporting workers' unions, creating make-work projects, establishing rent and price controls, and introducing social welfare programs. In short, government control of the economy and regulation of business. Of course, this meant higher taxes and less privilege for the wealthy. No wonder they objected! Neoliberal thought offered a switcheroo from growing equality to the inequality enjoyed by the wealthy one per cent today.

Backed by the super-rich with well-funded think tanks and lobbyists, the neoliberal ideology gradually took hold and reached its goals with the presidency of Ronald Reagan and the government of Margaret Thatcher in Britain. Backed by the Chicago School of Economics and its leading economist Milton Friedman the social democratic state was transformed into the competitive market-driven state we know today.

The basic principle of neoliberalism is that the economy is best run by a free and unregulated market, winner take all and last man out. Therefore, right-wing Conservative and Republican governments bring us deregulation, tax cuts benefitting corporate interests, balanced budgets, free trade, anti-immigration, competition, privatization, and efficiency or "cost effectiveness." For schools, this means competition for grades, relentless testing, and prepping the top students for university degrees in STEM and business administration while aiming the lower achievers at low-paying jobs. Those who end up on social assistance are written off as losers. Sickness, poverty, and addiction are disdained as "their own fault." How many times have you heard that someone dead of an overdose deserved what they got because, after all, they made the *decision* to become addicts? The idea of society as a community of people who care for one another is junked in favour of individualism.

Privatization of schools and other social services like hospitals, prisons, public transit, and telephones, are in the service of making more money for those who control them. Private schools offer what is known as "choice" to parents, choice is of course only available to those who can afford it. So-called research by well-funded think tanks provides press releases that look like their findings are actually news-worthy.[604]

Neoliberal policies have enabled corporations like *Walmart* and *Amazon* to take control of the market on the backs of underpaid labour while driving all competition off the board and thus undercutting privately owned businesses, reducing employment, and increasing the inequality that has given us the super-wealthy one per cent. A sad result is the undermining of social contact in everyday life. Instead of going to the local grocer or butcher where customers are known by name, and every purchase involves a friendly greeting and conversation (see Part One) people are enticed to big-box stores by the illusion of choice and low prices.

For such supply-side economic principles to be effective, a culture of believers must be created. What is needed is a well-trained population of ever- and over-consuming individuals whose spending habits can be manipulated by advertising and other forms of mass marketing, especially those bolstered by social media. They must be willing to assume crippling debt in the form of credit cards, education loans, and mortgages in support of rich banks and corporations. Success in competitive life is measured by wealth and possessions. Whoever has the most, wins.

School is the perfect place for such training to occur: everyone has to attend, success in competition is rewarded, individual interests are curtailed, and personal freedoms are non-existent. Children may be granted privileges but they have no rights. Authority is not to be questioned. As we have seen, high-stakes testing has become the only measure of success, and only those who are equipped to master the skills required are going to make it. Jessica Brathwaite sums it up nicely in an article in *Critical Sociology*:

> Neoliberal policy creates an illusion of meritocracy, where all students are perceived to have equal access to a high-quality education. Given this perceived equality of opportunity, poor outcomes are attributed to individual decision-making and not the state or any existing racial or socioeconomic inequalities. Good outcomes are attributed to individual merit and hard work.[605]

The idealistic goals of educators like Horace Mann, Heinrich Pestalozzi, and John Dewey were to offer equal opportunities to all by levelling the playing field of school so that every child could find his or her path to a satisfying future. Public schools were intended to create a democratic society with "Liberty and Justice for All." There was a time when we thought that any boy or girl, starting by selling newspapers, could become President of the United States or Prime Minister of Canada. It now takes wealth and privilege to aspire to such a goal. And, besides, no one sells newspapers anymore.

Idealism to one side, it didn't take long for compulsory universal schooling to be producing a disciplined workforce for the offices and factories of the late nineteenth and early twentieth centuries. Of course, there would be the high-achievers who were to become the bosses and managers of that workforce. There was money to be made. But that workforce isn't much needed anymore. We now have tech giants and powerful corporations that create and amass the wealth. The workers they employ in the few jobs they provide are taken by people without the certification of As and Bs, or by dropouts or recent immigrants. Only those who have acquired, often with crippling debt, a university degree in business or STEM may find a reasonably well-paying position that will enable them to acquire the cars, houses, and products that are the marks of success. Others will end up in poverty on some kind of minimal government support or on the street.

If school was there to create a just and equal society or even a disciplined workforce, it is now there to create consumers. The outspoken education critic Henry Giroux states bluntly:

> Under the current regime of neoliberalism, schools have been transformed into a private right rather than a public good. Students are now being educated to become consumers rather than thoughtful, critical citizens.[606]

And what could be better for this purpose than the standardized tests, textbooks, and lesson exercises that are produced *en masse* by four major publishing houses.[607] They even have a helpful newsletter *Educational Marketer*[608] showing that education is indeed a *market* where the big boys will win and the schools will buy in. So much so, that the test has become the determiner of what kids are supposed to be learning in school, and because teachers will be judged by how well their students do on the tests, they, too, have bought into the *education market*.

The neo-liberal creed of privatization has led to a proliferation of private and charter schools supported in one way or another by public funds as well as tuitions. Governments funnel money to these schools in a variety of ways: through direct grants, subsidized tuitions, vouchers, education savings accounts, and generous tax credits to individuals and corporations who subsidize schools with donations. As we have seen, though, the *choice* of a private school education is available only to the well-to-do.

If you can't afford a private school for your kids, you still have the "choice" of sending them across town to one of the "better" public schools. No need to throw them into the cauldron of immigrant, mixed race, and poor kids in the neighbourhood school if you live in one of the less prosperous but trendy parts of town. That is, as long as you can afford the transportation and the required wardrobe to match the fashions and tech hardware of the well-heeled upper classes. Christopher Tienken, a professor of education at Seton Hall University, looks at it this way:

> Education consumerism proponents allude that parents should be able to select their child's education delivery model as they see fit, regardless of the potential unintended consequences to democracy such as economic and racial balkanization or segregation. The message being sent is similar to telling parents that they should have the right to choose their schooling option like they can choose their fast food.[609]

Neoliberalism adopts the ideology of Social Darwinism, suggesting that the strongest and best-adapted people deserve to excel in society. In other words, survival of the fittest. The unrestrained free market will choose winners and losers.

The Disappearance of the Liberal Arts

Since the introduction of the ever-popular STEM, education systems have edged away from Dewey-inspired ideas of child-centred curricula including arts and music. Schools emphasize career-path studies instead of liberal education. A liberal education would mean a curriculum based on arts, music, literature, history, humanities, foreign languages, mathematics, and sciences as academic pursuits. We're talking about education as intellectual and personal development, not training for a job. This is in contrast to the belief that school should be preparing kids to follow a well-paid career path. "You have to do well in school if you ever want a good job," they say. Any study or training that does not lead in that direction will be derided as a waste of time. This is another lesson of school.

The universities complain that high school graduates are not prepared for post-secondary studies. This is not surprising if we consider that elementary and secondary schools are driven by two forces: STEM and high-stakes testing. These leave little room for liberal arts or traditional intellectual disciplines. And the universities, once known as communities of scholars, are now doing the work of the corporations by training future executives and technicians. In a speech given at the University of Toronto (Scarborough) Noam Chomsky said:

> There's, furthermore, no way to measure the human and social costs of converting schools and universities into facilities that produce commodities for the job market, abandoning the traditional ideal of the universities. Encouraging creative and independent thought and inquiry, challenging received beliefs, exploring new horizons, free of external constraints. That's an ideal that's no doubt been flawed in practice, but to the extent that it's realized is a good measure of the level of civilization achieved.[610]

In an article written for the web magazine *Truthout*, Chomsky reminded us of the hidden curriculum of school that has been there since the beginning:

> Mass public education is one of the great achievements of American society. It has had many dimensions. One purpose was to prepare independent farmers for life as wage laborers who

would tolerate what they regarded as virtual slavery.

The coercive element did not pass without notice. Ralph Waldo Emerson observed that political leaders call for popular education because they fear that "This country is filling up with thousands and millions of voters, and you must educate them to keep them from our throats." But educated the right way: Limit their perspectives and understanding, discourage free and independent thought, and train them for obedience.[611]

Elementary school curricula are still focused on training in secretarial skills like literacy and numeracy or, to use less-pretentious verbiage, reading and arithmetic; what used to be hand-writing, or penmanship, has become computer savvy and coding. Slice it however you like, it still adds up to job training.

Well, why do anything else? I'm suggesting that liberal education is about discussion, thought and, perhaps above all, curiosity. These are activities that are squeezed out by the urgency of preparing for tests and striving for good grades: As, Bs, and approval from the teacher.

There *has* been some concern and worry—I'm writing this during the COVID pandemic—over the fact that many kids were not attending school. The other day, I heard an interview with some high school students about how they were coping without attending classes. They didn't say anything about missing out on learning something, they were all afraid that they would not be able to get the good grades they wanted. In similar interviews, younger kids only cared about not hanging out with their school friends. School is about attaining certification or joining the peer culture. In a neoliberal society, these are the measures of personal development.

Not unexpectedly then, students entering a university are not ready for and probably not even interested in what we once called the "disinterested pursuit of knowledge." That simply means pursuing knowledge for its own sake, not because it will make more money for you. The universities have, accordingly, morphed themselves into institutions serving the needs of corporations and adopting the neoliberal ideals of competition and success in the marketplace. In a 2018 article, Professor Reshmi Dutt-Ballerstadt lamented the downsizing of liberal arts and humanities programs. She was writing about the trend characterized by the business-like sounding term "academic prioritization." The implication of this trendy-sounding euphemism is that college courses are to be "prioritized" based on market principles of who's buying.

> Silent alarms go off in our heads and red flags begin waving whenever the term is used, because we know such euphemisms usually mean departments that serve the public good, such as the humanities, social sciences and even some sciences like math and physics, are going to be sacrificed for a robust expansion of other job-oriented programs such as health sciences, business administration, sports management and various pre-professional and polytechnic programs that serve the market-driven, neoliberal interests and profit-driven model of education.[612]

And in case we need to be reminded of what we're losing:

> Indeed, higher education has become a business, and like in any business, there are winners and losers. The biggest losers are a generation of students who are being robbed of critically engaging with disciplines and materials within the arts, humanities, theater, music, history, religious studies and philosophy, political science, sociology, anthropology, and foreign languages. These disciplines have proven to contribute deeply to enhancing one's malleable intelligence, a sense of civic duty and social responsibility, and engagement in critical citizenship.[613]

The last sentence reflects what Emerson, as quoted by Chomsky above, said. Writing about the education of the time, Emerson went on to say:

> Our skill is expended to procure alleviations, diversion, opiates. We adorn the victim with manual skill, his tongue with languages, his body with inoffensive and comely manners. So have we cunningly hid the tragedy of limitation and inner death we cannot avert. Is it strange that society should be devoured by a secret melancholy, which breaks through all its smiles, and all its gayety and games?[614]

And here we have the triumph of mediocrity—the end of intelligence. When it comes to pliability there is nothing to beat a society dulled by shabby entertainment and the constant stimulation of digital media and sports. Remember *panem et circenses*[615] (bread and circuses) noted by Juvenal some 2000 years ago? He meant that the people could be lured by cheap entertainment away from civic duties as responsible citizens. A populace so lulled into complacency is readily available to a market-driven economy. Subject to the blandishments of advertising, they are the ready-made consumers provided by twelve years or more of schooling.

Grades, Marks, Rewards, and Punishments

Marking and grading students' work is one of school's most powerful and insidious methods of control. The compliant are rewarded with a false sense of accomplishment and superiority, and the non-compliant are punished with humiliation and the threat of failure. It is such an integral part of the system that we tend to assume that it has always been with us. It hasn't.

For thousands of years, the mentorship style of education that existed along with the one-room school was the way young people learned their trade, became literate—and educated. This had nothing to do with grades or the Grade Point Average (GPA) that figure so importantly in today's schooling. The mentorship style encouraged individuality and free thinking. What mattered was what you could do, what you thought, and with whom you had studied. The communal aspect of the one-room school was a part of this kind of education in rural communities.

In a book about the predominance of technology, Neil Postman notes, "To say that someone should be doing better work because he has an IQ of 134 or that someone is a 7.2 on a sensitivity scale, or that this man's essay on the rise of capitalism is an A- and that this man's is a C+ would have sounded like gibberish to Galileo or Shakespeare or Thomas Jefferson."[616]

The A, B, C, D, F grading system is so well established that, like compulsory school itself, we assume that it has been around forever. Of course, it hasn't and would have been irrelevant in earlier forms of education. The first, or one of the first, grading systems was introduced, in 1785, by Ezra Stiles, president of Yale University. It was a simple system using four Latin terms, *Optimi, second Optimi, Inferiores,* and *Perjores,* to rank students based on results of the exit exam. Other universities picked up on and expanded the idea. Number grades soon replaced the Latin descriptors. It seems that letter grades replacing numbers were first used by Mount Holyoke College in 1897,[617] but it wasn't until the 1940s that letter or per cent grades became common in public elementary and secondary schools. The concept was a good fit with the rising notion of efficiency.

When it comes to efficiency, the influence of Frederick Taylor cannot be overestimated. Grades, tests, and standardized curricula were readily adopted by schools as populations became urbanized, resulting in larger and more populous "egg-crate" school buildings with students segregated according to age and grade level. No longer were teachers part of a community, known by everyone and acquainted with everyone. Teachers were now professional *managers* who had to demonstrate control of large classes and show, by test results, the quality of their teaching, while maintaining standards set by school superintendents, school boards, and a growing body of university-based educationists.

Problems arose early on as it was recognized that not only was grading arbitrary, based on the teacher's judgment, but also that teachers tended toward "grade inflation," that is giving more high grades (As and Bs) than low grades (Ds and Fs), because *average* was getting a bad reputation. A way of dealing with this problem came in the form of the *bell curve*, which normalized grading by distributing marks such that the majority of students receive Cs, or average, which now had a scientific justification. The Cs at the top of the bell are followed by a small but equal number of students, on the downward slopes, receiving Bs and Ds, and, at the lowest point on each side, an even smaller number receiving As and Fs. This made a kind of sense because multiple tosses of coins arranged themselves very nicely on just such a curve. Scores on IQ tests also arranged themselves in such a way. If they didn't, the test would be revised so that they did. Assuming that there is a correlation between IQ scores and school performance seemed to eliminate, or at least reduce, subjective judgment by teachers. Using the curve also assumes that its predetermined distribution will be found in every classroom.

The *bell curve* was a scientific construct developed in the eighteenth century as a means of determining probability. It was then grasped by social scientists to determine normal or average and deviations therefrom. As with Taylor's scientific management, the *bell curve* demands that individual human characteristics be placed on graphs and charts as though they were randomly generated numbers or coins tossed with pass-fail on either end and the centre rising to mediocrity, reducing diversity to a simple average.

Writing for StateUniversity.com, Thomas Guskey and Howard Pollio summarize the justification for *bell curve* grading and tell us that its days are numbered:

> Grading on the curve was considered appropriate at that time because it was well-known that the distribution of students' intelligence test scores approximated a normal probability curve. Since innate intelligence and school achievement were thought to be directly related, such a procedure

seemed both fair and equitable. Grading on the curve also relieved teachers of the difficult task of having to identify specific learning criteria. Fortunately, most educators of the early twenty-first century have a better understanding of the flawed premises behind this practice and of its many negative consequences.[618]

In spite of criticism and various attempts to introduce alternative methods of grading, the bell curve is still used today. But of course you'll never know whether or not your school uses it. Here's a curious example from my teaching history. Kids in a grade seven class I was teaching were given some form of IQ test at the beginning of the year. Say two of them got top scores of around 125, five came in at 111 to 120, fifteen fell into the average category of 90 to 110, with the remaining kids distributed along the bottom at IQs of 79 to 89. So far so good—maybe. When it came to giving out grades these numbers were applied arbitrarily. Thus there were two As to be given, five Bs, fifteen Cs, and so forth, the grades bearing no connection to the individuals who got the various IQ scores. This left many of us scratching our heads, but the superintendent assured us that it all made sense, somehow. I would suggest that any form of grading on the curve is similarly nonsensical because it means that some students *always* must fail while a few others must get the top grades. Any deviations from this norm can be fixed by making the tests easier or harder.

When cast adrift from the secure and predictable bell curve, teachers are again faced with "the difficult task of having to identify specific learning criteria." Since universities and parents insist on letter grades, teachers are stuck with having to rate their students one way or another. Subjectivity is unavoidable. Guskey and Pollio, echoing the study cited earlier where students were randomly assigned IQ scores:

> Negative consequences result when subjectivity translates to bias. This occurs when factors apart from students' actual achievement or performance

affect their grades. Studies have shown, for example, that cultural differences among students, as well as their appearance, family backgrounds, and lifestyles, can sometimes result in biased evaluations of their academic performance. Teachers' perceptions of students' behavior can also significantly influence their judgments of academic performance. Students with behavior problems often have no chance to receive a high grade because their infractions over-shadow their performance. These effects are especially pronounced in judgments of boys. Even the neatness of students' handwriting can significantly affect teachers' judgments.[619]

I suppose that teachers can take consolation in the presumed impartiality of standardized tests. If we could assume that cultural and racial differences won't influence results or, if so, not enough to matter, test results can be used to guide the setting of final grades. However, do standardized tests actually measure learning, knowledge, intelligence, or responsible thought? Or do they simply measure the ability to take tests?

Parents and universities take letter grades seriously; kids are rewarded for getting As or Bs or reprimanded for getting Ds or Fs. No matter, because once the As and Fs are on the report cards, transcripts, and cumulative records, there is an illusion of impartiality, a belief that they mean something. The absurdity of this becomes obvious upon a moment's reflection: Because in school everyone is supposed to learn the same thing at the same time, no matter how demanding or difficult the subject matter, there will usually be a few who excel and few who fail, with a majority falling along the curve as percentages dictate. In other words, grading does not take into account the accomplishment or interest level of students, high or low. If too many students get As or too many fail, the problem may be that the teaching was too easy or too difficult, but it will more likely be attributed to the students; those on the bottom will be diagnosed with learning disabilities or psychologi-

311

cal problems of one sort or another while those at the very top will be considered "gifted" and given special treatment.

A pervasive notion among school people, fortified by neoliberal thought, is that competition encourages achievement. Therefore, they argue, every child who gets a low grade will strive to rise to a higher level; failure is assumed to stimulate effort to improve. Ironically, the bell curve determines that if one rises up a level another must fall. The flaws in this thinking are so obvious—even beyond those determined by the bell curve—that you would think, if schools were truly concerned with education, grading would have been abandoned decades ago.

In his Report on Education of 1845, Horace Mann warned about the risks of competition:

> If superior rank at recitation be the object then, as soon as that superiority is obtained, the spring of desire and of effort for that occasion relaxes. The pupil knows that the record, "perfect," set against his name, will stand whatever fading-out of the lesson there may be from his mind.[620]

Shouldn't we learn things because they are interesting and important to us, not to show that we are *better* than someone else or that we can *earn* approval from someone in authority? In other words, grades constitute an artificial measurement that has nothing to do with learning or the pursuit of knowledge. The competition that is encouraged is not about learning but about aiming for a higher grade. The As and Bs may get you into a top-ranking college or university but they, like the degree you'll end up with, are no guarantee that you've learned anything besides how to score well on the tests.

As we'll see, psychologists talk about intrinsic vs. extrinsic motivation. It's not hard to figure out that intrinsic motivation means doing something because it is enjoyable or out of a desire to satisfy curiosity and extrinsic motivation means doing something to get a reward. Striving for grades has nothing to do with real learning.

Reports and Report Cards

The semi-annual report card is the way you expect the school to inform you of your child's status or progress set against the school's standards. You may not know that the school also keeps a "cumulative record" of details about your child's years in school. If your child went to preschool, the record begins there and continues annually until graduation from grade twelve. If the student transfers to a different school, the record will follow. How long these documents are to be retained by the school varies from place to place, anywhere from five years to indefinitely. In British Columbia, for example, cumulative records are kept on file for fifty-five years(!).

What's in it and who can see it? The cumulative record contains anything relevant to your child's life in school and sometimes out of school: test results, grades, attendance records, medical reports, growth and development records, reports by any specialists involved (visits to a guidance counsellor for example), disciplinary records, extracurricular activities, and progress reports by teachers. Access to these records also varies. Access may be granted to parents (or legal guardians), school officials, university admissions departments, police, and unspecified others who may be deemed to have legal access or permission. Upon reaching the age of eighteen, the student is, or may be, allowed to see their own record.

When paper files were stored away in school cabinets They weren't so easy to retrieve, but with large digital repositories now storing records from multiple schools, access is available to anyone who can hack their way in, or if details are wanted, computer algorithms can sort out individual characteristics at the click of a mouse. An article in *The Atlantic* pointed out some of the dangers:

> Think about records of student activism being stored and made available to prospective employers when an individual applies for a job a quarter of a century later. Today past records are very

> hard to access, save for high-profile individuals. But in the future this information will be routinely accessible for everyone. And it may not be just "snapshot" data like standardized college admissions tests—it may be every scrap of data related to our progress as a student, from amount of sick days and visits to the guidance counselor, to number of pages read and passages underlined in Huckleberry Finn.
>
> Hence, the first significant danger with comprehensive educational data is not that the information may be released improperly, but that it shackles us to our past, denying us due credit for our ability to evolve, grow, and change.[621]

The permanency of the records means that they will follow an individual for life. Suppose you were a cutup in kindergarten, will this be a barrier to your becoming, say, a teacher or detective in later life? What if you belonged to a youth-action group or wrote an anti-authority article in a student paper? Will this cast a shadow on your future career or association prospects? Your performance in school will follow you for the rest of your life.

There was no need for anything like cumulate records or report cards in the days when schools were part of the community and parents were directly involved with training and educating their children. With the teacher as a member of the community, there could be open communication between parents, children, and the school. Within the school, informal records may have been maintained by the teacher, simply keeping track of what each child knew or had accomplished. Those records would not have been thought worth keeping beyond the school year.

As early as 1825, occasional school reports would be based on measurable accomplishments, like the number of biblical verses memorized or how many times you came up with the correct quotient in long division problems. Word would get around the community, so everyone knew who the top students were and who was lagging behind. It wouldn't have made much difference because those who weren't very good at "book larnin'" would have plenty of opportunity to be good at domestic and farm labours. Not only was "no child left behind," but every child was prized as an important part of the community.

The development of the large city school, with multiple classes and hundreds of students, meant that parents had less and less involvement in the school or indeed in their children's education. In graded city schools, teachers may have had as many as fifty pupils in one classroom. The only communication between school and parents would have to be some kind of written report.

As described earlier, the universities set the way for graded ranking of students. These grades were not directed at parents. Since the students were of age, there was no reason to enlist the aid of parents in getting sons and daughters to shape up. However, once elementary and high schools adopted recording and reporting student performance, parental participation was seen as important. Hence, the report card.

By the early 1930s, report cards with numbers, percentages, check marks, or letter grades rated a child's scholastic performance as well as matters like attendance, behaviour ("deportment"), and cleanliness. (I remember, around 1939, having to show that I had a clean handkerchief every morning.) Student progress in all areas (academic, social, personal) were graded in great, and sometimes cryptic, detail. Parents were left to figure out what the marks on the card meant, a problem that can still plague parents today.

Over the years, simple means like letters and numbers were not enough to acknowledge students' progress or lack thereof. The teacher was expected to provide a written comment, and space for this was allotted on the report card where explanatory—or *helpful*—comments, directed toward parents, could be written. These comments, from 1926, can be seen as typical: Mathematics: *Works well. He is still very untidy. He must try to improve in this respect.* Science: *He is keen & has a natural bent for science, but his work is badly spoilt by extreme untidiness.* English: *Without being lazy, he seems to do his work rather perfunctorily. I should like to see rather more life in him.* [622] Then, as now, it seems that

315

any positive comment must be tempered with a cautionary note, a bit of could-do-better-if-would-work-harder.

Since the advent of the internet, teachers struggling to write something on twenty or thirty cards two or more times per year will have no trouble finding help. *Education World*, for example, is ever ready: "Having a tough time finding the right words to come up with 'areas for improvement' comments on your students' report cards? Check out our helpful suggestions to find just the right one!" Apparently, comprehensive report card comments should indicate how well the pupil is meeting the character and behaviour standards as determined by the school. Ready-made categories and lists provided clarity. To be sure that nothing is missed, the teacher's comments should cover:

Attitude
Behavior
Character
Communication Skills
Group Work
Interests and Talents
Participation
Social Skills
Time Management
Work Habits

Appropriate comments are offered for each category. On the positive side, a student "tackles classroom assignments, tasks, and group work in an organized manner," or "demonstrates responsibility daily by caring for the materials in our classroom carefully and thoughtfully." [623] On the other hand, the "struggling" student, "has a difficult time staying on task and completing his/her work," "is not demonstrating responsibility and needs to be consistently reminded of how to perform daily classroom tasks," or "has a difficult time using the materials in the classroom in a respectful and appropriate manner."[624] Et cetera.

In the progressive times of the 1950s and 60s, letter grades were deemed too judgmental or harsh, not taking into account the psychology of the individual child. Consequently, many softer variations on the letter-grade report card have been tried more or less successfully. Hard judgments like Pass/Fail, A,B,C,D,F, and Could-do-better-if-would-work-harder fell into disfavour as the theories of Arnold Gesell (1880-1961) and Jean Piaget (1896-1960) were popularized by books, magazines, and publications about baby and child care. (Incidentally, it was Gesell who first had the idea that "You should get your child ready for school."[625] In other words send them to preschool.) Convenient lists of age-appropriate characteristics were readily available so that parents could check to be sure their child was on the right track. Growth could now be measured by checklists. This also meant that the school would now be taking an interest, and involvement, in your child's emotional, physical, and cognitive development. Simply counting verses memorized or arithmetic problems solved was no longer enough. In what has been called a "home-school partner-ship,"[626] parents are expected to engage with teachers in guiding their children to standards of normalcy.

The Center for Parenting Education provides a list of be-havioural characteristics for ages eighteen months to sixteen years.[627] Here are a few samples:

Typically, a 6-year-old:

- is expansive and out of bounds
- is dramatic and loud
- likes to show off
- can be very affectionate
- can be extremely enthusiastic and adventuresome
- asks a lot of questions
- is demanding, contrary or combative
- is competitive – needs to be the fastest, best, the winner
- may be aggressive
- is stubborn
- cries easily when hurt physically

- tends to fling clothes all over the house
- often loses shoes
- suddenly seems clumsy and uncoordinated
- may go through parents' private stuff

Emotions

- has a hard time dealing with any failure
- cannot bear to lose or be criticized
- loves to be flattered and praised
- can be ambivalent, may have trouble making choices
- is easily hurt emotionally

And by the time the child has turned twelve:

Typically, a 12-year-old:

- shows many changes for the better
- is less impulsive, more reasonable, more companionable, and shows better self-control
- can be more objective
- is more insightful
- doesn't want to be seen as a "baby" – works at being grown-up
- accepts correction and discipline
- can atone for guilt felt

Social

- can be excellent conversational company
- is friendly, out-going, cooperative, ready to please, spontaneous, positive and enthusiastic
- has a growing sense of humor, more cheerful, sociable
- is less naive in social relationships
- gets along better with all peers

- is influenced by the attitudes and interests of peer group
- shows empathy and can views things from the standpoint of others
- wants to win approval from others

School/Learning

- likes to learn
- shows warm admiration for firm, well-informed teacher who has sense of humor
- can work independently, but desires group activity
- seizes opportunities for discussion or debate of political and civic issues
- shows increase in conceptual thinking, in abstracts
- shows initiative (example: might start own newspaper)

But what if your twelve-year-old doesn't accept "correction or discipline" or doesn't seize "opportunities for discussion or debate of political and civic issues"? And what if your eight or nine-year-old in grade three doesn't like "asking and answering questions using details from the text" or "recounting/summarizing key ideas and details"? Or if your six-year-old isn't dramatic and loud" or doesn't love "to be flattered and praised"? Does that mean that your kids are not normal or are not shaping up? Parents and teachers might be dismayed, but since the kids had not read the books and magazines, they just went on growing and developing at their own rate and in their own way. Can intelligence be measured by a checklist?

Following in the footsteps of Arnold Gesell and his followers, schools devised similar checklists to assess a child's status in reading or any other school subject. Certain characteristics are set as "normal," and deviations are rated as "superior" or "causing concern." The terminology will vary, but checklists have become a convenient way to measure a child's progress in the various subject categories.

These samples are from School District 8 (Kaslo) in British Columbia and reflect a few of the details of the B. C. Curriculum. (The curriculum writers are fond of "competencies.")

Personal and Social Awareness and Responsibility (Core Competencies)
Competencies (Student is able to…)

- Use strategies to focus, manage stress, and accomplish personal goals
- Persevere with challenging tasks
- Identify when he/she is becoming angry, upset, or frustrated, and he/she has strategies to calm him/herself
- Interact with others and the environment respectfully and thoughtfully

Social Studies – Canadian Issues and Governance
Competencies (Student is able to…)

- Use inquiry processes and skills to: Ask questions, gather, interpret, and analyze ideas; and communicate findings and decisions
- Construct arguments defending the significance of individuals/groups, places, events, and developments (significance)
- Ask questions, corroborate inferences, and draw conclusions about the content and origins of a variety of sources, including mass media (evidence)
- Sequence objects, images, and events, and recognize the positive and negative aspects of continuities and changes in the past and present (continuity and change)

Science
Competencies (Student is able to…)

- Plan scientific investigation/inquiry

- Collect data and record observations
- Process and analyze data and information
- Evaluate the investigation
- Transfer and apply learning to new situations
- Communicate ideas, findings, explanations, processes, etc.[628]

The Ministry of Education in British Columbia has adopted its own terminology. Ratings that go from bad to good are tactfully named *Emerging, Developing, Proficient,* or *Extending.* In schools the *Emerging* student "demonstrates an initial understanding of the concepts and competencies relevant to the expected learning;" the *Developing* student demonstrates "a partial understanding;" the *Proficient* student "demonstrates a complete understanding;" And the *Extending* student "demonstrates a sophisticated understanding."[629] Throughout this document, we are repeatedly advised that the reporting is to be "strength-based," meaning accent positive rather than negative attributes. Your child's performance will be measured against the "Core Competencies"[630] that are given in the province's school curriculum. Letter grades "may" be given for grades five and above, though with a note of caution: "Traditional report cards (with letter grades) have been found to reduce motivation and diminish student learning. Assessment that is focused on student proficiency in relation to the established learning standards leads to improved reliability of assessment results and increased student engagement."[631]

A recent form of reporting, known as the "rubric" report card, lays out details of performance in wording similar to the comments above. You may recall that a rubric in a liturgical document is a side note, written in red, explaining how a certain action is to be carried out ("genuflect here") or for emphasis in a religious text. The somewhat arcane use of the term for a modern report card is evidence of an attempt to make things look more sophisticated and less judgmental.

In the *3rd Grade Reading Rubric, Lapeer Community Schools, District of Ottawa,*[632] each subject is broken into components. Grade three reading, for example, contains Phonics and Word Recognition, Reading Fluency, Comprehension, Literary Analysis, and Independent Reading. In each component the student is rated under four categories:

> 4. Exceeding (Above grade level);
> 3. Meeting (At grade level);
> 2. Developing (Below grade level),
> 1. Area of concern (Below grade level).

Notice how the numbers 4 to 1 are in the reverse order from the usual expectation of number "1." being on top. Could this be to illustrate the departure from the musty old-style ratings? At least if your kid is a disaster at school, you can say that he got a One!

Under each of the four-to-one categories will be found descriptive details. These samples are from *Comprehension*.

> 4 Exceeding:

> Consistently demonstrates understanding
> of above-level texts by:
> • asking and answering questions,
> using details from the text;
> • recounting/summarizing key ideas
> and details
> • using text features
> • determining central message or
> theme

The "rubrics" continue in less-flattering terms down to poor *1. Area of Concern*, who is summarily dismissed with:

> Student rarely meets the expectations
> for this trimester.
> Uses minimal, incorrect, or unrelated
> information; misinterprets message or
> information from text.

In many school districts, the rubric report card and variations on it have superseded letter-grade ratings, leaving many parents flummoxed as to just where their child stands. The Ministries of Education tell us that the report card is a way to inform parents of how the kids are doing in school, but as that's not enough, parents will be called to confer with the teacher at least once a year. This is when parents will be given *expert* advice on how to "cooperate" with the teacher to keep the kids toeing the line. Whether this is helpful or not may be open to question. If you found the report card confusing, you may have trouble deciphering statements like, "Kevin has good observations and is eager to share them in class, but he has a lot of trouble waiting his turn to speak." In other words, "Your kid is a nuisance because he won't shut up." Or "Michelle's not shy, but she gets upset and anxious when I call on her in class or ask her to read out loud. I'd like to add her to our response to intervention (RTI) program,"[633] meaning "Your kid has psychological problems and I'm calling in the shrinks." Of course I'm joking, but you'll find that remarks from teachers are cloaked in educational jargon or *teacherese*. However, given the litigious tendencies of some parents, you can hardly blame the teacher for being careful.

The report card and the teacher conference are there to extend the school's influence beyond the classroom and to keep parents working for what is to be perceived as the child's benefit. The goal is normalcy or average. "Just act normal. But not too normal."

A More Subtle Punishment

"In the middle of the last century, two young scientists conducted experiments that should have changed the world—but did not."[634] Daniel Pink is talking about Harry F. Harlow (1905-1981) and Donald R. Meyer. Harlow was an experimental psychologist known for his work with rhesus monkeys, on maternal dependency, but the experiments that "should have changed the world" were carried out to see how a food reward would influence performance in a puzzle-solving test.[635] The monkeys were first given puzzle devices which involved a series of manipulations leading to the opening of a compartment. In the first part of the experiment, the monkeys were simply given the devices and their actions were carefully recorded. It was noted that the animals showed considerable curiosity over the puzzles, played with them until they could open the compartment, then repeated the operation numerous times, showing a lively interest in the process of manipulation. In the second part of the experiment, the monkeys were shown that a few raisins were stashed in the compartment and could be retrieved by again solving the puzzle and opening the box. What happened was that the monkeys appeared to lose interest in the process of solving the puzzle. They now made many more errors and soon abandoned the puzzles. "Subsequent introduction of food in the puzzle situation tended to disrupt, not facilitate, the learned performance of the experimental subjects."[636] Often to the surprise of the researchers, countless other studies have shown that the promise of rewards tends to have an adverse effect upon performance.

What does the Harlow experiment suggest in the matter of using rewards—gold stars, praise, As and Bs—for enhancing performance? It suggests that the promise of a reward is no better than the threat of punishment when it comes to getting someone to do what you want them to do. In school, the praise and criticism handed out in the form of grades, good or bad, and privileges, granted or withheld, focuses attention on performance and away from the goal— "To offer a prize for doing a deed is tantamount to declaring that the deed is not worth doing for its own sake"[637]— and offers the dubious motivation of knowing that you are either better or worse than your fellow students. In a book "that should have changed the world—but did not," Alfie Kohn puts it this way:

The truth is that the problem is not just punishments but also rewards, not bad grades but the emphasis on grading per se. Anything that gets children to think primarily about their performance will undermine their interest in learning, their desire to be challenged, and ultimately the extent of the achievement. Small wonder that rewards have precisely those effects.[638]

Isn't there an ethical issue here as well? How can we justify trying to manipulate another person's thinking and behaviour by offering a reward or threatening punishment? Is there a difference? Either way, the focus is on striving for the reward or avoiding the punishment, and the content of the so-called lesson fades in importance. Further to that, Kohn observes:

The underlying principle can be summarized this way: *when we are working for a reward, we do exactly what is necessary to get it and no more.* Not only are we less apt to notice peripheral features of the task, but in performing it we are less likely to take chances, play with possibilities, follow hunches that might not pay off. Risks are to be avoided whenever possible because the objective is not to engage in an open-ended encounter with ideas; it is simply to get the goody.[639]

Is there a better way to discourage curiosity?

Harlow's experiment with monkeys prompted many researchers to carry out studies comparing the results of extrinsic vs. intrinsic motivation. Does the introduction of a reward increase or decrease interest and quality of performance in a given task? Almost universally both interest and quality were seen to decrease when an activity was carried out with the aim of achieving a reward of some sort, be it good grades, money, treats, or congratulatory approval.

The phenomenon was dramatically demonstrated in a study at Stanford University with a group of little kids in a campus preschool.[640] Some fifty-five children who had shown an interest in drawing were selected to participate. Having agreed to take part in a "fun activity," they were divided into three groups and then invited to come to a "surprise room" where magic markers and drawing paper were laid out on a table. One group was offered a prize for good work in the form of a certificate, introduced by the experimenter, who said, "It's got a big gold star and a bright red ribbon, and there's a place here for your name and your school. Would you like to win one of these Good Player Awards?" All of the children agreed that they would like to win. Of the other two groups, one was not offered any kind of reward as an incentive but given unexpected awards and congratulations when their drawings were completed. The third group was neither offered nor given any kind of reward. So far, so good.

So what do you suppose happened?

First, the pictures drawn in the experimental setting were examined and rated by three judges, none of whom had any knowledge of the experiment or why they were asked to judge the drawings. The drawings were rated by the judges as One (very poor) to Five (very good). Now some people will assume that the kids working for rewards would be more concentrated and produce better work. Exactly the opposite was true. The drawings of the expected-award group were notably inferior to those of both the unexpected-award group and the no-award group. "Thus the detrimental effects of the expected-award manipulation were apparent during the experimental sessions, as well as later in the classroom setting."[641]

When the children were observed "in the classroom setting" seven to fourteen days after the experiment had been carried out, the expected award group showed little interest in the magic markers and spent less time playing with drawing materials than either of the other two groups. The obvious conclusion was that the children who had worked for an award lost interest in drawing. It was not fun for them any longer. Incidentally, all the children participating in the experiment were chosen because of their initial interest in and enthusiasm for drawing.

The experimenters concluded:

> Many of the activities we ask children to attempt in school, in fact, are of intrinsic interest to at least some of the children; one effect of presenting these activities within a system of extrinsic incentives, the present study suggests, is to undermine the intrinsic interest in these activities of at least those children who had some interest to begin with. The quite limited manipulation employed in this study, involving a symbolic reward not unlike those routinely employed in the classroom, was sufficient to produce significant differences in the children's subsequent behavior in a natural preschool classroom. This is consistent with the complaint, from Dewey (1900)[642] and Whitehead (1929)[643] up to the time of Holt (1964)[644] and Silberman(1970),[645] that a central problem with our educational system is its inability to preserve the intrinsic interest in learning and exploration that the child seems to possess when he first enters school. Instead, as these authors have suggested, **the schooling process seems almost to undermine children's spontaneous interest in the process of learning itself.**[646] [emphasis added]

The answer to Sir Ken Robinson's question "Do schools kill creativity?"[647] is clearly, YES.

Getting the Kids to Read?

There have been numerous studies on reading incentive programs and how they have affected reading. Curiously, or perhaps significantly, such programs are applied only to children. I suppose we assume that adults either read or they don't, so who cares? When it comes to kids, however, there is a lot of ballyhoo over getting them to read more. Consequently, all kinds of clever incentives have been devised, all the way from pizza to popcorn. The Pizza Hut *Book it!* program offers pre-kindergarten to grade six kids an opportunity to win a free pizza. Teachers are advised to "Set monthly reading goals for your students. When they meet their goal, recognize them with a Reading Award Certificate, good for a free one-topping Personal Pan Pizza®."[648] A way to encourage reading while conveniently selling them on Pizza Hut's products. Another proffered prize that I found especially amusing was allowing kids to chew gum in class if they read a certain number of books.[649] A routinely forbidden activity is offered as a reward! Have another look at the scene from *Blazing Saddles* cited earlier[650]. Several other ever-so-clever incentives for schoolwork are described in The Gamified Classroom.

Alfie Kohn reminds us that "The reward buys us a behavior—in this case the act of checking out a book and reading it. But at what price? The quality of performance in general and of learning in particular tends to decline significantly when people are extrinsically motivated."[651] A 1982 study of rewards-for-reading by Barry Schwartz concluded:

> The rate of book reading increased astronomically . . . [but the use of rewards also] changed the pattern of book selection (short books with large print became ideal). It also seemed to change the way children read. They were often unable to answer straight-forward questions about a book, even one they had just finished reading. Finally, it decreased the amount of reading children did outside of school. [652]

"Think about it: reading has been presented not as a pleasurable experience but as a means for obtaining a goody. The experience of children in an elementary school class whose teacher introduced an in-class reading-for-reward program can be multiplied hundreds of thousands of times."[653]

It's easy to see that the influence of Skinner's behaviorism is still pervasive in the classroom. After all, it worked with pigeons, why not with kids? It's also easy to see that promised rewards or threatened punishments, whatever form they come in, produce an effect quite opposite from the intended one.

Why is it that schools continue to use reward and punishment systems regardless of how counterproductive they have been shown to be? Could it be that *counterproductive* is the underlying and unrecognized intent? We can assume that no one would deliberately discourage the enjoyment of learning for its own sake, but since that is exactly what happens in school, and anyone can see this, we can only judge that the true purpose of school is to do just that: to promote ignorance and the discounting of intellectual pursuits. Nobody does this on purpose, it's just there. And nobody questions it.

The First and the Last Day of School

To begin, let's consider what children have learned before they have to attend school. It's important to remember that all of this early learning has gone on without instruction. By way of language, the average six-year-old will have a speaking vocabulary of 2600 words and a vocabulary of words they understand of 20,000 to 24,000 words.[654] As we have seen earlier, though, these numbers are on the decline. Be that as it may, before the age of two, most children will have taught themselves how to walk. This seems like a nearly automatic process, so much so that we rarely comment on it. It's just one of the natural things, like learning to talk, that children seem to do automatically—and without teaching. But that's not all. Imagine the complexities of social interaction that children have absorbed by their keen observation of those around them. They already know, by the age of six, the rules and practices of eye contact and the observance of personal space. These, along with language, will be, with breath-taking precision, exactly those that are common to the culture in which they find themselves.

329

Howard Gardner has pointed out the "theories, under-standings and constraints" that children have figured out by the age of five or six:

> In the world of physical objects, they have developed a theory of matter; in the world of living organisms, they have developed a theory of life; and in the world of human beings, they have developed a theory of the mind that incorporates a theory of the self. These theories are supplemented by skill in different kinds of performances, mastery of a wide set of scripts, and an ensemble of more individualized interests, values, and intelligences.[655]

As Frank Smith points out repeatedly, all this learning is done without effort and without forgetting. "This is all learning without awareness, without effort, without guidance or direction."[656]

A friend of mine once said, "Children do not have unanswered questions," and as anyone who has been around children knows, they ask innumerable questions, often to the dismay of the grownups. If no answer is forthcoming, they will make one up. A little boy of three or four who lived next door to me was sitting on his tricycle, one pleasant day, reflecting upon the world. He observed to me, "The sun is up in the sky because it can't get down." This was a perfectly reasonable conclusion that made sense to him. He had asked himself a question and provided an answer. As he gained experience and learned more ways to satisfy his curiosity he would, given half a chance, have refined his answer to this question.

Children are endlessly curious, they are learning machines. Until the routines of school intervene.

One of the end-of-school-year duties of teachers, in the days when I was teaching, was to go through all the used textbooks and decide which ones could be reused and which ones had to be discarded. The results were significant.

The books that had been used by grade one and grade two kids were in nearly perfect condition, ready to be put back into service in September. Starting from grade three, though, damage ranging from torn and dog-eared pages, marginalia, and broken bindings began to creep in. By grade seven, half or more of the books were beyond repair and of no more use. If the book itself were not destroyed, we would be spending a good deal of time erasing obscenities and other scribblings. The teachers seemed to accept all of this with a tsk tsk and "boys will be boys." Yes, the books used by boys suffered the most severe damage. The meaning of all this was attributed to the recalcitrance of the kids. No one ever thought that it might indicate a problem with school itself.

Little children are usually quite keen on school during the first year or so. They're excited by the prospect of learning and discovering new things; they may look to the teacher with admiration. Let's just say that it takes some time to train this out of them.

> When they first get to school, they are endlessly fascinated by the world. They are filled with delight by their new-found ability to print their own names in huge, shaky letters, to count everything in sight, to decode the signs they see around them. They sit on the floor at story time, eyes wide and jaws slack, listening raptly as the teacher reads. They come home bubbling with new facts and new connections between facts. "You know what we learned today?" they say.
> By the time the last bell has rung, the spell has been broken. Their eyes have narrowed. They complain about homework. They count the minutes until the end of the period, the days left before the weekend, the weeks they must endure until the next vacation. "Do we have to know this?" they ask.[657]

A common question, from grade seven and up, is "Will this be on the exam?" By then, everyone has figured out that there is no reason for learning anything that will not result in a grade. Zachary Jason, writing in the *Harvard Education Magazine*, cites the results of a poll about students' attitudes toward school:

> A 2013 Gallup poll of 500,000 students in grades five through 12 found that nearly eight in 10 elementary students were "engaged" with school, that is, attentive, inquisitive, and generally optimistic. By high school, the number dropped to four in 10. A 2015 follow-up study found that less than a third of 11th-graders felt engaged. When Gallup asked teens in 2004 to select the top three words that describe how they feel in school from a list of 14 adjectives, "bored" was chosen most often, by half the students. "Tired" was second, at 42 per cent. Only 2 per cent said they were never bored. The evidence suggests that, on a daily basis, the vast majority of teenagers seriously contemplate banging their heads against their desks.[658]

This phenomenon is so well known that it hardly seems worth documenting. However, the more curious phenomenon is that teachers and educational experts don't seem to take it seriously. As usual, they blame the kids for not being *motivated*. Hence, as we've seen, they spend a lot of time figuring out ways, like rewards and punishments, to get the kids worked up about their lessons. The entire operation of school—from the university experts, to the school board, to the superintendents, to the principals, to the teachers, and to the parent advisory councils—is based on unexamined assumptions about young people, about learning, and about education. Instead of the effortless learning common to little kids, school teaches that learning is difficult, requires effort, and must be taught. Remember Illich's statement about the false assumption that learning is a result of teaching.

My own experience, as exemplified by what happened to the textbooks, was that the average six-year-old, entering school for the first time, as Alfie Kohn describes, approached this new experience with eager curiosity and a willingness to participate in classroom activities. But as these young people advanced through the grades, there was a noticeable deterioration in this attitude. Many of the older kids were sloppy and indifferent if not downright rebellious. An inordinate amount of time was spent on discipline or exhortations to pay attention, work hard, do your homework, etc.

There was a time, following my free-school years, when I tried substitute teaching. I stuck it out for twelve days, until I could take it no more. I was appalled by the stupidity of it all and by the way bright young kids were turned into dullards. One outstanding memory was a grade seven class for which the teacher had left a sample of a spelling test she was going to give. I told the kids that we could go through all these words so they would know what would be on the test and be prepared for it. I foolishly thought they would find this helpful. Not a chance. They continued to be inattentive, pretending not to understand, fidgeting, and acting dumb. "Wait a minute," I said, "I'm doing this for your advantage, so it will be easier for you when you have to take the test." This was greeted with blank looks and sniggers. Finally, I said, "What have they done to you to make you so stupid?" At the end of the day, I went home, phoned the school board office, and told them not to call me again. I suppose if I had been a stern disciplinarian the kids would have behaved differently. But would the spelling lesson have held any more meaning or purpose for them? No. Their behaviour was a clear indication of what they felt about the whole operation.

There is such a thing as "learned helplessness" that occurs when people are stuck in a situation that they cannot control. It is defined by the *American Psychological Association* as

A phenomenon in which repeated exposure to uncontrollable stressors results in individuals failing to use any control options that may later become available. Essentially, individuals are said to learn that they lack behavioral control over environmental events, which, in turn, undermines the motivation to make changes or attempt to alter situations.[659]

After a few months in school, children have learned that they have no control over the situation and that what they think and feel is of no consequence, so they give up and turn to subtle forms of resistance, like failing to comprehend the simplest concepts of arithmetic or grammar, suddenly having a broken pencil during some crucial bit of seat work, making up excuses for not doing required assignments, not being able to find a necessary textbook, daydreaming instead of hanging on the teacher's every word, needing to go to the washroom at some key moment, scribbling in textbooks, and other endlessly creative subterfuges to grasp at some shred of self-respect and self-determination.

But what about those few model students who cheerfully follow all the orders, do their homework, keep their desks and textbooks tidy, get As or Bs on all the tests, and are the delight of teachers? Are they becoming more educated than the rebellious and slovenly? No. Their experience of the world is still limited and controlled by the school and its hidden agenda. It all amounts to how school infantilizes young people, keeps them helpless, and, yes, ignorant.

PART SEVEN

In Conclusion

What Is Education?

We talk about going to school to *get* an education as though it's something like a suit of clothes or a disease. You also go to school to *get* grades; the higher the grades you *get*, the more certifiably "educated" you are. We also know that almost everything learned (or crammed) to pass examinations is quickly forgotten. Let's just say "schooled" instead of "educated" and you'll know what I mean.

Albert Einstein is famously quoted as having said, "I have no special talents. I am only passionately curious."[660] As we have seen, young children are endlessly curious and not easily discouraged. Enabling satisfaction of that innate curiosity should be the responsibility of adults everywhere. The more that young people can become acquainted with grown-ups who are pursuing passionate interests of their own—musicians, scientists, writers, artists, athletes, craftspeople, and workers of all kinds—who are articulate and enthusiastic, the more curiosity will be stimulated and satisfied. Any real learning will stimulate further learning. There is no end. But I'm saying that all real learning comes from curiosity and interest, not from being taught what someone else thinks you ought to learn.

If (by now) you've read Frank Smith's book that I keep referring to, you'll recognize that I agree with his mantra: *You learn from the company you keep and from the people you identify with.* He also makes it clear that you can't learn anything that you are not interested in and that you do not understand. What's the best way to discover things you might be interested in? What's the best way to learn about things you are interested in? From the company you keep, from other people. Hence, the best way to learn about music is to talk with musicians; the best way to learn about Shakespeare is to talk with actors, the best way to learn about science is to talk with scientists, the best way to learn about politics is to talk with politicians.

An educated person has a broad range of interests ranging through the liberal arts. An educated person will usually have one or two passionate interests of their own that they will pursue intently. An educated person will be creative, imaginative, thoughtful, articulate, and above all, curious.

Bear with me for two stories.

Number One: When I was around nine years old I developed an interest in opera. There were two reasons. One was that my parents, drawn by my paternal grandfather, attended the opera from time to time and had the opera broadcast on the radio every Saturday. The other, and perhaps the main reason, was that we had a copy of the 1921 edition of *The Victrola Book of the Opera*.[661] I was swept away by the photos of the great singers—Caruso, Farrar, Journet, Galli-Curci, Scotti, Tetrazzini—in full costume as opera characters. I read the stories and attempted pronunciation of Italian, French, and German titles. And of course, I wanted to hear the recordings that were described in the book. With our very fine Victor Orthophonic phonograph (wind-up version), I played the two or three records we had. My grandfather, who had been a great opera fan when he lived in New York, gave me his substantial record collection: 78 rpm, mostly 12-inch, many single-sided. I think I was only ten at the time. I played them all over and over. By the time I was thirteen or fourteen, I was going, on my own, to any opera performance available. That was almost eighty years ago, and a love of opera and a pursuit of knowledge about opera are still major parts of my life. I've directed performances of opera, worked with singers, and presented courses on opera for a major university. May I hasten to mention that I learned none of this in school? School was mostly disparaging, or at best condescending, of such "highfalutin" art forms. Remember the nun who said that arithmetic was more *ee*ssential than music.

Like all serious interests and endeavours in life, one thing leads to another. So, my love of opera led me to the discovery of all classical music as well as art and literature. I also met people, young and old, who shared the love of music and art. Thus, the most important part of my education came from my heart and from people who shared my interests.

Number Two: I have already mentioned my involvement with Vancouver Opera's *Opera-in-the-Schools* program. We presented our performances in over three hundred schools every year for eight years. But for the school kids, this was a once-a-year, forty-five-minute presentation, with no follow-up. From the teachers and principals we observed, there was no interest other than that it gave them an hour or so out of the classroom.

Years later, I was manager of the Pacific Baroque Orchestra in Vancouver. This was an ensemble of professional musicians who played early music in what is known as "informed performance practice," an attempt to get as close as possible to the way the music would originally have been played. We had often thought that it would be a good idea to present concerts in schools as a way of introducing kids to serious music by composers like Bach, Vivaldi, and Handel. After a couple of one-off school shows of the usual forty-five minutes with no follow-up, it occurred to me that it might be better if the kids could see how musicians worked rather than performed. The plan was to have the orchestra spend an entire day in one school, simply rehearsing for an upcoming concert. The teachers were to bring their classes, at their discretion, into the gymnasium to watch the musicians at work. The orchestra leader, violinist Marc Destrubé, would speak to each group explaining in his intelligent non-condescending way what the musicians were rehearsing and why. He or one of the musicians would answer any questions. Of course, the kids would also hear the music that was being rehearsed. So far, so good. But again, it was once-a-year, one-time-only, that kids got to see, hear, and talk with real musicians.

I want to look at school again as a small community that would be similar to the one-room school of the past. There could be many such schools, each serving a neighbourhood or portion of a neighbourhood. There could be one person in charge of that school, but there would be many "teachers," people, especially parents, who would come to read to the kids, play music, answer questions, talk and talk and talk. In a city, there would be many excursions to places of interest like museums, libraries, concert halls, parks, other schools, the list is endless. In rural areas, there would be as many excursions as possible similar to those listed. Above all, the school would have no tests and no grades, no divisions or ratings, all ages would play and work together. Throughout, learning would take place through mentorship, children learning from each other and from wise and caring adults. The school as an extended family.

Suppose the school had a resident musical ensemble like a small orchestra, a string quartet, or other chamber group? What if the school had a relationship with the local theatre company or group so kids could attend rehearsals and performances, so they could see how actors, set designers, directors, and coaches did the work it took to stage a full performance of a play? The same could be said of any other human endeavour. I'm now not talking about the usual school performance, lecture, or demonstration which purports to be "educational." What if there were writers, artists, mathematicians, carpenters, everything possible, at work in the school or nearby? The school is not a *school* any more, it is a village or community of children and adults. It is an expanded version of the one-room school of the past.

I'm talking about building relationships with intelligent and active people, people that kids can identify with and can learn from, and from whom they can discover interests of their own. *You learn from the company you keep and from the people you identify with.*

We need to ask ourselves, "What kind of people do we want in this world?" If we want people who are trained to be passive consumers of entertainment, who will follow orders without question, and who will be devoted followers of social media, all we have to do is to continue with the present form of schooling. On the other hand, if we want a populace of thoughtful, literate, and creative people, people who are *passionately curious*, it's time we did something completely different.

Starting from any one place, like wondering why the sun can't get down, you can learn everything there is to know. Your curiosity will never be satisfied and your pursuit of learning will be endless.

Why I Believe in Freedom

My last three years as a public school teacher were spent with a group of kids who had been identified as "slow learners."[662] The formal diagnosis of the time was "educable mentally retarded." (They didn't mince their words in those days.) As a teacher of grade seven in the school, I had watched this class walking, or was it shuffling, quietly and obediently in line through the halls. I thought how relaxing and effortless it would be to spend the days with this tractable and undemanding class. It didn't take long to discover how wrong I was.

There were thirteen kids, eleven boys and two girls, ages eleven to fifteen, in what was called Intermediate Special Class. When I started the first year with them I tried to do all the exercises and lessons that I had studied up on in preparation. A lot of it had to do with eye-hand coordination, phonics-style reading lessons, singing little songs, co-operative games, manual crafts, etc. Easy-peasy. I had even acquired the latest box of colourful programmed-reading cards, simple step-by-step Skinner-type lessons for individual use. Oh yes, there was even a beautiful brand-new woodwork table complete with a vise for holding woodwork projects to be fashioned with the few tools on hand.

Before long, it became apparent to me that all this paraphernalia was useless—or worse than useless. The kids played dumb with the eye-hand exercises as though they just couldn't understand the simple instructions. (Did I say *learned helplessness?*) Then, the cards in the box of reading lessons were soon mixed up and showing signs of wear and tear. Whatever they were being used for had nothing to do with learning to read. As for the worktable, the tools were being used to "fashion" *it* more than the presumptive woodwork projects. Interactions amongst the kids were showing more and more signs of poking, prodding, pushing, pinching, and every other subtle form of hostility—and getting more and more noisy.

Most teachers would—and I'm sure they did—say that the apparent disorder was **all my fault** because I failed to exert the usual control and discipline. Well, I never was much of a disciplinarian in the years I was a teacher; that was not much of a problem with so-called normal kids. By this time I had read A.S. Neill's *Summerhill* (more than once) and I was reading Carl Rogers on non-directive therapy. I believed in the goodness of human nature and the power to grow and to heal that was in every individual. I was convinced that the more that constraints and restraints were removed, the more the truth will come out. What I was seeing in my special kids was the emergence of their frustration and rage over the treatment they had received at school and, almost for sure, at home. They had been taught that they were stupid, slow, couldn't learn, and had little value as persons. And now that the lid was off, the pot was boiling over. We've already explained the *wild* period, and we were now in the middle of it.

There were months of chaos, hostility, violence, and racket. Months, yes, but there was also a change beginning to happen. The rage, for that's what it was, was subsiding. There were days of peace, congeniality, and quiet activity. By the end of the first year, the days were occupied with play, constructive projects, and lengthy discussions with me. They were asking me endless questions covering every imaginable topic. Time and effort were spent on cleaning up and repairing the damage that had been done during the wild period. These kids were becoming intelligent, creative, and co-operative human beings. No one could miss the obvious changes. The other teachers and the principal commented on what they saw but didn't contemplate how this might challenge their theories and practices. After all, they said, this "experiment" may be OK for the mentally retarded, but surely not for the normal kids.

There are a couple of things I want to tell about. One was that the older boys started getting interested in the maintenance of the school grounds. They got together with the janitor and persuaded him to let them mow the lawns around the school. They did this with pride and pleasure. On the playground, instead of being the outsider "dumb" kids, they began associating as equals with the other kids. They engaged in the games being played at recess and noon hour, especially tether ball, which was enormously popular at the time. They played happily, always insisting that the rules of fair play be observed. When there was an assembly at which some classes put on skits that they had learned, my gang cooked up a silly skit of their own and performed with great gusto, shocking, I'm sure, the other teachers because the skit involved a good deal of pretend drinking. When there was a science fair, they drew pictures and made models of various kinds of weapons—slingshots, guns, bombs—showing man's inhumanity to man. These boys and girls who had been ready to tear the world apart had now become thoughtful, sympathetic, and caring.

There was another truly remarkable occurrence that requires a bit of background. During the wild days, the boys wanted to play in the gymnasium, so I arranged with the principal that we could have access whenever it was free. In the gym, I would unlock the door to the room that held all the equipment: balls, nets, rackets, tumbling pads, hockey sticks, etc. Almost immediately, everything was removed from the room and tossed about helter-skelter in a disorganized and nutty way. That went on for a few weeks until I noticed that some of the boys were attempting to organize a game. Floor hockey was the going thing at the time, so they began to practise swatting the puck about, sometimes even in a playful way with each other. This kind of play became increasingly organized, teams were created, and their own version of the game was played. They asked me to tell them the rules of floor hockey, how it was scored and how it was played. I didn't know much, but I found out and explained as best I could. Now, the play got serious. Now, they were getting skillful, shooting the puck into the net with great zest.

Around this time, the school was organizing a floor hockey tournament for grade six and seven boys. My boys wanted to join, so I discussed this with the principal. He advised against it because, after all, the "dumb" kids would be so soundly beaten that they would be emotionally damaged. I was able to convince him that it would be worth the risk because my kids so loved playing the game. Need I mention the outcome of the tournament? My team of "slow-learner" boys trounced every other team and walked away as winners. Did they make a big thing of this, bragging about how good they were? No. They were pleased with having won, but they did not start thinking of themselves as better than the others. They enjoyed the game and that was enough.

After two and a half years of growth in an atmosphere of freedom and permissiveness, the Intermediate Special Class was reintegrated into the regular classes. For better or for worse I don't know, but I suspect for the worse. There was little or nothing there for them to gain. It was that the school, wouldn't you know it, thought this would be better for them. Let's just say that it was clear they were becoming too independent and too capable. Without all the teaching, the lessons, and the homework, these kids could figure out for themselves whatever they needed to know in order to do what they wanted to do.

This is why I believe in freedom.

Kids These Days—And Beyond

"Historically, human societies have been pro-child; modern society is unique in that **it is profoundly hostile to children**. We in the West do not refrain from childbirth because we are concerned about the population explosion or because we feel we cannot afford children, but **because we do not like children**."[663] [emphasis added]
—Germaine Greer

"*Sesame Street* appeared to justify allowing a four- or five-year-old to sit transfixed in front of a television screen for unnatural periods of time. Parents were eager to hope that television could teach their children something other than which breakfast cereal has the most crackle. At the same time, *Sesame Street* relieved them of the responsibility of teaching their pre-school children how to read—no small matter in a culture where **children are apt to be considered a nuisance.**"[664] [emphasis added]—Neil Postman

"By *potential helpers* I mean all those who do not shrink from unequivocally taking the side of the child and protecting him from power abuse on the part of adults. In **our child-inimical society** such people are still rare, but their number is growing."[665] [emphasis added]
—Alice Miller

"As the father of a three year old boy, I've become much more attuned to the way that people treat children. What astounds me is how much, as a society, **we tend to despise children.**"[666] [emphasis added]—James C. Kaufman

These statements may seem shocking until you consider the way children are treated in our society. Look at the shoddy cartoon-character entertainment posing as education. Look at the newly invented childcare devices and virtual babysitters. Look at the cheap and garish playthings that are sold. (A visit to Toys "R" Us will confirm this.) Look at the sexualized and arid manufactured music that is pushed off on the youth market. Look at the institutions that will relieve parents of the care of their children. Look at the way we believe that children have to be watched, controlled, and directed. Look at the way children are disciplined and schooled. Look at how many parents express relief when school starts and the kids get out of their hair. Look at the way children and young people are denied access to the working and professional world. Look at the way celebrities and sports heroes are the only role models offered to them. Look at the way industry is capitalizing on the youth market by pushing conformity in expensive clothing, makeup, jewellery, and cellphones. Look again at the statistics on youth depression, ADHD, and suicide. How can we avoid recognizing that we are a society that denies and suppresses the curiosity, intelligence, beauty, and vigour of children of all ages? Their young lives must be devoted to consumerism and preparation for getting a job and making money. The only escape available to them is through social media, and we know by now what that leads to.

Though I've said this many times already, it bears repeating: The only people who are subjected to the kind of treatment meted out to children in school are the convicted criminals in the penitentiary. Prison dehumanizes, so does school.

We think that intelligent and informed democratic citizens will emerge from twelve or more years under an authoritarian dictatorship. We think that young people will be curious and eager to learn when we convince them that the only reason to learn anything is to pass a test or get a grade. We think that kids will learn *critical thinking* in school when the main message is *do as you're told and don't ask questions.* We think that children will not be bullies when the biggest bullies in the school are the teachers. We think that our young people will make intelligent career choices when they are confined and kept out of the adult world of work and professions. We think we can encourage a love of literature when we give it to them as an *assignment*, with deadlines, book reports, and tests to follow. We think that students will take scholarship seriously when we present learning as a cartoon. We think that kids will learn the intelligent use of digital media when the use of computers is presented and extolled from the earliest years in school. We think that school is about education when it is about exactly the opposite. School is the end of intelligence.

I started this book more than thirty years ago as *Ten Arguments for the Elimination of School*. It morphed into its present form some three years ago. When I mention the *elimination* of school, people invariably ask What will you replace it with? My semi-facetious answer was always What will you replace cancer with once a cure is found? The truth of the matter is that school will not be eliminated any more than a cure for cancer will be found in the foreseeable future. Any change in the way we raise our children will happen as a change in society itself and in the way people regard child-rearing. Over the past hundred years or so child-rearing practices have been slowly changing from the harsh disciplinary rigours of the nineteenth and early twentieth centuries to the softer and more permissive methods as characterized by Dr. Spock. Compare these two statements and you'll see what I mean: "Parenthood, instead of being an instinctive art, is a science, the details of which must be worked out by patient laboratory methods."[667] and "TRUST YOURSELF—You know more than you think you do."[668]

The basic attitude that children are incomplete creations that must be trained and molded still prevails, and our society is constructed in such a way that children have little or no part in it and must, therefore, be cared for by professionals in some kind of institution or institutional setting like school or daycare. How will this change? I don't know. That's why, unlike most of the books I've read about school and education that are full of recommendations about what should be done, I have no blueprint to offer. I know that everything about school as it now exists is wrong and damaging to kids and that it serves the purposes of corporations and governments. School won't change until they do.

We need a new Renaissance, a new Enlightenment, in which the curiosity and intelligence of children are nurtured and where play is regarded as important work. Where children are integrated into society and have meaningful involvement in social and personal interaction.

The Beginning of Intelligence

Most of this book has been devoted to negativity and criticism of school and its deleterious effects on children and youth. I think I've made a case against school as a purveyor of learning and intelligence. But there are people around us who are both learned and intelligent; where did they come from and how did they survive the depredations of school? Let's now go back to where intelligence is first developed.

We know that the brain is formed, we could even say created, by associations with other people. A human brain does not automatically click through the stages of development, it grows and creates itself by means of attachment to mothers, fathers, siblings, caregivers, and everybody else who has an impact on the baby and small child. I don't have to tell you that the personality that eventually emerges will not be unlike those inhabitants of the child's world. After all, that world is the only world the little child knows, and he or she will have to figure out how to make a go of it.

If figuring out how to make a go of it becomes an urgent and pressing need of existence—of survival—how can intelligence, co-ordination, curiosity, confidence, and ability ever be part of the grownup person that the child will become? The brain cannot reach its potential in the presence of anxiety and frustration.

Intelligence begins with love. Intelligence comes from the security of an intimate and dependable connection or attachment with a primary caregiver, most often the mother. It is the love of nutrition, warmth, and human contact.[669] It is this security that enables the body and the brain to thrive. Independence grows out of dependence. To deny the satisfaction of the baby's needful demand for contact and attention is to guarantee prolonged dependency. Independence will develop naturally and organically as dependency needs are satisfied.

In his 2022 book *The Myth of Normal*, Gabor Maté quotes Gordon Neufeld:

> "The question," Gordon Neufeld said to me, "becomes, What are the irreducible needs of the child?' By "irreducible" he means a need that the child cannot do without if she is to reach her Nature-endowed potential; one that, if not met, will incur negative consequences. As he told the European Parliament, "It is true maturation, not schooling, learning or genetics that is key to be-

> coming fully human and humane." We cannot teach maturity, nor can we cajole, entice, or coerce a child into it. What is required of us to ensure the developmental conditions that satisfy the child's nonnegotiable needs; from there, Nature more or less takes care of the rest.[670]

How and when the human brain develops is well known, at least to the extent that the major part of that development takes place during the first three years of life. Not only does the brain increase in size, but more importantly, there are as many as one thousand trillion synapses ready to join into cognitive development. Those synapses will consolidate and be put to use as a result of input from the little child's experiences with the world. If those experiences are of frustration and fear, that development will be thwarted.

> Babies learn an enormous amount from direct experience with the world. This early learning occurs as a result of, among other things, seeing events transpire, manipulating objects, moving through space, and interacting with the most interesting category of entities around—other people.[671]

The "other people" the researchers refer to are, or should be, loving parents, grandparents, siblings, and other relatives and friends. The more children are talked to, read to, played with, fondled, and enjoyed, the more they will develop into social, verbal, and intelligent beings full of curiosity and a desire to participate. These interactions all involve real people, not images on a screen. They will adopt and adapt to the customs and practices of "their people." What can we expect if *their people* are cartoon ducks, cute animated characters, confusing ever-changing images, and peers?

Babies and young children have a very clear way of expressing their needs. What could be more loving than responding to the baby's cries with attention and tenderness? It's the same as

351

the beauty of holding your baby in your arms, rocking and singing, as she falls asleep, then when soundly sleeping laying her gently into the crib. And you'll be there ready to pick up and comfort her should she wake up and cry at any time during the night. Love, attention, and security allow growth to happen.

Psychologists and psychiatrists are now "discovering" what cats, dogs, apes, and primitive people have always known: that what babies need is care, attention, physical contact, feeding, and, in the case of human babies, vocal and verbal contact. Mothers everywhere sing and coo to their babies. In indigenous societies babies are constantly carried about, observing and participating in whatever the mother and other people around are doing. In more developed societies, people also read to babies and children. Simply enough, the babies are welcomed as a part of the community! If it's a literate community, so much the better. They learn what being human is all about through attachment to parents and other members of their community.

John Bowlby's extensive studies of what he calls "attachment theory" have emphasized and clarified the crucial importance of a close and dependable relationship (or attachment) between parent and child.

> A young child's experience of an encouraging, supportive, and co-operative mother, and a little later father, gives him a sense of worth, a belief in the helpfulness of others, and a favourable model on which to build future relationships. Furthermore, by enabling him to explore his environment with confidence and to deal with it effectively, such experience also promotes his sense of competence.[672]

Exploring with confidence and competence of course means intelligence.

What are you going to do as the child grows and starts moving about in the world? It is a time of exploration and discovery, a time when curiosity begins to flourish. In her book *Cycles of*

Power,[673] Pam Levin calls this age "The Power of Doing," meaning that it's the stage in a child's growth when he can move about. He begins exploring and testing the world around him. He will also, given half a chance, ask endless questions: why, what, when, how? This is a time of endless curiosity, and of course you will answer every question with forbearance and respect, often with "I don't know, let's see if we can find out." This conveys the notion that there is an intelligent way of finding out about the world around us. At the same time, let's not forget the endless creativity of a young developing mind. Remember my little friend who answered his question about why the sun was up in the sky? It is equally important to allow the little explorer to make discoveries and figure things out on his own.

Emphasizing the importance of attachment at this stage of life, Levin goes on to say:

> To do this, we need continued bonding, support and affection while we learn about the world and get our feet on the ground. We need a continued abundance of food and touching to feel safe enough to explore. As long as we can return or tag in, touching base with our loving caretaker at will, we feel secure enough to move freely and satisfy our curiosity without having to inhibit our developing sensory appetite.[674]

This is why I am opposed to daycare for children of any age.[675] A strong and nurturing attachment to a primary caregiver will be interrupted and usurped by so-called experts who are there to direct the child into compliance with institutional values. Need I say that a disoriented and mystified child will be more susceptible to the demands of school, where independent intelligence and curiosity are not welcome? As a loving and caring parent, you would not subject your child to the soul-destroying influence of daycare or school.

When the law demands school attendance, the available answer is homeschooling. This is a misnomer, the word "schooling" should be replaced with "unschooling" or simply "home learning." Yes, you may have to comply with the curricular demands of the department of education, but once the content is removed from the absurdities of the classroom it is revealed to be ridiculously simple. Many years ago, I knew a father who was homeschooling his two sons, one eleven and the other fourteen. They were with him almost always. He took them to concerts, lectures, meetings, everything possible. The boys also engaged in sports and other activities with other kids their age. The dad told me that they averaged less than fifteen minutes per day on what he called "schoolwork." The result was two highly confident lads, comfortable in all adult situations, interested in everything, and fully engaged with their father, mother, and other parent figures. Intelligent? You bet!

What I've noticed about the home-schooled kids I've met is that they are comfortable talking with and associating with grownups. They have not been tossed into the maelstrom of the peer-oriented youth culture that school creates. They don't feel compelled to wear the *right* clothes or have the latest technological gizmos. They are free to be individuals, living their lives freely and pursuing their own interests.

Sometimes "pursuing their own interests" means that kids can be noisy and demanding. How do you deal with this? Remembering that it's simply a matter of living together and that children do not need to be "disciplined," you will simply say "That noise is driving me crazy, please stop," "This is the way we talk to grandma," or "Try this instead." My belief is that children want to be part of the family and that they will adopt the behaviours and customs they observe. If the parents are polite, the kids will be polite. They don't have to be told to say "Thank you" because they will have learned that that is what *my* people say when someone gives them something or does something for them. If they are loved, they will love in return. Love is "unconditional positive regard," and it is never withdrawn for any reason.

In their splendid book *Hold On To Your Kids*, Gordon Neufeld and Gabor Maté describe *connection before direction*, saying, "Most approaches to discipline are devoid of any sensitivity to emotional vulnerability, lack any consciousness of attachment and possess little understanding of the dynamics of development."[676] The internet and dozens of books about parenting will offer the latest clever tricks for disciplining your child. Time-outs, shunning, "tough love," withdrawing privileges, going to bed without supper, etc., etc. are all ways of distancing ourselves from our children, or "showing them who's boss." Threatening the withdrawal of love is threatening the destruction of attachment; we put the child into the position of having to "buy" our love. This can only create anxiety and fear that will block the development of intelligence.

This book is about school and its effects on children and society. Parents who care about the intelligence of their children and the benefits of a civilized society will stay away from school. They will find a wealth of richly interesting and educational resources all around. Children already know *how* to learn, all we have to do is provide them with opportunities to discover the world and to develop curiosity. Robert Louis Stevenson wrote, "The world is so full of a number of things, I'm sure we should all be as happy as kings." That's all you need to know.

Epilogue

EPILOGUE

I'd like to think that this book is finished just because I got to the point of saying to myself "No more," but that hasn't stopped me from thinking about all the things I should have said. At least I hope it's clear that I think school should be done away with, though that doesn't mean that education should be done away with, quite the contrary. A society that prized learning would provide a means of introducing its young to the achievements and practices of the best of its people. It would encourage curiosity, questioning, intelligent discourse, and individual initiative. I'm talking about a social revolution, a different way of thinking about children and education. It's not a question of what kind of workers or consumers we want, but of what kind of people we want. This would mean a revolution of thinking about childhood and what we mean by education.

How that will occur, I don't know. If and when the world comes out of its present parlous state, there may well be new ways of thinking about our relations with each other, our history, and about the natural environment around us.

I've written about the deterioration of popular entertainment and social communication. People will say that old people (I was born in 1931) go around complaining about young people (Kids these days!) and how bad things are now and about how good things used to be. ("Why can't they be like we were, perfect in every way. What's the matter with kids today?"[677]) I think we'd better be careful about discounting the perspective of a person who has witnessed the coming and going of innovation and technological advances. New is not necessarily better. When the automobile came along it seemed like a great idea. Every family could have a car and go anywhere they pleased in comfort and convenience. People could live in the suburbs and work in the city. It was all fine until farms and parklands were paved over and tailpipe emissions were destroying the planet. A portable telephone was something of science fiction until the smartphone started dominating people's lives. People are willing to abandon civilized travel by train—you are aware of ground covered—in favour of being handled like cargo to get there faster. Technical advances have a way of taking on lives of their own. People lose control and forget what life was like before. The very structure of society is refashioned without planning or consideration of consequences.

Don't get me wrong, I am far from a Luddite. I drive a car, I have a cellphone, I use a computer. You can see from the more than six hundred footnotes below that much of the research for this book was done on the internet. Digital technology can make a huge contribution to the enrichment of intellectual and social life. But, for many people, especially for youth, it has taken over, not contributing to life but running it. Unlike the printing press, automobiles, telephones, and airplanes, computer technology advances at breakneck speed. Almost daily it seems that there is some new device or platform that one cannot do without. The pace of life is dashing along (to disaster?) as never before.

I said earlier that we need a new Renaissance, a new Enlightenment. Both of these philosophical developments brought about a widespread rediscovery of art, music, science, and literature—the liberal arts. People thought in new ways about themselves and about human nature. In the 1960s, we talked about "the revolution." It was to be a new world of peace, love, and harmony. The young people I knew—freeschoolers, dropouts, hippies— were thoughtful and idealistic, attributes that should be trademarks of youth. But that "enlightenment" fizzled out, extinguished by established economic, religious, and political values that enforced conformity and competition.

If we are going to have education—not school—it will be in the liberal arts, meaning a perspective of the past on the movements and trends of the present. Instead of rushing blindly into a world dominated by social media, video games, and huge corporations, an educated populace would slow down and take into account where we're going, what we're gaining, and what we're losing.

If school continues its promotion of digital media and neo-liberal ideologies, we can look forward to a society dominated by far-right regressive politics and the end of democracy—the end of intelligence.

Appendix

FROM 1966

The following article was published in the 1966 issue of *The Challenge of Capacity*, the annual publication of the Provincial Association of Teachers of Special Education. It was then published by Free School Press, May 30, 1970. At that time I was director of the Saturna Island Free School.

This paper represents an attempt to describe some of the experiences I have had with my class in Williams Lake, B.C. It is an Intermediate Special Class consisting of eleven boys, aged 12 to 15, and two girls, both aged 14. Most of the youngsters in the class have been in Special Classes for about six years. They have all been "diagnosed" as "slow learners". This is my second year with the group.

Through these two years, I have found my way of dealing with youngsters tending toward greater permissiveness and freedom. I have tried to describe the effects and results of this approach. Naturally, my evaluation of the success of this venture is a personal one based on my daily contact with these youngsters over the two-year period. The names used in this paper are not the actual names of the youngsters being described.

Much of the activity of the group, noisy and boisterous as it often is, has been possible because the class is housed in a portable classroom separate from the main school building. We are also grateful to the other teachers and administrators who have regarded our class, though not without philosophical reservations, With interest and indulgence.

Tom Durrie
Williams Lake, B.C.
April 9, 1966

My special Class in Williams Lake has been described as "unique" and "experimental." It is unique because I have taken what many would describe as a radical approach to dealing with children, an approach which probably would not be found, at least to this degree, in any other classroom in British Columbia. And because it is unique it is called experimental. If it is an experiment, it is only to the extent that life itself is an experiment, for I have tried, not to induce my youngsters to follow a program of learning or activities, nor to guide or foster growth in any predetermined direction, but to give them the freedom to discover their own directions and to come face to face with life itself as they meet it daily in its infinite variety.

I have tried to establish for each child the feeling that he was an individual of worth, that I prized and loved him for what he was, and that I wished no more for him than that he should be himself. I hoped that he would know that I had an unshakeable faith in his ability to conduct his own life in the best possible way for himself.

Among the reasons I have for departing from traditional methods was the feeling that learners were having trouble in school for emotional and psychological reasons rather than, if the distinction exists, intellectual reasons. I had often seen infants who were inadequately loved develop more slowly and less fully than those whose needs were more nearly satisfied. The thwarted infant is too busy using his energy in anger and frustration to learn to talk and walk with much efficiency. The timid, enigmatic faces and awkward bodies of many "slow learners" reminded me of the doughy bodies of such infants.

For a long time, I have believed that every individual is best able to direct his own life, and that any external direction was likely to thwart and pervert this natural and constructive drive.

I felt that life was good and learning and exploring the world were desirable aspects of living. It seems ridiculous to me that anyone should have to be forced to learn to read since reading is such a vital form of contact among human beings and that as social beings such communicative contact is natural to us. Perhaps, then, "slow learners" were dull because they were thwarted and frustrated, too wrapped up in inner suffering to be able to view their environment clearly and effectively. Therefore, I reasoned, it is vital to provide a situation which would be therapeutic, which would enable them to discover and accept themselves as they were. Painful though this self-discovery might be, it would make further growth possible.

In my classroom then, each youngster is free to be himself as he truly is and to direct his own affairs in whatever way he chooses as long as he doesn't harm or unduly interfere with others. My own role is that of provider of material and information, and as a kind of reflective listener. As a provider, I find I must be ready to search out all kinds of supplies and raw materials for building, for art projects, and for reading or study. When the creative urge arises, action must be its immediate outcome. As an information-giver, I am called upon to answer questions on and to explain the multitudes of topics that arise when active, curious children are free to pursue whatever interests them. It may be history, anatomy, social problems, psychology, sex, religion, jet propulsion, or banking. Again, the time to answer is when the question is asked, not after the length of time it takes to prepare a lesson. Children are eager to know what they want to know, but if you try to turn a simple question into a "learning situation" by developing the topic beyond their original inquiry you might as well save your breath, they simply don't listen--and I suspect this is what happens to most of what adults say to children.

As a reflective listener, I attempt to be open and responsive to whatever the children may express to me. As I listen to what they say, I try to put myself in their place. Instead of trying to see things my way, I try to see things his way. This doesn't mean that I have to do as he does or take on his way of thinking for myself, but it does mean that I, as a fellow individual, will give myself without judging, leading or advising to understanding and empathy with the child. Because they do not need to seek my approval (they have it already), and they need not fear my disapproval, they can and do express themselves on any matter they choose and in any manner they choose.

What do children do all day when they can decide for themselves what to do? A typical day might run something like this: The kids usually come into the room as soon as they get to school in the morning -and. a number of them have a standing race on to see who can get there first, as they arrive, they stand around in the room talking about what they have done, seen or heard since the previous day. By the time the nine o'clock bell rings everyone is assembled in the room or just outside. We have no opening exercises because I discovered long ago that the children paid no attention to them and only went through the motions of listening, reciting and singing because they had to. Life has enough artificiality in it already, I feel I cannot afford to force any more on these youngsters.

So the day begins, or rather, evolves without a formal beginning. Now that the weather is fine, three or four boys may start out with a friendly and earnest game of marbles. Another small group may get to work excitedly on a model car that some lucky soul has been able to afford. Two or three studious types will pull their desks together into some corner and settle down for work on arithmetic or language. In another corner you may find Billy holed up with a book for the day. Comic books are well-loved, and if someone brings a stack of them, they will make the rounds throughout the day. If all activities were quiet ones, the day would be a smooth as butter. But, as likely as not, one of the two girls, very much teenagers, has brought her favorite records which she must play at full volume. Joe decides to make himself a wooden rifle and commences sawing and hammering full blast. Mike, who had a rough weekend at home, lets loose his anger with volleys of loud bragging and knocking desks around, eliciting cries of protest from those offended. In the midst of this, Danny and Jerry may tear through the room, one in hot pursuit of the other, knocking into the model-builders and jiggling the needle from its path on the record. The situation, though a bit rugged on the nerves at times, gives the kids a chance to find out what they are really like and just what it takes to live with other individuals.

Such conflicting interests as these are problems which have to be dealt with. As I have lived with and observed these children over the months, I have seen their approach to problems change. At first, they fought and squabbled constantly. Some of them begged me to "make us behave", but I knew they didn't really want this. They resented being told what to do. They were simply lost souls, loosed from their hated moorings but unable to set a course to steer by. The only way they seemed to be able to deal with problems was with violence. Consequently, the stronger and louder youngsters usually had their way and the smaller ones fought among themselves and wept. But gradually I think they learned that it is more satisfying to help another person than it is to dominate him; that it is more rewarding to co-operate with and sympathize with others than it is to have one's own way. Youngsters who a few months ago spent every day in bitter, violent and hateful fighting now fight no more. Jerry, who was known around the school for years as a tough little fighter with a perpetual chip on his shoulder, said to me recently, "The one thing I don't want to do in life is fight." Where, in September and October, a. group of boys would hurl invectives at each other and provoke a fist fight or mercilessly pick on some under-dog, they will now engage in a hilarious, noisy and thoroughly friendly game of tag, or they may be found huddled up in the back of the room talking about their plans for the future. They are happy kids, full of interest in and affection for each other.

If the girls' record-playing interferes with someone's studying, he will now either simply go elsewhere to study or ask the girls to turn it down. If Joe's hammering and sawing get to be too much, he may be asked to quit or to hurry up and get it over with. Above all, I find that as problems are created by conflicting interests, there is now a willingness to see the other fellow's point of view, to regard him as a person worthy of consideration, not just an annoying object to be hated and removed. In my opinion, no amount of disciplining by authority, or lecturing or fatherly advising could have produced growth in human relations like this.

So the day continues. Activities and groupings change freely whenever the need arises. I may spend some time helping with a model, sharing the enthusiasm and excitement as the tiny automobile takes shape in its awe-inspiring perfection. John is yelling for help in figuring out an arithmetic problem. He will try on me every devious means he has used on other teachers to wangle the solution, but he knows that I will only attempt to understand what he is saying and that my understanding will somehow help him to understand and feel able to solve the problem himself. I find that if I try to explain or try to lead him to the solution, however subtly, I will only convince him that he is incapable of doing it himself. So part of our conversation may run something like this:

John: I can't get this one.

Me: This problem is especially hard for you.

John: Yeah, it says, Bob took $5.00 to the store and bought $3.55 worth of school supplies. How much did he have then?" Oh, I know, you would add, wouldn't you?

Me: You think you might add to find the answer.

John: No, I guess you have to divide.

Me: It looks to you now as though you should. divide.

John: Yeah, that's it. Divide $5.00 into $3.55.

Me: If you divide $5.00 into $3.55 you will get the answer.

John: No, you can't do that.

Me: That's not possible, is it?

John: Tell me how to do it.

Me; You would just like me to tell you how to do it, wouldn't you?

John: Oh, I guess I'll have to figure it out myself.

And nine times out of ten, he will figure it out for himself. And his satisfaction is deep and quiet. His is the satisfaction of accomplishment, not of manipulating another person, or of winning praise or avoiding disapproval.

Next I may be called upon to hold Mike on my knee and read to him. He is a big boy, aged thirteen, but he has a deep need to be loved and given attention. Before he came to my class he was an incorrigible bully, a straight F student, and a constant behavior problem at home and school. He used to make loud, bragging threats to the other boys and then "chicken out" if anyone called his bluff. Now he is much less obnoxious, and less of a "chicken" than he used to be. He is a serious student and his achievement has risen several grade levels in the past few months. And Mike, like the others, talks about himself honestly and realistically. "I don't know why, but I'm sure scared of high places." Fears, which were previously kept hidden by layers of defenses, gradually come out into the open to be talked about, accepted, and dealt with. Paper tigers lurking in the murky recesses of the mind are seen for what they are in the light of love, acceptance, approval, and self-esteem.

We eat lunch together in the room these days, commenting on what we have to eat and what we like and dislike, sharing with each other something a little special—marshmallow cookies or bites of dill pickle. The kids find out that others have tastes different from theirs but just as important to them. Every experience like this pushes the horizon a little bit and reveals the world as a friendly and warm place where Mike or John or Jerry can have importance and ability as an individual. Self-esteem is, to me, the key to ability. And it cannot be taught, it must be discovered.

The afternoon goes along pretty much as did the morning. Individuals and small groups busy themselves with their own affairs. What if big fifteen-year old John is lying on the floor playing with a toy truck and making loud truck noises? He is living out his own fantasy life, he must never have been free to do it before. Playing trucks is terribly important to him and I know he will not grow beyond this stage until he is free and able to live it out. If Sally tells me in emotional terms how much she hates her mother, I can best help her by listening, by putting myself in her position. "Yes, I see how it must feel to be you," is what I say to her in effect. And seeing how it is to be her, I find she is a person worthy of love and esteem. Finally, when her hate is expressed openly and found to be acceptable, Sally will begin to see that she has other feelings for her mother as well, that her mother is a person with feelings too, and that there are possibilities for understanding and love. If I had given Sally advice or tried to point out to her that she should look for her mother's good qualities, she would have reacted defensively. She would have felt that I didn't understand. She would have gone on hating, now adding me to her list.

What the children say is: "Love me as I am and for what I am!" They are not to be denied.

The end of the day usually brings much farewell hand-shaking, back-patting, and hugging as the children set out for home. The warmth and affection that passes between us is not a sign of dependence; in fact, I find the youngsters far more independent than they were previously. Many of them have friends and belong to groups outside the Special Class. They will confidently set out for town or on an errand where before they would have needed support and assistance. Their affection is simply the warmth of fellow living creatures for each other.

I have heard a great deal lately about developing co-ordination, kinesthetic control, and visual perception in "Slow Learners". I have seen many exercises which are designed to develop these traits in children deficient in them. A year ago, I felt that my children lacked co-ordination, that their physical development was slow, that they lacked. "tone." To my amazement, I have watched the youngsters develop and practice their own co-ordination "exercises." From the simplest chasing games and hammering, through setting up their own obstacle courses for running and jumping, tracing pictures, and using chisels, to inventing games of their own, requiring a high degree of co-ordination, guiding toy cars over board "highways" and following diagrams and instructions. If long division has no personal significance to him, he will not learn it - not really - no matter how hard I "teach"? it at him. All I am doing is keeping him from being active in ways that are important to him. When long division becomes necessary to him, he will learn it in the most efficient way, and he will remember it as long as he needs to--unless, of course, my "teaching" has forever turned him against learning of all kinds.

The youngsters in my class actually do very little academic school work. They are much too busy growing and living. There are two or three who have stuck with their books fairly consistently, and while this has been motivated by a genuine desire to get ahead in school and not just because parents are putting on pressure, there has been real progress. Some of them have shown a significant rise in achievement even though they have done no "school work" whatever all year. Others have remained at about the same level and a few have gone down slightly. However, who is to say that this would not have happened had I been "teaching" them all year. And there is the inescapable fact that Achievement Tests, like Intelligence Tests, measure only the ability to write that particular test in the myriad conditions, inner and outer, under which it was given. No, what my children are learning cannot be measured by tests. They are learning that life is a process of growing and becoming, and of learning. They are finding out that they can deal effectively with reality, that they can make decisions, and that they are responsible for their actions. They are learning some of the millions of scraps of information that make up an education. Above all they are learning to live life with joy and vigour, and to face its limitless possibilities with confidence and enthusiasm.

Tom Durrie

What's this?

A symbol of ignorance. It is the symbol of Mara or Marzanna, the pagan Slavic goddess of death, rebirth, rural places, and young plants.

Acknowledgements

Bibliography

Notes

ACKNOWLEDGEMENTS

This is where the author thanks all the people who provided help and encouragement through the process of creating a book. If I could, I would say thanks to my wonderful editor, to mom and dad, and to my friends who stood by me. Well, I couldn't afford an editor, mom and dad are long gone, and of friends there are few because I didn't go around telling everyone I was writing a book. However, let me thank Gail and Anita for offering encouragement, Seth McDonough for sharing his publishing experiences, and Charles Barber for donating the first proofreading and a few editorial suggestions. My son Miles, to whom this book is dedicated, edited as much as he was able, up to around the first fifty pages. As a respected professional editor and writer, he would have done a fabulous job had a fatal illness not intervened. His absence is felt keenly by all who knew him and worked with him. By the way, though he advanced rapidly as a journalist, he had no official credentials, never having attended much school. He always wanted to be involved in writing. He just went ahead and did it.

As for my dad, he would have said what he said around 1968 when I was arguing in favour of free schools: "I don't like what he says, but I like the way he says it." R.I.P.

The real people to whom I owe thanks are the children and young people, including my own, that I have known, over the years, as friends, co-workers, and students. It is from them that I learned that intelligence and curiosity emerge from acceptance, freedom, and positive regard.

Fond memories must go to those wonderful boys and girls who formed the "special class" in Williams Lake those many years ago. They were indeed special.

BIBLIOGRAPHY OF BOOKS CITED AND REFERENCED

Anderson, Chris. *TED Talks: The Official TED Guide to Public Speaking* (London: Headline Publishing Group, 2016)

Bauerlein, Mark. *The Dumbest Generation: How the Digital Age Stupefies Young Americans and Jeopardizes Our Future: Or, Don't Trust Anyone Under 30,* (New York: Tarcher Perigee, 2006)

Bobbitt, John Franklin. *What Schools Teach and Might Teach* (Ithaca: Cornell University, 1915)

Bowlby, John. *Attachment* (Pimlico, an imprint of Random House, London, 1973)

Callahan, Raymond E. *Education and the Cult of Efficiency* (Chicago: University of Chicago Press 1962)

Campbell, Don G. *The Mozart effect: tapping the power of music to heal the body, strengthen the mind, and unlock the creative spirit* (New York: Avon Books, 1997)

Carnegie, Andrew. *The Empire of Business* (New York: Doubleday, Page & Company, 1902*

Carr, Nicholas. *The Shallows: How the internet is changing the way we think, read and remember* (London: Atlantic books, 2010)

Cook, Henry Caldwell. *The Play Way, an Essay in Educational Method,* (New York: Frederick A. Stokes Company, 1917)

Coulter, Natalie. *Tweening the girl, the crystallization of the tween market* (New York: International Academic Publishers, 2014)

Cubberley, Elwood Patterson. *Public Education in the United States, A Study and Interpretation of American Educational History, an Introductory Textbook Dealing with the Larger Problems of*

Present Day Education in the Light of Their Historical Development (New York, Houghton Mifflin, 1919)

Davis, Michael. *Street Gang: The Complete History of Sesame Street* (New York: Viking Press, 2008)

Dawson, Christopher. *The Crisis of Western Civilization*, (Washington, D.C.: Catholic University of America Press, 1961)

Dewey, John. *Experience and Education*, (New York: Touchstone, 1938)

Dewey, John. *The school and society* (Chicago: University of Chicago Press, 1900)

Dewey, John. *The School and Society*, (Chicago: University of Chicago Press, 1902)

Du Pont de Nemours, Pierre. *National Education in the United States of America*, translated from the second French edition of 1812 and with an Introduction by B. G. Du Pont (Newark: University of Delaware Press, 1923)

Durant, Will & Ariel. *The Story of Civilization: Rousseau and revolution; a history of civilization in France, England, and Germany from 1756, and in the remainder of Europe from 1715 to 1789*, (New York: Simon & Schuster, 1967)

Flesch, Rudolf. *Why Johnny Can't Read—And What You Can Do About It*, (New York: Harper and Brothers, 1955)

Gardner, Howard. *The Unschooled Mind, How Children Think and How Schools Should Teach*. (New York: Basic Books, 1981)
.

Gladwell, Malcolm. *The Tipping Point: How Little Things Can Make a Big Difference* (New York: Little, Brown and Company, 2000)

Golding, William. *Lord of the Flies*, (London: Faber and Faber, 1954)

Green, John Alfred. *The Educational Ideas of Pestalozzi. 3rd edition (Baltimore: Warwick & York, 1900)*

Greer, Germaine. *Sex and Destiny, The Politics of Human Fertility* (New York: Harper & Row. 1984)

Hayes, Dade. *Anytime Playdate, Inside the preschool entertainment boom, how television became my baby's best friend* (New York, Free Press, 2008)

Hobbes, Thomas. *Hobbes's Leviathan Reprinted from the edition of 1651* (London: Oxford Clarendon Press, 1909

Holt, John. *How children fail* (New York: Dell, 1964)

Illich, Ivan. *Deschooling Society* (New York: Harper & Rowe, 1972)

Klein, Naomi. *This Changes Everything: Capitalism and the Climate* (New York: Simon and Schuster, 2014)

Kohn, Alfie. *Punished by Rewards, The Trouble with Gold Stars, Incentive Plans, A's, Praise, and Other Bribes* (Boston, New York: Houghton Mifflin Company, 1993)

Laing, Samuel. *Notes of a traveller: on the social and political state of France, Prussia, Switzerland, Italy and other parts of Europe during the present century. 2nd ed.* (London: Printed for Longman, Brown, Green, and Longmans, 1842)

Levin, Pamela, *Cycles of Power: A User's Guide to the Seven Seasons of Life* (Health Communications, Inc., Deerfield Beach, Florida, 1988)

Liu, Ziming. *Reading behavior in the digital environment, Changes in reading behavior over the past ten years*, (San Jose, California: School of Library and Information Science, 2005)

Locke, John. *Some Thoughts Concerning Education* (New York: Teachers College, Columbia University. 1964)

Mander, Jerry. *Four Arguments for the Elimination of Television* (New York, HarperCollins Publishers Inc., 1978)

Maté, Gabor, with Daniel Maté, *The Myth of Normal: Trauma, Illness & Healing in a Toxic Culture* (Toronto: Penguin Random House, Knopf Canada, 2022)

McGonigal, Jane. *Reality Is Broken: Why Games Make us Better and How They Can Change the World* (London: Jonathan Cape, 2011)

McGuinness, Diane. *Why Our Children Can't Read and What We Can Do About It* (New York: Simon & Schuster, 1997)

Mill, John Stuart. *On Liberty, ed. Elizabeth Rapaport* (Indianapolis: Hackett Publishing Company, 1978)

Miller, Alice. *Banished Knowledge, Facing Childhood Injuries, trans. Leila Vennewitz* (New York: Doubleday 1991)

Miller, Alice. *For Your Own Good, Hidden cruelty in child-rearing and the roots of violence* (New York: Farrar, Straus, Giroux, third edition 1990 by The Noonday Press)

Monbiot, George. *How Did We Get into This Mess?* (London: Verso, 2017)

Neill, Alexander Sutherland. *Summerhill, A Radical Approach to Childrearing* (New York: Hart Publishing Company, 1960)

Neill, Alexander Sutherland. *The Free Child* (London: Herbert Jenkins, 1953)

Neufeld, Gordon. *Hold on to your kids: why parents matter/Gordon Neufeld and Gabor Maté* (Toronto: Alfred A. Knopf Canada, 2004)

Ortega y Gasset, José. *The Dehumanization of Art and Other Essays on Art, Culture and Literature, trans. Helene Wyel* (Princeton: Princeton University Press, 1948, 51. Original, *La Dehumanización del Arte e Ideas sobre la Novela* published by Revista del Occidente, Madrid, 1925)

Pestalozzi, Johann Heinrich. *How Gertrude Teaches Her Children, trans. Lucy E. Holland and Frances C. Turner, and edited with introduction and notes by Ebenezer Cooke* (London: Swan Sonnenschein & Co., 1894)

Pestalozzi, Johann Heinrich. *Leonard and Gertrude, translated and abridged by Eva Channing* (Boston: D.C. Heath & Co., 1908)

Pink, Daniel H. *Drive, The Surprising Truth About What Motivates Us* (New York: Riverhead Books, 2009)

Postman, Neil. *Amusing Ourselves to Death, Public Discourse in the Age of Show Business* (New York: Viking Penguin Inc., 1985)

Postman, Neil. *Amusing Ourselves to Death, Public Discourse in the Age of Show Business* (New York: Penguin Books USA Inc. 1986)

Postman, Neil. *Building a Bridge to the 18th Century, How the Past Can Improve Our Future*, (New York: Knopf 1999)

Postman, Neil. *Technopoly, The Surrender of Culture to Technology* (New York: Random House, Vintage Books, 1993)

Putnam, Robert D. *Bowling Alone, The Collapse and Revival of American Community* (New York: Simon & Schuster, 2000)

Richler, Mordecai. *Cocksure* (Toronto: McClelland and Stewart, 1968)

Rosenthal & Lenore Jacobsen, Robert. *Pygmalion in the Classroom: Teacher Expectation and Pupil's Intellectual Development.* (Williston, VT: Crown House Publishing, 1968, revised and expanded 1992)

Rousseau, Jean-Jacques. *Emile or On Education, trans. Allan Bloom* (New York: Basic Books Inc., 1979)

Ryerson, Egerton. *Report on a System of Public Elementary Instruction in Upper Canada* (Montreal: Lovell and Gibson, 1847)

Silberman, Charles. *Crisis in the classroom* (New York: Random House, 1970)

Smith, Frank. *Insult to Intelligence: The Bureaucratic invasion of our Classrooms* (New York: Arbor House, 1986)

Smith, Frank. *Reading Without Nonsense, fourth edition* (New York: Teachers College Press, 2006)

Smith, Frank. *The book of learning and forgetting* (New York: Teachers College Press, 1998)

Spitzer, Michael. *The Musical Human, A History of Life on Earth* (London: Bloomsbury Publishing, 2021)

Spock, Dr. Benjamin. *Baby and Child Care* (New York: Pocket Books, Inc. 1946)

Taylor, Frederick W. *The Principles of Scientific Management* (New York: Harper & Brothers, 1911)

Tomatis, Alfred. *Pourquoi Mozart?* (Paris: Éditions Fixot, May 23 1991)

Vaughn, Robert. *The age of great cities; or, Modern civilization viewed in its relation to intelligence, morals and religion. Second Edition* (London: Jackson and Walford, 1843)

Verhaeghe, Paul. *Says Who? The Struggle for Authority in a Market-Based Economy trans. David Shaw* (Victoria, Aus. Scribe Publications, 2017)

Vygotsky, L. S. *Mind in Society, The Development of Higher Psychological Processes*, Michael Cole, Vera John-Steiner, Sylvia

Scribner & Ellen Souberman, eds., (Cambridge, Mass.: Harvard University Press, 1978)

Watson, John B. *Behaviorism* (New York: People's Institute Publishing Company, 1925)

Watson, John R. *The Psychological Care of Infant and Child* (London: George Allen and Unwin Ltd. 1928)

Watson. John R. *The Psychological Care of Infant and Child* (London, George Allen and Unwin Ltd. 1928)

Whitehead, Alfred North. *The aims of education* (New York: Mentor, 1929)

Wolf, Maryanne. *Proust and the Squid, The Story and Science of the Reading Brain* (New York: Harper Perennial, 2008)

Wolf, Maryanne. *Reader Come Home, The Reading Brain in a Digital World.* (New York: Harper-Collins, 2018)

NOTES

Introduction: Something About Me

1
https://open.library.ubc.ca/soa/cIRcle/collections/ubctheses/831/items/1.0
086416.
2
https://open.library.ubc.ca/soa/cIRcle/collections/ubctheses/831/items/1.0
055476.

Part One—What School Has Done For Us

3 Robert Longely, "Neoliberalism is a political and economic policy model that emphasizes the value of free market capitalism while seeking to transfer control of economic factors from the government to the private sector. Also incorporating the policies of privatization, deregulation, globalization, and free trade," ThoughtCo, accessed May 18, 2022, https://www.thoughtco.com/what-is-neoliberalism-definition-and-examples-5072548.

4 Horace Mann, *Twelfth Annual Report of the Board of Education together with the Twelfth Annual Report of the Secretary of the Board* (Boston: Dutton and Wentworth, 1849), 15-16, accessed May 15, 2022, https://archives.lib.state.ma.us/bitstream/handle/2452/204731/ocm07166 577_1848.pdf?sequence=1&isAllowed=y.

5 "National Assessment of Adult Literacy," *National Center for Education Statistics*, accessed June 10, 2021, https://nces.ed.gov/naal/kf_demographics.asp.

6 "What's the latest U.S. literacy rate?" *Wylie Communications*, accessed June 10, 2021, https://www.wyliecomm.com/2020/11/whats-the-latest-u-s-literacy-rate/#_ftn4.

7 "Literacy at a Glance," *ABC Life Literacy Canada*, accessed June 11, 2021, https://abclifeliteracy.ca/literacy-at-a-glance/.

8 Question #45780, Asked by Linus 337, "How many words make up the vocabulary of an average seven year old and an average adult?," *Fun-Trivia*, last updated Sep. 2016, https://www.funtrivia.com/askft/Question45780.html/.

9 Mark Bauerlein, *The Dumbest Generation: How the Digital Age Stupefies Young Americans and Jeopardizes Our Future: Or, Don't Trust Anyone Under 30,* (New York: Tarcher Perigee, 2006).

10 Jean M. Twenge et al, "Declines in vocabulary among American adults within levels of educational attainment, 1974–2016," *Intelligence*, Volume 76, Sep.–Oct. 2019, Article 101377.

11 Maggie Gilmour, "Students can't write," *MacLean's*, Nov. 19, 2010, https://www.macleans.ca/education/uniandcollege/students-cant-write/.

12 Nicholas Dion and Vicky Maldonado, "Making the Grade? Troubling Trends in Postsecondary Student Literacy," *Higher Education Quality of Ontario*, Issue Paper No. 16 Oct. 31, 2013, https://heqco.ca/wp-content/uploads/2020/03/HEQCO-Literacy-ENG.pdf.

13 Julia Martin Burch, "Back to school Anxiety," *Harvard Health Publishing*, Aug. 23, 2018, https://www.health.harvard.edu/blog/back-to-school-anxiety-2018082314617.

14 "American Psychological Association Survey Shows Teen Stress Rivals That of Adults," *American Psychological Association (2014)*, https://www.apa.org/news/press/releases/2014/02/teen-stress.

15 Matt Huston, review of *Freedom to Learn* by Peter Gray, "The Danger of Back to School, Children's mental health crises plummet in summer and rise in the school year," *Psychology Today*, Aug. 7, 2014, https://www.psychologytoday.com/ca/blog/freedom-learn/201408/the-danger-back-school.

16 Guifeng Xu, et al, "Twenty-Year Trends in Diagnosed Attention-Deficit/Hyperactivity Disorder Among US Children and Adolescents, 1997-2016," *Jama Network* (The Journal of the American Medical Association), Aug. 31, 2018, https://jamanetwork.com/journals/jamanetworkopen/fullarticle/2698633.

17 Heather M. Jones, "The benefits of ADHD medication for teens," *The Checkup, by Single Care*, Oct. 2019, https://www.singlecare.com/blog/adhd-medication-for-teens/.

18 "How ADHD Became a Multi-Billion Dollar Industry," WIRED.com, Dec. 9, 2015.

19 Toni Morrison, *Paradise* (Alfred A. Knopf, 1998), 254.

20 Sandra Graham, "Bullying: A Module for Teachers," *American Psychological Association*, accessed June 11, 2021, https://en.wikipedia.org/wiki/School_bullying.

21 "School Bullying affects us all," *Stop Bullying Now Foundation*, accessed June 11, 2021, http://www.stopbullyingnowfoundation.org/main/.

22 "All the Latest Cyber Bullying Statistics and What They Mean in 2021," *BroadbandSearch*, accessed June 11, 2021, https://www.broadbandsearch.net/blog/cyber-bullying-statistics.

23 Justin W. Patchin, "School Bullying Rates Increase by 35% from 2016 to 2019," *Cyberbullying Research Center*, accessed June 11, 2021, https://cyberbullying.org/school-bullying-rates-increase-by-35-from-2016-to-2019.

24 Nick Morrison, "Anti-Bullying Programs In Schools May Do More Harm Than Good," *Forbes*, Oct. 20, 2020,

https://www.forbes.com/sites/nickmorrison/2020/10/20/anti-bullying-programs-in-schools-may-do-more-harm-than-good/?sh=2318fefd38e0.

25 "11 Facts About High School Dropout Rates," *Do Something.org*, accessed June 12, 2021, https://www.dosomething.org/us/facts/11-facts-about-high-school-dropout-rates.

26 "Why Kids Drop out of High School and How to Prevent It," *Learning Liftoff*, accessed June 12, 2021, https://www.learningliftoff.com/why-kids-drop-out-of-high-school-and-how-to-prevent-it/.

27 Caitlin Curley, "How Standardized Testing Pushes Out Students," *Genbiz*, Sep. 12, 2016, https://genbiz.com/standardized-testing-pushes-students.

28 Michael Savage, "Almost a quarter of teachers who have qualified since 2011 have left profession," *The Guardian*, July 8, 2017, https://www.theguardian.com/education/2017/jul/08/almost-a-quarter-of-teachers-who-have-qualified-since-2011-have-left-profession.

29 Economic Research Institute, "Elementary School Teacher Salary in British Columbia, Canada," last updated Nov. 18, 2022, https://www.erieri.com/salary/job/elementary-school-teacher/canada/british-columbia.

30 CBC News, "B.C. teachers' union warns of possible staff shortages this year," Sep. 3, 2022, https://www.cbc.ca/news/canada/british-columbia/bctf-teachers-shortage-bc-1.6571191.

31 Chritopher Balow, PhD, "Teacher Attrition: A Critical Problem for America's Schools," June 2021, https://schoolmint.wpenginepowered.com/wp-content/uploads/Teacher-Attrition-Whitepaper.pdf.

32 Benjamin Kutsyuruba, Lorraine Godden, and Leigha Tregunna, "Curbing Early-Career Teacher Attrition," *Canadian Journal of Educational Administration and Policy*, Issue #161, Aug. 6, 2014, https://files.eric.ed.gov/fulltext/EJ1035357.pdf.

33 Lindsay Holmes, "Suicide Rates for Teen Boys and Girls Are Climbing." *Huffpost*, Sep. 4, 2017, https://www.huffpost.com/entry/suicide-rates-teen-girls_n_59848b64e4b0cb15b1be13f4.

34 Hilary Brueck and Shayanne Gal, "Suicide rates are climbing in young people from ages 10 to 24," *Insider*, Sep. 12, 2020, https://www.insider.com/cdc-suicide-rate-in-young-people-10-24-continues-climb-2020-9.

35 Steven Singer, "Middle School Suicides Double As Common Core Testing Intensifies," *Huffpost*, updated Aug. 2, 2017, https://www.huffpost.com/entry/middle-school-suicides-double-as-common-core-testing_b_59822d3de4b03d0624b0abb9.

36 Kerry McDonald, "At Back-To-School Time, the Childhood Suicide Rate Rises," *Intellectual Takeout*, Aug. 31, 2017, https://www.intellectualtakeout.org/article/back-school-time-childhood-suicide-rate-rises/.

37 Line Dalile, "How Schools Are Killing Creative," Huffpost, updated June 12, 2012, https://www.huffpost.com/entry/a-dictator-racing-to-nowh_b_1409138.

38 Sir Ken Robinson, Mar. 4, 1950 to Aug. 21, 2020.

39 Sir Ken Robinson, "Do schools kill creativity?" *TED2006 Video*, Feb. 2006, 18:12, https://www.ted.com/talks/sir_ken_robinson_do_schools_kill_creativity.

40 Howard Gardner. *The Unschooled Mind, How Children Think and How Schools Should Teach*. (New York: Basic Books, 1981), 3.

41 Gardner, *The Unschooled Mind*, 4.

42 Gardner, *The Unschooled Mind*, 4.

43 I'm not the only one who has come to this conclusion. See, for example, the writings of John Taylor Gatto, Peter Gray, Diane Ravitch. Ken Robinson, and many others.

44 Quoted in *The Free library: The case for public schools*, accessed May 8, 2022, https://www.thefreelibrary.com/The+case+for+public+schools.-a016706078.

Part Two—The Erosion of Civilized Society

45 Robert C. Putnam, "Bowling Alone: America's Declining Social Capital," *Journal of Democracy*, Jan. 1995, https://www.journalofdemocracy.org/articles/bowling-alone-americas-declining-social-capital/.

46 Robert D. Putnam, *Bowling Alone, The Collapse and Revival of American Community* (New York: Simon & Schuster, 2000).

47 Wikipedia, "L.J. Hanifan," Last modified May 9, 2021, https://en.wikipedia.org/wiki/L._J._Hanifan.

48 L.J. Hanifan (1916), "The Rural School Community Center," *Zenodo*, accessed Nov. 19, 2022, https://zenodo.org/record/1448664, 130.

49 Hanifan, "The Rural School Community Center," 131.

50 According to Hanifan, out of 1,409 adult residents, some 45 were illiterate. That's three per cent of a rural population, looking pretty good compared to the approximately 50 per cent of today's population that are functionally illiterate. See also Neil Postman on 18th century literacy in America.

51 Putnam, *Bowling Alone*, 218 (Putnam's source: *Statistical Abstract of the United States* (Various years) and *Historical Statistics of the United States.*)

52 , Douglas McLennan & Jack Miles, "A once unimaginable scenario: No more newspapers," The Washington Post, Mar. 21, 2018, https://www.washingtonpost.com/news/theworldpost/wp/2018/03/21/newspapers/.

53 Putnam, *Bowling Alone*, 218.

54 Wikipedia, "Astor Market," last modified May 16, 2021, https://en.wikipedia.org/wiki/Astor_Market.

55 Oana Vasiliu, "Supermarkets story," PR Pret-a-Porter, August 3, 2011, https://prpretaporter.wordpress.com/2011/08/03/supermarkets-story/.

56 Paco Underhill, "Why We Buy-The science of shopping," *Academia.edu*, accessed June 13, 2021, https://www.academia.edu/6789902/Why_We_Buy_The_science_of_sho pping_Paco_Underhill_Qwerty80_.

57 John Matson, "Is Pop Music Evolving, or Is It Just Getting Louder?" *Scientific American*, July 26, 2012, https://blogs.scientificamerican.com/observations/is-pop-music-evolving-or-is-it-just-getting-louder/.

58 Mike Floorwalker, "10 Surprising Ways Music Can Be Bad For You,", LISTVERSE, June 25, 2015, https://listverse.com/2016/06/25/10-surprising-ways-music-can-be-bad-for-you/.

59 Chris Morris, "Songs are getting shorter. Blame the economics of streaming music." FORTUNE, Jan. 17, 2019, https://fortune.com/2019/01/17/shorter-songs-spotify/.

60 John Philip Sousa, "The Menace of Mechanical Music," Appleton's Magazine, Vol. 8 (1906), 278-284, https://ocw.mit.edu/courses/music-and-theater-arts/21m-380-music-and-technology-contemporary-history-and-aesthetics-fall-2009/readings-and-listening/MIT21M_380F09_read02_sousa.pdf.

61 Arthur Sullivan, "Sir Arthur Sullivan Speaking 1888," *Archive of Recorded Church Music*, YouTube Video, 1:21, accessed Nov. 19, 2022, https://www.youtube.com/watch?v=v5-oe3GkpVk.

62 José Ortega y Gasset, *The Dehumanization of Art and Other Essays on Art, Culture and Literature, trans. Helene Wyel* (Princeton: Princeton University Press, 1948, 51. Original, *La Dehumanización del Arte e Ideas sobre la Novela* published by Revista del Occidente, Madrid, 1925).

63 cleonje, "The North has Spoken! Toronto Raptors 2019 NBA Champions," *Never Dated*, June 14, 2019, https://neverdated.ca/2019/06/14/the-north-has-spoken-toronto-2019-nba-champions/ accessed May 10, 2022.

64 "2019/20 Toronto Raptors Salaries" *Hoops Hype*, accessed May 10, 2022.

65 Ortega y Gasset, *Dehumanization of Art*, 51.

66 Carmen Ang, "How much does it cost to host the Olympics?" *Visual Capitalist*, Feb. 3, 2022, https://www.visualcapitalist.com/how-much-does-it-cost-to-host-the-olympics/.

67 Louis Menard, "Show them the money: Is the sports business a bubble?" *New Yorker*, May 16, 2016. Also: https://www.newyorker.com/magazine/2016/05/16/the-professional-sports-bubble.

68 Fran Lebowitz, "Right off the top of my head, I would say math," (Quoted in George Gurley, "What I don't know," *Observer*, April 3, 2002, https://observer.com/2002/03/what-i-dont-know/).

69 Wikipedia. 2021, "Automated teller machine," last modified May 6, 2021, https://en.wikipedia.org/wiki/Automated_teller_machine.

70 Justine Jordan, "According to a New Report, Last Year Was a Very Bad Year for Print Magazines," The Fashion Spot, Aug. 9, 2018, https://www.thefashionspot.com/runway-news/799011-print-magazines-in-decline/.

71 "U.S. media use: time spent reading magazines 2010-2018." Statista Research Department, June 13, 2016, https://www.statista.com/statistics/186944/us-magazine-reading-habits-since-2002/.

72 Wikipedia, *Time* (magazine), accessed June 15, 2021, https://en.wikipedia.org/wiki/Time_(magazine).

73 Jeffrey A Trachtenberg, "Time Magazine Sold to Salesforce Founder Marc Benioff for $190 Million," *The Wall Street Journal*, updated Sep. 16, 2018, https://www.wsj.com/articles/time-magazine-sold-to-salesforce-founder-marc-benioff-for-190-million-1537137165.

74 Sydney Ember & Michael M. Grynbaum, "The Not-So-Glossy Future of Magazines," *The New York Times*, Sep. 23, 2017, https://www.nytimes.com/2017/09/23/business/media/the-not-so-glossy-future-of-magazines.html.

75 Maryanne Wolf. *Reader Come Home, The Reading Brain in a Digital World.* (New York: Harper-Collins, 2018).

76 Maryanne Wolf. *Reader Come Home.* 41.

77 *There is no frigate like a book/To take us lands away,/Nor any coursers like a page/Of prancing poetry.//This traverse may the poorest take/Without oppress of toll,/How frugal is the chariot/That bears a human soul!*—Emily Dickinson.

78 Ziming Liu, *Reading behavior in the digital environment, Changes in reading behavior over the past ten years,* (San Jose, California: School of Library and Information Science, 2005), 700.

79 Anne Mangen, Bente R.Walgermo & Kolbjørn Brønnick, *Reading linear texts on paper versus computer screen, Effects on reading comprehension,* (Amsterdam: International Journal of Educational Research, Volume 58, 2013), 61-68.

80 Erik Wastlund, Henrik Reinikka, Torsten Norlander & Trevor Archer, "Effects of VDT and paper presentation on consumption and production of information: Psychological and physiological factors," accessed Nov. 19, 2022,

https://www.researchgate.net/publication/220495600_Effects_of_VDT_a
nd_paper_presentation_on_consumption_and_production_of_informatio
n_Psychological_and_physiological_factors.

81 Gemma Walsh, *Screen and Paper Reading Research--A Literature Review* (Kingston: Australian Academic & Research Libraries, 2016), 160-173, https://www.tandfonline.com/doi/full/10.1080/00048623.2016.1227661.

82 Nicholas Carr, *The Shallows: How the internet is changing the way we think, read and remember* (London: Atlantic books, 2010).

83 Maryanne Wolf, *Proust and the Squid, The Story and Science of the Reading Brain* (New York: Harper Perennial, 2008).

84 Barry Cull, *Reading Revolutions*: *Online digital text and implications for reading in academe* (Fredericton: First Monday, Peer-Reviewed Journal on the Internet Volume 16, Number 6. 2011).

85 *Blazing Saddles* (10/10) Movie CLIP Boy, Is He Strict (1974) HD, YouTube Video, 2:42, accessed June 22, 2021, https://www.youtube.com/watch?v=bcokL59jeqU.

86 Peter Schjeldahl, "Garry Winograd and Jeff Wall: Photography in Two Phases," *New Yorker*, May 13, 2019.

87 The Halo Group, *Snackable Content: Short, sweet, and extremely filling*, accessed June 22, 2021, https://www.thehalogroup.com/snackable-content-short-sweet-extremely-filling/.

88 *MediaBUZZ,* "Snackable content manages the balancing act between pleasing content and monetarization," accessed June 22, 2021, https://www.mediabuzz.com.sg/archive/2017/february.

89 Kevin McSpadden, "You Now Have a Shorter Attention Span Than a Goldfish," *Time*, May 14, 2015.

90 Nick Salerni, "Microsoft Study: Tech is Shortening the Average Human's Attention Span," accessed June 22, 2021, https://www.iphoneincanada.ca/news/microsoft-study-tech-is-shortening-the-average-humans-attention-span/.

91 Neil A. Bradbury, "Attention span during lectures: 8 seconds, 10 minutes, or more?" *Advances in Physiology Education* Vol. 40, No. 4, 509-513, November 8, 2026, https://doi.org/10.1152/advan.00109.2016.

92 W.S. Gilbert & Arthur Sullivan, *The Mikado or The Town of Titipu* (First produced at the Savoy Theatre in London, March 1885).

93 Ariel Schwartz, "What it's like to attend the TED talks, where attendees pay $10,000 to learn the next big ideas, *INSIDER*, Apr 13, 2018, https://www.businessinsider.com/ted-2017-conference-photos-2017-4.

94 *Chris Anderson, TED Talks: The Official TED Guide to Public Speaking* (London: Headline Publishing Group, 2016).

95 Sir Ken Robinson, "Do schools kill creativity?" YouTube Video, 20:03, Jan. 6, 2007, https://www.youtube.com/watch?v=iG9CE55wbtY.

96 Neil Postman, *Building a Bridge to the 18th Century, How the Past Can Improve Our Future*, (New York: Knopf 1999), 64.

97 Pierre Du Pont de Nemours, *National Education in the United States of America,* translated from the second French edition of 1812 and with an Introduction by B. G. Du Pont (Newark: University of Delaware Press, 1923), 3-4, *)Quoted in Susan Alder,* "Education in America," *Foundation for Economic Education,* 1993), https://fee.org/articles/education-in-america.

98 Frank Smith, *Reading Without Nonsense, fourth edition* (New York: Teachers College Press, 2006), 12.

99 Frank Smith, *The book of learning and forgetting* (New York: Teachers College Press, 1998), 25.

100 Andrew Marantz, "The Anti-coup," *New Yorker,* Nov. 23, 2020.

101 Joni Mitchell, "Big Yellow Taxi." Recorded 1969-1970, Side 2, Track 4, on *Ladies of the Canyon.* Reprise-Warner Bros., 1970, Long-play record.

102 "Teenagers are a great group for businesses to target because they have the potential to really help your business grow. They are part of a large group of consumers who are obsessed with the consumer market. They are also a group that you can strategically cater to and plan your marketing methods behind. Teenagers are a very specific group that needs a particular way of engaging with," accessed Nov. 18, 2022, https://thelogocompany.net/blog/branding-guides/5-easy-ways-target-teens-marketing/.

103 See Booth Tarkington's *Penrod,* comic strips like *Harold Teen,* and *Archie Comics,* radio, movies, and later television shows such as *The Aldrich Family and* the series featuring the character Andy Hardy.

104 Natalie Coulter, *Tweening the girl, the crystallization of the tween market* (New York: International Academic Publishers, 2014).

105 Smith, *Learning and Forgetting,* 9.

106 Smith, *Learning and Forgetting,* vii.

Part Three—The World of Fun and Games

A. Shoot To Kill

107 Naomi Klein, *This Changes Everything: Capitalism and the Climate* (New York: Simon and Schuster, 2014).

108 Connor Williams, "Gaming: Study reveals how much of the global population now plays video games," *Givemesport,* Feb. 24, 2021, https://www.givemesport.com/1653435-gaming-study-reveals-how-much-of-the-global-population-now-plays-video-games.

109 Note that this is the second Doom movie. The first, simply titled *Doom,* had a theatrical release in 2005. Comment by Miles Durrie.

110 Universal Home Entertainment, "Doom Annihilation, Own it on Blu-ray, DVD & Digital Now," accessed June 22, 2021, https://www.uphe.com/movies/doom-annihilation.

111 Doom was developed by a Dallas company called id Software LLC, founded in 1991. That company was acquired in 2009 by ZeniMax Media, a video-game conglomerate based in Rockville, Md. Comment by Miles Durrie.

112 This statistic refers to the number of registered Fortnite accounts. The highest number of active players in a single month was 78.3 million, and the record of people logged in simultaneously was 10.8 million before and during a live in-game concert by American DJ Marshmello on Feb. 2, 2019. (I'd bet all those numbers will be eclipsed during the pandemic lockdown.) Comment by Miles Durrie.

113 "Is Fortnite dying? How many people play Fortnite in 2022?" last updated Aug. 5,1011, https://techacake.com/is-fortnite-dying/.

114 Iain Wilson, Sam Loveridge & Ford James, "How to play Fortnite advice for absolute beginners," *gamesradar*, accessed June 22, 2021, https://www.gamesradar.com/how-to-play-fortnite/.

115 Frannie Ucciferri, "Parents' ultimate guide to 'Fortnite'," *Salon*, Oct. 19, 2018, https://www.salon.com/2018/10/19/parents-ultimate-guide-to-fortnite_partner/.

116 KidsPost, "What is Minecraft?" *Washington Post*, accessed Aug. 16, 2021, https://www.washingtonpost.com/lifestyle/kidspost/what-is-minecraft/2013/03/14/98c54514-8a57-11e2-a051-6810d606108d_story.html.

117 Elissa Strauss, "The argument for playing video games with our kids," *CNN Health*, Feb. 18, 2019, https://www.cnn.com/2019/02/18/health/video-games-parenting-strauss/index.html.

118 Christina Barron, "Minecraft spawns classroom lessons," *Washington Post*, Mar. 14, 2013, https://www.washingtonpost.com/lifestyle/kidspost/minecraft-spawns-classroom-lessons/2013/03/14/717aed66-87b8-11e2-98a3-b3db6b9ac586_story.html?tid=a_inl_manual.

119 Luke Morgan Britton, "'Grand Theft Auto V' has made more money than any movie ever," *NME News*, Apr. 11, 2018, https://www.nme.com/news/grand-theft-auto-v-most-successful-entertainment-title-ever-2289320.

120 Keith Stuart, "GTA 5 review: a dazzling but monstrous parody of modern life," *The Guardian*, Sep. 16, 2013, https://www.theguardian.com/technology/2013/sep/16/gta-5-review-grand-theft-auto-v.

121 Tom Hoggins, "Grand Theft Auto V is designed deliberately to degrade women," *The Telegraph*, Oct. 4, 2013,

https://www.telegraph.co.uk/women/womens-life/10355275/Grand-Theft-Auto-V-is-designed-deliberately-to-degrade-women.html.
122 I think in this era we do need to say, because there's a real and growing expectation of female characters as key players, heroes and bad guys across pop culture. Comment by Miles Durrie.
123 Tom Hoggins, "Grand Theft Auto V."
124 That was 2013 when it was first released. Do I need to say that the trend has continued, with more realistic video, more violence, more sexism?
125 Mark Serrels, "17 awesome video games to play with your kids," *cnet*, June 1, 2020, https://www.cnet.com/pictures/17-awesome-video-games-to-play-with-your-kids/.
126 Daphne Bavelier, "Your Brain on Video Games," YouTube Video, 17:41, Nov. 19, 2012, https://www.ted.com/talks/daphne_bavelier_your_brain_on_video_games/transcript?language=en#t-68565.
127 "A song from Walt Disney's 1964 film and 2004 musical version of *Mary Poppins*, composed by Robert B. Sherman and Richard M. Sherman," https://en.wikipedia.org/wiki/A_Spoonful_of_Sugar.
128 Daphne Bavelier, "Your Brain on Video Games."
129 Drew Guarini, "9 Ways Video Games Can Actually Be Good For You," *Huffpost*, updated December 6, 2017, https://www.huffpost.com/entry/video-games-good-for-us_n_4164723.
130 Drew Guarini, "9 Ways Video Games Can Actually Be Good For You."
131 Daphne Bavelier, "Your Brain on Video Games."
132 Drew Guarini, "9 Ways Video Games Can Actually Be Good For You."
133 inf9YbR3, "'8 Cognitive Benefits of Playing Video Games for Kids," *Inferno Group*, May 20, 2019, https://inferno-group.com/8-cognitive-benefits-of-playing-video-games-for-kids/.
134 Jane McGonigal, *Reality Is Broken: Why Games Make us Better and How They Can Change the World* (London: Jonathan Cape, 2011).
135 Craig A. Anderson, PhD, "Violent Video Games: Myths, Facts, and Unanswered Questions," *American Psychological Association, Psychological Science Agenda, Oct. 2003, https://www.apa.org/science/about/psa/2003/10/anderson.*
136 Jane McGonigal, "Gaming can make a better world," YouTube Video, 20:31, Mar. 12, 2010, https://www.ted.com/talks/jane_mcgonigal_gaming_can_make_a_better_world/transcript.
137 Jane McGonigal, "Gaming can make a better world."
138 Dimitri Christakis, "TEDxRainier - Dimitri Christakis - Media and Children," YouTube video, 16:11, Dec. 28, 2011, https://www.youtube.com/watch?v=BoT7qH_uV.

139 SingleCare Team, "ADHD statistics 2021," Updated on Jan. 21, 2021, https://www.singlecare.com/blog/news/adhd-statistics/.

B. Learning As Fun or The Erosion of Childhood

140 Loadmaster, "Einstein, Top Definition," Urban Dictionary, July 29, 2005, https://www.urbandictionary.com/define.php?term=Einstein.
141 State of the Union 2007, "President Bush Delivers State of the Union Address," *The White House,* Jan. 23, 2007, https://georgewbush-whitehouse.archives.gov/news/releases/2007/01/20070123-2.
142 Joel Schwarz, "Baby DVDs, videos may hinder, not help, infants' language development," *University of Washington, UW News*, Aug. 7, 2007, https://www.washington.edu/news/2007/08/07/baby-dvds-videos-may-hinder-not-help-infants-language-development/.
143 Jay L. Hoecker, "Can Baby Einstein videos and similar programming promote a child's development?" *Mayo Clinic*, accessed July 26, 2021, https://www.mayoclinic.org/healthy-lifestyle/infant-and-toddler-health/expert-answers/baby-einstein/faq-20058099.
144 Campaign for a Commercial-Free Childhood, https://fairplayforkids.org/.
145 American Academy of Pediatrics, https://www.aap.org/en-us/Pages/Default.aspx.
146 Drea Knufken, "After Controversy, Disney Issues Baby Einstein Recall." *Business Pundit*, Oct. 26, 2009, https://www.businesspundit.com/after-controversy-dinsey-issues-baby-einstein-recall/.
147 Liz Gumbinner, "Breaking news – Baby Einstein is issuing full refunds on their DVDs," *Cool Mom Picks*, Oct. 23, 2009, https://coolmompicks.com/blog/2009/10/23/baby-einstein-dvd-refund/.
148 Wikipedia, "Baby Einstein," accessed July 25, 2021, https://en.wikipedia.org/wiki/Baby_Einstein.
149 Tamar Lewin, "'Baby Einstein' Founder Goes to Court," *New York Times*, Jan/ 12, 2010, https://www.nytimes.com/2010/01/13/education/13einstein.html.
150 Ruth Graham, "The Rise and Fall of Baby Einstein," *Slate*, Dec. 19, 2017, https://slate.com/technology/2017/12/the-rise-and-fall-of-baby-einstein.html.
151 "Kids II Purchases Baby Einstein," *License Global*, Apr. 6, 2018, https://www.licenseglobal.com/toys-games/kids-ii-purchases-baby-einstein.
152 https://www.kids2.com/
153 https://www.kids2.com/collections/baby-einstein-toys-gear.
154 https://www.kids2.com/collections/baby-einstein-toys-gear/products/30974-bendy-ball-rattle-toy.

155 https://www.kids2.com/collections/baby-einstein-toys-gear/products/60184-neighborhood-friends-activity-jumper.

156 https://www.babyprodigy.com/.

157 Fleischer Studios v. Ralph A. Freundlich, Inc., *Opinion 1934*, accessed May 19, 2021, https://casetext.com/case/fleischer studios-v-ralph-a-freundlich-inc-2.

158 ChuChu TV, "Chubby Cheeks Rhyme with Lyrics and Actions" 1/47, Feb.14, 2013, https://www.youtube.com/watch?v=Ul3nQsM-Hmc.

159 Alexis C. Madrigal, "Raised by YouTube, The platform's entertainment for children is weirder—and more globalized—than adults could have expected," *Atlantic*, Nov. 2018.

160 Julian CELEBRITY NET WORTH "How Much Money ChuChu Tv Makes On YouTube" *Nailbuzz*, Feb. 3, 2022, https://naibuzz.com/much-money-chuchu-tv-makes-youtube/.

161 ChuChu TV Nursery Rhymes & Kids Songs Net Worth & Earnings, "What is ChuChu TV Nursery Rhymes & Kids Songs's net worth?" *Net Worth Spot*, May 1, 2022, https://www.networthspot.com/chuchu-tv-nursery-rhymes-kids-songs/net-worth/.

162 Don G. Campbell, *The Mozart effect: tapping the power of music to heal the body, strengthen the mind, and unlock the creative spirit* (New York: Avon Books, 1997).

163 Don G. Campbell, *The Mozart Effect for Children: Awakening Your Child's Mind, Health, and Creativity with Music* (New York: Harper Collins Publishers, 2000).

164 Published by The Children's Group, Waterdown, Ontario, 2002.

165 Alex Ross, "CLASSICAL VIEW; Listening To Prozac . . . Er, Mozart," *New York Times*, Aug. 28, 1994, https://www.nytimes.com/1994/08/28/arts/classical-view-listening-to-prozac-er-mozart.html.

166 Nicholas Till, "And God created Mozart—archive, 1991," *The Guardian*, Dec. 5, 2017, https://www.theguardian.com/music/2017/dec/05/mozart-god-created-archive-1991.

167 Available from Amazon: https://www.amazon.com/Baby-Mozart-Music-Stimulate-Babys-Brain/dp/B00000I6MF/.

168 Baby Einstein, "Baby Mozart Music Festival, Classical Music for Toddlers,Full Episode," YouTube Video, 26:13, accessed Nov. 18, 2022, https://www.youtube.com/watch?v=_HbEejSqE9Y. 5:49 / 26:13.

169 Alfred Tomatis, *Pourquoi Mozart?* (Paris: Éditions Fixot, May 23 1991).

170 Frances Rauscher, Gordon Shaw & Katherine Ky, "Music and spatial task performance," *Nature* **365,** 611 (1993), Oct. 1993, https://doi.org/10.1038/365611a0.

171 Kevin Sack, "Georgia's Governor Seeks Musical Start for Babies," *New York Times*, Jan. 15, 1998.

172 Dr. Benjamin Spock, *Baby and Child Care* (New York: Pocket Books, Inc. 1946), 304.

173 "Good Toys for Young Children by Age and Stage," National Association for the Education of Young Children, accessed June 19, 2022, https://www.naeyc.org/resources/topics/play/toys.

174 "Mattel's nabi® Brand Introduces First-Ever Connected Kids Room Platform In Tandem With Microsoft And Qualcomm – Aristotle," CISION, PR Newswire, accessed Oct. 30, 2022, https://www.prnewswire.com/news-releases/mattels-nabi-brand-introduces-first-ever-connected-kids-room-platform-in-tandem-with-microsoft-and-qualcomm---aristotle-300385221.html.

175 "Re: Aristotle" (Letter to Mattel), Campaign for a Commercial-Free Childhood, The Story of Stuff Project, Oct. 2, 2017, https://fairplayforkids.org/wp-content/uploads/archive/Letter%20to%20Mattel.pdf,

176 "Meet Hello Barbie," Hello Barbie, accessed July 28, 2021, http://hellobarbiefaq.mattel.com/.

177 Rachel Rabkin Peachman, "Mattel Pulls Aristotle Children's Device After Privacy Concerns," *New York Times*, Oct. 5, 2017, https://www.nytimes.com/2017/10/05/well/family/mattel-aristotle-privacy.html#commentsContainer.

178 "Echo Dot (4th Gen) Kids | Designed for kids, with parental controls," *Amazon*, accessed July 28, 2021. https://www.amazon.com/Echo-Dot-4th-Gen-Kids/dp/B084J4QQK1.

179 Caribu, "Playtime is Calling," accessed July 28, 2021, https://caribu.com/.

180 Ms. Rachel, "Speech Practice Video for Toddlers and Babies," YouTube video, 1.02.05, July 9, 2020, https://www.youtube.com/watch?v=41vocyDRhLs.

181 Malcolm Gladwell, *The Tipping Point: How Little Things Can Make a Big Difference* (New York: Little, Brown and Company, 2000).

182 Michael Davis, *Street Gang: The Complete History of Sesame Street* (New York: Viking Press, 2008), 8.

183 Melissa S. Kearney & Phillip B. Levine, "Early Childhood Education by MOOC: Lessons from Sesame Street," *National Bureau of Economic Research*, June 2015, https://www.wellesley.edu/sites/default/files/assets/site/files/wellesleysesamestudy_full.pdf.

184 Neil Postman, *Amusing Ourselves to Death, Public Discourse in the Age of Show Business* (New York: Viking Penguin Inc., 1985), 144.

185 Saga Briggs, "Refuse to Be a Boring Teacher: 15 Ways to Have More Fun," *informED*, Oct. 10, 2015, https://www.opencolleges.edu.au/informed/features/refuse-to-be-a-boring-teacher/.

186 Presidential Speeches Lyndon B. Johnson Presidency, "January 8, 1964: State of the Union," *UVA—Miller Center*, https://millercenter.org/the-presidency/presidential-speeches/january-8-1964-state-union.

187 One of the most remarkable (and creative?) commercial enterprises would have to be "Caribbean Adventures with Sesame Street.--Our exclusive partnership with Sesame Street makes Beaches Resorts the only Caribbean resorts where kids can play every day with their favorite furry friends! At Camp Sesame, children can participate in fun-filled activities like *Baking with Cookie Monster, Puppet Making with Bert & Ernie, Move and Groove with Zoe and Rosita* and so much more!" accessed July 20, 2021, https://www.beaches.com/activities/sesame-street/.

188 "Tickle Me Elmo is a children's plush toy from Tyco Preschool, a division of Tyco Toys, of the Muppet character Elmo from the children's television show *Sesame Street*," *Wikipedia*, accessed Nov. 19, 2022, https://en.wikipedia.org/wiki/Tickle_Me_Elmo.

189 Dade Hayes, *Anytime Playdate, Inside the preschool entertainment boom, how television became my baby's best friend* (New York, Free Press, 2008).

190 Marketing Charts, "The State of Traditional TV: Updated With Q3 2020 Data," May 12, 2021, https://www.marketingcharts.com/featured-105414.

191 PA Media, "Most children own mobile phone by age of seven, study finds," *The Guardian*, Jan. 30, 2020, https://www.theguardian.com/society/2020/jan/30/most-children-own-mobile-phone-by-age-of-seven-study-finds.

192 Health News, "Most 2-Years-Olds Use Mobile Media Devices," *healthline*, accessed July 20, 2021, https://www.healthline.com/health-news/most-2-year-olds-use-mobile-media-devices-042515.

193 Brent Lang, "Netflix hopes to popularize the concept of 'must-binge'," *Variety*, Nov. 6, 2018.

194 Sanj Awal, "SpongeBob SquarePants is still the most popular children's TV show," *KIDS*, Mar. 17, 2022, https://kids.guinnessworldrecords.com/news/2022/3/spongebob-squarepants-is-still-the-most-popular-childrens-tv-show-695586.

195 "As of late 2017, the *SpongeBob SquarePants* media franchise has generated _____ in merchandising revenue for Nickelodeon," *QuizGriz*, accessed Mar. 15, 2021, https://grizly.com/question/as-of-late-2017-the-spongebob-squarepants-media-franchise-has-generated-in-merchandising-revenue-for-nickelodeon.

196 News Room, "American Academy of Pediatrics Announces New Recommendations for Children's Media Use," *American Academy of Pediatrics*, Oct. 21, 2016, https://services.aap.org/en/news-room/news-releases/aap/2016/aap-announces-new-recommendations-for-media-use/.

197 Jerry Mander, *Four Arguments for the Elimination of Television* (New York, HarperCollins Publishers Inc., 1978), 192-193.
198 Mander, *Four Arguments*, 200.
199 Dorothy G. Singer & Jerome L. Singer, *Television, Imagination, and Aggression, A Study of Preschoolers* (Milton Park, Abingdon, UK: Routledge, 1981), 1.
200 Emily Sohn, "What Video Games Can Teach Us," *Science News for Students*, Jan. 19, 2004, https://www.sciencenewsforstudents.org/article/what-video-games-can-teach-us.
201 Kira Leigh, "This is Why Video Games are the Future of Education," *GamerSensei*, June 28, 2018, https://blog.gamersensei.com/article/gaming-and-education/.
202 Caitlin Uttley, "10 Educational Video Games Your Kids Will Love," *HowStuffWorks*, accessed June 24, 2021, https://electronics.howstuffworks.com/family-tech/tech-for-kids/10-educational-video-games-your-kids-will-love.htm.
203 LY203 Productions, "Reader Rabbit Preschool (Carousel Version) Full Walkthrough," YouTube video, 3:01:51, Feb. 17, 2017, https://www.youtube.com/watch?v=YRSbXuKSKBk.
204 Reader Rabbit Wiki, "Reader Rabbit: Learn to Read With Phonics," accessed June 24, 2021, https://readerrabbit.fandom.com/wiki/Reader_Rabbit:_Learn_to_Read_With_Phonics.
205 Frank Smith, *Insult to Intelligence: The Bureaucratic invasion of our Classrooms* (New York: Arbor House, 1986), 2.
206 Phil Edwards, "9 myths you learned from playing Oregon Trail," *Vox*, Updated June 2, 2015, https://www.vox.com/2015/2/6/7987697/oregon-trail-game-real-life.
207 Bill Bigelow, Brenda Harvey, Stan Karp, & Larry Miller, eds., *Rethinking Our Classrooms, Volume 2, Teaching for Equity and Justice*, (Milwaukee: A Rethinking Our Classrooms Publication, Feb. 13, 2004).
208 Bill Bigelow, "On the Road to Cultural Bias, A critique of 'The Oregon Trail'," accessed June 25, 2021, http://www1.udel.edu/educ/whitson/897s05/files/OregonTrail.pdf.
209 Colin Campbell, "The Oregon Trail was made in just two weeks," *Polygon*, July 31, 2013, https://www.polygon.com/2013/7/31/4575810/the-oregon-trail-was-made-in-just-two-weeks.
210 The Oregon Trail Card Game, *Pressman*, accessed June 25, 2021, https://www.pressmantoy.com/product/the-oregon-trail-card-game/.
211 Steve Kamb, "Life Lessons Learned from Oregon Trail," *NerdFitness,* https://www.nerdfitness.com/blog/life-lessons-learned-from-oregon-trail/, last updated Jan. 9, 2013.

212 MECC, "The Oregon Trail, Diskette and Instruction Booklet," accessed Nov. 18, 2022, https://oldgamesdownload.com/wp-content/uploads/The_Oregon_Trail_AppleII_Manual_EN.pdf.
213 "Their imagination glows, their energies rise up at the idea of death, these people: they love it; and the more horrible it is the more they enjoy it," George Bernard Shaw, *Man and Superman*, Act 3, Scene 2, (Westminster: Archibald and Constable & Co., Ltd, 1903).
214 Phil Edwards, "9 myths you learned from playing Oregon Trail."
215 "You Have Died of Dysentery T Shirt Funny Gamer Shirts Video Games Nerdy Cool 80s," *Amazon*, accessed June 25, 2021, https://www.amazon.com/Dysentery-Shirt-Funny-Gamer-Shirts/dp/B0064CH6NW.
216 They don't distinguish between the Greek *Odysseus* (Roman *Ulysses*) and the Roman *Hercules* (Greek *Heracles*). But I suppose this is nitpicking. After all, we're selling something here, not bothering with details.
217 Assassins Creed Odyssey, "Discover Assassin's Creed Valhalla," *Ubisoft*, accessed June 25, 2012, https://www.ubisoft.com/en-ca/game/assassins-creed/odyssey.
218 Assassins Creed Odyssey, "Discover Assassin's Creed Valhalla."
219 Louise Blaine, "Best single player games to play in 2019." YouTube video, 10:24, Apr. 2, 2019, https://www.youtube.com/watch?v=ZTXHrgNw2yM.
220 Ubisoft [NA], "Assassin's Creed Odyssey: Discovery Tour," YouTube video, 3:51, Sep. 10, 2019, https://www.youtube.com/watch?v=uh4Iy-p943M.
221 Ubisoft [NA], "Assassin's Creed Odyssey: Discovery Tour."
222 Ubisoft [NA], "Assassin's Creed Odyssey: Discovery Tour."
223 Colin Campbell, "Assassin's Creed Odyssey's Discovery Tour is an inspiring journey through ancient Greece," *Polygon*, Sep. 10, 2019, https://www.polygon.com/reviews/2019/9/10/20859403/assassins-creed-odysseys-discovery-tour-review-ancient-greece-education-game.
224 Andy Kelly, "Feel what it was like to live in Ancient Greece in Assassin's Creed Odyssey's new mode," *PCGamer*, Sep. 12, 2019, https://www.pcgamer.com/feel-what-it-was-like-to-live-in-ancient-greece-in-assassins-creed-odysseys-new-mode/.
225 W. S. Gilbert and Arthur Sullivan, *The Mikado* (1885), ActOne.
226 "Gamification in Learning Examples 2020," accessed July 30, 2021, https://skiglaciermt.com/0ji30/8174a8-gamification-in-learning-examples#.
227 Ryan Schaaf & Jack Quinn, "12 Examples Of Gamification In The Classroom," *Teach Thought*, accessed July 30, 2021, https://www.teachthought.com/the-future-of-learning/12-examples-of-gamification-in-the-classroom/.

228 Mordecai Richler, *Cocksure* (Toronto: McClelland and Stewart, 1968).

229 Ryan Schaaf & Jack Quinn, "12 Examples of Gamification In The Classroom."

230 Gabriela Kiryakova, Nadezhda Angelova, & Lina Yordanova, "Gamification in Education," accessed July 30, 2021, https://www.sun.ac.za/english/learning-teaching/ctl/Documents/Gamification%20in%20education.pdf.

231 Daphne Bavelier, "Your Brain on Video Games," YouTube Video, 17:41, Nov. 19, 2012, https://www.ted.com/talks/daphne_bavelier_your_brain_on_video_games/transcript?language=en#t-68565.

232 Tony Wan, "Now With Revenue, ClassDojo Raises $35 Million to Expand to Homes Across the World," *EdSurge*, Feb. 28, 2019, https://www.edsurge.com/news/2019-02-28-now-with-revenue-classdojo-raises-35-million-to-expand-to-homes-across-the-world.

233 Tony Wan, "ClassDojo Goes 'Beyond School' to Launch First Monetization Feature for Parents," *EdSurge*, Nov. 15, 2018, https://www.edsurge.com/news/2018-11-15-classdojo-goes-beyond-school-to-launch-first-monetization-feature-for-parents.

234 "Global Education Census Report 2018," *Cambridge Assessment International Education*, accessed July 30, 2021, https://www.cambridgeinternational.org/Images/514611-global-education-census-survey-report.pdf.

235 "School Days," song by Will D. Cobb and Gus Edwards, 1907.

236 TeachThought Staff, "Apps and Tools To Support And Improve Teacher-Parent Communication," *TeachThought*, accessed July 30, 2021, https://www.teachthought.com/technology/12-apps-smarter-teacher-parent-communication/,

237 Sidney Stevens, "10 Reasons Making Music Is Good for Your Brain," *Treehugger*, June 25, 2019, updated Nov. 4, 2019, https://www.treehugger.com/reasons-why-making-music-is-good-for-your-brain-4863852.

238 It's interesting that even Nicolas Maduro, who demonstrably thrives on drugs and violence, has maintained and supported El Sistema.—Note by Miles Durrie.

239 Quoted on "El Sistema: How the power of music helped change Venezuelan lives," rebroadcast of Playing for their Lives, *CBC Radio*, Oct. 23, 2017, https://www.cbc.ca/radio/ideas/el-sistema-how-the-power-of-music-helped-change-venezuelan-lives-1.4367337.

240 Xiomara Alemán, et al, "The Effects of Musical Training on Child Development: a Randomized Trial of *El Sistema* in Venezuela," *Prevention Science*, Nov. 28, 2016, https://www.ncbi.nlm.nih.gov/pmc/articles/PMC5602103/.

241 Michael Hopkins, Anthony M. Provenzano, & Michael S. Spencer, "Benefits, challenges, characteristics and instructional approaches in an El Sistema inspired after-school string program developed as a university–school partnership in the United States," *Sage Journals*, July 28, 2016, https://journals.sagepub.com/doi/10.1177/0255761416659509.
242 "El Sistema Programs Worldwide," *Sistema Global*, accessed Aug. 2, 2021, https://sistemaglobal.org/el-sistema-global-program-directory/.
243 A popular song about Pennsylvania Dutch cooking, with music by Guy Wood and words by Sammy Gallop. It was published in 1945.
244 Huang, Ping, Hanhua Huang, Qiuling Luo, & Lei Mo, "The Difference between Aesthetic Appreciation of Artistic and Popular Music: Evidence from an fMRI Study," *Plos One*, Nov. 4, 2016, https://journals.plos.org/plosone/article?id=10.1371/journal.pone.0165377.
245 Michael Spitzer, *The Musical Human, A History of Life on Earth* (London: Bloomsbury Publishing, 2021), 103.
246 Tom Jacobs, "Why Our Brains Respond Differently to Classical Music," *Pacific Standard*, Nov. 16, 2016, updated June 14, 2017, https://psmag.com/news/why-our-brains-respond-differently-to-classical-music.
247 Benjamin Zander, "The Transformative Power of Classical Music," Feb. 2008, TED Video, 20:14, https://www.ted.com/talks/benjamin_zander_the_transformative_power_of_classical_music?language=en.

C. Social Media

248 *Christa Melnyk Hines,* "5 Benefits of Social Media for Kids," *Atlanta Parent Editorial*, Feb. 6, 2019, https://www.atlantaparent.com/5-benefits-of-social-media-for-kids/.
249 "Facebook by the Numbers: Stats, Demographics & Fun Facts," *Omnicore*, last updated Jan. 25, 2021, https://www.omnicoreagency.com/facebook-statistics/.
250 Aubre Andrus, "FAQs of (Web) Life: Managing Your Online Identity," *tom's guide*, Jan 26, 2012, https://www.tomsguide.com/us/linkedin-facebook-blogging-email-hacked,review-1727-6.html.
251 At the time of writing, June 2021, we know that Facebook use by teenagers has been steadily decreasing, though Facebook revenues have clearly not been.
252 "Facebook Revenue 2009-2021 | FB," *macrotrends*, accessed June 25, 2021, https://www.macrotrends.net/stocks/charts/FB/facebook/revenue.

253 Ryan Robinson, "The 7 Top Social Media Sites You Need to Care About in 2020." *Adobe Spark*, accessed July 13, 2021, https://www.adobe.com/express/learn/blog/top-social-media-sites.
254 Judi Ketteler, "When Is a Child Instagram-Ready?" *New York Times*, Feb. 21, 2018, https://www.nytimes.com/2018/02/21/well/family/children-technology-instagram-youtube.html.
255 "Instagram by the Numbers: Stats, Demographics & Fun Facts," *Omnicore*, last updated: Jan. 6, 2021, https://www.omnicoreagency.com/instagram-statistics/.
256 Instagram Help Center, "Search and Explore," *Instagram*, accessed June 28, 2021, https://www.facebook.com/help/instagram/325395640916015.
257 "30 seconds: the time it takes to find porn on Instagram," *family zone*, accessed June 28, 2021, https://www.familyzone.com/anz/families/blog/instaporn.
258 Louise Myers, "100 Most Popular Emojis on Instagram for Killer Comments," *Louise Meyers Visual Social Media*, Aug. 6, 2019, https://louisem.com/19309/most-popular-emojis-instagram.
259 "Community Guidelines," *Instagram*, accessed June 29, 2021, https://www.facebook.com/help/instagram/477434105621119.
260 Nicole Harris and Anna Halkidis, "Is Instagram Safe for Kids?," *Parents*, updated Mar. 16, 2021, https://www.parents.com/parenting/better-parenting/advice/how-instagram-is-helping-you-protect-your-child-from-social-media/.
261 Amy Morin, "How to Prevent the Media from Damaging Your Teen's Body Image," *verywellfamily*, updated on June 29, 2020, https://www.verywellfamily.com/media-and-teens-body-image-2611245.
262 Amanda MacMillan, "Why Instagram Is the Worst Social Media for Mental Health," *Time*, May 25, 2017, https://time.com/4793331/instagram-social-media-mental-health/.
263 Heather R. Gallivan, "Teens, Social Media And Body Image," *Park Nicollet Melrose Center*, accessed June 28, 2021, https://www.macmh.org/wp-content/uploads/2014/05/18_Gallivan_Teens-social-media-body-image-presentation-H-Gallivan-Spring-2014.pdf.
264 Paediatric Child Health, "Dieting in adolescence," *Canadian Paediatric Society*, Sep. 9, 2004, https://www.ncbi.nlm.nih.gov/pmc/articles/PMC2720870/.
265 Shirley Cramer, "Instagram Ranked Worst for Young People's Mental Health, Our Comments," *Royal Society for Public Health*, May 19, 2017, https://www.rsph.org.uk/about-us/news/instagram-ranked-worst-for-young-people-s-mental-health.html.
266 Alex Hern, "Instagram is supposed to be friendly. So why is it making people so miserable?" *The Guardian*, Sep. 17, 2018,

https://www.theguardian.com/technology/2018/sep/17/instagram-is-supposed-to-be-friendly-so-why-is-it-making-people-so-miserable.

267 Andrew K. Przybylski, Kou Murayama, Cody R.DeHaan, & Valerie Gladwell, "Motivational, emotional, and behavioral correlates of fear of missing out," *ScienceDirect*, June 2013, https://www.sciencedirect.com/science/article/abs/pii/S0747563213000800.

268 Victoria Rideout & Michael B. Robb, "THE COMMON SENSE CENSUS: Media Use By Tweens and Teens," *Common Sense*, accessed June 29, 2021, https://www.commonsensemedia.org/sites/default/files/uploads/research/2019-census-8-to-18-key-findings-updated.pdf.

269 Rideout and Robb, "THE COMMON SENSE CENSUS: Media Use By Tweens and Teens."

270 Jean M. Twenge, "Have Smartphones Destroyed a Generation?" *The Atlantic*, Sep. 2017, https://www.theatlantic.com/magazine/archive/2017/09/has-the-smartphone-destroyed-a-generation/534198/.

271 casadeliziosi, "Hot & Sexy Girls," accessed June 28. 2021, www.instagram.com/casa.deliziosi.

272 "Male Poses for Instagram Photos," *Payday Pickups*, Aug. 5, 2020, https://www.youtube.com/watch?v=EW6qnqSyeWU.

273 Wikipedia, "Thigh gap," accessed June 30, 2021, https://en.wikipedia.org/wiki/Thigh_gap.

274 Harris & Halkidis, "Is Instagram Safe for Kids?"

275 Wikipedia, "List of suicides that have been attributed to bullying," accessed July 1, 2021, https://en.wikipedia.org/wiki/List_of_suicides_that_have_been_attributed_to_bullying.

276 Hilary Brueck & Shayanne Gal, "Suicide rates are climbing in young people from ages 10 to 24," *INSIDER*, Sep. 12, 2020, https://www.insider.com/cdc-suicide-rate-in-young-people-10-24-continues-climb-2020-9.

277 Gordon Neufeld. *Hold on to your kids: why parents matter/Gordon Neufeld and Gabor Maté* (Toronto: Alfred A. Knopf Canada, 2004).

278 Neufeld, *Hold on to your kids: why parents matter/Gordon Neufeld and Gabor Maté*, 8.

279 As one of the originators of Facebook, Parker held presidency of the organization from its beginning in 2004, but resigned a year later because of pending charges, that were never laid, of cocaine possession. His association with Zuckerberg and influence on Facebook continued.

280 Subsequent to his Facebook presidency, Parker formed the Parker Institute for Cancer Immunotherapy.

281 Olivia Solon, "Ex-Facebook president Sean Parker: site made to exploit human 'vulnerability'," *The Guardian*, Nov., 2017,

https://www.theguardian.com/technology/2017/nov/09/facebook-sean-parker-vulnerability-brain-psychology.

Part Four—How Did We End Up With School?—And Why.

A: How and Why It All Started

282 Markham Heid, "We Need to Talk About Kids and Smartphones," *Time*, updated: Oct. 10, 2017, https://time.com/4974863/kids-smartphones-depression/.
283 Henry Wadsworth Longfellow, "The Day Is Done," in *The Waif, a collection of poems* (Boston: William D. Ticknor, 1846).
284 Karl A. Schleunes, *Enlightenment, Reform, Reaction: The Schooling Revolution in Prussia (Central European History)*, 12(4), 315-342, accessed Jan. 24, 2021, http://www.jstor.org/stable/4545874).
285 See also Johann Georg Sulzer below.
286 Stephen Hicks, "Obedience in education in 1700s Germany," Sep. 28, 2012, https://www.stephenhicks.org/2012/09/28/obedience-in-education-1700s-germany/.
287 Quoted in Alice Miller, *For Your Own Good, Hidden cruelty in child-rearing and the roots of violence* (New York: Farrar, Straus, Giroux, third edition 1990 by The Noonday Press), 10-13.
288 Paul Verhaeghe, *Says Who? The Struggle for Authority in a Market-Based Economy trans. David Shaw* (Victoria, Aus. Scribe Publications, 2017), 82.
289 "Frederick William II of Prussia" *Encyclopædia Britannica, Volume 11, 1911,* 64, https://en.wikisource.org/wiki/1911_Encyclop%C3%A6dia_Britannica/Frederick_William_II._of_Prussia#top.
290 *Encyclopædia Britannica, Volume 11*, 65.
291 Fichte, Johann Gottlieb. *Addresses to the German nation by Johann Gottlieb Fichte; trans. by R. F. Jones and G. H. Turnbull* (Westport, Conn: Greenwood Press, 1979).
292 Fichte, *Addresses, Second Address*, §13.
293 Fichte, *Addresses, Second Address*, §16.
294 Fichte, *Addresses, Second Address*, §18.
295 Fichte, *Addresses, Second Address*, §19.
296 Fichte, *Addresses, Second Address*, §14.
297 Fichte, *Addresses, Second Address*, §15.
298 Fichte, *Addresses, Eleventh Address,* §67.
299 Fichte, *Addresses, Ninth Address*, §177.

300 "Why a new Curriculum?" *New Westminster Schools*, accessed Aug. 9, 2021, https://newwestschools.ca/about-us/learner-success/bcs-redesigned-curriculum/.

B. Visitors from North America

301 Horace Mann, "Mr. Mann's Seventh Annual Report—Education in Europe," *The Common School Journal, Vol 6, No. 5*, (Boston: Antioch College, March 1, 1844), 117, https://books.google.ca/books?id=jWIKAAAAMAAJ&printsec=frontcover&vq=%22come,+unite+their+voices+in+an+appeal+to+us+%3B+%E2%80%94+they+implore+us+to+think+more+of+the+character%22&source=gbs_quotes&redir_esc=y#v=onepage&q=%22come%2C%20unite%20their%20voices%20in%20an%20appeal%20to%20us%20%3B%20%E2%80%94%20they%20implore%20us%20to%20think%20more%20of%20the%20character%22&f=false.
302 Egerton Ryerson, *Report on a system of public elementary instruction for Upper Canada* (Montreal: Lovell and Gibson, 1847).
303 Ryerson, *Report,* 9.
304 Mann, *Seventh Report*, 86.
305 Mann, *Seventh Report*, 119.
306 Mann, *Seventh Report*, 48.
307 Ryerson, *Report*, 180.
308 Calvin Ellis Stowe, *Report-on-Elementary-Public-Instruction-in-Europe--Made-to-the-Thirty-Sixth-General-Assembly-of-the-State-of-Ohio--December-19—1837*, (Sydney, Aus: Wentworth Press, 2016).
309 Stowe, *Report*, 57.
310 Stowe, *Report*, 29-30.
311 Stowe, *Report*, 40.
312 Stowe, *Report*, 51.
313 Stowe, *Report*, 52.
314 Stowe, *Report*, 41.
315 Samuel Laing, *Notes of a traveller: on the social and political state of France, Prussia, Switzerland, Italy and other parts of Europe during the present century. 2nd ed.* (London: Printed for Longman, Brown, Green, and Longmans, 1842).
316 Laing, *Notes*, 171.
317 Laing, *Notes*, 166.
318 Laing, *Notes*, 171.
319 Mann, *Report*, 22.
320 Robert Vaughn, *The age of great cities; or, Modern civilization viewed in its relation to intelligence, morals and religion. Second Edition* (London: Jackson and Walford, 1843).
321 Vaughn, *Age of Great Cities*, 189.

322 Vaughn, *Age of Great Cities*, 190.

C. Locke and Friends: The Philosophy of Education

323 See: John Locke. *An Essay Concerning Human Understanding, Book I: Innate Notions.*
324 John Locke, *Some Thoughts Concerning Education* (New York: Teachers College, Columbia University. 1964) §1, 19.
325 Locke, *Some Thoughts* §9, 21.
326 Benjamin Spock & Steven Parker, *Dr. Spock's baby and child care, Seventh edition* (New York: Pocket Books, 1998).
327 Locke, *Some Thoughts* §4, 20.
328 Locke, *Some Thoughts* §9, 21.
329 Locke, *Some Thoughts* §38, 28.
330 John R. Watson. *The Psychological Care of Infant and Child* (London, George Allen and Unwin Ltd. 1928).
331 Locke, *Some Thoughts* §43, 31.
332 Locke, *Some Thoughts* §46, 32.
333 Locke, *Some Thoughts* §54, 36.
334 Locke, *Some Thoughts* §44, 31.
335 Thomas Hobbes, *Hobbes's Leviathan Reprinted from the edition of 1651* (London: Oxford Clarendon Press, 1909), 97.
336 Locke, *Some Thoughts* §52, 35.
337 Locke, *Some Thoughts* §52, 35.
338 See also on this subject: Alfie Kohn. *Punished by Rewards, The Trouble with Gold Stars, Incentive Plans, A's, Praise, and Other Bribes* (Boston: Houghton Mifflin, 1993) and Daniel H. Pink, *Drive, The Surprising Truth About What Motivates Us* (New York: Riverhead Books, 2009).
339 Locke, *Some Thoughts* §74, 56.
340 Locke, *Some Thoughts* §76, 58.
341 Smith, *Learning and Forgetting*, 3.
342 Locke, *Some Thought* §70, 51.
343 Locke, *Some Thoughts* §70.
344 Locke, *Some Thoughts* §70.
345 Locke, *Some Thoughts* §78.
346 Locke, *Some Thoughts* §78.
347 Locke, *Some Thoughts* §147.
348 Locke, *Some Thoughts* §148.
349 Locke, *Some Thoughts* §148.
350 See above "The Gamified Classroom" etc.
351 Locke, *Some Thoughts* §162.
352 Locke, *Some Thoughts* §162.
353 Locke, *Some Thoughts* §163.

354 Locke, *Some Thoughts* §164.
355 Locke, *Some Thoughts* §180.
356 Locke, *Some Thoughts* §174.
357 Locke, *Some Thoughts* §196, 162.
358 Locke, *Some Thoughts* §197, 162.
359 Though the age of the English baroque (Purcell, Handel) had not yet arrived when Locke was writing this book, there had been a lively period of English keyboard music in the early seventeenth century. Composers such as Orlando Gibbons, William Byrd, and John Bull composed numerous pieces for an instrument known as the *virginals*. The term virginals applied to any keyboard instrument similar to a harpsichord or clavichord. The instrument, especially in its smaller home-style version, was popular with young ladies, hence the probable origin of the name.
Around 1612 a collection of pieces for the virginals was published with the title *Parthenia or the Maydenhead of the first musicke that ever was printed for the Virginalls.* The cover of this delightful collection is dominated by the picture of a rapturous young woman seated at the aforesaid instrument. It is interesting, at this point, to note that music was (and still is in some quarters) thought of as beneath the occupations of men, while at the same time, the professional public performance and creation of music was exclusively the domain of men. Fortunately, this is now changing. Even such strongholds of tradition as the Vienna Philharmonic now include women players.
360 Locke, *Some Thoughts* §198.
361 Locke, *Some Thoughts* §199.
362 Locke, *Some Thoughts* §199.
363 Locke, *Some Thoughts* §204.
364 Locke, *Some Thoughts* §207.
365 Quoted in Will & Ariel Durant, *The Story of Civilization: Rousseau and revolution; a history of civilization in France, England, and Germany from 1756, and in the remainder of Europe from 1715 to 1789*, (New York: Simon & Schuster, 1967), 191.
366 Rousseau, *Le devin du village*, YouTube Video, 37:48, Jan.17, https://libanswers.snhu.edu/faq/48007.
367 Ruth Kotinsky, "Jean-Jacques Rousseau on nature, wholeness and education," *Infed.org*, accessed Aug. 4, 2021, https://infed.org/mobi/jean-jacques-rousseau-on-nature-wholeness-and-education/.
368 Jean-Jacques Rousseau, *The Reveries of the Solitary Walker, trans Anonymous 1796* (Project Gutenberg Australia, posted Sep. 2019), http://gutenberg.net.au/ebooks19/1900981h.html#ch1.
369 *Rousseau's Social Contract, Etc. trans. G. D. H. Cole*, (London: Everyman's Library, J. M. Dent & Sons Ltd. n.d.), 5, accessed Nov. 20, 2022, http://files.libertyfund.org/files/638/0132_Bk.pdf.
370 *Rousseau's Social Contract, Etc.*, 147.

371 The outrage was caused by a section of the book titled "Profession of Faith of the Savoyard Vicar" in which Rousseau claims that morality and belief in God are not innate but learned.

372 Jean-Jacques Rousseau, *Emile or On Education, trans. Allan Bloom* (New York: Basic Books Inc., 1979), 116.

373 For a startling example, see *Your Baby Can Read*, accessed Aug. 5, 2021, https://yourbabycanread.ca/. For a mere two or three hundred dollars you can get a set of CDs and DVDs that will get any two-year old or younger to read. That will impress the neighbours. So what are the kids going to read, *War and Peace*?

374 Rousseau, *Emile*, 117.

375 Rousseau, *Emile*, 79.

376 Rousseau, *Emile*, 91.

377 Rousseau, *Emile*, 84.

378 Rousseau, *Emile*, 118.

379 Rousseau, *Emile*, 125.

380 Rousseau, *Emile*, 207.

381 Marcel Schwante, "This Famous Albert Einstein Quote Nails It. The Smartest People Today Display This 1 Trait," accessed July 5, 2021, https://www.inc.com/marcel-schwantes/this-1-simple-way-of-thinking-separates-smartest-people-from-everyone-else.html.

382 John Alfred Green, *The Educational Ideas of Pestalozzi. 3rd edition* (Baltimore: Warwick & York, 1900), 61.

383 Johann Heinrich Pestalozzi, *How Gertrude Teaches Her Children, trans. Lucy E. Holland and Frances C. Turner, and edited with introduction and notes by Ebenezer Cooke* (London: Swan Sonnenschein & Co., 1894), 75, https://archive.org/stream/howgertrudeteach00pestuoft/howgertrudeteach00pestuoft_djvu.txt.

384 Pestalozzi, *How Gertrude Teaches*, 31.

385 Iselin, a philosopher in his own right, was a great supporter of Pestalozzi and his ideas about education. He published a fund-raising appeal for the Neuhof school.

386 In astronomy and celestial navigation, an *ephemeris* (plural: *ephemerides*) gives the trajectory of naturally occurring astronomical objects as well as artificial satellites in the sky, i.e., the position (and possibly velocity) over time.

387 Johann Heinrich Pestalozzi, *The Evening Hours of a Hermit, trans. Nobuko Ui*, accessed August 17, 2021, http://blessmingyu.blogspot.com/2016/09/the-evening-hours-of-hermit.html.

388 Pestalozzi, *Evening Hours of a Hermit*.

389 Johann Heinrich Pestalozzi, *Leonard and Gertrude, translated and abridged by Eva Channing* (Boston: D.C. Heath & Co., 1908), 118.

390 Pestalozzi, *Leonard and Gertrude*, 95.

391 Pestalozzi, *Leonard and Gertrude,* 130-131.

392 Pestalozzi, *Leonard and Gertrude,* 131.

393 Quoted in John Alfred Green, *The Educational Ideas of Pestalozzi, 3rd edition* (Baltimore: Warwick & York, 1900), 41.

394 Green, *Educational Ideas of Pestalozzi,* 47.

395 It's interesting that a radical approach to education, sometimes tolerated where not much is expected of the kids anyway, can turn out to have positive effects that even the most conservative cannot fail to notice. My own experience in this regard is reported later and in the appendix.

396 Quoted in Green, *Educational Ideas of Pestalozzi,* 52-53.

397 Typical of any house or institution where children are given freedom. It's usually just that the place is messy rather than dirty. Restrictive authorities insist that children be trained to be tidy and presentable at all times.

398 This was very much like our experience at the free school in the 1960s. There was widespread interest, or perhaps *curiosity* is a better word, many visitors, etc., etc. However, none of the principles of freedom were adopted by teachers or schools.

399 Famous now as the birthplace of the painter Paul Klee (1879-1940).

400 Green, *The Educational Ideas of Pestalozzi,* 62-63.

401 William Shakespeare, *Hamlet,* Act 4, Scene 5.

402 Green, *The Educational Ideas of Pestalozzi,* 64.

403 https://artvee.com/dl/pestalozzi-with-the-orphans-of-stans/

404 Pestalozzi, *How Gertrude Teaches,* 28.

405 Green, *The Educational Ideas of Pestalozzi,* 67.

406 Pestalozzi, *How Gertrude Teaches,* 145.

407 Pestalozzi, *How Gertrude Teaches,* 91.

408 Pestalozzi, *How Gertrude Teaches,* 105-106.

409 "I find I have fixed the highest, supreme principle of instruction in the recognition of sense-impression as the absolute foundation of all knowledge," Pestalozzi, *How Gertrude Teaches Her Children,* 139.

410 Pestalozzi, *How Gertrude Teaches Her Children, Appendix: The Method, a Report by Pestalozzi,* Burgdorf, June 27, 1800, 205.

411 Pestalozzi, *How Gertrude Teaches Her Children,* xvi.

412 I should also mention the idyllic location of the Saturna Island Free School and other such schools that sought a rural setting.

413 John Dewey, *Experience and Education,* (New York: Touchstone, 1938), 86.

414 John Dewey, *The School and Society,* (Chicago: University of Chicago Press, 1902), 75.

415 Dewey, *Experience and Education,* 17-18.

416 Dewey, *The School and Society,* 48.

417 Dewey, *The School and Society,* 20.

418 Dewey, *The School and Society,* 86.

419 Dewey, *The School and Society,* 34.

420 Dewey, *The School and Society,* 86.

421 L. S. Vygotsky, *Mind in Society, The Development of Higher Psychological Processes*, Michael Cole, Vera John-Steiner, Sylvia Scribner & Ellen Souberman, eds., (Cambridge, Mass.: Harvard University Press, 1978).

422 Vygotsky, *Mind in Society,* 90.

423 Vygotsky, *Mind in Society*, 73.

424 Smith, *Learning and Forgetting,* 9.

425 Anna Shvarts & Arthur Bakke, "The early history of the scaffolding metaphor: Bernstein, Luria, Vygotsky, and before," *Mind, Culture. and Activity, Vol. 26, 2019 Issue 1,* https://doi.org/10.1080/10749039.2019.1574306.

426 David Wood, Jerome S. Bruner, & Gail Ross, "The Role of Tutoring in Problem Solving." *The Journal of Child Psychology and Psychiatry, Vol 17 (1976)*, 89-100, https://acamh.onlinelibrary.wiley.com/doi/10.1111/j.1469-7610.1976.tb00381.x.

427 Wood, Bruner, & Ross, 93.

428 Wood, Bruner, & Ross, 96.

429 I have more to say about Watson in the following pages.

430 Rousseau, *Emile or On Education*, 85.

431 I'm using Neill's multi-gender term; I certainly prefer it to the gender-less but nonsensical *chair*.

432 Alexander Sutherland Neill, *Summerhill, A Radical Approach to Childrearing* (New York: Hart Publishing Company, 1960), 51.

433 "A great business is made of seeking the best methods of teaching reading. Desks and cards are invented; a child's room is made into a printing shop. Locke wants him to learn to read with dice. Now is that not a clever invention? What a pity! A means surer than all these, and the one always forgotten, is the desire to learn. Give the child this desire, then let your desks and your dice go. Any method will be good for him," Rousseau, *Emile*, 117.

434 Neill, *Summerhill*, 4-5.

435 Henry Caldwell Cook, *The Play Way, an Essay in Educational Method*, (New York: Frederick A. Stokes Company, 1917).

436 Neill, *Summerhill*, 27.

437 Neill, *Summerhill*, 62.

438 Neill, *Summerhill*, 62.

439 Peter Wilby, "Summerhill School: these days surprisingly strict," *The Guardian*, May 27, 2013.

440 Office for Standards in Education (Ofsted), "School Report, Summerhill School," accessed Jan. 31, 2021, https://files.ofsted.gov.uk/v1/file/50075777/.

441 National Bullying Prevention Center, *Bullying Statistics*, accessed Mar. 12, 2021, https://www.pacer.org/bullying/resources/stats.asp.

442 Angela Neustatter, *Summerhill School and the do-as-yer-like kids*, accessed Mar. 12, 2021, https://www.theguardian.com/education/2011/aug/19/summerhill-school-at-90.

443 A. S. Neill, *The Free Child* (London: Herbert Jenkins, 1953), 29.

444 Rousseau, *Emile* , 86.

445 Rousseau, *Emile,* 92.

446 Rousseau, *Emile,* 95-96.

447 Rousseau, *Emile,* 97.

448 New Teachers' Handbook, "Classroom Management," *British Columbia Teachers' Federation,* accessed Aug. 8, 2021, https://bctf.ca/NewTeachers.aspx?id=31827.

449 William Golding, *Lord of the Flies,* (London: Faber and Faber, 1954).

450 Rousseau, *Emile,* 92.

451 Neill, *Summerhill,* 110-111.

452 Alfie Kohn, *Punished by Rewards* (New York: Houghton Mifflin Company, 1993), 33.

453 "Summerhill (2008) -AMAZING- Best Freedom Movie Ever!!," YouTube video, 1:48:16, Nov. 2, 2016, https://www.youtube.com/watch?v=TxngqMavda0.

454 Hansard, *HC Deb 30 July 1833 vol 20 cc139-74.*

455 Hansard, *HC Deb 30 July 1833 vol 20 cc139-74.*

456 Hansard, *HC Deb 30 July 1833 vol 20 cc139-74.*

457 John Stuart Mill, *On Liberty, ed. Elizabeth Rapaport* (Indianapolis: Hackett Publishing Company, 1978), 53. *On Liberty* was originally published in 1859.

458 Mill, *On Liberty,* 53.

459 Tom Jacobs, "Tolerant Tykes, Small children aren't inherently racist. New research suggests we aren't born bigots. Racial prejudice is something we learn," *Pacific Standard,* Jan. 23, 2018, https://psmag.com/social-justice/small-children-arent-inherently-racist.

460 Mill, *On Liberty,* 9.

461 Mill, *On Liberty,* 104.

462 Mill, *On Liberty,* 104-105.

463 [52 & 53 Vict.] *Prevention of Cruelty to, and Protection of* [Ch. **44.**] *Children Act 1889.* clause 6-1.

464 *Protection of Children Act,* clause 14.

465 Mill, *On Liberty,* 105.

D. The Denial of Freedom

466 "Classroom Management, *The practice of teaching: A handbook for new teachers,* British Columbia Teachers' Federation, n.d., 28-30, ac-

cessed Nov. 5, 2022, http://www.ostu.ca/files/Docs%20-%20BCTF%20-%20ThePracticeofTeaching.pdf.
467 "School Corporal Punishment," *Repeal 43 Committee*, accessed Aug. 9, 2021, https://www.repeal43.org/school-corporal-punishment/.
468 Wikipedia, "School Corporal Punishment," accessed Aug. 9, 2021, https://en.wikipedia.org/wiki/school_corporal_punishment.
469 "Table 18 DSM-IV to DSM-5 Oppositional Defiant Disorder Comparison," *The National Center for Biotechnology Information*, accessed Nov. 20, 2022,
https://www.ncbi.nlm.nih.gov/books/NBK519712/table/ch3.t14/.
470 Simran Khurana, "Mark Twain Education Quotes," *ThoughtCo.*, June 21, 2019, https://www.thoughtco.com/mark-twain-education-2832664/.
471 "Student success through curriculum transformation," *BC's Curriculum*, accessed Aug. 1, 2021,
https://curriculum.gov.bc.ca/curriculum/overview.
472 W. S. Gilbert and Arthur Sullivan, *Patience* (1881), Act One.
473 "Unpacking Essential Learning Experience," *NESD Curriculum Corner*, accessed Aug. 1, 2021, http://curriculum.nesd.ca/Pre-Kindergarten/_layouts/15/WopiFrame.aspx?sourcedoc=/Pre-Kindergar-ten/Spiritual%20Experiences/SD%20P.1%20Experiencing%20a%20Sense%20of%20Wonder,%20Awe%20and%20Joy/Stage%201-Experi-ence/SD%20P.1%20Unpacked%20Experience.doc&action=default.
474 "Grade Six at a Glance," *Learn Alberta*, accessed Aug. 1, 2021, https://www.learnalberta.ca/content/mychildslearning/gradeataglance/grade6.pdf.
475 "English Language Arts Grade 6: Writing and Representing," *Curriculum Nova Scotia*, accessed Aug. 1, 2021,
https://curriculum.novascotia.ca/sites/default/files/documents/outcomes-indicators-files/English%20Language%20Arts%20P-6%20at%20a%20glance%20%282019%29.pdf.
476 "Curriculum Redesign: Key features of redesigned curriculum," *BC's Curriculum*, accessed Aug. 1, 2021,
https://curriculum.gov.bc.ca/rethinking-curriculum.
477 "Curriculum Redesign: Key features of redesigned curriculum," *BC'sCurriculum*.
478 https://www.google.ca/search?sxsrf=ALeKk003jjdoq8fO7OSnM7aVSGlptit2yg:1593114845283&source=univ&tbm=isch&q=BC+New+curriculum&safe=active&sa=X&ved=2ahUKEwjBtsGj353qAhXWl54KHd9WAp0QsAR6BAgIEAE&biw=1920&bih=938
479 "Curriculum Redesign: Key features of redesigned curriculum," *BC'sCurriculum*.

480 Explore English Language Arts curriculum: Kindergarten to Grade 9," *BC's Curriculum,* accessed Aug. 1, 2021, https://curriculum.gov.bc.ca/curriculum/english-language-arts.
481 "Mathematics 7: Core Competencies: Big Ideas," *BC's Curriculum,* accessed Aug. 1, 2021, https://curriculum.gov.bc.ca/curriculum/mathematics/7/core.
482 "Science 1: Core Competencies: Big Ideas," *BC's Curriculum,* accessed Aug. 1, 2021, https://curriculum.gov.bc.ca/curriculum/science/1/core.
483 "Science 9: Core Competencies: Big Ideas," *BC's Curriculum,* accessed Aug. 1, 2021, https://curriculum.gov.bc.ca/curriculum/science/9/core.
484 "Arts Education K-9 – Big Ideas," *BC's Curriculum*, accessed Aug. 1, 2021, https://curriculum.gov.bc.ca/sites/curriculum.gov.bc.ca/files/curriculum/continuous-views/en_arts_education_k-9_big_ideas.pdf.
485 "English Language Arts: Grade Six: Learning Standards," *BC's Curriculum*, accessed Aug. 1, 2021, https://curriculum.gov.bc.ca/sites/curriculum.gov.bc.ca/files/curriculum/english-language-arts/en_english-language-arts_k-9.pdf.

E. And Then What Happened?

486 Earl Schmit, *"Memory of a One-Room School,"* University of Wisconsin Extension's Yarns of Yesteryear Contest, 1994, https://imperfectwomen.com/memories-of-a-one-room-school/.
487 Named for two British educators Andrew Bell and Joseph Lancaster.
488 "Mae West teaches a room of school boys in *My Little Chickadee,*1940," YouTube Video, 4:45, Sep. 9, 2011, https://www.youtube.com/watch?v=YCja9HCzzH4.
489 National Center for Educational Statistics, "120 Years of American Education: A Statistical Portrait," accessed Feb. 2, 2021, https://nces.ed.gov/pubs93/93442.pdf.
490 Erin McCarthy, "11 Ways School Was Different in the 1800s," last modified Sep. 7, 2020, https://www.mentalfloss.com/article/58705/11-ways-school-was-different-1800.
491 Grace Shackman, "Memories of the One-Room Schoolhouse," *Community Observer Summer 2001*, https://aadl.org/aaobserver/36086.
492 Quoted in Raymond E. Callahan, *Education and the Cult of Efficiency* (Chicago: University of Chicago Press 1962), 51.
493 Callahan, *Education and the Cult of Efficiency,* 49-50.
494 Andrew Carnegie, *The Empire of Business* (New York: Doubleday, Page & *Company, 1902)*, 79-81.

495 Callahan. *Education and the Cult of Efficiency*, 8.

496 Isaac Asimov, "A Cult of Ignorance," *Newsweek,* Jan. 21, 1980.

497 Frederick W.Taylor, *The Principles of Scientific Management* (New York: Harper & Brothers, 1911), 17.

498 Eric Breitbart, *Clockwork, Frederick Taylor and His Theories on Scientific Management*, accessed Nov. 20, 2022, https://www.kanopy.com/en/product/139635.

499 Taylor, *Principles of Scientific Management, 12.*

500 Taylor, *Principles of Scientific Management, 46.*

501 Taylor, *Principles of Scientific Management, 55.*

502 Taylor, *Principles of Scientific Management, 59.*

503 Taylor, *Principles of Scientific Management, 36.*

504 When I see this name I can't help but wonder if Mary Chase had Cubberley in mind when she named the principal character in *Harvey,* her delightful play of 1944, Elwood P. Dowd.

505 Elwood Patterson Cubberley, *Public Education in the United States, A Study and Interpretation of American Educational History, an Introductory Textbook Dealing with the Larger Problems of Present Day Education in the Light of Their Historical Development* (New York, Houghton Mifflin, 1919).

506 John Taylor Gatto, "The Prussian Connection to American Schooling (Part 1)," YouTube video, 10:58, Aug. 28, 2014, https://www.youtube.com/watch?v=G3nVwrSk1p4.

507 Cubberley, *Public Education in the United States*, 278.

508 Cubberley, *Public Education in the United States*, 281-292.

509 Cubberley, *Public Education in the United States*, 449.

510 Cubberley, *Public Education in the United States*, 298.

511 Cubberley, *Public Education in the United States*, 449.

512 Cubberley, *Public Education in the United States*, 689.

513 Cubberley, *Public Education in the United States*, 689.

514 Elwood P. Cubberley, Public School Administration, A Statement of the Fundamental Principles Underlying the Organization and Administration of Public Education (Boston: Houghton Mifflin Company, 1916), 338.

515 Taylor, *Principles of Scientific Management, 46.*

516 J. B. Watson, "Psychology as the behaviorist views it," *Psychological Review, 20(2)*, 158–177, accessed July 30, 2021, https://psychclassics.yorku.ca/Watson/views.htm.

517 John B.Watson, *Behaviorism* (New York: People's Institute Publishing Company, 1925), 82.

518 B. F. Skinner, "The science of learning and the art of teaching," *Harvard Educational Review, 24*, 86–97, accessed July 30, 2021, https://psycnet.apa.org/record/1955-02985-001.

519 Audrey Watters, "Pigeons, Operant Conditioning, and Social Control," *Hack Education,* June 15, 2018, http://hackeducation.com/2018/06/15/pigeons.
520 B. F. Skinner, "Teaching machines," *Scientific American*, Sep. 1961, Vol 205: 91-102, ps://www.scientificamerican.com/article/teaching-machines/.
521 Smith, *Learning and Forgetting*, 59.
Smith goes on to say "All of these involve *values* that can only be acquired from people with whom you identify, from the company you keep. Unless learners *see* people demonstrating such values as part of their own daily lives, there is no way the values can be learned. To the extent that any of these values are officially regarded as having educational relevance they are taught as academic *subjects*, as the right answers to questions not as ways of life. The effort to teach them fails—and the usual suspects are rounded up."

Part Five—The Next Big Thing

522 Christopher Dawson, *The Crisis of Western Civilization*, (Washington, D.C.: Catholic University of America Press, 1961), 62-63.
523 Benjamin Spock, *The common sense book of baby and child care*, (New York: Duell, Sloan & Pearce, 1946).
524 Rudolf Flesch, *Why Johnny Can't Read—And What You Can Do About It*, (New York: Harper and Brothers, 1955).
525 The National Commission on Excellence in Education, "A Nation at Risk: The Imperative for Educational Reform, April 1983," https://edreform.com/wp-content/uploads/2013/02/A_Nation_At_Risk_1983.pdf.
526 Richard Nixon, "Special Message to the Congress on Education Reform, March 03, 1970," *The American Presidency Project*, https://www.presidency.ucsb.edu/documents/special-message-the-congress-education-reform.
527 "A Nation at Risk - April 1983 Recommendations," accessed July 30, 2021, https://www2.ed.gov/pubs/NatAtRisk/recomm.html.
528 William Shakespeare, *As You Like It*, Act 2, Scene 7.
529 Committee on Science U.S. House of Representatives, "Unlocking our Future: Toward a New National Science Policy," Sep, 1998, https://www.aaas.org/sites/default/files/s3fs-public/GPO-CPRT-105hprt105-b.pdf.
530 David F.Robitaille & J. Stuart Donn, "TIMSS: The Third International Mathematics and Science Study," *Springer Link*, accessed Nov, 20, 2022, https://link.springer.com/chapter/10.1007/978-94-017-1974-2_15.

531 Committee on Equal Opportunities in Science and Engineering, "1998 Biennial Report to The United States Congress," https://www.nsf.gov/pubs/2000/ceose991/ceose991.html.

532 Jerome Christenson, "Ramaley coined STEM term now used nationwide," *Winona Daily News,* Nov. 13, 2011, https://www.winonadailynews.com/news/local/ramaley-coined-stem-term-now-used-nationwide/article_457afe3e-0db3-11e1-abe0-001cc4c03286.html.

533 Richard Adams, "Girls lack self-confidence in maths and science problems, study finds," *The Guardian*, Mar. 5, 2015, https://www.theguardian.com/education/2015/mar/05/girls-lack-self-confidence-maths-science-oecd-school-engineering.

534 "Employment in STEM occupations," U.S. Bureau of Labor Statistics, last modified Apr. 9, 2021, https://www.bls.gov/emp/tables/stem-employment.htm.

535 "The STEM Imperative: Preparing Students for Tomorrow," *Smithsonian Science Education Center*, accessed July 30, 2021, https://ssec.si.edu/stem-imperative.

536 Tala Salem, "Study: Boys' Interest in STEM Careers Declining," *US News*, June 8, 2018, https://www.usnews.com/news/stem-solutions/articles/2018-06-08/study-boys-interest-in-stem-careers-declining.

537 "Why is STEM Education Important?" *Stem Village*, accessed Nov. 20, 2022, https://www.stemvillage.com/blog/why-is-stem-education-important.

538 Ryan, "The state of STEM education told through 18 stats," *Blog & News*, May 20, 2022, https://www.idtech.com/blog/stem-education-statistics.

539 Attributed to Albert Einstein, https://www.scientificamerican.com/article/einstein-s-parable-of-quantum-insanity//.

540 Michele McNeil & Alyson Klein, "Obama Offers Waivers From Key Provisions of NCLB," *Education Week*, Sep. 27, 2011, https://www.edweek.org/policy-politics/obama-offers-waivers-from-key-provisions-ot-nclb/2011/09.

541 Ray Hart, et al, "Student Testing in America's Great City Schools: An Inventory and Preliminary Analysis," *Council of the Great City Schools*, Oct. 2015, https://www.cgcs.org/cms/lib/DC00001581/Centricity/Domain/87/Testing%20Report.pdf.

542 Owen Davis, "No Test Left Behind, How Pearson Made a Killing on the US Testing Craze," *TPM Features*, accessed July 31, 2021, https://talkingpointsmemo.com/features/privatization/four/.

543 Sir Ken Robinson, "Bring on the Learning Revolution," Sep. 15, 2015, TED Video, 17:54, https://www.youtube.com/watch?v=kFMZrEABdw4.

544 Mehran Ebadolahi, "Why The Test Preparation Industry May Finally Get Out Of The Classroom," *Forbes Technology Council,* Apr. 29, 2020, https://www.forbes.com/sites/forbestechcouncil/2020/04/29/why-the-test-preparation-industry-may-finally-get-out-of-the-classroom/?sh=518d3dd678de.

545 "The Gift of Learning that Keeps on Giving," *Sylvan,* accessed Nov. 20, 2022, https://www.sylvanlearning.com/.

546 Sylvan Learning Home, "Pricing-Fit any Sylvan learning program into your budget," accessed No. 20, 2022, https://www.sylvanlearning.com/pricing?sharedcontent.

547 "Our Approach to Personalized Learning," *Sylvan,* accessed Nov. 20, 2022, https://www.sylvanlearning.com/personalized-tutoring/sylvan-method/our-technology.

548 "Practice Makes Possibilities," *Kumon,* accessed Nov. 20, 2022, https://www.kumon.com/ca-en/.

549 Sara Holbrook, "I Can't Answer These Texas Standardized Test Questions About My Own Poems," *Huffpost,* Jan. 4, 2017, https://www.huffpost.com/entry/standardized-tests-are-so-bad-i-cant-answer-these_b_586d5517e4b0c3539e80c341.

550 Lisa Guernsey, "TESTING; None Of the Above," *New York Times,* Apr. 24, 2005, https://www.nytimes.com/2005/04/24/us/testing-none-of-the-above.html.

551 Meredith Kolodner, "City students are passing standardized tests just by guessing," *New York Daily News,* Aug. 11, 2009, https://www.nydailynews.com/new-york/city-students-passing-standardized-tests-guessing-article-1.396883.

552 "Increase your Score with Multiple Choice Secrets!" *Complete Test Preparation,* accessed July 31, 2021, https://www.test-preparation.ca/multiple-choice/.

553 Emmie Martin, "4 ways to outsmart any multiple-choice test," *Insider,* June 26, 2015, https://www.businessinsider.com/4-ways-to-outsmart-any-multiple-choice-test-2015-6.

554 "School Performance," *Fraser Institute,* accessed Aug. 9, 2021, https://www.fraserinstitute.org/school-performance.

555 Tom Durrie, "Fraser Institute Says Private Schools Are OK," *Rants and Raves of Tom Durrie,* July 19, 2016, https://tdurrie.wordpress.com/2016/07/19/fraser-institute-says-private-schools-are-ok//, See also: Tom Durrie, "Why the Fraser Institute Likes Private Schools, *Rants and Raves of Tom Durrie,* July 20, 2016, https://tdurrie.wordpress.com/2016/07/20/why-the-fraser-institute-likes-private-schools/

556 "STAAR Released Test Questions," *Texas Education Agency,"* accessed July 31, 2021, https://tea.texas.gov/student-assessment/testing/staar/staar-released-test-questions.

557 Stephen J. Dubner, "What Should Be Done About Standardized Tests? A Freakonomics Quorum," *Freakonomics*, Dec. 20, 2007, https://freakonomics.com/2007/12/20/what-should-be-done-about-standardized-tests-a-freakonomics-quorum/.

558 H. L. Mencken, "The Little Red Schoolhouse," *The American Mercury, Vol 1, No. 4, Apr. 1924*, 504, https://babel.hathitrust.org/cgi/pt?id=mdp.39015030748613&view=1up&seq=44&skin=2021.

559 "STEM jobs: the good, the bad and the ugly," *Randstad*, May 10, 2019, https://www.randstad.ca/job-seeker/career-resources/tech-jobs/stem-jobs-the-good-the-bad-and-the-ugly/.

560 "About Canada-Wide Science Fair Virtual 2022," *Canada-Wide Science Fair, Expo Sciences Pancanadienne*, accessed Aug. 9, 2021, https://youthscience.ca/science-fairs/cwsf/virtual-2022/.

561 Canada 2067, "What is Canada 2067?" accessed Nov. 20, 2022, https://canada2067.letstalkscience.ca/en/about/.

562 Canada 2067, "National Leadership Conference," accessed July 31, 2021, https://canada2067.ca/en/conference/national-leadership-conference/.

563 Canada 2067, "Regional Youth Events," accessed Nov. 20, 2022, https://canada2067.letstalkscience.ca/en/conference/regional-youth-events/.

564 Canada 2067, "The Learning Framework," accessed Nov. 20, 2022, https://canada2067.ca/en/the-learning-framework/.

565 "The State of STEM: Educating Canadians for the Next 50 Years," *Mowat Centre*, June 25, 2019, https://munkschool.utoronto.ca/mowatcentre/the-state-of-stem-educating-canadians-for-the-next-50-years/1.

566 Ivan Illich, *Deschooling Society* (New York: Harper & Rowe, 1972), 14.

567 Council of Ministers of Education, Canada, *PISA*, https://www.cmec.ca/712/PISA_2022.html.

568 Tim Johnson, "Does standardized testing really evaluate your kid's learning?" *Today's Parent*, Aug. 11, 2015, https://www.todaysparent.com/family/does-standardized-testing-really-evaluate-your-kids-learning/.

569 "ADHD Numbers: Facts, Statistics, and You," *The A.D.D. Resource Center*, Oct. 11, 2017, https://www.addrc.org/adhd-numbers-facts-statistics-and-you/.

570 "Isadora Duncan > Quotes > Quotable Quote," *Good Reads*, accessed Nov. 20, 2022, https://www.goodreads.com/quotes/62793-if-i-could-tell-you-what-it-meant-there-would.

Part Six—The School and Its Agenda

571 John Franklin Bobbitt, *What Schools Teach and Might Teach* (Ithaca: Cornell University, 1915).

572 Egerton Ryerson, *Report on a System of Public Elementary Instruction in Upper Canada* (Montreal: Lovell and Gibson, 1847), 21.

573 The Free Library. S.v. "The case for public schools." accessed Feb. 2, 2021, https://www.thefreelibrary.com/The+case+for+public+schools.-a016706078.

574 World Inequality Report, accessed Nov. 25, 2022, https://wir2022.wid.world/.

575 BC's Curriculum, "Curriculum Redesign," accessed Feb. 2, 2021, https://curriculum.gov.bc.ca/rethinking-curriculum.

576 "Many forms of Government have been tried, and will be tried in this world of sin and woe. No one pretends that democracy is perfect or all-wise. Indeed it has been said that democracy is the worst form of Government except for all those other forms that have been tried from time to time...." Winston S Churchill, Nov. 11, 1947. *International Churchill Society*, Feb. 26, 2016, https://winstonchurchill.org/resources/quotes/the-worst-form-of-government/.

577 Diane McGuinness, *Why Our Children Can't Read and What We Can Do About It* (New York: Simon & Schuster, 1997), 142-143.

578 Mann, *Seventh Report*, 161.

579 Je'Quan Sailes-Irving, "5 Reasons Why: One Should Go To School," May 30, 2017, https://wybeaconnews.org/6320/college/5-reasons-why-one-should-go-to-school/.

580 "Reasons why kids should go to school," *Classroom*, accessed Nov. 20, 2022, https://www.livestrong.com/article/256375-reasons-why-kids-should-go-to-school/.

581 "6 reasons children should go to primary school," *Garden Conejo School,* accessed May 12, 2021, https://www.cardenconejo.com/private-school-blog/6-reasons-children-should-go-to-primary-school/.

582 Naia Lee, "The Young and the Zestless, Young people are increasingly skeptical of our political system. Here's how to restore our trust," *The Tyee*, Sep. 14, 2021, https://thetyee.ca/Topic/The_Run_Archive/2021/09/17/The-Run-The-Young-And-The-Zestless/.

583 Ivan Illich, *Deschooling Society* (New York: Harper & Rowe, 1972), 14.

584 Michael C. Zwaagstra, Rodney A. Clifton & John C. Long, *What's Wrong With Our Schools and How We Can Fix Them*, (Lanham Maryland: Rowman & Littlefield Education, 2010).

585 James H. Stronge, *Qualities of Effective Teachers* (Alexandria, Virginia: ASCD, 2002).

586 Rants and Raves of Tom Durrie, *"When a Highbrow Meets a Lowbrow,"* https://tdurrie.wordpress.com/2012/03/10/when-a-highbrow-meets-a-lowbrow/.

587 "Digest of Education Statistics," *National Center for Education Statistics*, accessed Nov. 20, 2022,
https://nces.ed.gov/programs/digest/d10/tables/dt10_153.asp.

588 Walter E. Williams, "Educational Ineptitude," Mar. 10, 1004,
http://walterewilliams.com/educational-ineptitude/.

589 Statistics Canada, *Back to school... by the numbers 2014*,
https://www.statcan.gc.ca/eng/dai/smr08/2014/smr08_190_2014#a5.

590 Statistics Canada, *Back to school... by the numbers 2018*,
https://www.statcan.gc.ca/en/dai/smr08/2018/smr08_220_2018#a9.

591 Statistics Canada,
https://www.statcan.gc.ca/eng/dai/smr08/2014/smr08_190_2014#a5.

592 R. V. Jordon, "The Intelligence of Teachers" (Chicago: University of Chicago, *The Elementary School Journal*, Volume 33, Number 3, Nov. 1932, 195-204), https://www.jstor.org/stable/i241362.

593 Based on Harmon-Nelson IQ Distributions.

594 Robert M. Hauser, "Meritocracy, Cognitive Ability, and the Sources of Occupational Success" D*epartment of Sociology Center for Demography and Ecology*, The University of Wisconsin,-Madison, Aug.17, 2002.

595 Quora, "How do the average IQs rank by profession. Which professions have the highest IQs?" accessed May 21, 2021,
https://www.quora.com/How-do-the-average-IQs-rank-by-profession-Which-professions-have-the-highest-IQs.

596 Amadora M. Tschechtelin, "A Study in Teacher Personality," accessed Nov. 20, 2022, https://www.jstor.org/stable/27529323?seq=1.

597 the Homeroom, "Regulations and Courses of Study for Provincial Normal Schools 1928-1929," accessed Nov. 13, 2022,
http://curric.library.uvic.ca/homeroom/content/topics/programs/curriclm/nschool.htm.

598 "The secret to classroom seating arrangements – How to decide what's right for you," *Differentiated Teaching*, accessed Nov. 23, 2022,
https://www.differentiatedteaching.com/classroom-seating-arrangements/.

599 Robert Rosenthal & Lenore Jacobsen, *Pygmalion in the Classroom: Teacher Expectation and Pupil's Intellectual Development*. (Williston, VT: Crown House Publishing, 1968, revised and expanded 1992).

600 Jere E. Brophy, "Research on the Self-Fulfilling Prophecy and Teacher Expectations," *Journal of Educational Psychology, Vol. 75, No. 5 (1983)*, 631-661.

601 "Teacher Expectations of Students, A Self-fulfilling Prophecy," accessed Nov. 20, 2022, https://www.ecs.org/clearinghouse/01/05/51/10551.pdf.

602 George Monbiot, *How Did We Get into This Mess?* (London: Verso, 2017).

603 George Monbiot, "Neoliberalism—the ideology at the root of all out problem," *The Guardian*, Apr. 15, 2016, https://www.theguardian.com/books/2016/apr/15/neoliberalism-ideology-problem-george-monbiot.

604 Tom Durrie, "Fraser Institute Says Private Schools Are OK," *Rants and Raves of Tom Durrie* (blog), July 19, 2016. https://tdurrie.wordpress.com/2016/07/19/fraser-institute-says-private-schools-are-ok/. See also: Tom Durrie, "Why the Fraser Institute Likes Private Schools," *Rants and Raves of Tom Durrie* (blog), July 20, 2016, https://tdurrie.wordpress.com/2016/07/20/why-the-fraser-institute-likes-private-schools/.

605 Jessica Brathwaite, "Neoliberal Education Reform and the Perpetuation of Inequality," *Critical Sociology, vol. 43, No. 3*, 429-448, first published June 1, 2016, https://journals.sagepub.com/action/doSearch?ContribAuthorStored=Brathwaite%2C+Jessica&SeriesKey=crsb.

606 Henry A. Giroux, "Can democratic Education Survive in a Neoliberal Society?" *Truthout*, Oct. 16, 2012, https://truthout.org/articles/can-democratic-education-survive-in-a-neoliberal-society/.

607 These are: Harcourt Educational Measurement, CTB McGraw-Hill, Riverside Publishing (a Houghton Mifflin company), and NCS Pearson.

608 Educational Marketer, "The pre-eminent source of business news and analysis for educational publishing and marketing for over 40 years, delivering alerts to upcoming adoptions, mergers and acquisitions intelligence, and tested success strategies for PreK-12 and college markets," accessed Nov. 20, 2022, https://www.educationalmarketer.net/about-em.

609 Christopher H. Tienken, "Neoliberalism, Social Darwinism, and Consumerism Masquerading as School Reform," *Research Gate, Interchange 43(4) DOI: 10.1007/s10780-013-9178-y*, May 2013, accessed June 6, 2021, https://www.researchgate.net/publication/257572784_Neoliberalism_Social_Darwinism_and_Consumerism_Masquerading_as_School_Reform.

610 Noam Chomsky, "Public Education Under Massive Corporate Assault—What's Next?" *Guernica/15 years of global arts & politics,* Aug. 9, 2011, https://www.guernicamag.com/noam_chomsky_public_education/.

611 Noam Chomsky, "The Assault on Public Education," *Truthout*, Apr. 4, 2012, https://truthout.org/articles/the-assault-on-public-education/.

612 Reshmi Dutt-Ballerstadt, "Academic Prioritization or Killing the Liberal Arts?" *Inside Higher Ed*, Mar. 1, 2019,

https://www.insidehighered.com/advice/2019/03/01/shrinking-liberal-arts-programs-raise-alarm-bells-among-faculty.

613 Dutt-Ballerstadt, "Academic Prioritization or Killing the Liberal Arts?"

614 Ralph Waldo Emerson, "Essays: Second Series (1844) New England Reformers," *American Transcendentalism, Web,* https://archive.vcu.edu/english/engweb/transcendentalism/authors/emerson/essays/nereformers.html.

615 Juvenal, *Satire 10,* 77–81.

616 Neil Postman, *Technopoly, The Surrender of Culture to Technology* (New York: Random House, Vintage Books, 1993), 13.

617 Dr. Mark W.Durm, "An A is not an A is not an A: A History of Grading," *The Educational Forum, Volume 57, 1993, Issue 3.*

618 Thomas R. Guskey & Howard R. Pollio, "Grading Systems—School, Higher Education," accessed Nov. 20, 2022, https://education.stateuniversity.com/pages/2017/Grading-Systems.html.

619 Guskey and Pollio, "Grading Systems."

620 Horace Mann, *Annual Reports on Education,* (Boston: Lee and Shepard Publishers, 1872), 504, https://books.google.ca/books?id=1Dk4AAAAYAAJ&pg=PA504&lpg=PA504&dq=&redir_esc=y#v=onepage&q&f=false.

621 Viktor Mayer-Schönberger, Kenneth Cukier, and Quartz, "Your High School Transcript Could Haunt You Forever, How big data could create an inescapable 'permanent record,'" *The Atlantic,* Mar. 11, 2014, https://www.theatlantic.com/education/archive/2014/03/your-high-school-transcript-could-haunt-you-forever/284346/.

622 JF Ptak Science Books Post 1770, "Alan Turing--Report Card Teachers' Comments, 1926-1931," accessed Dec. 2, 2022, https://longstreet.typepad.com/thesciencebookstore/2012/03/alan-turing-report-card-teachers-comments-1926-1931.html.

623 "125 Report Card Comments," *Education World,* accessed June 28, 2021, https://www.educationworld.com/a_curr/profdev/profdev148.shtml.

624 "50 'Needs Improvement' Report Card Comments," *Education World,* accessed Nov. 20, 2022, https://www.educationworld.com/a_curr/profdev/Needs-Improvement-Report-Card-Comments.

625 "Get your child ready for school is a new slogan on which we can hang a new philosophy of education, which will recognize the value of the pre-school years and use them more farsightedly . . ." from Arnold Gesell, "Pre-School Development and Education," *The Annals of the American Academy of Political and Social Science, Vol 121, Issue 1,* Sep. 1925.

626 Andrea Canter, "Teacher Conferences—A Guide for Parents," *Child Mind institute*, updated on July 23, 2021., https://childmind.org/article/teacher-conferences-a-guide-for-parents/.

627 "Child Development by Age," *The Center for Parenting Education*, accessed Nov. 26, 2022, https://centerforparentingeducation.org/library-of-articles/child-development/child-development-by-age/.

628 Homelinks, "Kaslo, Reporting on Learning, BC Curriculum, Curriculum Checklists, Grade Five Checklist," accessed Dec. 3, 2022, https://homelinks.sd8.bc.ca/kaslo/curriculum-checklists.

629 "Draft K–9 Student Reporting Policy (2019): Handbook for Piloting Schools and Districts," British Columbia Ministry of Education, accessed Nov. 27, 2022, https://curriculum.gov.bc.ca/sites/curriculum.gov.bc.ca/files/pdf/reporting/student-reporting-policy-pilot-handbook.pdf.

630 "Core Competencies," BC's Curriculum, accessed Nov. 27, 2022, https://curriculum.gov.bc.ca/competencies.

631 "Informed Directions: Foundations for the DRAFT K-9 Student Reporting Policy (2019) and Pilot," British Columbia Ministry of Education, accessed Nov. 27, 2022, https://curriculum.gov.bc.ca/sites/curriculum.gov.bc.ca/files/pdf/reporting/informed-directions-k-9-policy-pilot.pdf.

632 "Report Card Rubrics, For Parents," *Lapeer Community Schools*, accessed Nov. 26, 2022, https://www.lapeerschools.org/for_parents/report_card_rubrics.

633 Amanda Morin, "How to decode what teachers say about your child," *Understood*, accessed Dec. 3, 2022, https://www.understood.org/en/articles/how-to-decode-what-teachers-say-about-your-child.

634 Daniel H. Pink, *Drive, The Surprising Truth About What Motivates Us* (New York: Riverhead Books, 2009), 1.

635 Harry F.Harlow, Margaret Kuenne Harlow & Donald R. Meyer, "Learning Motivated by a Manipulation Drive," *Journal of Experimental Psychology, Vol 40(2), Apr 1950*, 228-234.

636 Harlow, et al, "Learning Motivated by a Manipulation Drive," Summary and Conclusions.

637 A. S. Neil, *Summerhill*, 162.

638 Alfie Kohn, *Punished by Rewards, The Trouble with Gold Stars, Incentive Plans, A's, Praise, and Other Bribes* (Boston, New York: Houghton Mifflin Company, 1993), 159.

639 Kohn, *Punished by Rewards,* 63.

640 Mark R. Lepper, David Greene & Richard E. Nisbett, "Undermining children's intrinsic Interest with extrinsic reward: A test of the 'overjustification' hypothesis," *Journal of Personality and Social Psychology, 1973, Vol. 28, No. 1*, 129-137.

641 Lepper, Greene & Nisbett, "Undermining children's intrinsic Interest," 135.

642 John Dewey, *The school and society* (Chicago: University of Chicago Press, 1900).

643 Alfred North Whitehead, *The aims of education* (New York: Mentor, 1929).

644 John Holt, *How children fail* (New York: Dell, 1964).

645 Charles Silberman, *Crisis in the classroom* (New York: Random House, 1970).

646 Lepper, Greene & Nisbett, "Undermining children's intrinsic Interest," 136.

647 Sir Ken Robinson, "Do schools kill creativity?" *TED2006 Video*, Feb 2006, https://www.ted.com/talks/sir_ken_robinson_do_schools_kill_creativity.

648 The BOOK IT! Program, "A free reading incentive program for PreK-6th grade classrooms, parents and homeschool families," *Book it!*, accessed July 2, 2021, https://www.bookitprogram.com/.

649 Stacy Tornio, "28 Reading incentives That Really Work," *We Are Teachers*, Feb. 9, 2016, https://www.weareteachers.com/28-reading-incentives-that-really-work/.

650 *Blazing Saddles* (10/10) Movie CLIP Boy, Is He Strict (1974) HD, YouTube Video 2:42 https://www.youtube.com/watch?v=bcokL59jeqU.

651 Kohn, *Punished by Rewards,* 73-74.

652 Barry Schwartz, "Reinforcement-induced behavioral stereotypy: How not to teach people to discover rules," *Journal of Experimental Psychology: General*, Vol *111*(1*), Mar. 1982, 23-59.

653 Kohn, *Punished by Rewards,* 74.

654 Susie Loraine, "Vocabulary Development," *Handy Handouts No. 149*, accessed Nov. 20, 2022, http://www.handyhandouts.com/viewHandout.aspx?hh_number=149.

655 Gardner, *The Unschooled Mind*, 85.

656 Smith, *Learning and Forgetting,*" 16.

657 Kohn, *Punished by Rewards,*142.

658 Zachary Jason, "Bored Out of Their Minds," *Ed. Harvard Ed. Magazine*, Winter 2017, https://www.gse.harvard.edu/news/ed/17/01/bored-out-their-minds.

659 APA Dictionary of Psychology, "Learned Helplessness," *American Psychological Association*, accessed Nov. 20, 2022, https://dictionary.apa.org/learned-helplessness.

Part Seven—In Conclusion

660 Marcel Schwante, "This Famous Albert Einstein Quote Nails It. The Smartest People Today Display This 1 Trait," accessed Nov. 20, 2022,

https://www.inc.com/marcel-schwantes/this-1-simple-way-of-thinking-separates-smartest-people-from-everyone-else.html.

661 *The Victrola Book of the Opera, Sixth Edition*, (Camden, New Jersey: Victor Talking Machine Company, 1921).

662 You'll find a fuller account of this, written in 1966, at the end of this book.

663 Germaine Greer, *Sex and Destiny, The Politics of Human Fertility* (New York: Harper & Row. 1984), 2.

664 Neil Postman, *Amusing Ourselves to Death, Public Discourse in the Age of Show Business* (New York: Penguin Books USA Inc. 1986), 142.

665 Alice Miller, *Banished Knowledge, Facing Childhood Injuries, trans. Leila Vennewitz* (New York: Doubleday 1991), 7.

666 James C Kaufman, "Why does our society hate children?" *Psychology Today*, Oct 31, 2009, https://www.psychologytoday.com/ca/blog/and-all-jazz/200910/why-does-our-society-hate-children.

667 John R. Watson. *The Psychological Care of Infant and Child* (London: George Allen and Unwin Ltd. 1928), 16.

668 Dr. Benjamin Spock, *Baby and Child Care* (New York: Pocket Books, Inc. 1946), 3.

669 It is well known that babies who are deprived of physical contact fail to thrive. See the studies cited in this article from the National Library of Medicine: "To have and to hold: Effects of physical contact on infants and their caregivers." https://www.ncbi.nlm.nih.gov/pmc/articles/PMC7502223/

670 Gabor Maté with Daniel Maté, *The Myth of Normal: Trauma, Illness & Health in a Toxic Culture* (Toronto: Penguin Random House Knopf Canada, 2022) 131-132

671 Judy S. DeLoache &, Cynthia Chiong, "Babies and Baby Media" American Behavioral Scientist, Volume 52 Number 8. April 2009 1115-1135

672 John Bowlby. *Attachment* (Pimlico, an imprint of Random House, London, 1973) 378

673 Pamela Levin. *Cycles of Power: A User's Guide to the Seven Seasons of Life* (Health Communications, Inc., Deerfield Beach, Florida, 1988)

674 Levin, *Cycles of Power*, 55

675 Tom Durrie. *Is Daycare a Good Idea? Should We Institutionalize Our Children?* https://tdurrie.wordpress.com/, April 15, 2022.

676 Neufeld, *Hold on to your kids: why parents matter/Gordon Neufeld and Gabor Maté*, 271.

Epilogue

677 Charles Strouse and Lee Adams, "Kids," from *Bye Bye Birdie*, 1961, https://www.google.com/search?q=Why+can%E2%80%99t+they+be+lik e+we+were%2C+perfect+in+every+way.+What%E2%80%99s+the+matt er+with+kids+today%3F%E2%80%9D&source=hp&ei=9xWeY6-aI- Wz0PEPq5ezyA0&iflsig=AJiK0e8AAAAAY54kBy3AeSf2z1iR50v7fsn IL3AEGNiS&ved=0ahUKEwjv8cOVr4H8AhXlGTQIHavLDNkQ4dUD CA4&oq=Why+can%E2%80%99t+they+be+like+we+were%2C+perfect +in+every+way.+What%E2%80%99s+the+matter+with+kids+today%3F %E2%80%9D&gs_lcp=Cgdnd3Mtd2l6EAxQvxVYvxVgzx1oAXAAeA CAAWWIAWWSAQMwLjGYAQCgAQKgAQGwAQA&sclient=gws- wiz#fpstate=ive&vld=cid:00fa043c,vid:T3PvcpWbUIg.